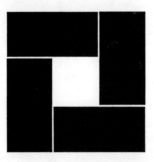

Project Management: Risks and Productivity

Project Management:
Risks and
Productivity

M. M. Obradovitch, MSME, MBA, P.E.
Program Manager
Hughes Aircraft Company
El Segundo, California

S. E. Stephanou, M.S., Ph.D
Professor Emeritus, Systems Management
University of Southern California

Daniel Spencer Publishers

Dedication

To our families

Printed in the United States

International Standard Book Number: 0-936496-10-X

Library of Congress Catalog Card Number: 90-61398

Artwork and Composition: Laserset
Cover and Text Design: Natalie Herse

Daniel Spencer Publishers
2264 N.W. Seventh, Bend, Oregon 97701 • (503) 385-1001 • 800-733-9210

———————— Author Biographies ————————

M.M. (Mike) Obradovitch has twenty five years of diversified technical and management experience including profit/loss responsibility. He has been accountable for a variety of projects and programs worth over half a billion dollars and has had hands-on experience in key positions involving design and development, marketing, production and product line management. In the latter capacity his recent experience has encompassed coordination, direction and integration of functions including: marketing, contracts, business management, design and systems engineering, manufacturing and logistics support. His project management experience spans all phases of product development from R&D through and including production.

Mike Obradovitch has fifteen years of concurrent experience as a seminar leader and member of the part time faculty of four universities at the graduate and undergraduate levels in the schools of business and engineering. An outspoken and engaging speaker, he is the author of a project/product management workbook and the co-author of a previous text on this subject. Mike is a graduate of the University of Southern California with BSME, MSME and MBA degrees. He is registered in California as a Professional Engineer in mechanical engineering. Prior to joining Hughes Aircraft Company, he was employed by Bendix Electrodynamics. He currently reside in Orange County, California with his wife and four children.

Dr. S. E. Stephanou has been a Professor of Systems Management for the last 18 years at the Institute for Safety and Systems Management at the University of Southern California. He is presently Professor Emeritus and continues to teach and consult. His academic experience in teaching the Management of Technology, Project Management and related subjects was preceded by over 20 years of industrial experience with major U.S. companies including Dupont; Herculer, Inc.; Rockwell International and McDonnel-Douglas. This experience included working on two of the largest projects of the century, namely the Manhattan Project and the Apollo Project. He also has managed a number of projects in Advanced Technology and Propulsion as well as owning and operating his own business, Newport Research Associates. He is the author or co-author of four books and has published numerous articles appearing in leading national and internationally distributed technical and management journals and periodicals. Dr. Stephanou has had extensive experience in consulting, conducting seminars and heading up extensive research and development programs. He received his bachelor of science degree from the Massachusetts Institute of Technology and his Ph.D. from the University of Kansas.

─────────── Preface ───────────

We were pleased and grateful for the positive comments received from students, faculty, consultants, practitioners and executives regarding our first text. Among the first and most generous were those of Professor Hans J. Thamhain of Worcester Polytechnic Institute that appeared in the Project Management Journal in September 1986. We are indebted to him and all others. The seemingly broad based appeal of our initial effort was most rewarding. We remain convinced of the need for a text that combines theory with practical reality and promotes the consideration and discussion of relevant issues.

From our perspective, project/program management is an important and integral part of the management of the overall industrial process. The Project/Program Manager is not only directly affected by the process, but he is also in a unique position to affect this process and contribute materially to its improvement. If he is to become an effective contributor to this process, he must develop an understanding and an appreciation for its various aspects and the issues involved. Correspondingly, he must have a broader view and appreciation of his function. Our selection and approach to the presentation of material was governed accordingly.

We recall reading an article (nearly twenty) years ago in which the author suggested that the Project/Program Manager was "the man in between" the executive and the engineer. He went on to say that the Project Manager was neither executive nor engineer yet had to be comfortable in both roles; this made him different and it is precisely this quality that makes him so very uniquely valuable. Hopefully, the author will forgive us for the lack of attribution and find solace in the knowledge that his insight has had such a lasting and significant impact. It is with the above in mind that we have selected and organized the material presented in this text.

Clearly, there is a difference between theory and practice. Given this difference, we have attempted to account for it in our treatment of the material and thus make this text of value to the student and the practitioner. Specifically, this text should provide the student with a perspective as to why theory is not generally applied in practice and the practitioner with an opportunity to rediscover the importance of applied theory in practice. We hope that both will eventually be encouraged to focus on and attack dysfunctional organizational and programmatic practices.

To our knowledge, this book has been used as a text or primary reference for courses and seminars on "Project Management", "Management of RDT&E" and "Entrepreneurship" by both business and engineering schools. It is divided into five parts as follows:

Part 1: Introductory Basics. Part 1 is made up of the first three chapters and deals with the history of projects, common terminology, organizational advantages and disadvantages. It covers a chronological description and a discussion of the activities involved in the initiation and execution of projects, including identification of need, preliminary studies, proposals, organization and staffing in both the commercial and governmental sectors.

Part 2: Making the Most out of Tools and Techniques. Part 2 consists of three chapters dealing with Project Planning and Scheduling, Monitoring and Control as well as Risk Analysis and Management. It provides a combination of theoretical and *practical* information that will be of interest to the student and the practitioner in improving the likelihood of project success. It presents reasons why a majority of projects are inadequately planned, controlled and monitored and identifies typical danger signs along with techniques and approaches for reducing and managing business and career risks.

Part 3: Getting the Most out of People and the Organization. Part 3 also consists of three chapters. Whereas Part 2 deals primarily with the "mechanical" aspects of project management, Part 3 deals with the equally, if not the more, important "organic" aspects of management. The importance of *both* to the success of the project and the organization along with their interdependence is underscored through chapters such as Making Project Management Work, Conflict Management and Productivity Improvement. Project success depends on a combination of *skill* and *will*. In other words, the *effective application* of various tools and techniques is as important as the *effective integration* of people to the accomplishment of an objective at hand. One cannot be achieved without the other. This part discusses the "how's" and the "why's" involved.

Part 4: Legal and Ethical Aspects of (Project/Program) Management. As a professional, we believe that the Project/Program Manager must become more sensitized to a host of legal, ethical and moral issues and obligations towards society, his/her employer, suppliers and fellow employees. Given the media and legislative attention these subjects have received based on recent developments in both public and private sectors, we cannot conceive of any course on this general subject matter failing to include coverage and vigorous discussion of these subjects. Our treatment of the legal aspects of project management include contracting principles, patents and licensing, proprietary data, warranties and products liability. Our discussion of ethics covers most of the major belief systems and provides a recommended approach to the analysis/syntheses of ethical problems.

The above frequently involve highly complex and technical questions and issues. While our treatment may appear thorough, it is not a substitute for competent and qualified counsel on issues of real and practical significance.

Part 5: Project Management and the Industrial Process. Project management can and does deal with a broad range of issues involving the overall management of an industrial process. *Strategic Planning* is a key to the successful management of this overall process. It is of critical importance in assuring the survival of the enterprise and is ultimately a determinant of the degree of project management success.

In general, *Strategic Planning involves the development of a cohesive plan of action based on the dovetailing of long range, medium range and short term organizational plans*. It is important, therefore, for a Project/Program Manager to have a general understanding of how his effort "fits in the big picture" as well as what influences and affects the "big picture". The rapid transitioning of an idea into production has received a great deal of attention in both the commercial and defense sectors based on obvious cost and competitive considerations. It is as dependent on the quality of the strategic planning as it is on the quality of *tactical implementation* by project/program management. It is thus part and parcel of an overall industrial process with which the project/program manager should be intimately familiar. This part also includes a discussion of future trends in project/program management. Finally, a number of appendices summarize subject areas of special importance to the project manager.

We are indebted to Dr. Ivan Sommers of the U.S. Department of Energy for reviewing the chapter on Risk Analysis and Management; to Ms. Julie A. Leib for reviewing Transition to Production and Timothy J. Otto, J.D. for reviewing Legal Aspects of project management; both Ms. Leib and Mr. Otto are with Hughes Aircraft Company. We are also indebted to Professor Robert P. Keller, J.D., Systems Management Department of the University of Southern California for his review of the Legal Aspects of project management; to Dr. William Yost of The Anderson Graduate Schol of Management at U.C.L.A. for his review of the chapter on ethics; to Robert M. Krone of the University of Southern California for reviewing the Appendix section on Total Quality Management. All of their comments and suggestions were invaluable and greatly appreciated.

Finally, we extend a very special thank you to our families for their patient support and understanding extending over far too many evenings and weekends.

M.M. Obradovitch
S.E. Stephanou

———————————— Contents ————————————

Part Two — Making the Most of Tools and Techniques

Part Three — Getting the Most out of People and the Organization

---------- **Part One** ----------

Introductory Basics

Chapter 1: Introduction

1.1   History of Projects: The Past and the Present

Increases in technological complexity along with the need for a multi-disciplinary approach to the development of new products have given rise to the need for a goal-oriented management technique to cut across existing organization lines. The setting up of projects and the use of project management has been successful in fulfilling this need. The project concept is not new to industry and business. Chemical companies, for example, in developing new products have projectized to make first small batches and then large quantities of the desired product in pilot plant operations. A project leader is designated who works with the originating chemists and chemical engineers, then with pilot plant personnel, and finally with the production engineering and manufacturing groups to make the transition to full-scale production. In this case, as in most projects, what is required is leadership over groups that normally work separately from each other but must be coordinated toward a common goal, namely, the development of a manufacturing technique for producing the desired product.

In a similar manner, construction activities have used modified versions of the project approach throughout history to build aqueducts, bridges, cathedrals, and so on. In present-day construction, a cadre of knowledgeable supervisors lead the effort and labor is recruited locally to fill the needs of the project. The necessary subcontracts are let and when the construction is complete, laborers are dismissed and the cadre of "hard-core" supervisors and management remains to go on to the next project.

With the advent of complex military, civilian, and space systems, the project approach has taken on a new significance, since it now appears to be the most effective technique available for managing the development of large, complex systems involving many different technologies and often extensive subcontracting. Outstanding examples of the success of this approach include the Manhattan Project for the development of the atomic bomb, numerous missile programs of the fifties and the sixties including the development of the ICBM, and the development of new aircraft, weapons, space, computer, and communication systems. The application of the project approach has by no means been limited to the aerospace industry and government procurements; it has found extensive application in civilian industry. The examples of the chemical and construction industries have already been cited, and to these can be added project activity in other technically oriented industries such as electronics, computers, utility, and automobile industries, to mention a few. Also, many banks, financial, service, and non-manufacturing organizations are now set up to carry on project-type activities.

There are several trends that affect management philosophy and encourage the use of projects in today's era of technological revolution. These trends, which were noted as early as 1962 by A.K. Wickesberg and T.C. Cronin,[1] include the following:

- Higher rates of technological innovation, its dissemination and broader-based adaptation, which drive product life cycles (market life) progressively shorter.

- The cost price and resulting profit squeeze fueled by competitive pressures and the complexity of our technology. Current trends are typically and understandably toward smaller production lots and discontinuous runs, given present rates of innovation. In addition, designs and processes that embody the latest in technology are in a continual state of flux and thus seldom reach classical (traditional) stages of production maturity. Under the circumstances, the question is no longer how much profit can be made as much as whether any profit will be realized at all.

- Increasing demand for a higher proportion of specialists and professionals in all phases of product creation throughout the business, industrial, and governmental communities.

As a result of these trends, four distinct forces have developed that drive companies and organizations towards the formation of projects or task teams. These forces and their organizational implications are listed in Table 1.1. In addition, the pressures of national and international competition along with the constant flow of technological improvements and occasional technological breakthroughs further exacerbate the need for a fast response and multidisciplined team approach to product improvement, new product, and process development.*

Although the project approach (including both "pure" projects and "Matrix"-type organizations) has been relatively successful, there have been failures and disappointments. This has been particularly true in the aerospace

---

* For further reading, see David L. Wilemon, "Project Management and Its Conflicts: A View from Apollo," *Chemtech* (September, 1972), p.531.

—— **Table 1.1: Forces Driving Companies Toward the Use of Projects and Task Teams** ——

Factor	Organizational Implications
Rate of change	Adaptable/responsive and temporary structure
Complexity	Multidisciplinary approach/interaction of distributed expertise
Risk	Focus on predetermined requirements and means of reducing attendant risks
Scarcity of resources	Flexibility in allocation and management of limited available resources

industry where high media visibility and congressional scrutiny have revealed and highlighted overruns and failures to meet schedule and performance requirements. In the private sector such failures at the project level (and there are many) do not usually surface and therefore industry is somewhat insulated from public criticism, except perhaps by the stockholders. Nevertheless, the overall advantages of the project approach are sufficient enough to warrant continued use of this approach in special endeavors of the type that are described in the following pages.

1.2   Definition, Concepts, and Terminology

(a)   The Project Approach

In the project approach a project leader (project manager) is designated and a specialized group of people is assigned to work under the leader to carry out a sequence of activities dedicated to the attainment of a goal within the constraints of time, budget, and predetermined performance specifications.

The project approach in modern companies and organizations arose because of the difficulties encountered in trying to carry out the development of a complex system working around and through the usual functional or discipline-oriented groupings of most organizations. Questions of priorities and control arose and often a project had to wait in line for attention from a particular expert or group of experts busy with other work. Subcontracting for various components was more difficult if various product groups were involved. Access to expertise needed in purchasing, manufacturing, finance, quality control, and reliability had to be achieved through appropriate organizational channels. Working in the traditional type of organization, such conditions often made accomplishment, cost, and control unnecessarily difficult and inefficient.

The principal advantage of the project approach is that it provides efficient use of resources with a focal point, namely, the project manager, for the direction, monitoring, and control of the work that has to be done. This approach may be contrasted with that of the functional manager who has to supervise the carrying out of a number of recurring tasks. If special projects are brought to his group, he* must prioritize the various jobs that have to be done, since sufficient resources are not usually available. Thus the project manager has one project with which he is concerned, whereas the functional manager may have responsibility for a number of ongoing operations. Some organizations use the same project manager for several different projects, but this tends to defeat one of the primary purposes of the project approach, which is 100% concentration of the project leader on the tasks to be performed for a particular project. If the projects are small, however, it is possible for a project manager to direct two or possibly three projects.

The project approach is an excellent example of the systems approach, as it considers all of the components and subsystems of a problem and concentrates on the integration of these to produce the optimum system. The components and subsystems may be "soft" such as people and groups in organizations or "hard" such as hardware components subsystems and total assemblies.† The interactions among components and subsystems are identified, evaluated, and adjusted to optimize the performance of the total system. Similarly, the performance of different interdisciplinary groups are integrated by the project manager with respect to cost, schedule, and output so that the best overall effort is attained. Finally, the final system is implemented or tested to provide feedback for evaluating and improving its performance. These are the key characteristics of the systems approach.[2]

The term *systems approach* can be described as the approach to the solution of complex problems or the development of complex systems that ties together the pertinent disciplines in a logical manner. It can be used in the building of all types of systems (hardware, software, social, and so on) or the development of an operational procedure for a complex system. It brings together subsystems in an orderly and efficient manner to accomplish some predetermined goal. More generally, it can be considered to be a management technique or method for problem solving or developing a procedure or system. The systems approach looks at a problem in its entirety and uses all the available science and technology to solve it. Key references in the theory and application of the systems approach are the treatises of Kast and Rosenzweig[3] and Churchman.[4]

(b) Projects and Programs

Projects are often confused with programs, and the two terms can be, and often are, used synonymously. Projects sometimes become programs and programs can end up being projects if life spans are shortened or funding is decreased.

---

* To avoid the awkwardness of *he/she*, we have chosen to use the personal pronoun he throughout. It is understood, of course, that this gender distinction is not applicable in real-life situations.

† The term *soft* as used here is not to be confused with *software*, which usually refers to computer tapes, discs, programs, and the like.

Projects usually have the following notable characteristics:

- They are typically unique nonrecurring undertakings.
- They generally involve a degree of urgency and are of importance to the organization.
- They have special, precise requirements with respect to performance, schedule, and cost.
- They involve the development of a relatively complex operation, product, or system with clear-cut goals and objectives.

These characteristics may be contrasted with those of a product development program where the technical activity is ongoing and can have an unspecified lifetime with continuous funding. For example, a paint company has a product improvement program that employs scientists and engineers in a continuing effort to improve the quality and durability of its line of paints. Improvements in the pigments, vehicles, and other ingredients of the paint are constantly being sought through testing of new materials and mix compositions. The objectives may be quite specific over the period of a year but may change from year to year. The overall objective remains the same, however, namely, to improve the salability and profitability of the paint. The overall technical effort can continue year after year despite changes.

Although the term *project* is customarily applied to the study, development, or operation of relatively complex systems, it can and is used to describe any goal-oriented effort that has a time and cost constraint. It may involve only a few personnel over a short time span at a relatively small cost or hundreds or even thousands of people with commensurate major time and cost expenditures. Although major projects costing into the millions, sometimes billions, of dollars get the most publicity, minor projects of less than $1 million outnumber large projects by at least 1,000 to 1.

As we noted, programs are often called projects and vice versa; this is understandable since they are so closely related. In government contracting, projects may be subsets of programs or they can be one and the same, depending upon the complexity of the effort, the dollar value, and the time involved.

(c) Project Life Cycle

Projects have a finite time span and the emphasis of activity varies with time. The several ways that the overall life cycle of a project or a system development can be described are summarized in Table 1.2. Each phase can be sequential or there may be overlap; for example, the conceptual phase may overlap with the definition phase, and so on.

The actual carrying out of a project occurs after the completion of a feasibility of preliminary study and the acceptance of the proposal. The variation in level of personnel used throughout the different phases of a project is shown in Figure 1.1. The curve showing the use of personnel parallels to a considerable extent the use of funds and other resources, particularly when

—————————— Table 1.2: Life Cycle Phases of Projects and Systems ——————————

Stuckenbruck et al[a]		Kerzner[b]		Archibald[c]	Cleland & King[d]
Nongovt. Project	Govt. Project	System/ Project	Project	Project	System
Initiation	Conceptual	Conceptual	Project formation	Concept	Conceptual
Growth	Definition	Definition	Project buildup	Definition	Definition
Production	Production or acquisition	Production	Production	Design	Production or acquistion
Shutdown	Operational	Operational	Phase-out	Manufacture	Operational
	Divestment	Divestment	Final audit	Installation	Divestment

[a] L.C. Stuckenbruck, et al., *The Implementation of Project Management* (Reading, Mass.: Addison-Wesley), 1980), p. 20.

[b] H. Kerzner, *Project Management: A Systems Approach to Planning, Scheduling and Controlling* (New York: Van Nostrand Reinhold, 1979) pp. 25-26.

[c] R.D. Archibald, *Managing High-Technology Programs and Projects* (New York: John Wiley, 1976), p. 22.

[d] D.I. Cleland and W.R. King, *Systems Analysis and Project Management* (New York: McGraw-Hill, 1975), pp. 185-190.

the project has high engineering content. Where many projects are involved or the company is completely project oriented, personnel use can vary as in Figure 1.2.

—————— Figure 1.1: Personnel Growth and Decline During the Execution of a Project ——————

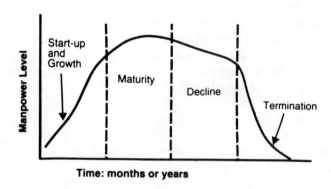

Time: months or years

Note: 1. The curves for other resource use such as facilities, materials, and services often parallel the manpower-level curve.

2. The curve could also be applicable to a product life cycle. For some high-technology industries, the total lifetime of a product can be as little as 10 months or even less.

Source: S.E. Stephanou, *Management: Technology, Innovation & Engineering*, (Malibu, Calif.: Daniel Spencer, 1981), p. 192.

Figure 1.2: Multiproject Management (Project-Oriented Organization)

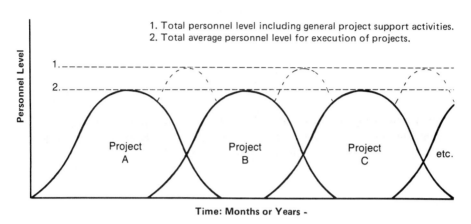

1. Total personnel level including general project support activities.
2. Total average personnel level for execution of projects.

Personnel Level

1. -
2. -

Project A   Project B   Project C   etc.

Time: Months or Years -

Notes: 1. In this example a stable work force is assumed with the projects of the same size.

2. In real-life situations, the projects are not exactly the same size nor is the timing equally spaced and predictable, so that strategic planning and a high level of management control is needed.

3. This set of curves could also be applied to product development, where each project would be a product and the time span would be the product life-cycle.

For a project in which a large, complex hardware system involving technical improvements is being developed, the following activities during the various phases are typical:

Start-Up and Growth Phase. The start-up and growth phase includes staffing, ordering materials, making make-buy decisions, sending out requests for bids, selecting subcontractors and vendors, and arranging for the required technical and other support from within the company. The detailed planning for the project is the first order of business. It may have been done in outline form in the feasibility study, but, at this point there are usually insufficient funds to allow for complete planning and programming. The term programming is used here to mean planning the sequence or chronology of events and expenditures, not program monitoring or computer programming.

Maturity Phase. In the maturity phase the project is well under way and major inroads have been made on the principal problems (critical issues), although there are still residual questions to be answered. Most of the components and subsystems are well along in development, and deliveries of the first of the components and subsystems are being received from the vendors. Subcontractors should have advanced in their technical and development work and already achieved a major degree of success. However, there still remains engineering work to be done, which may involve testing, systems integration, pilot plant operation, and a host of other development activities.* During the maturity phase, staff and other expenditures reach their maximum values. The critical issues have been attacked, alternative solutions examined, and the most promising solutions selected and implemented.

Components and subsystems are assembled and tested by the specific systems groups and the subsystems integrated into the total system by the systems integration groups. There may also be some mock-up and experimental prototypes set up depending on the project. If the project involves the development of new technology, morale of the engineers and scientists can be high in this stage since technical activity is still intense and there remain problems to be solved.

Decline Phase. Following the maturity phase, technical activity begins to ebb gradually and emphasis shifts to hardware or process development, including testing, pilot plant, and production engineering problems. The project manager and his staff must see to it that personnel are gradually released to other projects or other operations in the company or returned to their original group.

Termination Phase. This phase of the project marks the conclusion of the technical and other efforts. The total system has been fabricated and the system is being delivered to the customer. A certain amount of continuing technical support is needed to solve minor problems in systems performance and provide technical consulting, but these problems are more of an operational than a design nature. Final documentation is prepared to furnish the necessary information for future reference, modification, and product or system improvement. This phase of the project can involve wholesale "destaffing" with all the attendant problems of relocating personnel.† The project manager and his staff usually remain to close out the project and make certain that customer requirements are fully met. If large, operational systems are the product, a cadre of personnel may be retained to service them.

It is also important that the logistic support requirements of the system be summarized and documented. This aspect of project management may persist well after the main effort of project execution has been accomplished and the product is operational. It must be planned for in the design, development, and production of the system. Unfortunately, there have been instances where

---

* This can include support activities such as logistics planning and implementation.

† In the past there have been cases of large government-funded projects where mass layoffs occurred during the decline and termination phases. This condition is presently mitigated by a number of factors including better planning by both government agencies and the companies involved and better company policies and practices.

——————————————— Figure 1.3: The Systems Life Cycle ———————————————

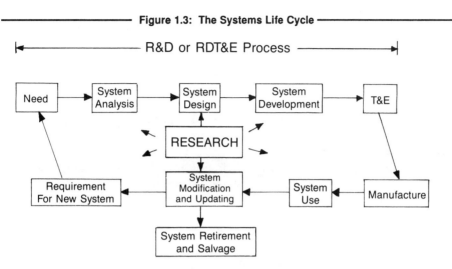

Notes: 1. All of the steps in the systems life cycle may have feedback and iteration.
2. Systems analysis can drive the need or vice versa.
3. Need can arise from strategic planning.
4. Research is really the hub of the activity in a high-technology system development and can provide input during all phases and steps of the systems life cycle. However, in most system developments, the major portion of research is done in the earlier stages along with or preceding the system analysis.

Source: Adapted from S.E. Stephanou, *Management: Technology, Innovation & Engineering* (Malibu, Calif.: Daniel Spencer, 1981), p. 30.

products have been successfully developed but logistics support was lacking in the operational phase.

For major systems, particularly government-funded systems such as Department of Defense, there is a system life cycle (Figure 1.3) comparable to the product or project life cycle. For such systems obsolescence must be planned for and included in forecasting and predictions of resource allocations. The research and development (R&D) process or, for DOD systems, the research, development, test, and engineering (RDT&E) process can be included in the system life cycle.

(d) Systems Development and Related Concepts

The term *systems development,* often used synonymously with project management, is the design, development, and manufacture of complex systems; it also can involve design, development, and implementation of complex operations or the solution of complex problems. Hard systems as well as soft systems may be developed. Hard systems primarily involve hardware, whereas soft systems involve operational techniques or procedures that may be inherent to or embodied in the hardware. An example of a hard system would be a new type of coal excavation equipment; an example of a soft system would be a new operational procedure for processing checks in a bank.

The term *systems development* is also often used interchangeably with *systems management, systems integration* and *systems engineering.* They relate to the same general type of activity but have different emphases. The meaning of each term must be determined from the context in which it is used.

For example, systems management can involve not only the development of the system but also its implementation, operation, and management, including feedback, further improvement, and logistics support requirements, either singly or in combination. In this context it is a much more encompassing term than the others.

Systems integration emphasizes bringing together components into subsystems and subsystems to form systems. It often involves coordination of diverse technical efforts and hardware developments that culminate in the successful testing and operation of the total system. An example of system integration would be the bringing together of the components of a special-purpose computer, such as input, output, processing, and memory units, into a compatible physical volume, properly packaged or encased, that worked harmoniously to operate as designed. It is particularly concerned with the identification and correction of any interface problems between components of subsystems and the optimization of the subsystems to give maximum performance of the total system.

Systems engineering is also used synonymously with systems development, systems integration, and systems management.[5] It emphasizes the application of the various engineering disciplines needed to carry out the systems development process, especially in the design of the product or system. A.W. Wymore defines it as the professional, intellectual, and academic discipline that has as its primary concern the analysis and design of large-scale, complex, human/machine systems.[6]

Aerospace companies and DOD have slightly different interpretations: Hughes Aircraft considers systems engineering a necessary and effective technique used by the company to achieve the most efficient and orderly development and production of the grouped physical products that together compose a product system. The Air Force in its directives refers to systems engineering as the engineering management of a total system to ascertain and maintain technical integrity over all the elements of the system. In this context, systems engineering is synonymous with systems management.

The foregoing terms are so closely related that it is no wonder they are commonly used interchangeably with project management to describe project effort, particularly hardware development.

1.3 Advantages and Disadvantages of the Project Approach

Advantages of the project approach can be summarized as follows:

1. The designation and use of a project manager provides a focal point for leading, monitoring, and controlling the work that has to be done.

2. The project approach answers the need for developing a complex product or system within a specified period of time, within predetermined cost and performance parameters.
3. The project can be operated as a financially independent unit from the rest of the company so that information gathering, execution, and termination of the project can be achieved with the least disturbance of other company operations.
4. Numerous components, subsystems, and systems can be developed in parallel with various groups or entities within or outside the company.
5. Performing development or special jobs for another company or organization may require closer or differently prescribed control of cost, schedule, and performance than is customary in the company.
6. The project concept allows for cutting across the organizational lines and technical disciplines so that technical and other required expertise can be drawn from different functional parts of the company and used 100% for the needs of the project. These experts can be released when their services are no longer needed.
7. The working toward definite goals, the charisma of an effective project leader, the technical challenge, and the potential benefits if the project succeeds can provide a high level of personnel morale and camaraderie. Personnel tend to identify themselves with the project and its success.

Like any system, the project approach is not perfect. Ignoring these imperfections might create the impression that the formation of a project is a panacea for all organizational problems.

There are in fact important disadvantages to the project approach. These can include the following:

1. Weakening of the functional organizations through loss of key personnel
2. Disruption of mainline product support functions owing to special needs of projects
3. Dilution of company resources
4. Development of conflicts within the organization
5. Designation and setting up of projects in situations where regular functional groups could accommodate the need (overprojectizing)

Often a series of tasks or the development of a product can be successfully carried out within a functional group without setting up a project. In fact, the latter may "red-flag" a situation and mask the real source of the problem, causing a delay in the correction of what should have been a simple line management problem.[7] Project management should not be used to salvage what are basically unsound or hopeless situations, although it sometimes may require a project to determine this. The role played by the manager of such a project would be that of trouble shooter; this role should be recognized from the outset. Project management should not be used to provide artificial growth opportunities (promotions) for deserving personnel where no real growth and new projects exist.

Conflicts that can develop within a functioning organization (item 4) as a result of the introduction of the project approach is a serious potential disadvantage; it is discussed in Chapter 8.

1.4 Reasons for Project Failures

There are any number of documented reasons why projects can fail. A few of the most frequently mentioned are as follows:

1. The basis for the project is not sound (inadequate planning).
2. There is a lack of management/company support (including money and other resources).
3. Tasks are inaccurately defined.
4. Management techniques/systems are misused (or not used at all).
5. Communications are inadequate (faulty information system).
6. There is too much shifting of personnel owing to changing priorities.
7. There is failure to take into consideration the varying relative importance of performance, cost, and schedule during the project.
8. The wrong person is chosen as project manager.
9. The manager falls prey to temptations of expedience.
10. Staffing is poor.
11. Project termination is not planned.

These reasons do not stand alone since several are intimately related; nor are they arranged in order of importance or applicability since one or more can precipitate the downfall of a project. Probably the lack of appropriate planning and the failure to attain full management support are the principal reasons; these two can catalyze the onset of other failure characteristics. It may be that the effort should never have been projectized to begin with but should have been handled within a functional group.

We deal with methods of recognizing and overcoming these potential sources of project failure in subsequent chapters of this book.

1.5 Alternative to Projectizing

A logical question in considering project management is: What alternatives are available to a manager or executive for accomplishing a non-typical task in the organization when the task has special requirements of time, effort, skills, facilities and cost? The question could be asked in another way: How were special tasks with the preceding characteristics carried out before project management became recognized as a cost-effective and efficient method of carrying out complex jobs? There are several answers to this question:

a. The executive may determine the detailed tasks that must be accomplished by each of the various function groups and any outside groups that may be involved. He can do this himself, he can use his staff people, or he can require that the functional and other groups submit descriptions of what their tasks would be for the particular job. After he or one of his staff has reviewed, modified, and approved the tasks, he can direct the groups to proceed with their specific segments of the job. Following completion of all work, the output is collected and evaluated and the system integrated by direction of the executive with or without assistance from his staff.

b. The executive can assign a functional head to act in his place to see that the tasks are developed and the various portions of the work are assigned to the functional and other groups. The designated functional head would collect, evaluate, and integrate the system.

c. The executive can designate a member of his staff or a coordinator to act in his place and see that the tasks are developed, and so on. The coordinator may also be selected from within the functional organization and should have talents that make him particularly suited for the job.

d. The work may be subcontracted to an organization outside the company.

These four alternatives have distinct disadvantages. Method (a) has the disadvantage of requiring the valuable time and energy of the executive. How many such jobs can he take on and still effectively carry out his principal job of directing and managing the overall operation of the functional organization? This disadvantage can be avoided by assigning a staff person to the task of collecting and coordinating the input, although the staff person would not have the authority of the organizational leader. However, if the project is important enough and the executive can spare the time, this procedure is not as disadvantageous as it might appear. Many small companies follow this procedure where there aren't many projects to be carried out. Method (a) resembles project management in that the organizational leader acts as the project manager, although the functional heads have the responsibility of carrying out the particular work that has to be done in their group.

Method (b) has the same disadvantages as (a) as it dilutes the overall activity of the supervisor, in this case the functional head, and this results in his having less time for the customary, but not unimportant, day-to-day op-

erations. A further disadvantage of method (b) is that the functional head
may have difficulty imposing his authority on another functional head who is
normally his peer. This could place him in an undesirable role and jeopardize
future relations with the particular peer. What usually happens is that whatever input is furnished by other functional groups is accepted by the functional head who is leading the effort. The alternative is to resort to higher
management assistance, which may create problems in future relations with
peer functional heads.

Method (c) suffers from the fact that staff people are specialists, usually
not as well versed in organizational operations as functional personnel and
often lacking the image of authority needed for leading an important project-
type effort that calls for maximum effort from all the concerned segments of
the company.

Subcontracting the special job to an outside organization—method (d)—is
a kind of project management. It can be considered analogous to the formation of a pure project except that none of the participating team members are
drawn from the functional organization. However, there are the potential
disadvantages of increased cost and less control. The in-house management
may have to depend on the outside organization's wishes in carrying out the
work.

1.6 Project Management, Strategic Planning, and Productivity

Project management is intimately related to strategic planning since appropriate long-range planning is needed to determine what continuing or new
areas of products or systems should be developed, at what level of funding
and in what sequence, and which organizational segments should be involved
and how. The ultimate output of strategic planning is a series of efforts or
projects that will ensure the survival of the company in a highly competitive
and constantly changing market. High productivity ensures that the projects
will be carried out in a successful manner with maximum cost effectiveness
and also that revenues will be adequate to supply the various system development and other basic needs of the company. These relationships are discussed
in Chapters 9 and 12.

——— Questions and Topics for Discussion ———

1. The term *project management* may create semantic confusion, particularly
    when it is used along with certain related terms. Discuss project manage-
    ment as it relates to the following: (a) systems engineering, (b) task force
    operation, (c) systems development, (d) systems management, (e) pro-
    gram management, and (f) systems integration.

2. How are projects carried out by a construction company usually different

from those performed within an industrial firm as part of a new process development?

3.   The construction of the Egyptian pyramids can be considered to have been a major project. What do you think the major criteria for successful completion of this project were and how do they compare with those for the construction of a nuclear plan today? Develop a table showing your comparison of these two projects based on the criteria you have selected.

4.   How is the project approach similar to the systems approach?

5.   Under what conditions can a project become a program and a program become a project?

6.   How does strategic planning relate to the maintenance and support of a steady stream of projects over an extended period of years?

7.   Describe conditions in a company where the setting up of a project to handle a special complex problem would not be desireable.

8.   Discuss how lack of management support could cause a project to fail.

9.   Some experts in management have referred to the general field of management (included project management) as a "social" rather than a "mathematical" activity. What is meant by this assertion?

--------------------------------- **References** ---------------------------------

1.   A.K. Wickesberg and T.C. Cronin, "Management by Task Force," *Harvard Business Review* (November-December 1962).

2.   S.E. Stephanou, *Systems Approach to Societal Problems* (Malibu, Calif.: Daniel Spencer, 1982), pp. 3-12.

3.   F.E. Kast and J.E. Rosenzweig, *Organization and Management* (New York: Dell, 1968).

4.   C.W. Churchman, *The Systems Approach* (New York: Dell, 1981).

5.   S.E. Stephanou, "Semantic Problems in Systems Engineering," *International Symposium on Systems Engineering,* Vol. 2, (Columbus, Ohio: Purdue University, 1972), p. 338.

6.   A. Wayne Wymore, *Systems Engineering Methodology for Interdisciplinary Games* (New York: John Wiley, 1976), p.1.

7.   C.C. Martin, *Project Management, How to Make it Work* (AMACOM, New York: 1976), p.273.

——————————————— Chapter 2 ———————————————
Project Initiation and Preproject Activities

Before the actual execution of a project, certain decisions and actions take place. In this chapter we examine the specifics of those events that trigger or precipitate the project effort.

The following general sequence usually occurs. In industry the sequence is

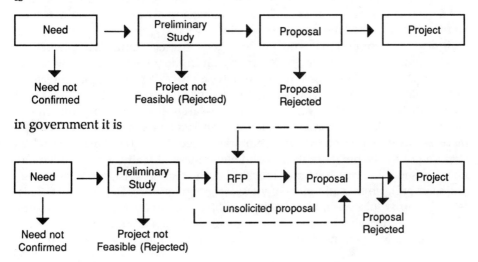

in government it is

There are several variations in the preceding series of steps in the case of government agencies: (1) An unsolicited proposal can be followed by a request of proposal (RFP) to competitive companies (the originally proposing company would have an advantage in such an instance). (2) The government agency can issue an RFP for the preliminary study. (3) The preliminary study can be part of the proposal.

2.1 Need and Need Analysis

First, a need must be recognized by company personnel, another company or organization, a government agency, or the public; then the need must be confirmed and funding obtained for a preliminary or feasibility study. The confirmation of the need may be carried out as a separate effort (need analysis) or a preliminary study may be initiated to evaluate the need. If the need is valid, the study must evaluate in a preliminary way how the need can be met.

The need for an improved product, a new product, or improved process or operation can arise from within the company or from outside the company. Within the company the requirement may be identified by technical personnel or supervision. This is sometimes referred to as "technology-driven" need or "technology-push," the important feature being that the need for the work has originated with the technologists. In contrast with "market-driven" need or "technology-pull," the need for a new product or capability is observed by someone outside the development organization and the technologists are asked to perform research and development to answer the need. An example of technology-push was the discovery of lasers in a research laboratory and their subsequent application to communications, weaponry, and medicine. An example of technology-pull was the recognition by consumer groups and the government of the need for improved driver and passenger safety in motor vehicles and the resulting applied research that was carried out to develop seat belts, air bags, collapsible bumpers, and other protective devices. In the case of technology-push, what technical personnel consider desireable may not necessarily be what can sell. There have been many cases of products that were technically challenging and professionally satisfying to those involved in their development but, that were not commercially successful. It is interesting here to contrast the two ends of the spectrum in the generation of new ideas. At one end is the technologist who promotes an idea or product that is technically challenging while having less than adequate knowledge of marketability, whereas at the other end is an executive (research director, vice president of engineering, sales director, or the like) who insists on a new product development because of potential profit or market need while having little understanding of the technical problems of development. Ideally, a symbiotic relationship should exist between management, the technologist, manufacturing, and marketing so that all points of view are given appropriate emphasis. This relationship would resemble that reported for the Japanese style of management where idea and product development decisions are arrived at over an extended period of time and with a great deal of interplay and discussion between all segments of the company.[1] This subject is discussed more extensively in Chapter 12.

———— **Figure 2.1: Cumulative Expenditures In the Development of a New System** ————

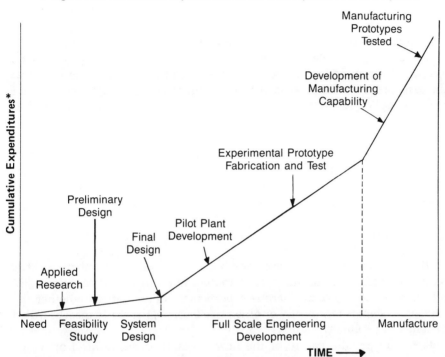

* Depending upon the particular product, this could be a logarithmic scale. Early steps in the development process are at least one order of magnitude less in cost than subsequent steps.

Soucre: S. E. Stephanou, *Management: Technology, Innovation & Engineering*, (Malibu, Calif.: Daniel Spencer, 1981), p. 184.

There are many factors that must be taken into account in the confirmation of a need or a need analysis. Questions include the following:

- Will the need still exist and will the customer be willing to pay the price for the product when it is developed and ready for sale? (This may be as far away as three years or more.)
- Will government action (legislation) affect the need or sale of the product?
- How will competitors respond to the new product?
- What will the economic climate be when the system or product is mass produced and marketed?
- Are observations and needs expressed by salespeople and marketing personnel accurate and reliable?
- Are the technical personnel too enthused about the technical challenge rather than the economic payoff (technology-push)?

For commercial products, market research is necessary to establish the need. Carrying out market research is a specialty in itself, requiring experts who have been trained in the art of consumer and customer sampling. Will the product be sold to the public, industry, or the government? What segment of the population will buy the item? Answers to these and other questions will affect the decision to initiate a project. If the need is not confirmed, the project must be stopped as quickly as possible; otherwise unnecessary costs are incurred. The cumulative costs of developing a product or carrying out a project are diagrammed in Figure 2.1. It is evident that costs are relatively low at the early stages of the process but rise rapidly as the product development goes from applied research to the hardware, prototype, pilot plant, and process development stage.

Although this discussion has emphasized the identification and confirmation of the need, need analysis may be included as part of a feasibility or preliminary study, which is normally carried out before embarking on a major product or system development. Such a study can not only confirm the need but also investigate in a preliminary way how the need can be met.

2.2 Preliminary Studies

After the need for the project has been identified and confirmed, it is necessary to make a preliminary study to determine what will be involved in satisfying the need. Where there is a particular concern about whether the product or system is technically or otherwise feasible, the study may be called a feasibility or exploratory study.

Depending on the nature of the new product or technical effort to be accomplished, the preliminary study can include several or all of the following factors:

- Development of alternative concepts to fit the need
- Identification of critical issues, technical and nontechnical
- Possible solutions to the critical issues
- Technical feasibility
- Economic feasibility including cost estimates for resources needed
- Make-or-buy decisions (including subcontracting requirements)
- Enumeration of tasks and subtasks (work breakdown structure)
- Development of preliminary specifications or system requirements
- Environmental impact and other societal or public effects (technology assessment)
- Product liability possibilities of a new product to be sold to the public

The study can be a short, preliminary type of effort indicating estimated levels of personnel, facilities, materials, and costs, or it can be a complete evaluation of what is needed to carry out the project. Logistic support requirements may be included if the project is a complex new system requiring considerable maintenance and support. If the funding allows, the preliminary study can include detailed planning such as the preparation of a work break-down structure, work flow charts, GANTT and estimated expenditure versus time charts, and so on. The results of the feasibility study are usually docu-mented in a report or they can be incorporated into a full-fledged solicited or unsolicited proposal to the funding organization or customer.

In the case of a project effort or system development requiring a major expenditure, the customer often requests the preliminary study before full funding of the project. In such cases the preliminary study itself can be treated as a project. In the past, government agencies like the Department of Defense (DOD) have included development of information of this type in a program definition phase (PDP) or a cost definition phase (CDP) for a system develop-ment. In industry the preliminary study is usually carried out by a special project group, a new product development group, a technical and economic studies group, or some other group experienced in making this type of study. For large projects that will involve many people and major costs, company management designates a study leader who then selects or is assigned key personnel to assist him in making the preliminary or feasibility study. It is better if the group making the study is together in the same physical location to enhance communication and interaction among the participants and the project leadership. The effect of physical distance has been borne out in the studies of Allen and Fusfeld (Figure 2.2). Although the data deal with commu-nication between R&D personnel, the principle of co-location is equally appli-cable to project study teams and similar groups.

If after the preliminary study the decision is made to proceed with the project, then the study leader usually becomes the project manager and the key personnel who assisted him become his deputies and key supervisors in the project.

2.3 Requests for Proposals (RFPs)

If the project is to be carried out by an outside organization, an RFP can be used. The purpose of the RFP is to identify organizations that are qualified and cost effective in building the system, carrying out the operation, testing, or in other ways executing the work. If a government agency is to fund the project, a formalized RFP is issued to a selected list of bidders who have already been established as qualified. In the private sector the RFP has a much less standardized format than in the public sector; each company will have its own special type of document, information request format, and proce-dure for soliciting project work.

The RFP is called different names by different government agencies and companies, for example, request for bid (RB), procurement request (PR), pro-curement invitation (PI), and invitation for bid (IB).

Regardless of whether the organization is public or private, the RFP must ask for key information on costs, technical and management capability, and schedule; in addition, it must supply background information on the project.

— Figure 2.2: Probability of Communication Versus Distance Between R&D Personnel —

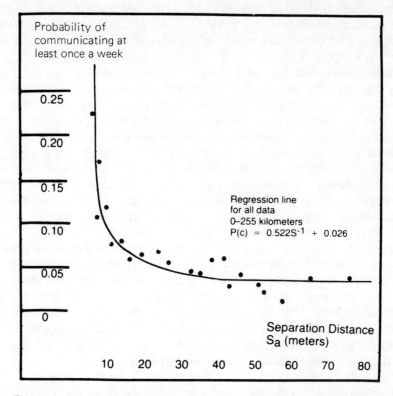

Note: The graph shows the probability that two people will communicate as a function of the distance separating them. The authors studied the relationship between the communication patterns of professional people and the separation of their offices in seven research and development organizations to obtain the data shown here. Though intuition suggests a curve of this shape, the fact that the probability of communication falls so rapidly as separations approach only 10 meters was surpising.

Source: Thomas J. Allen and Alan R. Fusfeld, "Design for Communication in the Research and Development Lab," *Technology Review* (May 1976), p. 66. Massachusetts Institute of Technology, Cambridge, Mass. Reprinted with permission from *Technology Review*, copyright 1976.

Typically, the contents of an RFP include the following:

- Discussion giving background of problem and reasons why work or system is needed
- Description of the deliverable end product along with the delivery schedule—when tasks are to be completed or hardware or software delivered
- Design/product specifications—what is required in terms of detailed product performance specifications and acceptance criteria
- Funds available (not usually given, although level of engineering hours expected may be indicated)

- Reporting requirements:
  - Design reviews (preliminary and critical)
  - Frequency of reports depends upon nature and size of contract. Written reports could include monthly letters, accomplishment reports, quarterly status reports, or final reports.
- Boilerplate*
  - Contract data requirements list
  - Special facilities needed or furnished
  - Format for reporting progress
  - How the proposal will be evaluated
  - Instructions regarding inventions and trade secrets
  - Special instructions
- If the RFP is for a project that is to be funded by a government agency, there are many additional requirements in the boilerplate sections, such as the following:
  - Certification that facilities are nonsegregated
  - Implementation/support of equal opportunity/affirmative action programs
  - Penalties for false statements (for example, currency of cost/pricing data)
  - Statement of what government furnished equipment (GFE) and facilities will be provided
  - Compliance with OSHA and other government regulations
  - Proposal preparation instructions

It is essential to supply sufficient information so that the organization receiving the RFP can respond in the most complete and pertinent manner.

RFPs for a government agency project may be advertised in the Commerce Business Daily (CBD), a publication of the Department of Commerce. This publication lists brief descriptions of all government procurement invitations, contract awards, and R&D and technical work, as well as subcontracting possibilities and foreign business opportunities. The CBD furnishes a brief summary of the work and an address where an interested organization can write for the complete RFP or for more information.

2.4 Project Proposals

(a) General Requirements

The proposal presents the plan for the full-fledged execution of the project. It may be a proposal to company management for work to be carried out within the company or a plan for work to be done for another company or

---

* The term *boilerplate* refers to certain clauses that are usually included with every RFP or request for work to be done by an outside contractor. The exact boilerplate clauses used vary with the organization seeking the work and the nature of the project.

organization. In the case of government projects, the proposal may be written in response to an RFP. This is referred to as a solicited proposal in contrast to an unsolicited proposal where no RFP has been written and the company has perceived a need that the customer may wish to fulfill. Unsolicited proposals are often efforts to influence anticipated customer requirements in the direction that the company may consider to be to its advantage.

The arrangement of a project proposal varies with the organization; in some cases the specific subject areas and even the format may be dictated by the customer. This is more often the case in the government than in the private sector, although industrial and business undertakings can be quite specific with respect to requirements and information that must be supplied. There are some subjects, however, that must be addressed in any proposal. These include description of the technical approach, a list of tasks and subtasks, a schedule of individual task and overall project completion dates, personnel and facilities that will be used, organization of the project, past experience and key personnel, estimated costs, delivery dates if there are deliverables, and a schedule of reporting. If the project has a high-technology content, the proposal will usually be developed in two sections or volumes, a technical section and a management section; there may also be a separate cost section or cost proposal. Procedures and details for pricing a proposal are given in Chapter 4. Figure 2.3 shows a sample proposal format for a small R&D project.

————————————— **Figure 2.3: Sample Proposal for a Small Project** —————————————

Technical Section

    (a) Introduction and background of problem or system requirement

    (b) Technical approach
- Technology required
- Indentification of critical issues and how they are going to be resolved

    (c) Work statement
- Spells out exactly what is going to be done
- Tasks and subtasks are itemized concisely

    (d) Schedule
- Bar charts showing initiation and completion dates for various tasks (as already discussed)
- Milestone table giving important events and estimated completion dates

Management Section

    (a) Previous experience of company in the particular project area

    (b) Organization chart showing delegation of authority and division or work
- Project organization—project manager, task leader, scientists, and engineers, consultants—showing how technical effort is tied into the company organization
- Biographies of key personnel showing pertinent experience

    (c) Costs—personnel
- Personnel—scientists, engineers, technicians
- Computer/programmer costs
- Materials
- Travel
- Documentation (costs of reports)

    (d) Delivery dates of hardware or software, or completion dates, if a non-hardware system

    (e) Company facilities that will be utilized

    (f) Quality control and reliability considerations

Source: S.E. Stephanou, *Management: Technology, Innovation, & Engineering* (Malibu, Calif.: Daniel Spencer, 1981), p. 187.

A proposal for a large project can be quite extensive and can include some or most of the following:

One- or two-page executive summary or cover letter
Technical approach and discussion
Work statement
GANTT and milestone charts
Work breakdown structure
Work flowcharts (CPM, PERT, and the like)
Estimated cost versus time plots
Percentage of work planned versus time plots
Performance measurement procedure
Cost control techniques
Schedule of personnel use
Biographies and experience of key personnel
Delivery dates of hardware or software
Schedule of task completion dates
Quality control and reliability considerations
Organization charts
Contractual and cost data
Company qualifications and experience
Facilities
Boilerplate

Some of the items may have already been considered in the preliminary or feasibility study but in less detail.

Most of the preceding items, with the exception of the cover letter and the biographies of key personnel, will be part of the project plan that is developed during the planning phase (Chapter 4). The cover letter and work statement are particularly important for the presentation and acceptance of a proposal. They are discussed in the following sections.*

(b) Summary or Cover Letter

Since at the higher levels of management there is often insufficient time for complete reading of the proposal, a short "executive" summary (one or two pages) or cover letter can be effective in describing its important aspects.

The summary should describe the capability and experience of the proposing organization by (1) recounting briefly previous or related experience in the subject area of the proposal; (2) describing the special capabilities of the project team and the organization in key areas of the proposed work; (3) identifying and showing an understanding of the critical issues involved in

---

* R.D. Stewart and A.L. Stewart have published a book, *Proposal Preparation* (Somerset, N.J.: John Wiley, 1984), which claims to provide step-by-step guidance on how to prepare a "winning" proposal.

the project through a discussion of how they will be solved; (4) indicating briefly the approach the program that will be carried out (often this is amplified by a brief discussion of the relative shortcomings of other competitive approaches); and (5) giving reasons why the proposing organization should be granted the work.

(c) Work Statement

The work statement can be part of the technical or the management section of the proposal depending upon the type and magnitude of the proposal. It should set forth accurately and succinctly what work is to be done, usually in a task and subtask format (Figure 2.4). It may or may not include delivery or task completion dates; this information is usually given in the schedule of performance. Particular attention should be given to the work statement if the proposal is to another company or organization since it involves commitments of work that have contractual implications. The amount of work promised must be carefully evaluated to ensure compatibility with the available funds.

Although there are factors other than the proposal itself that can determine whether or not a proposal in a competitive situation is successful, the writing and development of the proposal should be as close to perfect as possible. Previous experience and contacts with the particular customer, company prestige and track record, as well as other factors (not always predictable) can affect the final selection decision of the customer. Certainly, "brochuremanship" in the preparation and finalization of a proposal cannot be ignored, although it can be and often has been overdone. The special requirements and procedures for proposals specifically directed toward government agencies such as the DOD are included in Section 2.7 and 2.8 and Chapter 10.

Figure 2.4: Sample Work Statement for the Development of an Improved Financial Control System for a Small Company

Task 1.0	Examine literature for previous work on financial control systems of small companies.
	1.1 Review company archives to study previous financial control systems used by the company.
	1.2 Review archive and trade journals for articles on financial control systems.
Task 2.0	Based on findings of Task 1.0, develop a system suitable for the present operations of the company.
Task 3.0	Develop suitable software to implement the system using existing company computer capability.
	3.1 Evaluate existing available software packages.
	3.1 Modify existing software or develop special software package.
Task 4.0	Test software package using actual company data and compare results with existing system.
Task 5.0	Modify program as needed based on results of Task 4.0.
Task 6.0	Summarize this system development in appropriate documentation.

Note: Detailing the various costs associated with the individual tasks and subtasks is helpful in delineating the resources required and arriving at the total cost of the
project (see Chapter 4, Section 4.3)

(d) "Straw-Man" Proposals

Knowing the customer's needs and requirements increases the probability of winning a competitive bid. In private industry such needs and requirements are transmitted through marketing, sales, and service representatives or even technical personnel in constant touch with customers. Companies dealing with government agencies maintain permanent personnel in Washington D.C., and near large government facilities just to be in close communication with customers. This is particularly true if the company is already engaged in work for a particular government agency.

When word is received through company representatives of an upcoming procurement, the company can set up a "straw-man" proposal.* The straw-man proposal responds to the requirements of the customer as gleaned from all possible intelligence sources. If the response time to the RFP when it is issued is relatively short and if the requirements assume considerable previous preparation and related work, this technique can be quite effective.

In the aerospace industry, for example, companies have been known to involve hundreds of engineers for many months in preparation for an RFP for a large system development that the company anticipates a government agency will request. A "mock" RFP that includes anticipated system requirements and a responding straw-man proposal in such a situation can be highly advantageous. Similar activities occur in non-aerospace industries.

2.5 Project Evaluation and Selection

In organizations where a number of candidate proposals for projects are presented for consideration, the allocation of resources becomes an important consideration. Aggressive and creative laboratories and system, product, and process development groups, as well as feedback from customers, will result in more ideas for projects than can possibly be financed.

The methods used by management to make the optimum selection of projects and decide whether to proceed on a proposed project are varied indeed. Each company or organization has its own special procedures, and a constant flow of articles appears in academic journals giving theoretical treatment of the subject.[2,3] Inevitably, an economic evaluation must be made, although there are certainly other considerations. For both the project itself and the anticipated product or system, that can result, consideration must be given to company compatibility, appropriate allocation of resources, safety and liability aspects, government regulations and policies, and environmental impact (if any). Some evaluation techniques that can be used are described in the following sections.

---

* The "straw-man" proposal is drawn up to respond as completely as possible to the actual RFP as it will appear when it is finally issued. In an ideal situation the final proposal submitted in response to the official RFP will only be a slightly modified version of the "straw-man" proposal.

——————— **Figure 2.5: Product Life Cycle and Recovery of Development Costs** ———————

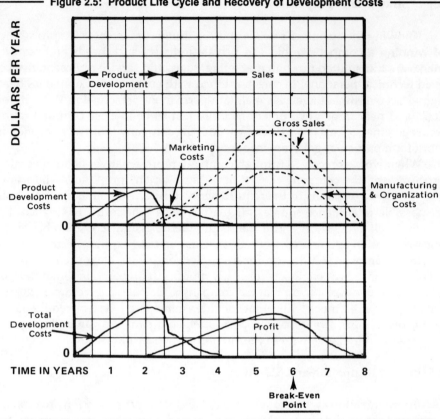

Source: S.E. Stephanou, *Management: Technology, Innovation & Engineering* (Malibu, Calif.: Daniel Spencer, 1981), p. 96.

(a) Determination of Profit and Related Evaluation Factors

For a new product or system development, each project must be evaluated for its profit potential. Such a calculation requires estimation of all product or system development costs, including the development of manufacturing capability, marketing, general and administrative costs, and so on. Profit can be calculated from the gross sales estimate for the lifetime of the product. This must be done for each potential project and the projects compared on a profit basis. For a particular product development, the set of curves shown in Figure 2.5 indicate the time sequencing of the various costs, cost recovery (break-even point), and return on investment (ROI). Although cost is an important factor in the evaluation of projects, the time required for the development and the probability of its technical and commercial success must also be considered, as well as the opportunity cost of alternative money use.

A variation of the determination of profit technique is to develop for each candidate project the ratio of gain expected from the resulting product to the money that will be invested in the project. The money invested can be either the cost of the technical development alone or the total costs associated with the product development. The latter include the estimated manufacturing, marketing, and other costs and provides a more meaningful ratio. Also, the effect of inflation and the loss of interest on money used over the lifetime of the project must be determined and included in the calculation. The candidate project is evaluated and compared with respect to the gain/risk ratio criterion. In this context, gain represents the profit to be derived and risk is the total cost. The company can arbitrarily establish a limit of 2.5 or some even high ratio as acceptable for further consideration of a project. This method is relatively simple and straightforward but suffers from the same disadvantages as the previous method; namely, it does not consider the probability of technical and commercial success, nor does it take into account development time or overall longer-range contribution to the company's well being.

A formula developed by Carl Pacifico for chemical products overcomes the first objection:[4]

$$\text{Project rating} = \frac{R_t \times R_c \times (P_n - C) \times V \times L}{\text{Total costs}}$$

where R_t = probability of technical success (0.1 to 1.0)
         R_c = probability of commercial success (0.1 to 1.0)
         P_n = price of product ($/lb)
         C = manufacturing plus selling costs ($/lb)
         V = sales volume (lb/year)
         L = commercial life (years)

Total costs =   the sum of research, engineering, plant cost, marketing, working capital, and other ancillary costs

The formula can be readily adapted to a per unit (system) rather than a per pound basis. In using this formula, a project rating of 1 is considered the break-even point and is obviously not acceptable. A project with a rating of 2 or better can be considered worthy of further consideration and should be compared with other candidate projects having similar high ratings. Disadvantages of this technique are that it does not include consideration of the time required for completion of a project, nor does it differentiate between low-risk/low-profit and high-risk/high-profit combinations.

A formula developed by Sidney Sobelman takes into account both the development time and the commercial lifetime of the product:[5]

$$z = pT - ct$$

where z =   product value or comparison factor
            p =   average net profit per year

$$T = \text{estimated life of the product or process}$$
$$c = \text{average development cost per year}$$
$$t = \text{years of development}$$

The loss of interest due to development time can be corrected for by applying the following formula to each cost item:

$$C_i^{\cdot} = C_i(1 + r)^t$$

where $C_i^{\cdot}$ = future cost calculated to present time for each element

C_i = actual cost before correction for interest loss

r   = prevailing average interest rate over the time period involved

t   = number of years elapsing from the time effort was initiated

For all the cost items the formula becomes:

$$\text{Total costs} = \sum_{i=1}^{n} C_i^{\cdot} = \sum_{i=1}^{n} C_i (1+r)^t$$

The Sobelman formula then takes the form:

$$Z = PT - \sum_{i=1}^{n} C_i^{\cdot}$$

This method takes into account development time but neglects the probability of commercial success. Many companies will not undertake a project if it has less than a certain probability of commercial success and a reasonable payback time. Average payback times for a wide range of industries have been reported as having values of three to seven years, depending upon the particular industry.[6] For high-tech industries, payback times are at the lower end of the scale and can be even shorter. An important consideration in the use of payback time as a criterion is the high cost of resources including personnel, facilities, and equipment. Even the payback method has some very serious limitations (see Chapter 12, Section 12.4).

In addition to the preceding methods of estimating new product costs, quite sophisticated parametric models, such as the RCA PRICE model, have been developed for making cost calculations (see Chapter 4, Section 4.3b and Chapter 6).

(b) The Rating Matrix

In this technique, key criteria for evaluating the candidate projects are

——————— Figure 2.6(a): Simple Rating Matrix for Evaluating Candidate Projects ———————

Key Criteria	Design				
	A	B	C	D	E
1. Cost to develop	5	2	1	3	4
2. Development time	4	3	1	2	5
3. Technical feasibility	3	1	2	4	5
4. Market potential	3	2	1	5	4
5. Adequacy of facilities	5	2	3	1	4
Totals	20	10	8	15	22

——————— Figure 2.6(b): Weighted Rating Matrix for Evaluating Candidate Projects ———————

Key Criteria[a]	Max. Value	Max. Value Normalized	Project			
			A	B[b]	C	D
1. Cost to develop	10	0.18	3	8	6	1
2. Development time	4	0.07	1	3	4	2
3. Technical feasibility	10	0.18	4	7	5	6
4. Customer acceptance	20	0.37	10	15	8	7
5. Manufacturing facilities	6	0.11	4	5	3	4
6. Technology assessment	5	0.09	3	4	1	2
Totals	55	1.00	25	42	27	22

(a)   A maximum value for a key criterion indicates the optimum or most desirable situation. The value assigned reflects the importance or weight of the particular criterion.

(b)   Project B with a total of 42 is the most attractive project to pursue based on these criteria and weighting factors.

Source: S.E. Stephanou, *Management: Technology, Innovation & Engineering* (Malibu, Calif.: Daniel Spencer, 1981), p. 104.

developed and each project rated according to these criteria (Figure 2.6 (a)). For example, an arbitrary score ranging rom 1 to 5 could be given for each criterion, where 5 would be the highest score and 1 the lowest. In the example of Figure 2.6 (a), projects E and A would be selected first since they had the highest total scores. The criteria used in the evaluation would be decided upon by a committee of knowledgeable individuals who could properly assess the organizational, technical, economic, marketability, and other important aspects of the projects.

A variation of this method is to assign maximum values (weighting factors) to the various criteria reflecting their importance. Such a matrix array is shown in Figure 2.6 (b). The number value can be broken out into constituent components based on criteria characteristics, for example:

Development Time	Points
1 year	4
2 years	3
3 years	2
Greater than 4 years	1

Cost to Develop	
Less than $100,000	10
$100,000 - $300,000	8
$300,000 - $500,000	6
$500,000 - $800,000	3
Greater than $800,000	1

The totals can be readily determined for the various projects and the most promising projects selected based on the chosen criteria.

(c) The Checklist Approach

In a checklist evaluation, both technical and economic considerations are taken into account (Figure 2.7). The example shown in relatively simple. In some organizations this evaluation can include many pages of questions about the technical development, use of company funds, marketing, and saleability. Answering such a questionnaire can be a project in itself. The assumption is that judging these factors separately is superior to averaging all the factors, as is done in the rating matrix technique, and that if a majority of knowledgeable evaluators separately perceive a project to be worthwhile based on the important factors in its development, the company can have a high level of confidence in proceeding with it.

(d) Other Methods

The foregoing techniques are by no means the only ones that can be used to evaluate candidate projects. Every large company has its particular ritual and procedure that it carries out every year to select projects that seem best suited to its future needs.

For projects whose goal is commercial products, some companies examine the estimated expenditure and sales curves (Figure 2.5) for the estimated life cycle of the product and use the break-even point as a criterion for deciding whether to go ahead. If the break-even point is very far in the future, the candidate project is scrapped. The tolerable length of time for the break-even point to occur depends on company policy and thinking at the time of the decision. The results of various surveys to determine R&D policy on this subject indicate that payback times of an average of three to four years and anticipated probability of technical success of at least 70% are acceptable.[7]

A relatively simple screening procedure that some companies use is to consider the net profit that the product can yield. If it is below some arbitrary amount, the project is not pursued. For example, a large company could use a

Figure 2.7: Project Evaluation Worksheet

Proposal number   *P-22*   Title *PORTABLE POWER UNIT*

Name of Evaluator   *JOHN SMITH, DIRECTOR OF ENGINEERING*

Technical Factors:	Favorable	No Opinion	Unfavorable
Long term objective(s)	✓		
Interim objectives	✓		
Technical approach	✓		
Availability of technology within Company			✓
Availability of technology outside Company	✓		
Availability of scientific skills			✓
Adequacy of facilities			✓
Adequacy of support manpower			✓
Tie-in with existing projects			✓
Anticipated output of current approach	✓		
Innovation or novelty of output	✓		
Estimated chance of technical success	✓		
Patent situation	✓		
Production capabilities	✓		
Totals	**9**	**0**	**5**

Economic Factors:	Favorable	No Opinion	Unfavorable
Competitive environment	✓		
Market potential	✓		
Market stability	✓		
Marketing advantages of project output	✓		
Promotional requirements		✓	
Capital expenditure requirements	✓		
Research investment payout time	✓		
Totals	**5**	**2**	**0**

Timing Factors:	Favorable	No Opinion	Unfavorable
Time to accomplish interim objective(s)	✓		
Time relative to supporting marketing objectives	✓		
Totals	**2**	**0**	**0**

Source: Burton V. Dean, *Operations Research in Research and Development* (New York: John Wiley, 1963), p. 179. Reprinted by permission of John Wiley & Sons, Inc.

figure of $10 million as the estimated annual profit that is necessary from the resulting product before a candidate project would be undertaken.

There have been a number of project selection models reported in the literature.[8,9] Such models are designed for computerization and have been described in sufficient detail that they may be used generally for the evaluation of candidate projects. Attractive and fashionable as these models appear initially, they have not gained the general acceptance hoped for by their authors. In a report Maher and Rubenstein offer reasons for the lack of acceptance of early models.[10] The important factor was the assessment of the out-

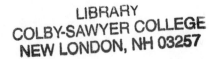

put data generated by the technique; the R&D managers sampled did not really believe the results of the computerized evaluation and selection process. Nevertheless, if the program logic and input are sound, there is no reason why such selection programs should not be applicable.

2.6 Other Project Activities

(a) Bid/No-Bid Decisions

The decision to bid on a contract to perform a project is a key decision for the viability of an organization that depends entirely or primarily on project-type work for its survival. For major projects considerable money can be consumed just in the preparation of the proposal. This is particularly true in government contracting where the requirements are extensive and a number of companies are competing. The same can be true in the private sector, but there a company does not usually bid unless the customer indicates favorable sponsorship and the probability of obtaining the work is relatively high.

If the company decides to bid, several conditions must be present:

1. The company should have a competitive edge over other prospective bidders (this may be due to previous favorable experience with the customer or specialized knowledge of the system or work to be accomplished).
2. The work should be suited to the organization, personnel, facilities, and product lines of the company.
3. The company should have sufficient intelligence available to reveal that the proposed project is not "wired," that is, the customer does not already have a preferred supplier or a supplier who has expended a great deal of "missionary work" promoting the project.
4. The company wants to maintain good working relations with the contracting agency or customer.

There may also be situations where the company may wish to become involved in a certain product area and is willing to invest (buy in) to acquire the capability. Such an investment can lead to lucrative follow-ons but can also be disadvantageous (see Section 4.1 (a)).

Having an edge on the competition can result from specialized or singular knowledge of the particular system or job, a record of successful previous contracts with the customer, or other factors, some subjective and some objective.

(b) Make-or-Buy Decisions and Subcontracting

In preparing for a major project involving complex system or operation, it is often necessary to make decisions about what work is to be performed by the company (the prime contractor) and what work should be subcontracted to outside firms. These make-or-buy decisions and the selection of the subcontractors may be done during the proposal phase or even in the preliminary or feasibility study phase. The timing of the decisions depends on how committed the customer is to the project.

As development costs become increasingly high, buying technical and other types of expertise, as well as components and subsystems, can be a cost-effective alternative. There are many pros and cons to going to an outside firm. The matter of secrecy, proprietary rights, and the desirability of building up in-house capability are important factors that mitigate against the purchase of technology. Nevertheless, because of the high cost of systems development, many companies use new technology in their products that is developed by others. This is accomplished by studying the pertinent technical, professional, and trade journals; attending trade shows, product meetings, and symposia; acquiring personnel skilled in the new technology; studying government agency reports; and purchasing patents and know-how through licensing agreements with individual inventors or companies.

If hardware items are involved, a number of factors must be considered in arriving at the make-or-buy decision, such as the following:

1. Can the item be made or the work be done within the company; that is, does the company have the necessary manufacturing capability, technical personnel, and available facilities?
2. What is the relative cost of making the item or doing the work in-house as against having it made by an outside firm?
3. Would it be advantageous in the long run for the company to make the capital outlay and acquire or develop the capability for doing the work or making the particular component or subsystem?
4. If the company chooses to develop the capability for making the particular component or subsystem, would it have any undesirable effects on other units of the company or the sales of other company products? Would there be any threat to products made by present customers?

(c) Subcontracting

If the company decides to have some work done by an outside vendor, the first need is to set up specifications or requirements. There are many types of specifications, but in system development and R&D work the most common types are *design* and *performance* specifications. *Design* specifications usually give dimensions, materials, and configuration of the item; they may also specify weight, size, and other physical properties. *Performance* specifications describe what the product must do to be acceptable. The ability of the product to perform these functions is usually determined by testing. After setting up specifications and requirements, requests for information or requests for pro-

Figure 2.8: Simple Matrix for Evaluating Subcontractors

Key Criteria	Company				
	A	B	C	D	E
1. Responsiveness to system requirements	5	2	1	3	4
2. Knowledgeable technical personnel	4	3	1	2	5
3. Available facilities	3	1	2	4	5
4. Previous experience of company	3	2	1	5	4
5. Schedule	5	2	3	1	4
6. Cost	4	2	3	5	1
Totals*	24	12	11	20	23

* Companies B and C would be the leading contenders.

posals are solicited from bona fide producers of the item or engineering firms that can perform the required technical work. This usually means making up a preferred list of those suppliers with whom the company has had previous experience. If the component or subsystem needed is an off-the-shelf item, then a request for quote (RFQ) can be issued to qualified suppliers.

Following receipt of proposals from the prospective subcontractors, the company evaluates the proposals and selects the winner. In larger companies this is typically an activity within the purview of the procurement organization, but it can be accomplished in a number of ways: (1) The project or procurement manager alone makes the decision. (2) The project or procurement manager distributes copies of the proposals to key members of his staff for evaluation. At a joint meeting the project or procurement manager and his staff decide the winner of leading contenders. (3) The project or procurement manager appoints an evaluation committee made up of experts in the particular fields and asked them to make the evaluation and recommendations. The experts may make evaluations only in their specialties or they may evaluate all the criteria, depending on their capabilities and the nature of the work.

For a major subcontracting effort, the third technique is particularly effective and commonly used. It can be systematized and used to its full potential by having the committee first determine the most important criteria in the fulfillment of the work. These criteria are confirmed by the project/procurement manager and a matrix is set up of the type shown in Figure 2.8. In this simple type of matrix evaluation, the candidate subcontractors are given a rating of 1 through whatever number of respondents there were to the RFP. In the example of Figure 2.8, there would be ratings of 1 through 5 since there were five respondents. Each committee member would be given a blank form listing the criteria and he would then proceed to evaluate the proposals and rate them. The results from all the evaluators would be totaled and the companies with the lowest number ratings would be the leading contenders.

————————— Figure 2.9: Weighted Matrix for Evaluating Subcontractors —————————

Key Criteria	Maximum Value	Company A	B	C	D
1. Responsiveness to system requirements	10	7	9	7	8
2. Knowledgeable technical personnel	6	3	5	3	4
3. Available facilities	4	3	4	4	4
4. Previous experience of company	4	2	3	2	2
5. Schedule	6	4	4	3	5
6. Cost	10	9	6	7	8
Totals*	40	28	31	26	31

* Companies B and D would be the leading contenders.

A more detailed matrix technique can be used that assigns maximum values or weights to each criterion (Figure 2.9). The maximum value of weight reflects the importance attached to the criterion by the committee and is determined by the committee at the time of making up the criteria list. The value of the weight should also reflect the importance of the criterion to the project manager and the company. The value given a particular company for each criterion can be broken down into components. For example, for the criterion "previous experiences of company," an evaluator could allocate points in the following manner:

Contractor has no experience in this field 0
Contractor has limited experience 1
Contractor has built similar items for
        other companies 2
Contractor has built similar items for this
        company with satisfactory performance 3
Contractor has built similar items for this
        company with outstanding performance 4

The maximum value or weight in this case would be 4.

Although a contractor could be selected on the basis of the highest total score obtained, it is better to contact the two or three high scorers and arrange for stand-up briefings during which they can present the highlights of their proposal and how they plan to perform the work. The project/procurement manager or the key personnel listens, evaluates, and asks pertinent questions to determine the true credibility and competence of the bidding firm. It sometimes happens that the company scoring highest on the proposal evaluation does not fare as well in the face-to-face briefing. Another company may have greater familiarity with the technical issues, greater understanding of the developmental problems, and generally be more knowledgeable and experienced. Something may surface at the briefing that was not evident from the proposal, and the decision reached by the committee as a result of the decision matrix may be reversed. This possibility is more the exception than the rule, however.

Because of the importance of the cost criterion, the cost portion of the proposal is often considered separately. Representatives of the accounting or financial group of the company evaluate the cost data, including the accounting methods to be used, and make a judgement as to which candidate companies are acceptable from a cost standpoint. A company that is rated first technically may be asked to reduced its costs in certain areas of work, and cost negotiations and trade-offs may be initiated between the contractor and the vendor or subcontractor. With a government contract, the lowest competent bidder is acceptable; this could be the firm that was rated third in the evaluation but was nevertheless acceptable technically. Government contracting is discussed in Chapter 10.

(d) Contract Negotiations

In addition to the preproject activities already mentioned, there are negotiations with the customer that can involve changes in the level of effort and direction of the project and a number of other matters (see Chapter 10, Section 10.3 and 10.4).

Contract negotiations is an area that requires the special expertise of individuals trained in contract law (usually, but not necessarily, lawyers). In contract negotiations the two parties strive to arrive at a mutually acceptable agreement on requirements for performance, type of contract and pricing, and related contractual matters. Each party seeks to achieve an agreement that optimizes his own individual position according to the various options and risks. Various types of project contracts, patents, trade secrets, know-how, and copyrights, that can be involved in projects are discussed in Chapter 10. These are usually included as part of the contract negotiated with a customer prior to the startup and execution of the project. For large projects, particularly with government agencies, contractual and legal aspects play an important role in the determination of fees, patent rights, subsequent benefits, and penalties. In regard to legal aspects, there is always the Damocles sword of product liability and potential lawsuit hanging by a thread over the company, not to mention the problems of union relations, government labor laws, and agency rules and regulations that must be recognized and adhered to.

2.7 Government Projects

For many years government agencies have funded projects in a variety of areas ranging from public health and transportation to complex hardware development programs. Almost all major government agencies have been involved, including the Department of Defense (DOD), the National Administration for Space and Aeronautics (NASA), the Department of Energy (DOE), the Department of Transportation (DOT), and the Department of Health, Education, and Welfare (HEW). Of these, DOD has been the largest spender, particularly in the last several decades during which the Soviet threat has appeared increasingly ominous. Because of major dollar expenditures required in the procurement of a complex weapon system, the use of projects has been standardized by DOD to deal with the large number of contractors involved. In the last decade approximately 40 to 50% of federal R&D funds have gone to the military for design and development of new and better weapon systems and substantially greater amounts for the purchase and improvement of systems already developed. With the political changes in the Eastern Bloc countries that have occurred, substantial reductions in DOD expenditures, including R & D, can be expected.

The entry of government into the project area began with the Manhattan Project in the 1940s when the devastating potential of nuclear energy as a weapon system was dramatically demonstrated. Since then, government agencies have turned again and again to private industry for setting up projects to develop and produce complex systems—new missiles, communication, space, and energy systems—the list is endless.

Federal R&D spending today accounts for a little less than half of the total U.S. R&D spending (industry and government). The major portion of this spending will be on R&D projects to develop new systems. A much larger amount of government funds over and above R&D expenditures is committed to the procurement of major systems (particularly in the military). The goal of such projects is to develop the manufacturing capability to produce a large number of identical systems. Here the requirements of performance, reliability, maintainability, and logistics support are an important part of the project activities and objectives.

Because of the large dollar volume of government-funded projects, it is essential for project managers employed by companies doing business with government agencies to understand the process whereby procurements are initiated and acquired.

2.8 R&D and Systems Acquisition Practices

(a) Introduction

Since the Departments of Defense, Space, and Health, Education, and Welfare spent most of the federal funds for R&D and systems procurement in the last decade, the procedures they set up and have been using were modified and adopted by the newer government agencies as a starting point for development of their own procurement and R&D funding procedures. However, the government has attempted to standardize systems procurement and contracting procedures for all government agencies in accord with Public Law 93-400 which was enacted on August 30, 1974. This law established the Office of

Federal Procurement Policy (OFPP) in the Office of Management and Budget (OMB) to provide overall direction of procurement policy and to prescribe procurement practice*, regulations, and procedures. The new federal agency developed and issued a major systems acquisition policy (OMB circulr A-109) on April 5, 1976. One of the key requirements of this policy was early competition among both large and small firms to identify and explore alternative system concepts to meet government requirements. In their 1977 report to Congress, the OFPP administration stated, "Emphasis will be on investigation of innovative system design concepts." Previously, industry had responded to specific technical requirements defining a system to perform a stated task. OFPP has developed and promoted a policy that would establish a uniform government-wide approach for systems acquisition and the support of research and development.[12]

As has been the case for most government procedures for systems acquisition, each new administration has modified A-109 to further emphasize cost saving and cost effectiveness. The elusive goal of projects that are on schedule and on cost with full achievement of performance goals is constantly pursued by organizations in both the public and private sector. To date, the setting up of new organizations, procedures, and directives has not succeeded in achieving this euphoric condition, but the need continues.

(b) The Solicitation and Bidding Process

If the company is engaged in work for government agencies, it will have technical representatives or marketing personnel in constant touch with the customer either in Washington, D.C., at various government installations around the country, or even in foreign countries where this is permitted by the State Department. Marketing and sales personnel will also be examing the Commerce Business Daily (CBD) for possible new procurement contracts, awards and subcontracting opportunities. This publication is primarily for public information purposes, since major procurements are usually known about well in advance so that eligible companies have sufficient time to do the homework required for a competitive proposal. If the procurement for major systems is not known about until it is seen in the CBD, it is usually too late to compete successfully.

In seeking suitable contractors for carrying out R&D work and developing new systems, government agencies can employ one of two acceptable procedures: First, they can set up specifications of work requirements, select a specific company or organization to do the work, and then proceed to negotiate a contract with that company. This is referred to as sole-source procurement and can only be executed under special conditions. Such conditions would include a statement of why this company should be the only firm contacted. Normally, government regulations require that bids for work should not only be publicized in the CBD but also that open bidding be allowed so that any qualified organization can bid. The CBD, which is issued by the Department of Commerce, provides a daily list of government procurement invitations, subcontracting leads, contract awards, sales of surplus property, and foreign business opportunties. Conditions that would justify sole-source procurement include special capability or facilities for doing the work. For example, if the firm has already been involved in doing the particular type of work or building the particular system, it would be wasteful of public funds or time to bring in an inexperienced firm. In the case of sole-source awards, the information is published in CBD to furnish subcontracting leads and to inform the general public of government contracting activities.

Second, the government agency can set up specifications or work requirements and send these to qualified bidders for their examination and decision about whether to bid. A notice of the requirement must be placed in the CBD. Companies interested in bidding can send for a request for proposal (RFP), which gives the detailed specifications and work requirements.

The RFP is a request for a bid to (a) perform technical work (applied research), (b) perform engineering design and development, (c) supply equipment of an advanced or novel nature, or (d) perform special studies, evaluations, and the like. It is not to be confused with the proposal to do the actual work and is called different names by different government agencies and companies: request or proposal (RFP), request for bid (RB), procurement request (PR), procurement invitation (PI), invitation to bid (IB), request for quotation (RFQ). RFQs are used when there is little or no R&D involved. A more detailed discussion of RFPs is given in Section 2.3.

RFPs are issued by companies as well as government agencies when there is a need for R&D work in the development of a new componenet or system. An outline of the contents of a typical RFP is shown in Section 2.3. The actual headings will vary, but certain key information is necessary so that the bidders can respond properly. Some of the questions that must be addressed by the prospective bidder in making the important bid/no-bid decision are as follows:

- Does the company have competitive capability in this technical area?
- Does the work fit the company's interests?
- Are personnel and facilities available?
- Is the contract already "wired"—that is, is a known competitor the most likely winner because of previous experience or preference by the contracting agency?
- What previous experience has the company had with the funding agency?
- Will future relations with the customer be affected by not bidding?

If the company is particularly interested in the technical area of the contract work because of potential lucrative follow-on or if an educational institution is involved and has special interest, there may be cost sharing. The contractor may contribute in one or more ways: (1) he may contribute engineering labor and materials; (2) he may contribute a specific percentage of the total cost; (3) he may provide materials or test facilities. "Buying in" can occur by the prospective contractor bidding an amount less than the true cost of executing the contract. This can also be accomplished by foregoing the fee.

The interesting situation that arises in governement contracting is that there is only one buyer (the government agency seeking the work, product, or system) and many sellers. This unusual relationship between buyer and seller is referred to as monopsony as contrasted to monopoly where there are many buyers and only one seller.

Proposals, types of contracts, subcontracting, and negotiations are discussed in Chapters 2 and 10.

(c) Design-to-Cost (DTC) and Life-Cycle Costing (LCC)

In response to an increasing cost consciousness in developing new products/systems for governement agencies, companies have pursued several new management techniques showing promise of cost effectivenes. One of these techniques is designing a system to a predetermined cost (DTC) and considering life-cycle costs (LCC) to determine the total cost of a system. In simple terms, DTC means tailoring the design, development, and manufacturing process so that the ultimate cost is equal to the money available for building the required number of systems or units (Figure 2.10). A design to cost goal is a specified dollar cost for a specified number of systems at a defined production rate; this is the DTC concept applied to systems procurement. In a broader context, DTC must also consider life-cycle cost (LCC), that is, it must include not only system development and production costs but also costs incurred during the life of the product or system.

In its totality, then, a DTC/LCC approach would include the following costs:

- Applied research
- Design and development
- Testing and evaluation
- Manufacturing
- Implementation or installation (delivery)
- Operation
- Support and maintenance

Such total considerations are particularly important when operation and support costs are three to ten times the acquisition costs and the system is used beyond its initially planned lifetime. Practical trade-offs must be made among operational efficiency, reliability, maintainability, and cost, as well as system capability, cost, and schedule. Performance, production, operating, and support costs must be evaluated in setting up the design requirements.

In the past, design, development, and acquisition costs alone were considered in making decisions concerning alternative systems. A cheaper system

———— Figure 2.10: Contractor's Target Cost Model for Communication Subsystem ————

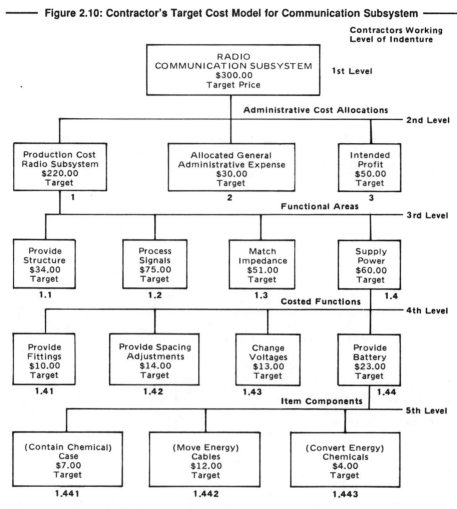

Source: R.L. Bidwell, "Selecting Design to Cost Goals Requires Realism and Flexibility," *Defense Management Journal* (September 1974), p. 30.

could also be less reliable, having higher maintenance and operating costs, a shorter lifetime, and more "down time" than a more expensive system as shown by Table 2.1. Here the initially more expensive product in acquisition cost is less expensive when life-cycle costs are considered. The concept is illustrated in a more general way in Figure 2.11 where improved design efficiency, represented by large expenditures in R&D, can be traded off against decreasing costs of system operations and support costs.

Although the objectives of DTC and LCC are clearly desireable, the implementation of the technique in government contracting has been difficult. DTC/LCC has been required for many major systems procurements but contractors have been having problems implementing the requirements. For governmental systems it is easier to obtain initial funding for acquisition than it is

———————— Table 2.1: Cost Comparison for Two Competitive Products ————————

A. COST DATA FOR LCC ANALYSIS

Cost Item	Data Source	Estimate Vendor A	Estimate Vendor B
Product price	Manufacturer	$200,000	$170,000
Equipment life	Customer's Specification	2 years	2 years
Installation.	Owner	$3,000	$4,000
Manning	Manufacturer	1 man	2 men
Manning labor rate	Owner	$8/hr.	$8/hr.
Mean time between failures . . .	Manufacturer	500 hrs.	300 hrs.
Mean time to repair.	Manufacturer	1 week	2 weeks
Preventive maintenance cycle	Manufacturer	160 hrs.	180 hrs.
Preventive maintenance down time	Manufacturer	4 hrs.	8 hrs.
Maintenance labor rate	Owner	$6/hr.	$6/hr.
Parts & supplies cost (% of product price)	Manufacturer	1%	2%
Input power	Manufacturer	8.0 kw.	9.0 kw.
Cost per kwh.	Owner	$.025	$.025

B. LCC TRADE-OFF ANALYSIS FOR 2 YEARS

Cost		Vendor A	Vendor B
Product price		$200,000	$170,000
Installation.		3,000	4,000
Manning labor (2 years)		46,720	93,440
Preventive maintenance (2 years)		912	1,632
Corrective maintenance (2 years)		2,800	9,344
Power requirements (@ .025/kwh.)		1,168	1,314
Parts & supplies cost (@ 1% & 2% of product price respectively).		2,000	3,400
Total		**$256,600**	**$283,130**

Source: S.E. Stephanou, *Management: Technology, Innovation & Engineering* (Malibu, Calif.: Daniel Spencer, 1981), p. 227.

to ensure adequate funding for the total life of the system. Expressing DTC and LCC requirements in an RFP and obtaining adequate response from contractors to fulfill these difficult requirements poses serious problems. Estimation of operational, support, and maintenance costs for a new system can be difficult, particularly when another organization is going to be the user. Nevertheless, the concept has obvious merit and contracts of this type continue to be solicited and granted.

(d) Other Procurement Practices

Since the Department of Defense has been responsible for a major portion

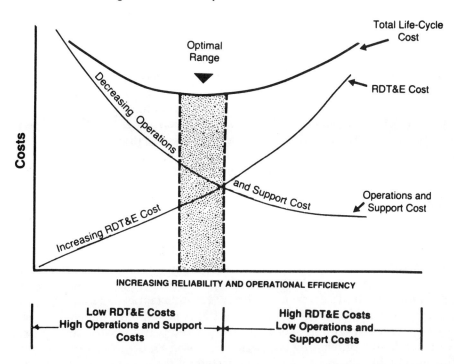

Figure 2.11: Unit Acquistion Cost Trade-Off Chart

Source: S.E. Stephanou, *Management: Technology, Innovation & Engineering* (Malibu, Calif.: Daniel Spencer, 1981), p. 228.

of the government's R&D and systems procurement spending, it is relevent to review some important changes that have occurred in DOD's procurement policies, particularly in the area of major systems development. During the period after World War II when Robert McNamara was Secretary of Defense, the total package procurement (TPP) concept was introduced. This procurement practice required bids from qualified suppliers covering all phases of the system development process including prototype fabrication and test and final manufacture of a finite number of systems. A cost definition phase (CDP) usually preceded letting the contract; it detailed all the research and development costs, most of the production costs, and even deployment and operational support for the system. In theory, the cost definition phase was to estimate costs of the system from its inception to the end of its life-cycle (from birth to grave). It was assumed that there would be no drastic changes in the state of the art during the course of the system development.

Use of the TPP concept led to serious overruns in major systems procurements such as the Air Force transport C-5, the Air Force SCRAM missile, and the Army Cheyenne helicopter. A number of seemingly logical reasons have been advanced for the failure of this concept. Outstanding among these are the lack of accomodation in the contracting for technical problems and changes in the state of the art during the time of the system development, lack of close monitoring by the government agency involved, and unrealistically low bidding by the winning contractor. Whatever the reasons, the ultimate result was serious cost growth in almost all of the contracts funded using the TPP concept. In 1973 the General Accounting Office (GAO) in a study of 45 major weapon system developments reported cost overruns of $31 billion over orginal planned estimates. The GAO gave the following reasons for the cost growths: (1) changes in requirements by the Pentagon or its corporate contractors (45%), (2) inflation (30%), (3) estimating errors (25%). There were no comments made about mismanagement by the contracting agency or contractor.

Because of the disappointing performance of TPP and resulting congressional and public disapproval, the prototype concept* was revitalized as a technique for the development and procurement of advanced systems. This was not a new technique since it had been used by the United States and foreign countries for many years. The Century series of fighter aircraft (for example, the F-100) was developed using this procurement procedure. The concept works as follows: The government agency requests one or more companies to design and build a working model or a manufacturing prototype of the system. The technical effort and system fabrication may be funded in part or wholly by the government. After completion of the working system, there is a demonstration of the operation and performance witnessed and evaluated by the purchasing organization. Based on the results of the prototype testing, the system is bought or rejected. If the system is an aircraft and there are several companies involved, there would be a "fly-off" to determine which aircraft met the design goals of speed, climb rate, load capability, and so on. Although this procurement technique has many advantages, it is not a panacea for all government hardware contracting. It must have specific applicability. For example, in the case of the first Air Force B-1 bomber contract, prototyping by several competing firms would have been prohibitively expensive. However, the prototype concept does offer economic benefits that preclude or at least decrease the seemingly excessive overruns that have occured in the past. The civilian sector of the economy has for many years used prototype buying: One company asks another company to develop a new system, then the purchasing company purchases the prototype and tests or uses it for a period of time before ordering addtional copies.

According to present DOD policy, the systems acquisition ofmajor, multi-million-dollar systems proceeds chronologically according to the following phases:

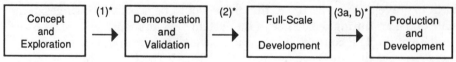

* Designates decision milestones. Milestone (0) starts at completion of Justification for Major Systems New Start (JMSNS).

---

* Also called the "fly-before-you-buy" concept.

Figure 2.12: Detailed Model of the Systems Acquisition Process for an Industrial Hardware System Development or Innovation

Phases	Conceptual & Definition		Development		Production	Implementation
Steps	Need →	System Analysis →	System Design →	System Development →	Manufacture →	Use
Activities	• Identification of a need	• Technical & economic studies	• Alternative concepts	• Pilot plant	• Manufacturing facilities completed	• Product distributed
	• Confirmation of need	• Input/output analysis	• Experimental models	• Development of manufacturing capability	• Manufacturing prototypes tested	• Servicing made available
	• Sponsorship of work	• Market analysis	• Computer stimulations	• Continued market evaluation	• Full-scale manufacturing initiated	
			• Servicing needs studied	• Development of sales capability & outlets	• Sales campaign implemented	
Milestones	• Funding approved	• Feasibility study completed	• Preliminary design completed	• Prototype completed & tested	• First system completed	• Market introduction
			• Final design completed			

Note: 1. Applied research by central research and engineering laboratory and product research and development laboratories of the organization is continuously fed into the system development process as needed.

2. Microinnovation can occur to enhance the effort during any of the steps of the process.

3. Go/no-go decisions about whether to proceed with the system development can be made anytime during the innovation process. It is best to have a design freeze as early as possible, optimally after the final design is completed.

Figure 2.13: Concept Based Requirements Systems (CBRS)
Used by the Army in the Systems Acquisition Process

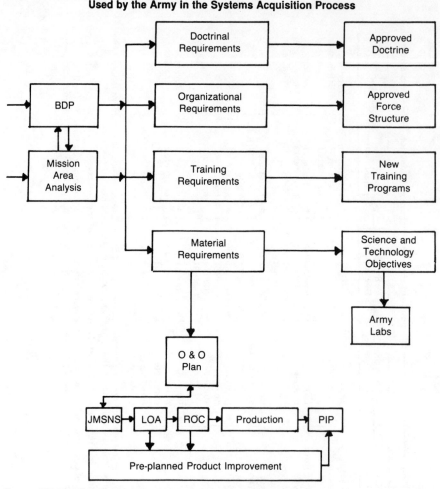

Source: TRADOC Regulation 11-7. Army Program, Operational Concepts and Army Doctrine.
Headquarters, United States Army Training & Doctrine Command. (16 July 1982), p. 10.

Each phase is followed by a high-level evaluation by the Defense System
Acquisition Review Council (DSARC). Each evaluation, which is designated a
milestone, determines whether funds should be allocated for carrying out the
next step or whether the program should be cut off completely, modified or
postponed. The complexity of DOD vis-a'-vis private sector procurement is
illustrated by considering the various activities involved in the two processes.
Figure 2.12 presents a detailed model of the systems acquisition process for
private sector hardware system development while Figure 2.13 shows a portion of the process for a major DOD system. (In this case, an Army System.)
Because of page size limitations, the complete details of the Army process
could not be shown since over 100 steps and decision points are involved.

──────────────── **Table 2.2: Acquisition Improvement Intitiatives** ────────────────

1. Reaffirm acquistion management principles
2. Increase use of preplanned product improvement
3. Implement multiyear procurement
4. Increase program stability
5. Encourage capital investment to enhance productivity
6. Budget to most likely cost
7. Use economical production rates
8. Assure appropriate contract type
9. Improve system support and readiness
10. Reduce administrative costs and time
11. Budget for technological risk
12. Provide front-end funding for test hardware
13. Reduce governmental legislation related to acquisition
14. Reduce the number of DOD directives
15. Enhance funding flexibility
16. Provide contractor incentives to improve reliability and support
17. Decrease DSARC briefings and data requirements
18. Budget for inflation
19. Forecast business base decisions
20. Improve source selection process
21. Develop and use standard operation and support systems
22. Provide more appropriate design-to-cost goals
23. Implement acquistion process decisions
24. Reduce DSARC milestones
25. Submit MENs with service POM
26. Revise DSARC membership
27. Retain USDRE as defense acquisition executive
28. Raise dollar thresholds for DSARC review
29. Integrate DSARC and PPBS process
30. Increase PM visibility
31. Improve reliability and support
32. Increase competition

Source: G. Dana Barbson, "Department of Defense Acquistion Improvement Program," *Concepts*, Vol. 4, No. 4 (Autumn 1981), p. 55.

(e) Multiyear Procurement

Faced with declining U.S. productivity, accentuated in part by anomolies in the DOD acquisition process, Deputy Secretary of Defense Frank Carlucci in 1981 chartered several working groups and assigned them the task of developing recommendations for improving the governement's acquisitoin process. As an outgrowth of the combined effort of government and industry, a total of 32 action items, including multiyear procurement, were identified for vigorous implementation by DOD. These action items, listed in Table 2.2, became generally known as the Carlucci initiatives.

In general, the suggested purpose of these initiatives was to promote (a) decentralized, participative management within DOD; (b) improved planning and execution of weapon system programs; (c) development of a stronger industrial base of support of DOD programs; (d) an increased degree of weapon system reliability, maintainability, and operational availability; and (e) a streamlined system acquisition process in terms of required administrative effort, time, and associated cost. [13]

Multiyear procurement, as embodied in the FY 82 Defense Authorization bill HR 3519, commits the government to longer-term contracts. It thus enables suppliers to pass on to the government savings resulting from the more cost-effective acquisition and use of requisite resources. In addition, the practice gives the contractor protection by authorizing recovery of recurring and nonrecurring expenses. A cancellation ceiling of $100 million has been established for certain candidate contracts in the event the governemnt is either unable or unwilling to meet the full extent of its multiyear committment.

To qualify, candidate programs must meet the following general criteria:[14]

- Provide the potential for a significant benefit to the governement.
- Be stable in terms of requirements, configuration, and projected funding.
- Reflect a high degree of confidence in projected cost estimates.
- Embody a high level of government confidence in the contractor's performance capabilties.

Each of the service secretaries is ultimately responsible for reviewing, deciding on candidate programs, and budgeting the cancellation ceiling. Initially, this could result in a significant reduction in the total number of programs that the individual secretaries could include within their total obligation authority. Inasmuch as wholesale annual cancellations are not likely to be instituted given program review and screening criteria, it has been proposed that in the future each service deposit a small percentage of the total contingent liability for the fiscal year into a common fund to meet any obligations that may result from program cancellations.[16]

Overall it has been projected that multiyear procurement could result in savings to the taxpayer in the range of 10 to 30% of the contract value. Considering the fact that the services manage many billions of dollars worth of contracts, the potential for savings is significant. This potential arises from two primary sources: (1) Contractors are increasingly willing and able to invest in productivity-enhancing equipment and programs given the improved prospect of recovering the requisite capital investment. The inclination to invest and the ability to recover tend to be largely influenced by the generally more favorable loan terms that the contractor can often negotiate with lenders based on longer-range stability. The by-product of such an investment, encouraged by competitive considerations and pressures, is invariably passed on to the government. (2) The prime contractor is able to procure new materials and other requisite commodities in larger, more economic quantities by avoiding, for example, set-up and retooling charges. A prime contractor is highly unlikely but more often than not unable to invest and risk huge sums of money in parts and materials that ultimately may not be covered contractually.

Multiyear procurement promotes savings to the government, not only through economies of scale, but also through the increased inclination and ability of lower-tiered contractors themselves to invest and recover their outlays in productivity-enhancing equipment and programs (see Section 9.4).

———— Questions and Topics for Discussion ————

1. Discuss the differences among a real need, a perceived need, and a created need. Give examples.

2. Market analysis to determine the need for a product or new system is a specialty field in itself. What are some of the evaluations that would have to be made in a market analysis? Select the product or system and the potential buyers.

3. Under what conditions would a preliminary or feasibility study be treated as a project?

4. Figure 2.2 presents results of a study of the effect of distance on the communication of technical personnel. Since there is no mention of telephone communication, it is assumed that only face-to-face conversations were considered in the study. What effect do you think the inclusion of telephone conversations would have on the results of this study.

5. Prepare a brief form RFP for a technology development that you feel is necessary in today's complex environment. It can involve hardware, software, or a social problem in the public sector.1

6. In cases of "sole-source" procurement, government agencies are required to list and give a brief description of the procurement in the CBD. Why is this?

7. Develop a work statement (two to three pages) for a project to study possible ways to alleviate the serious traffic situation on the freeways of many of our major cities.

8. Develop a work statement for a study on ways of improving and making more effective the information system presently being used in your organization to disseminate directive and policy changes.

9. What would be the advantages of setting up a straw-man RFP for an impending large project that your company expected to bid on?

10. Why do various companies and industries vary from (three to seven years) in their expectations of what is a reasonable payback time for a product resulting from a project effort?

11. What are the disadvantages of the laundry-list approach for evaluating new products or projects (see Figure 2.7)?

12. Name two ways of evaluating and selecting competing subcontractors for supporting a project. Discuss each method briefly.

13. Why do government agencies frequently request an explanation of no-bid decision on the part of a vendor who has been asked to bid (that is, who is on the qualified bidders list and has been sent an RFP)?

14. What are some essential business and economic factors that must be considered before a company makes the decision to embark on the venture of seeking government contracts for projects?

15. Government spending for R&D projects in the last 20 years has decreased from a maximum of 3% of GNP in the early sixties to a value of about 2% in the early eighties. How do you account for this continued decrease?

16. What explanations can be offered for the scope and complexity of documentation required for government agency contracts for projects compared with the private sector?

17. What are legitimate reasons for a government agency to make a sole-source procurement?

18. Most successful government contractors performing high-technology development for government agencies have a substantially higher success ratio with unsolicited proposals than with solicited proposals. Why?

19. Design-to-cost and life-cycle costing are *claimed by their proponents* to be highly successful; others involved with the nitty-gritty of writing, negotiating, and executing contracts that include DTC *and LCC requirements* have other opinions. What are some of the problems with the use of DTC and LCC and what are the benefits?

20. Prototyping has been found to be an *effective type of procure*ment for certain types of systems. What category of systems and products is *particularly suited to prototype* procurement? What categories are not?

21. What are the pros and *cons of multiyear procurement as* practiced by government agencies?

References

1. Marc S. Caspe *and Saburo Tamuro, "Making Productivity Soar*—Secret Ingredients for Blending American and Japanese Management Technology," Project Management Quarterly (September 1982), p.37.

2. B.J. Silverman, "Project A*ppraisal Methodology:* A Multidimensional R&D Benefit/Cost Assessment To*ol," Management Science, Vol. 27, No. 7 (July 1981),* p. 802.

3. P.M. Maher and A.M. Rubenstein, "Factors Affecting Adoption of a Quantitative Method for R&D Project Selection," Management *Science, Vol.21, No.* 2 (October 1974), p.119.

4. A.S. West, "How to Bud*get R&D Expe*nses," Chemical Engineering Progress, Vol. 66, No. 1, (1970), p. *160.*

5. *D.W. Karger* and R.G. Murdick, Managing Engineering and Research (New *York: Industrial Press, 1969*), p. 196.

6. A. Gerstenfeld, Effective Management of Research & Development (Reading, Mass: Addison-Wesley, 1970), p. 19.

7. Ibid.

8. B.J. Schuman, "Project Appraisal Methodology: A Multidimensional R&D Bene*fit/Cost* Assessment Tool," Management Science, Vol. 27, No. 7 (July 1981), p. 802.

9. J.F. Ramsey, Research & Development: Project Selection Criteria, (UMI Research Press, 1978).

10. Maher and Rubenstein, "Factors Al*fecting A*doption of a Quantitative Method for R&D Project Selection," Management Science, Vol.21, No. 2 (October 1974), p.119.

11. H. Gross, Make-or-Buy (Englewood Cliffs, N.J.: Prentice-Hall, 1966).

12. R.C. Cowen, Technology Review, (Cambridge, Mass.: MIT Press, November 1983), p. 10.

13. Report to the Congress 1976, Office of Federal Procurement Policy, Executive Office of the President, Office of Management and Budget, Washington, D.C., May 27, 1977.

14. G.D. Brabson, "Department of Defense Acquisition Improvement Program," Concepts, Vol. 4, No. 4 (Autumn 1981), p. 55.

15. Frank S. Carlucci, Memorandum for the Secretaries of the Military Department, April 30, 1981.

16. G.D. Brabson, "Can We Afford the DOD Acquisition Improvement Actions?" Concepts, Vol. 5, No. 1 (Winter 1982), p. 48.

——————————— Chapter 3 ———————————
Organizing and Staffing the Project

3.1 The Organizational Setting for Project Management

(a) The Line Organization

The organizational setting in which project management is implemented can have several forms, but the traditional line organization provides the usual framework. The line organization presents a hierarchy of authority relationships, which is manifested in an organization chart, in group charters, in documentation of executive and managerial responsibilities, and in job descriptions. The skeletal-type organization chart (Figure 3.1) shows the chain of authority from top to bottom of the organizational pyramid with each managerial or supervisory level indicated, including staff personnel (usually assigned to the higher levels of management). Line functions are those functions that concern the day-to-day operation of the company, as contrasted to staff functions, which refer to matters of general importance to the company but not directly related to day-to-day operations. According to Kast and Rozenzweig, the line organization is vested with the primary source of authority

─────────────── **Figure 3.1: Line Organization for a Small Company** ───────────────

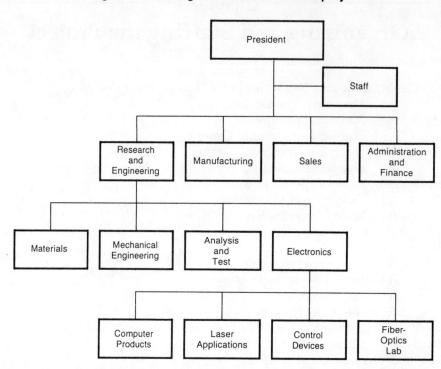

Notes: (a) Each main division such as manufacturing, sales, and so on, has a hierarchy of lower levels below the appropriate vice president or division head.

       (b) Depending on its nature and the size, a project can be attached to any of these levels with the project manager reporting directly to a president, vice president, division head, department, group, section, or laboratory leader.

in performing the major functions of the organization, whereas the staff supports and advises the line.[1]

The line organization stresses the vertical nature of authority, but project management organizations, as we discuss later, depends more on horizontal coordination and close working relations and less on formal lines of authority. Within the framework of the typical line organization, there are a number of possible groupings that can be used for project teams, (see Section 3.2). In the following sections (b) through (e), various groupings that can make up the line organization are described.

(b) Functional Grouping

This type of personnel grouping is most common as it clearly identifies and emphasizes the important aspects of the organization's operations (Figure 3.1). It also turns out to be the optimum grouping for a pure project (Section

3.2 (a)). If the principal function of a group is clearly defined, first in title and second in a group charter designating its responsibilities or the responsibilities of its leader, there is a focal point of capability and resources for carrying out that function. In the example of Figure 3.1, the function of the manufacturing group is to manufacture, that of the sales group to sell, and so on. All matters pertaining to manufacturing and sales logically fall into those groups.

For large national or multinational companies where facilities are geographically dispersed, decentralization of operations may require that each geographical unit has its own functional organization. For large and small companies the classical or functional format seems to be preferred, both for the overall company structure and for smaller segments of the company such as the division, department, section, and group. For example, the research and engineering division of Figure 3.1 is broken out into functional groups.

The number of levels in the line organization of a company varies with the size and complexity of the company's operations. A guiding principle is that the number of levels between the executive officer and the first-line supervision should be kept to a minimum. If there are too many levels of management, communication up and down the line organization become distorted and personnel at the bottom and top levels are seriously insulated from one another. Too many managers, just like too many management levels, can cause unnecessary expense and vertical communication problems. In technical organizations an average number of levels between the scientist or engineer and the engineering or research director seems to be about three to five. This range can allow for adequate information flow and a minimum number of supervisory levels and hence minimum management expense. General Electric claims six levels between the working engineer and the company president.[2]

The size of the group supervised varies with the level of the group in the line organization and the complexity and nature of the work. The number of people that the manager or supervisor is responsible for is referred to as the "span" of management. Professionals with degrees, usually engineers and scientists, require less supervision than personnel without degrees, such as technicians, laborers, and so forth. Professionals, however, do require considerable administrative support so that their time and effort are not spent performing duties that others who are paid less can do. For routine work where many tasks are repetitive, as in a testing laboratory or in construction work, a supervisor may be in charge of as many as 15 to 20 technicians or laborers. For less routine work where highly skilled personnel are involved, a span of five to six is common. Technicians are here defined as helpers to degreed professionals and are usually nondegreed, although they may have had a few years of college training.

(c) Product Line-Oriented Grouping

Some companies organize their principal divisions according to product lines. Figure 3.2, for example, shows an abbreviated format for a product line-

——————————— **Figure 3.2: Product Line-Oriented Company Grouping** ———————

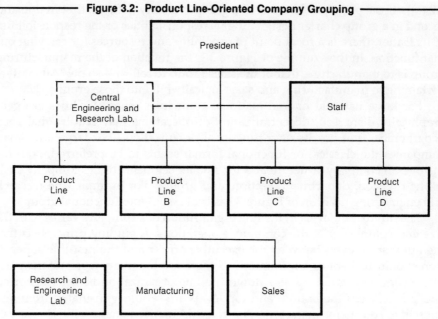

Notes: (a) There may be a central research and engineering laboratory or group, with the director as a vice president reporting to the president. Another arrangement is for each product division to have its own specialized research and engineering segment. Large companies often have both a central laboratory and specialized laboratories or engineering groups for each product division.

(b) Projects, as in the functional grouping example of Figure 3.1, can be attached to any of these levels with the project manager reporting to the appropriate head of that level.

---

oriented company. Each division can have its own functional groups including sales, manufacturing, research and engineering, and so on. Project groups can be attached to various levels of the organization depending on the functional groups and the size and nature of the project. The main effort of each product group is ongoing, year after year, rather than a one-shot, all-out effort with an identifiable termination date as in a project.

An advantage of this type of grouping is that the personnel are completely involved with the particular product area and are a permanent part of the product organization. From a company and the individual's standpoint this stability has certain advantages, vis-á-vis a project where individuals can be and are generally moved from project to project, as one project ends and another begins. On the other hand, there is the disadvantage that personnel can become stagnant and "grooved" in their thinking so that as years go by they cease to be innovative.

(d) Discipline-Oriented Grouping

This type of grouping, which brings together personnel according to their

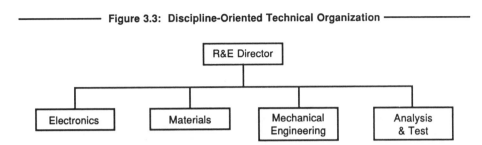

Figure 3.3: Discipline-Oriented Technical Organization

Note: There are many cases where discipline-oriented groupings are difficult to distinguish from functionally oriented groupings because it is sometimes difficult to differentiate between a discipline and a function, for example, engineering.

specialty areas of expertise or discipline (Figure 3.3), is popular for technology-oriented segments of the company; in research institutes and nonprofit organizations it is the principal mode. These specialized professionals carry out programmed work related to their discipline and also serve as in- house consultants for operational groups in the company to come to for the solution of product and processing problems. If other parts of the company are engaged in special projects, the technical problems can be farmed out to these discipline-oriented groups. Such work may require just a brief consultation with knowledgeable experts or may require the full-time effort of a specialist for an extended period. So the technical personnel in such organizations carry out continuing company-funded work in their area of specialization, and so serve the special needs of the company. In addition, customer problems— those having to do with products sold by the company—can be brought to such groups.

The main advantage of this type of group is that the same personnel are more comfortable working with peers who have the same professional background and general interests as themselves. This allows for discussion of issues related to their discipline, cross- fertilization of ideas, and an encouraging environment for keeping up to date in their particular field. Through discussion with peers, alternative solutions to a problem may be suggested that the individual working alone may not come up with. A possible disadvantage of this type of grouping is that the specialty groups tend to become insulated from other groups, particularly from sales groups that are close to market conditions and customer needs. Perhaps a more serious disadvantage is that the really competent scientists, engineers, and other professionals are in considerable demand by the various product, manufacturing, and service groups and are not able to give proper attention to company problems as they arise. A senior engineer, for example, may become so involved in solving a particular product or plant problem that a request from another part of the plant or a customer will have to remain unanswered for an inordinate amount of time. As more requests come in than can be accommodated by the personnel available, priorities may have to be set up, pressure exerted through ap-

—————————— **Figure 3.4: Hybrid Company Grouping** ——————————

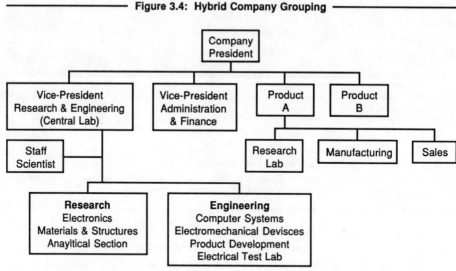

Notes: (a) The research and engineering portions of the organization are discipline- and functionally oriented.

(b) The level next to the chief executive officer contains both product and functional groups.

(c) The product divisions have a functional structure.

Source: S. E. Stephanou, *Management: Technology, Innovation & Engineering* (Malibu, Calif.: Daniel Spencer, 1981), p. 119.

propriate organizational channels, or additional personnel hired. In a product line-oriented grouping of a pure project, this is less of a problem.

(e) Hybrid Groupings

The line organizations of most major companies and organizations have a hybrid type of structure that includes most if not all of the previously mentioned types of organizational groupings (Figure 3.4). With a hybrid grouping, a large company can benefit from the advantages of the various arrangements (and also suffer the disadvantages). Special and long-range programs that cut across product lines can be initiated and carried out by the central research and engineering laboratory, and the specific problem areas of the products or projects can be investigated by the divisional or product laboratories. Often problems that cannot be solved by the product or project teams will be referred back to the central laboratory for more detailed study. The central research or engineering laboratory often has more sophisticated and extensive equipment for basic studies than do the product group laboratories. Companies that deal in complex systems and products with high technical content often maintain specialized groups for developing new systems, products, and projects. Such groups have been referred to as advanced systems or product development groups.

3.2 Types of Project Organizations

Given the line organization framework and its various possible organizational patterns, the introduction of projects into this mosaic is not a simple process. Nevertheless, to satisfy the need for a multidisciplinary approach to the complex problems faced by today's companies, the superimposition of projects on the existing organization structure has been found to be advantageous. As noted in Chapter 1, an organization's survival depends on its responsiveness and adaptability to today's sociotechnical and economic environments. Environmental factors and their associated organizational characteristics include:

Factor or Force   **Requiring**

- a high rate of change   adaptable/temporary structure
- increasing complexity   interaction of expertise
- high risk   focus on predetermined performance criteria
- scarcity of resources   flexibility in allocation and management of resources

There are two principal types of project organizations, the "pure" project and the matrix; there can also be intermediate variations between these two extremes.

(a) Pure Project Organization

The term *pure* describes a project that is sufficiently well funded that it can stand alone; that is, it need not share personnel with functional groups or with other projects. Sometimes pure projects can be large enough to support their own personnel, administration, and engineering departments. Large government- funded projects such as the Apollo project are examples. The aerospace and construction industries carry out many projects of sufficient magnitude to warrant such independent status.

In the formation of a pure project, the personnel needed for the project's fulfillment are completely under the control of the project manager (PM). For maximum effectiveness they should be physically located in one consolidated area with the PM. They may be hired from the outside or transferred from other parts of the company. The pure project can be considered an ad hoc group brought together to satisfy the need for a new development, operation, or system. Unlike the groupings previously discussed, the project group has a finite and specified lifetime, which may vary from a few months to several years.

Which level of management the PM reports to depends on the nature of the project, its size, importance, and the functional groups involved (Figure 3.5). The project would have to be of the utmost importance to the company for the PM to report directly to the president or chief executive officer, in

—— **Figure 3.5: Organizational Chart Showing Possible PM Reporting Relations** ——

Figure 3.6: Pure Project-Type Company

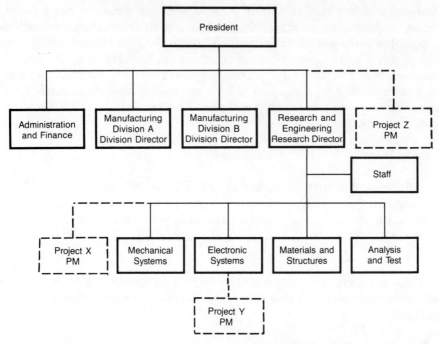

Note: There is also the possibility that one of the manufacturing divisions may have a special project. In that case the PM would report to that division director or manager.

Source: S. E. Stephanou, *Management: Technology, Innovation & Engineering* (Malibu, Calif.: Daniel Spencer, 1981), p. 117.

———————————— **Figure 3.6: Pure Project-Type Company** ————————————

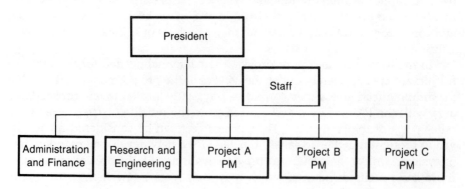

Notes: (a) Organizations that could have this type of structure are an engineering construction company, a think tank, and the like.

  (b) The R&D group could provide service to the various projects in a matrix-type operation (Figure 3.8).

Figure 3.7: Project Organization for a Satellite System Showing both Functional and System-Oriented Groupings (Pure Project)

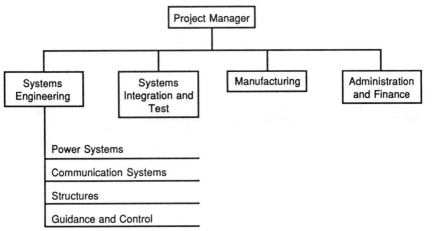

Note: The main organizational groups of the project are functional, whereas the systems engineering section is divided according to subsystems.

Source: S.E. Stephanou, *Management: Technology, Innovation & Engineering* (Malibu, Calif.: Daniel Spencer, 1981), p. 190.

which case the PM himself is often an executive of the corporation. The more frequent reporting level is below the top level of management, unless the company is completely project oriented (Figure 3.6). A construction company could be of this type, but even here a permanent management core would be needed to carry out the necessary administrative and information-processing functions.

The organization of personnel within a pure project is usually along functional lines, although lower levels can be discipline or system oriented (Figure 3.7).

The advantages of the pure project grouping compared with other modes of organizing the project effort include the following:

1. The PM has complete access and control of the personnel needed to perform the work of the project. There is no dilution of effort due to functional group or other project commitments.

2. High morale can be generated because of the intense level of activity, possible rewards if the project is successful, charismatic leadership of the PM, and requirements that are challenging from the standpoint of both performance and schedule.

3. Except for the personnel transferred to the project, there is no disturbance of the day-to-day line operations of the functional groups. Continuing or eliminating the project has minimum impact on the main line organization.

4. From the organization standpoint, the pure project can be an independent cost center and can be monitored as such. Profit or
loss are more visible.

5. Communication and information transfer can occur in a more efficient manner in the absence of organizational barriers. Response
times tend to be much faster than in matrix organizations since
the PM has all of the requisite resources under his direct control.

Disadvantages of the pure project are as follows:

1. Considerable cost is required to set up and maintain a pure project. Trade-offs must be made to determine whether other ways of
performing the work within the functional organization or use of
a matrix-type organization would be more cost effective.

2. Project personnel may experience a certain amount of insecurity
knowing that when the project ends there may be a change in
their status. This is particularly true for those that were hired
specifically for the project, although in well-managed companies
there are always other projects to work on or the personnel can be
returned to the functional groups.

3. If the same type of expertise is needed on several concurrent projects, there can be excessive duplication and inefficient use of personnel as specific project tasks are completed and projects phase
in and out.

4. Technical and other specialists are separated from their peer groups
and are not stimulated and kept current to the same extent as if
they were in their specialty group.

5. Setting up pure projects can be an excessive drain on the resources
of the functional groups, more so than a matrix or other type of
project arrangement.

(b) Matrix Organization

In the situation where the company has a number of projects, none of
which are sufficiently large to warrant the independent status and cost of a
pure project, a matrix organization may be used (Figure 3.8). A principal
feature of this type of organizational configuration is that personnel who are
normally in functional groups carry out work for one or more projects. These
personnel may physically remain in their functional group locations or they
may move their working location to that of the project operation. In the more
customary use of the matrix, personnel remain at their functional location

Figure 3.8: Matrix-Type Project Organization

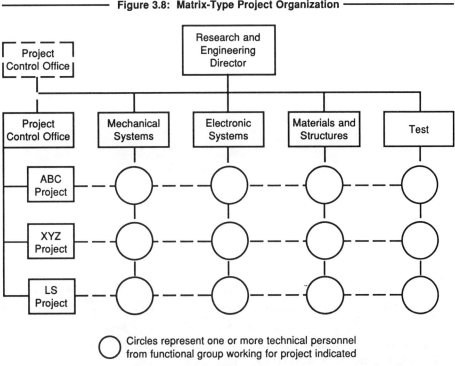

Circles represent one or more technical personnel from functional group working for project indicated

Source: S. E. Stephanou, *Management: Technology, Innovation & Engineering* (Malibu, Calif.: Daniel Spencer, 1981), p. 191.

because of the project's need for the facilities and other capabilities of the particular functional group. When their project work is complete, they can return to the work of the functional group or they can be transferred to another project.

In the example in Figure 3.8, the PMs report to the research and engineering director or to a project control office whose head can be at the same managerial level as the research and engineering director. The project managers are in charge of seeing that the work of their particular project is carried out by the personnel of the functional group. The relationship between the PM and functional group personnel may be a strong one; that is, they receive their work instructions directly from the PM or his deputy or they can receive them through their functional group leader. The latter mode of operation is called a "loose' or "weak" matrix, whereas the former is called a "tight" or "strong" matrix. In the loose matrix situation, the PM plays the role of a coordinator working through the functional head rather than directly with the nonsupervisory personnel. In the tight matrix, the PM deals directly with the functional personnel working on his project and does not interface with the functional head except where necessary to improve project results and coordinate his project and other work that the functional group is performing. We

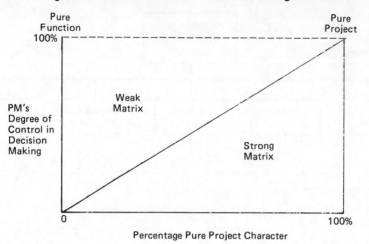

Figure 3.9: Balance of Power in Weak and Strong Matrices

Source: Adapted from L.C. Stuckenbruck, *The Implementation of Project Management* (Reading, Mass.: Addison-Wesley, 1981), p. 91. Reprinted with permission © 1981.

can say that in the strong matrix the balance of managerial power is on the side of the PM, whereas in the weak matrix the balance of power tilts in favor of the functional manager. (Figure 3.9).[3]

In terms of functions and objectives, the PM plays the role of a systems integrator, coordinating the efforts of the various functional groups so that the goals of the project are met and the customer is satisfied with the result. The functional heads have the responsibility for maintaining a high level of competence in their functional organizations and ensuring that the work done on the project is of the highest quality. This means overseeing the personnel doing project work to make sure that no errors or deficiencies occur.

There are a number of advantages of the matrix arrangement for carrying out projects:

1. Personnel are used only for the length of time they are actually needed on the project, making them a cost- effective resource.

2. Technical and other expertise of the various functional units can be fully used. Most present-day projects have multidisciplinary requirements. A functional manager might not be as effective in crossing organizational lines as a PM designated by a higher level of management.

3. The PM can give more attention to achieving the project objectives than can a functional manager who may have several project efforts underway in his group as well as the normal load of the line function.

4. The PM can achieve well-balanced use of all the functional groups needed to carry out the project, whereas a functional manager might tend to favor his particular discipline or specialty area. (This can also occur with a PM who is more of a specialist than a generalist.)

5. Sharing of resources (personnel, equipment, and facilities) among the various projects and functional groups can be more cost effective for the company than other arrangements (such as several pure projects).

6. The expertise of the functional or discipline-oriented groups is kept intact: Experts can consult with their peers and maintain proficiency in their discipline, unlike the pure project situation. The synergistic effect of maintaining teams of experts that are in physical proximity can be significant.

7. From a personnel standpoint, the matrix organization has advantages over the pure project because it solves the problem of what to do with the personnel when the project is over.

Disadvantages of the matrix organization are as follows:

1. The superimposition of the matrix on an existing line organization leads to a level of complexity of operation that can be cumbersome.

2. The "two-boss" situation faced by functional personnel working on projects can cause problems.

3. Close supervision of the overall matrix operation is necessary to make certain that resources are used to a degree that is optimum for the company rather than for a particular project or functional group.

4. Because of the demands for resources by the various projects and functional groups, as well as the problem of diverse objectives, there exists a great potential for conflict between individual PMs or between PMs and the functional heads.

3.3 The Project Manager

The central figure in a project is the project manager. He is the focal point for directing, monitoring, controlling, integrating, and bringing to a successful conclusion the work of the project. He has complete autonomy in the project and should have access to all the applicable experience available in the company. Ideally, he should also have access to all available resources of the company, including personnel and facilities. In actuality, this may not always be the case.

It is advantageous if he has already had experience in project management, either as a project manager or working at a level next to a project manager. He should be a generalist rather than a specialist, although he may have been a specialist at one time in one of the key technical areas of the project. The project manager should be responsible for the project from birth to completion and makes the ultimate decisions on all major project problems. Important personal characteristics include not only the usual managerial skills but also a flair for encouraging innovation and providing a creative environment. In addition to directing the project and maintaining coordination and communication with his staff and higher management, he must also maintain good relations with the customer, if an outside organization is funding the project. He must possess considerable tact and have strong persuasive powers to work across functional and organizational lines and accomplish the goals of the project. If there are subcontractors, he has to be concerned about their performance, delivery, schedule, and cost.

Careful distinction should be made between project manager as a title or ranking in an organization and project manager as a function. There is a deep-seated problem in many organizations born from two decades of declining R&D expenditures and consequent lack of real growth. In many cases the title of project manager has been bestowed upon individuals as a designation of level of achievement in the organization or as a reward or "pacifier," rather than because of the actual role they are carrying out. Such designated personnel are project managers in name only since, aside from a classification change, they have not been given any substantive changes in scope of work or real authority or responsibility. They should more appropriately and accurately be called senior project *engineers* rather than project *managers*.

A project manager can interface with several or all of the following:

- Deputies, assistants, and supervisors
- Higher management
- Working level professionals
- Other project managers
- Functional heads
- The customer
- Subcontractors and vendors
- The legal, marketing, and manufacturing staff of the company
- Union representatives

A project manager's base of authority is more tenuous than that of a functional head. The nature and size of his projects may vary so that he is more vulnerable to the ups and downs of the various projects to which he is assigned. Although he is given total responsibility for a project, he may not receive totally dedicated effort and support from functional heads and their

Figure 3.10: Job Requisition or Job Description

Title of Position:	Research Engineer.
Educational Requirements:	B.S. in Chemical Engineering.
Experience:	At least two years in chemical processing, particularly pilot plant operations and process development.
Description of Duties:	1. Supervise pilot plant operations for producing new organic intermediates.
	2. Identify and recommend process improvements including conversion of existing batch method to a continuous process.
	3. Work with production engineering to design manufacturing plant.
Salary Range:	$XX,xxx to $XX,xxx per year.

Source: S.E. Stephanou, *Management: Technology, Innovation & Engineering*, (Malibu, Calif.: Daniel Spencer, 1981), p. 129.

subordinates. As a result, an important requirement for a project manager is the ability to obtain by persuasion, rather than by authority, as high a level of support as possible from the involved personnel. The qualities that a project manager needs to obtain such support have been described variously as charisma, persuasiveness, high capability for instilling confidence, diplomacy, political astuteness, and the like. Certainly, these characteristics are not foreign to other types of manager, but they are particularly important in the project management context because of the special nature of the working relationships.

3.4 Staffing the Project

(a) Sources of Personnel

The personnel required for a project can be obtained from either within the organization or from outside sources. Many companies maintain a constant search for competent, talented professional personnel. In obtaining personnel from outside the company, the manager usually works with the personnel department, if the company is large, or personnel officer, if a small company. An abbreviated or short-form job description is prepared to furnish an accurate basis for selecting the required type of individual. An example of a job description, also called an employment requisition, is shown in Figure 3.10. It sets forth briefly the training and experience required for the position and the general nature of the tasks to be performed.

Job descriptions should be very carefully prepared. If the requirements are too broad or vague, too many persons will apply who do not meet the requirements. But if the job description is too narrow and specific, there may not be many candidates who feel qualified to apply. In hiring professional personnel, it is good practice to choose persons who have general capability in a particular area so that they can be used in a variety of projects rather than overly specialized individuals whose applicability may be limited to one or two specific types of problems.

The company personnel department has the principal responsibility for seeking personnel from outside sources. Common procedures include advertising in newspapers and professional magazines, recruitment at universities and colleges, and contacting employment agencies. Another source is professional meetings. The personnel departments of large companies usually have a continuing program of searching out and maintaining contact with promising candidates for employment. An organized, ongoing search is more cost effective for a large company than a sporadic although concentrated effort. However, if the company is primarily project oriented, hiring on an as-needed basis may be more economical if a core of supervisory and highly specialized personnel is permanently maintained. A select group of company personnel can become expert in starting, executing, and closing out projects in a cost-effective manner so that they become highly valuable to the company. Construction companies tend to operate in this manner because of the nature of their business. There are still additional ways that professional personnel from outside the organization or company can be obtained. Sometimes company personnel or customers may have friends or know of competent and eligible individuals who might be interested in the positions.

In fulfilling project requirements, it is usually quicker, more convenient, and more advantageous to obtain personnel from within the company. In such transfers it is customary for the manager to contact the supervisor of the person or type of person being sought. Formal negotiations should be made through the appropriate organizational channels. The supervisor may not be able to spare anyone at that time or the expert may be a nonexpendable member of the group. It is poor practice for the manager seeking personnel to contact the person directly and ask that he request a transfer without first contacting the person's supervisor. This could cause bad feelings since it would ignore the supervisor's needs and could lead to wholesale raiding of the best personnel from various groups. Such practices are generally prohibited by company policy as excessive personnel transfer could be harmful to the company's overall operation. Where the desired personnel cannot be spared from a particular group, other groups in the company can be contacted or outside sources solicited.

(b) Evaluation of Applications

Assuming that the personnel department does its job well, the project manager should soon receive a number of applications of prospective candidates for the position to be filled. These applications should be reviewed carefully and evaluated with respect to the following characteristics:

1. Is the application filled out neatly or is it filled out in a careless, slovenly manner? This is frequently an indication of the type of reports the person would write.

2. Are answers to questions complete and responsive or are they incomplete or evasive?

3. Are salary requirements excessive, that is, significantly above the allowable range for the position being filled?

4. Does the applicant have the desired educational training and experience?

5. Is the applicant a job hopper? This is a value judgement which varies with the manager. However, an applicant who has changed jobs every one or two years should be considered suspect.

6. Is the applicant overqualified for the position? If overqualified, he may not be happy at the level of the job and may seek another position shortly after being hired.

7. Is the applicant overly specialized? It is desirable to have some degree of versatility so that if the work area he is assigned to is reduced in personnel, he could be used in some other related work assignment.

8. Does the applicant indicate a geographical preference that would exclude him from consideration? This may indicate an unwillingness to locate in areas where the company might need employees.

These considerations can serve as a basis for eliminating a number of applicants so that the project manager is presented with a more workable group of candidates. Depending on company practice, contacts can then be made by the personnel department for plant or facility visits or the manager may further screen the potential new employees by phoning them personally. The latter technique tends to be more cost effective. During the course of the telephone conversation it may become apparent that the individual does not really want the position, is not immediately available for it, or is not suitable— factors that somehow have been obscured or not disclosed in the application. The company can realize appreciable savings in transportation, lodging, and other expenses that would have been incurred if the applicant had been needlessly brought to the company for an interview. Those applicants that still appear good prospects after the phone conversation are then asked to visit the plant or facility. Of course, common sense dictates that the applicant should not be contacted at his present place of employment, if he is still employed. This could jeopardize the individual's status in his present position, if the company is not aware that he is seeking employment elsewhere. Application forms should have a space where the applicant can indicate whether it is permissible to contact his present employer.

(c) Final Selection

With all the available data at his disposal, the manager can now select the candidate whom he wishes to hire. Before doing so, however, he can obtain still additional information on the applicant that may have an important bearing on his selection. A phone call to one or more former supervisors can be made to obtain their opinions of the individual and his performance in previous positions. Such calls, however, may yield little in terms of substantive information as many companies are exceedingly wary of giving out information that might be considered negative and thus an impediment to someone's ability to secure employment. As we noted, if he is presently employed, his present supervisory should not be contacted unless the candidate has given permission to do so.

In making the final selection, the manager should ask the following questions about the candidate:

1. Does he have the skills needed for carrying out the technical job?

2. Will he fit into the group or will his personality clash with those of others?

3. Is he sufficiently versatile so that he can be used in more than one job assignment?

4. Will he be happy in his environment?

5. Can his salary requirements be met? Are they out of line with comparable personnel already in the group?

Finally, the PM must take into account the immediate utility of the selected personnel to the objectives and work of the project, since there are usually insufficient funds for any substantial amount of training. Technical personnel must already be well versed in their specialty and be capable of immediately applying their expertise to their portion of the project effort. In acquiring project personnel, it must be kept in mind that their jobs with the project will eventually come to an end when the project winds down or is terminated. For hiring personnel with skills that require less advanced training and education, the job shop can be a valuable resource (see Section 3.4 (e)).

(d) Selection of Supervisory Personnel

In obtaining supervisory personnel the PM has several options: He can promote a worthy individual to a role of supervisor; he can look for an already trained supervisor who might be available for transfer within the organization; or he can bring in someone from outside the organization. It is highly desirable from a management standpoint to promote from within the organization, if possible. There are several reasons for this.

First, the morale of the individual promoted is given a big boost and that of the others is maintained as, hopefully, they could have the same experience some time in the future. The situation where supervisors are always brought in from outside the group or organization can demoralize and antagonize the personnel, most of whom are seeking organizational advancement.

Second, the individual selected from within the organization or group is a known quantity as evidenced by his performance in previous assignments. His weaknesses are also known and can be properly weighed against his attributes. In hiring an individual from outside the organization, his positive qualities are emphasized in his application and in his effort to make the best possible impression during the facility visit and interview. His weaknesses will become apparent only after he has been in the employ of the company for a while. It is human nature to give an applicant the benefit of the doubt and not consider his potential deficiencies.

Third, the individual selected from within the organization knows the operational procedures of the company, so that no time is lost in training him or allowing him to find out for himself how to get things done in the new environment.

Finally, the individual from within the organization is more likely to be accepted by the people in the group he is going to supervise. If properly selected, he has already proven his worth and demonstrated leadership capability while working in a peer relationship with them.

In support of hiring supervision from the outside, it can be argued that the new person could bring in new ideas that could improve the operation of the group. Also, sometimes an outside supervisor must be brought in when the assignment calls for a capability that is not present in available personnel, for example, if a mature, management-oriented individual is needed to supervise a young and inexperienced group. A judgement must be made whether this advantage would more than compensate for the disadvantages previously mentioned.

There are a number of professional management and executive placement firms who make a business of finding positions for managerial personnel. Such firms list professionals of many different backgrounds and talents including technical personnel. Their advertisements can be found in major newspapers as well as in professional, technical, and business magazines. More commonly, high-level competent managers in a particular industry are well known and are generally solicited directly by interested companies.

In selecting supervisory or managerial personnel, it is advisable to look for key qualities such as the following:

1. The person has good communicative skills. He articulates well, listens attentively, is responsive, and absorbs and retains information.

2. The person is a self-starter. He can initiate work and action on his

own rather than always being guided and directed. Ideally, the candidate should have some track record of accomplishment.

3. The person must have detailed knowledge of his field of supervision, but he does not have to be an expert in every area of applicable technology. In fact, there are advantages to the manager being a generalist, mainly he is less likely to overemphasize his particular field of specialization.

4. The quality of being energetic and dynamic seems to be a desireable characteristic although not a necessary condition of being an effective manager. A person with an apparently limitless amount of energy can be a tremendous asset in an innovative and successful organization; conversely, a lethargic manager will not tend to inspire or motivate personnel.

5. The person is perceptive and responsive to the needs of the people he will supervise. This is a difficult attribute to assess in advance, particularly for someone who has never supervised before.

Many companies have a trial period for breaking in a new supervisor and indicate this to the organization and the world by preceding his title by the word *acting*. One advantage of this procedure is to ensure that the individual will make every effort to fulfill the requirements of the position so that he can be accepted as a full-fledged supervisor. Another advantage is that the company is not committing itself permanently. If the individual makes serious errors, he can be demoted and readily transferred back to his previous assignment or another assignment. However, the term *acting* may also connote that the appointment is temporary and that the organization is looking for a permanent tenant to fill the position. Therefore the present appointee is there only until a suitable candidate is found. With this interpretation the supervisor may be treated with less deference by both peers and the people he supervises, weakening his position and authority. So the use of the term depends on the specific circumstances. There are situations when there is no suitable candidate for a supervisory position immediately available and a temporary appointment must be made. In such instances the term *acting* is justified and the temporary nature should be made clear when making the appointment.

(e) Short-Term Hiring

In staffing projects it is often not cost effective to bring new personnel with permanent status on board for carrying out tasks of relatively short duration. This is particularly true when the cost of fringe and other benefits given to permanent employees is considered. On such occasions the company may resort to employment agencies that have on tap specialized talent for short-term assignments. These free-lance individuals are interviewed and selected by the company in the same manner as other candidates, but it is understood at the outset that the length of employment is dependent on the work load, which is predefined, and there is no implied long-term commitment. From the standpoint of the company and the project manager, this procedure can be economically sound. With respect to performance, there is a slight risk since the individual hired under such circumstances has no long-range commitment or permanent ties with the company and hence may not be as conscientious and hard working as a permanent employee. However, there have been frequent instances where a temporary employee does his job so well that he is asked to remain with the company on a permanent basis. A temporary employee knowing of this possibility might tend to work harder and do a better job if he likes the working conditions and decides to seek permanent employment. In obtaining the services of temporary employees, the company must pay a premium rate, which means that their cost per unit of time is greater than that of comparable company personnel. Despite the increased pay rate, the overall cost is less than hiring full-time, permanent personnel, so the additional temporary expense can be justified.

Short-term hiring from employment agencies is most common for personnel such as draftpersons, machinists, and some types of engineers.

(f) Consultants

A project manager may use consultants when a specific type of expertise is not available within the company or the work load of available experts is too heavy. Sometimes the need can be fulfilled by a few visits on a short-term basis or the need may be recurring so that the consultant is scheduled for regular monthly or weekly visits. There are many specialists working individually or as part of consulting firms who are available for this type of duty. Such consultants can be used advantageously for solving special technical problems, providing guidance in complex, highly specialized areas, and making unbiased appraisals. However, there is usually a penalty of time and money in acquainting the consultant with the problem and the company environment. The company must make a cost/benefit judgement on such an expenditure.

3.5 Other Organizational Relationships

(a) Staff Personnel

In carrying out project tasks using complex technology, there is often a need for expertise in several different technical areas. The company may not be able to afford, or have a need for, a group of full-time people knowledgeable in a particular technology or specialty area. The presence of one individual who is highly expert in the field may be sufficient. Such an individual is usually a senior member of the technical staff, either a long- time, experienced specialist for the company with a proven track record or perhaps someone hired from the outside and given a permanent status. He can serve as an in-house consultant and can be used by the project manager to furnish guidance and direction in his area of expertise. He is not involved in the day-to-day operations of the project; that is, he is not in the direct chain of command (see Figures 3.2 and 3.4).

This type of position is referred to as staff. It is comparable to the position in which many companies place their legal counsels. On a large project a staff person may have a group of people working for him, but his authority and assignments are given to him by the project manager. Often the assignments entail special studies that cut across project organizational lines. The project manager may not want to disturb his line organization and therefore assigns his "special agent" to accumulate the information needed from the various groups and analyze it to assist him in making an important decision. Staff personnel can play important roles in the overall planning and operation of a large project.

(b) Committees and Task Forces

The appointment of a committee is an effective way to evaluate, plan, or make a decision on a matter about which the PM may not be sufficiently knowledgeable or have the time to investigate. The problem may be so complex that no one individual could possibly have all the information needed to make the decision or recommendation. The committee participants are usually selected on the basis of their knowledge of key areas of the problem since a number of work areas that cross organizational lines can be involved. A committee may be temporary (ad hoc) or permanent (standing) for the lifetime of the project depending on the nature of the problem.

Advantages of using a committee include obtaining informed input to the problem from several knowledgeable sources and the potential of arriving at a consensus decision. It has the additional long-range advantage of allowing the committee members to become better acquainted with each other and their respective work areas. Committees have the possible disadvantages that they are costly in terms of personnel time, possibly no agreement will be reached, personnel clashes may develop, a dominant personality may try to enforce his views on the other committee members, and time can be wasted in needless and spurious debate. Nevertheless, the PM should seriously consider the use of committees where the right conditions for them exist. The potential advantages outweigh the disadvantages.

A few rules that make use of a committee more effective are as follows:

1. Draw up and distribute an agenda to the invitees, preferably a day or two before the meeting.

2. The committee should not be too large—five is an ideal number. The more people there are, the more diverse are the opinions and the less likelihood of reaching an agreement on issues.

3. Specify the committee meeting time and duration at the outset to minimize unnecessary expenditure of time.

4. See that decisions are made on as many items as possible about what action is needed, who is responsible, and due dates for response.

5. Choose participants who are at comparable organizational levels, although the leader need not be.

6. Have the minutes of the meeting recorded and distributed. Conclusions and actions to be taken should be spelled out clearly.

Special task forces may be set up within the project. Task forces resemble committees in most ways except that the task force members are also expected to perform the work, whereas committee members in most cases are not. Also, as the task force must complete the mission within a specified period of time, there is often a greater urgency to the work of the task force than to that of a committee.

(c) Linear Responsibility Charts

To ensure that project supervisors and other personnel are informed about where responsibility lies and who should be consulted on important project activities, a linear responsibility chart (LRC) can be used (Figure 3.11). The LRC can clearly define the coupling of position with duties to be performed and responsibilities.[4] It offers a suitable technique for detailing the responsibility of the individual and whether the responsibility is advisory, informational, a responsibility for implementation, or some special responsibility. Responsibilities can be full or of varying degrees.

Although the LRC can spell out specific responsibilities of key project personnel, it cannot guarantee that these duties will in fact be carried out. It is up to the PM to monitor the project activities to make certain that these responsibilities are fulfilled.

(d) The Informal Organization

In addition to the formal organization, which can be charted, there is almost always an informal organization that develops during the growth and operation of the company and the carrying out of various projects. Personal ties develop among personnel and persist through the years as the individuals age and change positions in the organization. Such relationships can be particularly strong if the individuals worked together during the company's inception, during difficult times in the organization's history, or on the same projects at various times in the past. People with close personal relationships can work together informally and accomplish much without going through

———— Figure 3.11: Linear Responsibility Chart for Technical Support Contract ————

	Center Director	Marketing Manager	Proposal Manager	Contracts Manager	Accounting Manager	Project Manager	Task Leader(s)
Establish business objectives.	1	3		4			
Identifying business opportunities	2	1					
Decision to seek specific technical work.	1	3	4	4		4	
Prepare technical proposal	2	4	1				
Prepare cost proposal.	2	4	4	1	3		
Accept customer's contract	5	5	5	1	4		
Appoint project manager.	1					3	
Prepare technical plans	2					1	4
Organize technical team	2					1	3
Supervise technical work.						2	1
Submit technical reports	4					1	4
Submit cost invoices				2	1	3	
Deliver final end products	5			5	5	1	4
Submit final invoice	5			2	1	3	
Close the contract.	3	4		1	5		

Code:

1	actual responsibility	4	may be consulted
2	general supervision	5	must be notified
3	must be consulted		

Source: J.R. Wells, research paper "Institute of Safety & Systems Management," University of Southern California, 1979.

the "red tape" and paper work that is required by company procedures. It can also have undesired effects when the chain of command is circumvented or arrangements made by friends in different interfacing segments of the project organization or between projects without the PM's knowledge.

At its best, the informal organization can represent a group of truly "company-men" who have been successful at various levels in the organization and work for the best interests of the company. They also can have a hierarchy of authority (not documented but nevertheless present and operative). They represent the "memory" of the company and are true representatives of its culture as described by T.J. Peters and R.H. Waterman, Jr., in their best seller *In Search of Excellence.*[5] The astute PM should learn to recognize the informal ties that exist in his organization, try to use them to his benefit, and be aware of their potential pitfalls.

———— Questions and Topics for Discussion ————

1. What are various levels that a pure project can fit in a line organization, and what are the factors that determine the level and to whom the PM reports?

2. How are project and product line-oriented groupings in an organization similar? How are they different?

3. How would you explain the terms *loose* and *tight* as two extremes of a matrix-type organization?

4. What are the conditions in an organization that merit setting up a pure project? Under what conditions is a matrix-type organization more effective for carrying out projects?

5. What are the special attributes needed by a project manager compared with the attributes expected of a typical functional or line manager?

6. What are the trade-offs that a small-to-medium size company must make in maintaining a continued, programmed search for technical personnel, including visits to universities, employment clearing-houses, and the like, as opposed to making an occasional concerted effort when personnel needs accumulate or become acute?

7. What are the conditions for seeking personnel from job shops to fulfill project personnel needs? What are the advantages and disadvantages of such temporary hiring?

8. Under what conditions can hiring a consultant be justified (a) on an as-needed basis and (b) on a regularly scheduled basis?

9. What are the conditions that would justify setting up a standing committee versus those for setting up an ad hoc committee?

10. Set up a linear responsibility chart for a hypothetical project to develop a new mass transit system. (Hint: You will first have to draw up an organization chart for the project.)

11. Discuss the problems of destaffing when a large project is terminated and how you would cope with them. Discuss a general plan of attack.

12. The half-life of applicable knowledge (gained from college training) of say, an engineer or scientist is approximately four to five years. How can this affect company personnel hiring and pay policies? Discuss the significance of the preceding.

References

1. E.F. Kast and J.E. Rozenzweig, *Organization & Management* (New York: McGraw Hill, 1974), p. 213.

2. D.W. Karger and R.G. Murdick, *Managing Engineering & Research* (New York: Industrial Press, 1969), pp. 43-44.

3. L.C. Stuckenbruck, *The implementation of Project Management* (Reading, Mass: Addison-Wesley, 1981), p. 89.

4. D.I. Cleland and W.R. King, *Project Management Handbook* (New York: Van Nostrand Reinhold, 1983), pp. 364-382.

5. T.J. Peters and R.H. Waterman, Jr., *In Search of Excellence* (New York: Harper and Row, 1983).

Making The Most Out of Tools And Techniques

—————————————— Chapter 4 ——————————————
Project Planning and Scheduling

4.1 Introduction

Planning must provide answers to the following questions:

1. What are the specific goals and objectives of the project?
2. How is the project going to be structured?
3. What are the important tasks and events (milestones) of the project and how should they be sequenced and/or scheduled?
4. How will the personnel be used?
5. How are other resources (money, equipment, materials, facilities, and so on) going to be distributed among the various tasks?
6. How will the key elements of the project — namely, cost, performance, and schedule — be estimated and controlled? What management tools will be used?
7. What will be potential bottlenecks in carrying out the project and how will they be handled?

The answers to the last three questions are of particular importance. If they are not clearly defined, the approach to monitoring and control will be based on reaction and expediency rather than on well-conceived and carefully thought-out procedures.

If the project involves high technology, that is, substantial advancement of the state of the art (SOA), additional questions must be answered:

1. What are the critical technical issues (the known unknowns)? Invariably, there are also "unknown unknowns" that will surface as the project gets underway.
2. Is the technical expertise available in-house or is outside technical assistance needed?
3. How much supporting research effort can the company afford and how long will it take to solve the critical technical issues? How can such solutions be dovetailed into the problem at hand?

In answering these questions, the three inseparable elements of predefined performance, cost, and schedule must be considered. These elements, which characterize all projects and which, by definition, fall within the traditional purview of the project manager's accountability are an integral part of the planning and control functions. It is not unusual for project managers to expend a great deal of effort, encounter considerable difficulty, and experience significant frustration in juggling these elements to achieve even limited success. A lot of this stems from the PM not recognizing and accommodating factors that materially affect the soundness and effectiveness of the planning and control functions. He is thereby often forced into a precarious position from the outset.

Before discussing the various tasks and steps of the planning process, it is important to consider the forces under which project planning is carried out. Such factors can be classified as exogenous (externally instigated) or endogenous (internally instigated). They play a vital role in shaping the project manager's approach to the planning process and execution of the effort.

(a) Exogenous Considerations

Exogenous considerations include a host of factors such as customer needs and preferences, competitive conditions and pressures, technological considerations, and other external dictates that collectively influence the approach to a given effort. The evolving approach frequently tends to reflect what it takes to start an effort under current circumstances more than an in-depth consideration of what it takes to perform the effort. The tendency can be held in check through an ongoing process of long-range planning, since a go-ahead on the basis of what is most expedient may not steer the organization in the direction it necessarily wants or should be going. In the heat of launching the project, this is not always obvious.

Exogenous factors often foster unrealistic goals and expectations along with certain suspect practices that are not so much the by-products of malice of forethought as they are symptoms of shortsightedness and reactions. Such practices can occur when there is an absence of systematic assessment, coalescence, and transcription of longer-range plans and objectives into day-to-day activities. A number of fairly common tendencies, if not practices, illustrating this are as follows:

First is a tendency to make "buy-ins" or "management adjustments" whereby costs are scaled down from the accurately projected to the more acceptable to improve salability to the customer or sometimes even to upper levels of management. The financial lien created is often rationalized away on the basis of a need to invest in future business, economies of scale based upon anticipated follow-ons or other potential business, design to cost, producibility studies, or other such factors that may or may not ultimately prove valid.

The second tendency is to manipulate schedules depending upon how critical they are perceived to be and how they interact with other factors. Schedules may be manipulated or backed into to the extent that the projected period of performance is inconsistent with the customer's requirements or management's expectations. Costs under such conditions are seldom adjusted to reflect the well-accepted adage that "time is money." The treatment of schedule as an independent variable, be it inadvertent or not, invariably has a negative financial impact upon the effort.

The third tendency is to promote a technical approach either in response to customer requirements or organizational biases. This often tends to distort cost and schedule parameters beyond acceptable limits. As an example, what may be touted as the "lower-cost technical approach" may require more time to implement as the technology may not be fully developed. As a result, cost savings may prove purely illusory. However, it is not uncommon to have a more complex approach and correspondingly a more expensive solution propounded for no reason other than technical superiority, compatibility with ongoing programs, or other such reasons. Such general conditions can be similarly precipitated by the customer by way of his formulation and transcription of requirements.

Performance, cost, and schedule are often given varying relative weights during the various phases of a project. These variations tend to become more pronounced in the absence of long-range planning, the purpose of which is to provide detailed operational guidelines, ground rules, and evaluation criteria to inhibit such reactive tendencies.

The lack of long-range planning can promote a host of illnesses, among them the disruptive effect of varying managerial values, preferences, and interpretations (see Chapter 12). These in turn foster an obsession with the acquisition of new business or the redirection of on-going efforts as the ultimate proof of their validity. This pattern tends to be reinforced since within our corporate society, entrepreneurship is not only lauded but also often generously rewarded. Also, the motivations and emphasis of the proposal manager in securing a go-ahead on an effort may not necessarily be consistent with the requirements and constraints that the project manager will encounter in the course of the project's execution. Ultimately, a bad decision becomes an organizational cross as the blame can never really be fixed upon a single individual, considering the number of individuals that are required to approve a project prior to its initiation. A bad project is very likely to become a political football. A go-ahead to proceed with an effort, therefore, be it customer or company approved, does not in itself imply that the proposed effort is inherently sound, that is, consistent with respect to the constraints on performance, cost, and schedule.

Upon assuming accountability for an effort, a prudent project manager should consequently always undertake to develop a clear-cut understanding of any built-in biases and their likely impact. To the extent that an inconsistency does exist among the elements of performance, cost and schedule, it should be resolved by the project manager through solicitation and reclarification management's criteria of success. There tends to be an understandable but unfortunate reluctance on the part of the project manager to pursue this resolution even in cases where it is clearly warranted. However, it is essential to the formulation of realistic objectives as well as the establishment of appropriate trade-offs during the project's execution. Too often project managers tend to launch a project seemingly ignorant of built-in biases, harboring preconceived notions of the criteria of success, supremely confident of their attainability and thus predisposed to obdurate hammering of the project team to bring a flawed effort into compliance. In the process the PM promotes his own impotence through customer ill will, management's perplexity, and the project team's dismay.

(b) Endogenous Consideration

Endogenous considerations are encompassed by three basic operational issues:

- What factors should be the subject of managerial focus to promote the likelihood of project success?
- Why do these factors promote the likelihood of project success?
- How should these factors be approached to maximize the likelihood of project success?

Each of these issues has two associated aspects (1) the mechanical aspect, which deals with factors affecting the appropriateness of selected planning, scheduling, and control tools and procedures, and (2) the organic aspect, which deals with factors and practices that assure the effective implementation and application of tools selected for a given project through their effect on team involvement and commitment. Generally speaking , these aspects are separable only in theory. In practice, the success of a project will be largely dependent upon the extent of concurrent recognition and accommodation of the aforementioned by management. Their lack of concomitant accommodations and support is perhaps the most frequent general cause of project failure, the inherent soundness of the undertaking notwithstanding.

(c) Meeting Performance, Cost, and Schedule Criteria

Both exogenous and endogenous factors drive the performance, cost, and schedule constraints of a project and account for the great degree of difficulty often encountered in their fulfillment. To successfully accommodate these constraints, the project manager must direct his effort to the following areas:

- Definition (or acceptable redefinition) of the problem
- Development of alternatives leading to an acceptable solution
- Evaluation and allocation of all requisite resources
- Implementation of the effort
- Appraisal of progress and results
- Iteration of relevant parameters in line with the established constraints and stated objectives.

These are in effect the constituent elements of planning, scheduling, and control. It may be thought from the preceding that a project manager may need nothing more than a knowledge of the business and an understanding of the job. This would be erroneous since the project manager must also possess an understanding of people along with a certain degree of creativity and imagination with respect to what is, what can be, and what should be done. Since there are no standard recipes for successful project management, there must be a blending of the use of appropriate tools and techniques with actions that reflect an understanding of the human aspects and organizational interplay. The project manager's planning and actions must be directed toward objectives of attaining the performance, cost, and schedule goals of the project.

4.2 Scoping, Detailing, and Scheduling the Work

Three key areas of a project that require careful and ongoing consideration are *objectives, effort,* and *organization.* Planning for these key areas must be tailored to the specific requirements and characteristics of each project. Although it is highly desirable to transfer lessons learned on one project to another, this doesn't mean that a formerly successful approach to the organization of an effort necessarily ensures success on subsequent efforts. Each project must be evaluated and structured on the basis of its own unique requirements and constraints.

(a) Defining Objectives

The importance of clearly defined and stated objectives cannot be overemphasized. A clear definition and transcription of objectives into operationally meaningful terms is the first and perhaps most important step on the road to the successful execution of the effort. The apparent simplicity of this prerequisite is deceptive and tends to detract from the seriousness with which it should be treated.

The objectives may be expressed in the form of a statement of work or they may be enumerated as project objectives (there may be primary and secondary objectives). At a minimum such documentation must do the following: [1,2]

- Give explicit operational direction delineating the overall intent, limits on scope, specific constraints, and preferably a concrete description of the desired and deliverable end result(s). Such direction must be both attainable and realistic.
- Resolve the issue of organizational priority to be placed on the effort relative to other ongoing efforts in the likely and often unavoidable conflict over both human and physical resources. Establishing priorities and resolving conflicts must be accomplished in consultation with higher management.
- Provide the basis as well as guidelines for a course of action and the decision-making process. Among the relevant issues in this area are the order of required trade-offs among the key parameters and constraints likely to be encountered in the course of executing the effort.
- Indicate how attainment of project objectives is to be measured using the management information system established to monitor and gauge actual performance. This suggests that objectives must be formulated so that progress in their attainment can be accurately and consistently measured.

These objective requirements are essential in coping with problems generally arising from: (1) inconsistencies fostered by varying interpretations, preferences, commitments, and values of individuals throughout the organization; (2) continual changes in priorities owing to incompatibilities between requirements, resource availability, and allocations; and (3) frequent confusion of activity with accomplishment or paperwork completion with actual output.[3,4]

The importance of the above factors is highlighted by the fact they constitute some common and frequent causes of project failures (in addition to and part of those enumerated in Section 1.4).

(b) The Work Breakdown Structure*

The basic and most effective tool in planning and integration of a project is the work breakdown structure (WBS). The WBS has been defined in a number of ways, although the key concepts are the same:

- Project Work Breakdown Structure is a *family tree subdivision* of a project, beginning with the end objective and then subdividing these objectives into successively smaller work packages.[5]
- The WBS is an *end item oriented* family tree composed of hardware, services and data. The WBS displays and *defines the product* or

---

*Although the discussion of WBS in this section refers to its use in government agency contracting, it is commonly used in nongovernment related projects for delineating the details of the project work load. In such applications it often assumes a simpler format than that show in Figure 4.1, with tasks and subtasks enumerated as in Table 4.3.

Figure 4.1: Integration of WBS and Organizational Structure

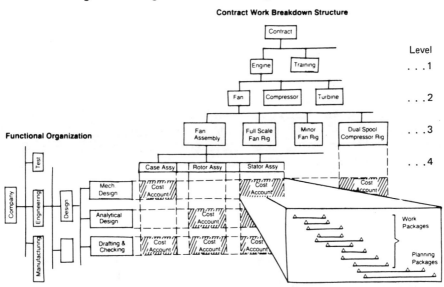

Source: Cost/Schedule Control Systems Criteria Joint Implementation Guide (Washington, D. C.: U.S. Department of Defense, October 1, 1976), p. 30.

products to be developed or produced and relates the elements of work to be accomplished to each other and to the *end product.* [6]

- The WBS is a skeletal *outline of program objectives..* It subdivides these into successively smaller segments until manageable units of work are reached which program management can assign to the responsible supporting organizations.[7]

The example of a WBS shown in Figure 4.1 depicts the successive subdivision of the end product into logical and more manageable units of work.
Applications of the WBS as a planning tool include the following:[8]

- Defining and/or limiting the general scope of the effort. This involves identifying the levels at which various subsystems and components will be developed. The levels can also be based on the type of effort arranged in hierarchical order according to the importance of the effort and its relationships to other efforts.
- Suggesting or outlining the preferred approach to the effort.
- Describing and underscoring the importance of prevailing or mandated relationships and interfaces.
- Communicating responsibilities and providing the framework for the subdelegation of effort.
- Estimating, allocating, and accumulating costs.

- Carrying out necessary configuration and data management.
- Monitoring overall performance through integration of specific responsibilities for costs, schedules, and technical accomplishments.

The specific configuration, contents and detail of the WBS will generally vary depending on a number of factors: (1) nature and size of the effort, (2) structure of the organization, (3) combination of technical and organizational interfaces, (4) technical and managerial complexity of the effort, (5) reporting requirements and associated cost considerations, (6) degree of visibility and control desired by project management, and (7) the type of resources available to maintain the data base and resources accessibility.

The hierarchy of the WBS is usually based on systems, subsystems and components, tasks, subtasks, and work packages and sometimes is related to the functional organization shown in Figure 4.1. The structural character depicts the true nature and purpose of the WBS.

For maximum visibility and control, good practice calls for subdividing the effort and extending the degree of detail of the WBS to the work package level. The work package is typically defined as a unit of work that does not lend itself to any further logical subdivision of effort and is assignable to either the lowest level of the organization or a specific individual. Various rules of thumb have been proposed for the optimal size of the work package, such as that the package should not exceed 80 hours' worth of effort or should be achievable within the time span of a single reporting period. The latter perhaps has a greater degree of merit than the former. In practice, the desired degree of visibility should generally be traded off against a qualitative assessment of the added cost and administration effort to provide such a degree of visibility and potential control.

The effectiveness of the WBS as a tool will be largely, if not exclusively, determined by how creative the project manager is in developing its configuration and detail. There is no substitute for such creativity. The starting point in developing the WBS should be the manager's recognition that the WBS is an end item-oriented structure whose primary usefulness lies in its potential to communicate, clarify, and link objectives as well as transcribe these objectives in terms of successively smaller subdivisions of the deliverable end result.

A common error in structuring and developing the WBS is a tendency to pattern it along the lines of what effectively amounts to an organizational chart like that in Figure 4.2(a). In so doing, the WBS is typically relegated to a financial accounting tool, namely, an effective repository for the accumulation of costs and time charges that attempts to provide questionable control over the operation of organizational functions rather than the outputs of such functions. Under such conditions cost duplication, padding, or omission is inevitable in the planning and programming stages of an effort. Outputs of the various functions, rather than functions as such, are and should be the primary focus of project management's concern, particularly within the matrix

Figure 4.2: Structuring of the WBS

(a) Incorrect Structuring

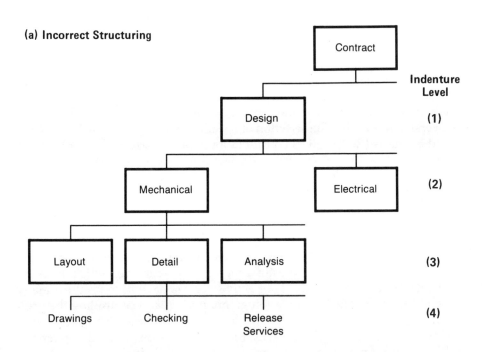

(b) Correct Structuring

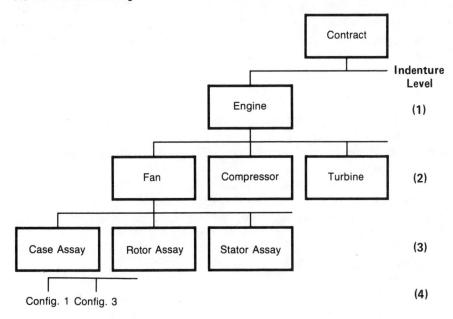

environment.[9] It is the end-item orientation of the WBS, as shown in Figures 4.1 and 4.2 (b), that promotes its proper use as a management tool. This tool not only prompts "score card" questions but also furnishes attention-directing and problem-solving inputs for the elements of the end products as well as associated functions requiring management action.[10]

The WBS ultimately affects the extent of downstream visibility and control that the project manager is likely to possess. Once the WBS has been properly developed, it provides, the framework not only for the subsequent planning, scheduling, and budgeting of the constituent elements of the effort but also for the overall effort itself. The selection of specific planning and scheduling tools should be guided by practical considerations such as size and complexity of the effort, availability of resources (in terms of money, people, and equipment), customer and/or upper management requirements or dictates, and user training, experience, and acceptance.

(c) Task Charts and Milestones

An important part of the development of the WBS is setting forth the various tasks and subtasks and estimating the time span over which the work will be done. Task bar, GANTT, or activity charts have been used for many years and are still valuable in planning, monitoring, and controlling the project effort (Figure 4.3). They are most applicable and effective at the lower levels of the WBS for work packages, for simple projects, or as status-reporting tools. In estimating the time frame for each task and the personnel required, the manager can plan the allocation of labor and sequencing of the work. Task bar charts are best developed by personnel that will be involved in doing the actual work and subsequently reviewed by the project manager.

An important output of the development of task bar charts is that they can help in arriving at milestones or key events in the program or project (Figure 4.3). Milestones can be used to signal initiation of an effort, but more important, they give an estimated date at which a task or significant segment of the total job is to be completed. Key milestone dates may be determined from task bar charts by the project manager and his staff or they may be dictated by the customer for delivery of hardware, software, subsystems, and systems or completion of services such as testing. Milestones can also be dates at which the program/project is to be reviewed. Task bar charts and milestone dates are important guideposts to indicate the status of the work. Tasks completed, slippages in time, and percentages of work accomplished can be indicated as the project progresses. Furthermore, task bar charts and milestone tables can serve as the basis for setting up network diagrams.

(d) Network Analysis (Work Flowcharts)

Although task bar charts are necessary in planning since they set forth tasks and subtasks and the time span over which they are to be carried out, they have several disadvantages for complex projects with many systems,

Figure 4.3: Sample Task Bar Chart for Planning a Small Project

Task	J*	F	M	A	M	J	J	A	S	O	N	D
1. Development of Preliminary Design	①											
2. Development of Final Design				②								
3. Fabrication fo Experimental Model					③							
4. Testing of Experimental Model						④						
5. Setting up of Pilor plant Manufacturing Facility									⑤			
6. Operation of Pilot Plat Facility											⑥	
7. Testing of Advanced Prototype												⑦
Personnel Loading												
Designers	2	2	2	1	1							
Model Shop				2	3	1						
Development Engineering		1	3	3	3	3	3	3	3	3	3	2
Test Group												1
TOTALS	2	3	5	6	7	4	3	3	3	3	3	3

Milestones	Date
1. Completion of Preliminary Design	March 1
2. Completion of Final Design	April 15
3. Experimental model fabricated	June 1
4. Testing of experimental model completed	July 1
5. Pilot plant completed	Sept. 1
6. Pilot plant operated successfully for 3 months	Dec. 1
7. Testing of advanced prototypes	Jan. 1

* Instead of names of months, numbers can be used to indicate months after start.

Source: S.E. Stephanou, *Management: Technology, Innovation & Engineering* (Malibu, Calif.: Daniel Spencer, 1981), p. 45.

subsystems, and components.

First, they do not show the relations among various tasks and events and second, the project manager requires not only the work package task bar charts but also overall and intermediary sets of bar charts for the various subsystems and systems. In addition, he requires a summary bar chart showing the most important tasks or systems for the whole project. This leads to a plethora of bar chars, which in itself is not an overwhelming disadvantage, but network analysis can handle such complex systems more easily and is more amenable to computerization.

The use of network analysis is closely allied to the need to projectize. The factors that make the project team approach to a given effort operationally desirable and economically justifiable are the same factors that require the use of network-based techniques in planning. In Table 4.1 these are contrasted

——————————— **Table 4.1: Comparison of the Need to** ———————————
Projectize with the Characteristics of Network Analysis

Factors Promoting the need to Projectize	Characteristic Attributes of Network-Based Techniques
• Typically involves a higher degree of complexity	• Forces more thorough planning
• Requires more and faster decision making within the constraints of specific scope	• Permits simulation and iteration of alternative courses of action based on constraints
• Relies upon more effective use of limited resources	• Allows flexible scheduling of requisite resources
• Demands greater visibility and interaction	• Promotes improved communication through delineation of interdependencies
• Entails a one-of-a-kind effort	• Applies to nonrepetitive, nonrecurring activities

with the complementary attributes of network-based techniques such as program evaluation and review technique (PERT), critical path method (CPM), and precedence diagraming method (PDM).

In the past the unavailability or inaccessibility of computers along with the cost and effort of implementing and updating network-based plans and schedules, especially by hand, have served as convenient excuses for avoiding these techniques. Today with the proliferation of personal computes and the availability of a wide range of software, there is no practical reason for the exclusion of network-based plans and schedules. Selective application of network analysis appears to be a function of the extent of antiplanning bias that exists within an organization rather than the accessibility to or cost of computer-based planning and scheduling tools. In the long run these tools more than pay for themselves. The possible applications to which network-based tools can be adapted are many and varied. Among the more widely recognized and accepted are the following:

- Communication of interdependencies and involvement of the project team
- Estimation of project duration (through establishment of the critical path)
- Identification and resolution of potential conflicts and problem areas (bottlenecks)
- Simulation of alternative courses of action
- Project schedule acceleration (crashing)
- Optimal cost scheduling of projects
- Resource allocation and personnel smoothing (through manipulation of float times associated with noncritical activities)
- Cash flow management (based on float-time management)

———— Figure 4.4: Use of CPM for the Planning and Development of a Minicomputer ————

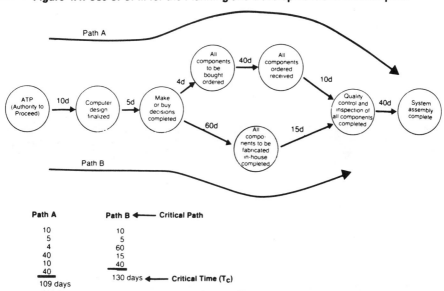

Path A	Path B ◄——— Critical Path
10	10
5	5
4	60
40	15
10	40
40	
109 days	130 days ◄——— Critical Time (T_c)

There are other network analysis techniques that have been and are being used but CPM, PERT, and PDM seem to be the most prevalent. These techniques are discussed in a minimum fashion so as to provide important essentials rather than a complete description of the many intricacies and ramifications of their use.[11, 12]

Critical Path Method (CPM)

The development of this early network technique has been attributed to a group set up by the E. I. duPont deNemours Company in 1956 to study possible ways of improving the planning and scheduling of construction projects.[13]

In developing the network, the principal activities (tasks) and events (milestones) must be identified and arranged in chronological order, preferably in table form. These can be derived from the WBS, work packages, and task bar charts. Events are indicated by circles on the diagram and activities by arrows. The event is an anticipated or planned occurrence at a specified date, an activity is the work required toachieve that event, and the activity time is the time required to proceed from one event to another. The activity time is estimated by an individual or individuals who have had experience with that particular type of activity and use previous performance as a basis for the estimate. Events, activities, and activity times are charted as in Figure 4.4. By adding the estimated times for the activities along various paths or sequences of events, the total time for each path can be arrived at. The path that requires the greatest length of time is referred to as the critical path, and the total length of time for that path is the critical time.

———————— Figure 4.5: Use of CPM Showing "Slack" or "Float" Times ————————

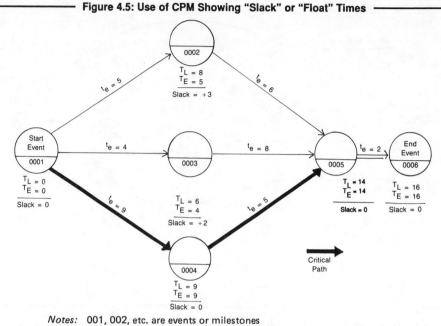

Notes: 001, 002, etc. are events or milestones

T_L is the latest time the event can occur without delay of the project

T_E is the earliest time the event can occur

Any slippage in time to complete an activity along the critical path will mean a slippage in the final event or the total time to carry out the project. Since CPM preparation is a part of the planning and programming phase, there is time to make changes to decrease the critical path time. In the example of Figure 4.4, it might be possible to decrease the critical path time by purchasing more components rather than fabricating them in-house or by granting overtime. Perhaps revamping the manufacturing operation, including the use of new or better equipment, might be the answer to reducing the critical path time for that activity. Another possible way might be to start quality control of the components being fabricated in-house just as rapidly as they are manufactured, rather than waiting until all the components are fabricated. These are just a few of the ways that the overall project could be accelerated as a result of analyzing the CPM network. The effect of an alternative on cost would have to be considered, and there would have to be a trade-off between increased cost and the value of the time saved.

In the CPM example in Figure 4.5, the earliest possible time for completion, the latest possible time, and the "slack" or "float" time for each event are calculated. The float time for a particular event is defined as the difference between its latest and earliest time for completion. It indicates how much delay in carrying out that activity can be tolerated without delaying the completion of the project. Since the critical path is the minimum time for project completion, all events along that path have zero float and represent potential bottleneck activities.

Calculation of float times requires the establishment of early start, early finish, late start, and late finish times for each of the activities within the network. These times are defined as follows:[14]

Early start (ES):   The earliest an activity can be initiated based upon the completion of the preceding activities

Early finish (EF):   The earliest an activity can be completed assuming preceding activities are initiated at their earliest start times and do not slip

Late start (LS):   The latest an activity can be initiated without adversely affecting project duration

Late finish (LF):   The latest an activity can be completed without adversely affecting project duration

Mathematically the relationship between these times can be expressed as:
ES+Duration=EF (forward pass)
LF-Duration=LS (backward pass)
Float time=LS-ES=LF-EF
This reflects the normal order of computation and is a part of routine output in computer-based planning and scheduling along with the identification of the project's critical path.

This information can be used not only in allocating and smoothing personnel requirements, scheduling facilities and equipment but also in projecting cash flow requirements based on the time phasing of costs associated with the various activities. The effects of float time upon some of these factors are shown in Figure 4.6. In this example, delaying certain tasks not on the critical path to a later date can change the schedule of cash flow requirements.

Program Evaluation and Review Technique (PERT)

PERT is similar to CPM, with the exception that the activity time is arrived at analytically and takes into account the fact that such times are variable depending upon the circumstances. It was developed by the consulting firm of Booz, Allen and Hamilton in conjunction with the Navy's Special Project Office and the Lockheed Missile System Division for the U.S. Navy's Polaris missile in 1958. It achieved considerable notoriety and favorable attention as a result of that program.[15]

In PERT, as in CPM, the important ingredients are events, activities, and activity times. To determine the activity times, the following formula is used:

$$T_{exp} = \frac{T_{opt} + 4T + T_{pess}}{6}$$

— Figure 4.6: Adjustment of Personnel and Cash Flow Requirements Using Float Times —

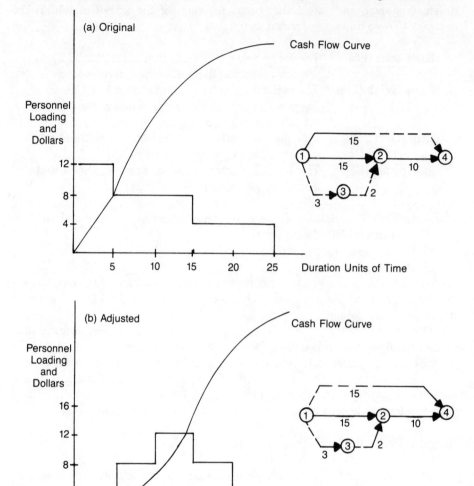

where

T_{exp}	is the expected time
T_{opt}	is the optimistic time
T_{pess}	is the pessimistic time
T	is the most likely time

    The formula provides a means of giving greatest weight to the most likely time and yet takes into account the optimistic and the pessimistic times. The optimum time is arrived at by looking at the previous history of such activities and observing what the shortest time for carrying out that or a similar activity has been in the past. The pessimistic time reflects the longest possible time that has been consumed by the activity in the past and takes into account major changes in approach or technical difficulties. To be truly realistic, the pessimistic time should probably be given a weighting greater than 1, possibility 2 or 3, since difficulties are more likely to occur than not. If the activities are relatively new and there is little experience to draw on, a formula such as

$$T_{exp} = \frac{T_{opt} + 4T + 2T_{pess}}{7}$$

is more realistic.

The steps in the development of a simple PERT chart are as follows:

1. Decide on key events and activities.
2. Set up the network of events and activities in proper sequence of occurrence.
3. Determine and tabulate the optimistic, pessimistic, and most likely activity times.
4. Calculate the expected or mean activity time from the preceding formula.
5. Determine the total times for the various paths.

Where the system to be developed is very complex — for example, where there are hundreds, even thousands, of components and sub-systems — the process is computerized and the effect on completion time of various options and variations can be determined. The final PERT chart would have the same form as the CPM charts shown in figures 4.4 and 4.5 except that calculated activity times (T_{exp}) would be used rather than estimated activity times.

An advantage of PERT over the CPM technique is that it allows for the calculation of the probability of meeting the schedule or potential schedule slippage. Assuming that the likelihood of predicting the activity time follows a beta-type statistical distribution, the standard deviation for one activity time would be[16]

$$\sigma \text{ (stand)} = \frac{T_{pess} - T_{opt}}{6}$$

For the critical path the total standard deviation (*σ (stand)) would be

$$\sigma_i \text{ (stand)} = \sqrt{\sum_{i=1}^{n} \sigma_i^2 \text{ (stand)}}$$

where n is the number of activities on the critical path and $_i$ refers to the particular activity and can have values equal to 1, 2, 3, 4,...$_n$. The term

$$\sum_{i=1}^{n} \sigma_i^2 \text{ (stand)}$$

in the equation represents the sum of the squares of all the standard deviations of the activity times in the critical path.

To calculate the probability of completing the project in a certain scheduled time, T_s, we can use the expression

$$Z = \frac{T_s - T_c}{\sigma \text{ (stand)}}$$

where Z is a factor indicating the number of standard deviations expressed by the difference $(T_s - T_c)$; T_s is the scheduled or desired project time, and T_c is the critical path time.

From probability tables, a sample of which is shown in Table 4.2, the probability of meeting the schedule time T_s can be found. For the example of Figure 4.4 where T_c was 130 days the probability of meeting a completion time of 140 day scan be calculated. If a value of five days is assumed for the total standard deviation of the critical path (* σ (stand)), then

$$Z = \frac{140 - 130}{5} = +2$$

From the table, a Z factor of +2 corresponds to a probability of 98%. If a schedule completion time of 120 days was desired, a Z factor of -2 would result, and the probability of meeting that curtailed schedule time would be 2% (not a very likely prospect).

──────────── Table 4.2: Probability for Various Values of the Z Factor ────────────

Z Factor		Probability
3.0	. . . .	0.9987
2.5	. . . .	0.9938
2.0	. . :	0.9772
1.5	. . . .	0.9332
1.0	. . . .	0.8413
0.5	. . . .	0.6915
0.0	. . . .	0.5000
-0.5	. . . .	0.3085
-1.0	. . . .	0.1587
-1.5	. . . .	0.0668
-2.0	. . . .	0.0228
-2.5	. . . .	0.0062
-3.0	. . . .	0.0013

Thus far we have been using the term PERT for scheduling events and activities with respect to time. More accurately, this use of PERT is referred to as PERT/TIME. There is also PERT/COST, which can be used to determine the most expensive rather than the most time-consuming path. The costs for various activities are estimated and the paths that are most expensive are identified. In the planning stage, resources, including personnel, materials, and facilities, may be adjusted to investigate possible ways of reducing the cost of the more expensive paths.

Precedence Diagraming Method (PDM)

This method, also known as the activity-on-node precedence system, is considered by many to be the most effective of the network planning techniques currently being used. As with CPM and PERT, it requires the systematic delineation of interdependencies and the logical sequencing of all significant activities or events that comprise a project, thus forcing thorough planning. Since a project is defined as an effort with a concretely identifiable beginning and end, PDM, like its analogues, must be constructed to reflect specifically identifiable events or activities such as completion of preliminary and final designs, completion of testing, customer acceptance of hardware, and so on. Figure 4.7 gives an example of the use of PDM and also shows the early start and finish times and the late start and finish times. With this information, float times can be calculated for each activity. The "forward pass" referred to in Figure 4.7a consists of going through the network from start to finish and adding up the durations to give the earliest starts and finishes for each activity. The "backward pass" of Figure 4.7b determines the latest start and finish times by starting from the end of the network, subtracting duration times, and working backward.[17]

The difference between PDM and CPM/PERT is that activities instead of events are considered nodes or tally points and the arrows connecting nodes show dependencies, not time. The advantages and disadvantages of the PDM method vis-á-vis CPM/PERT are discussed in detail in a number of texts which are specifically focused on description and comparisons of these techniques (see for example, reference 17).

Depending on the nature and type of effort, it is possible to have more than one logically acceptable activity sequence and interconnection pattern between the designated start and finish of a project. The general approach to and the duration of a project will thus be largely influenced by the individuals doing the planning and the extent to which these plans are iterated within the constraints of feasibility. Figure 4.8 presents two different approaches to the same effort, the duration of which is determined by the selected approach. We must remember that network-based techniques are management tools, not substitutes for management.

Figure 4.7: Precedence Diagram Showing
Early Start and Finish Times and Late Start and Finish Times

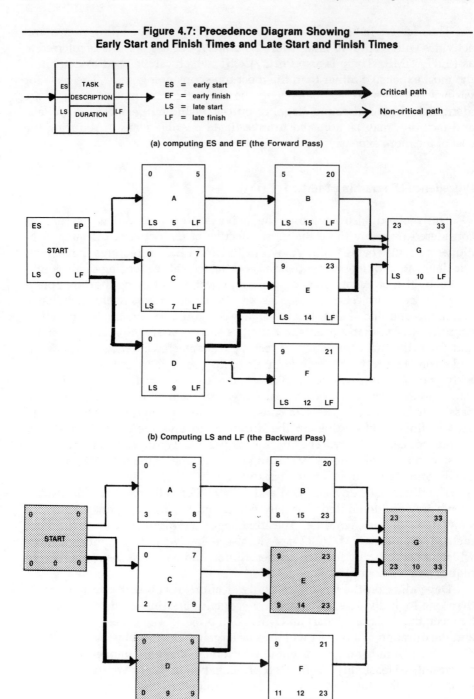

(a) computing ES and EF (the Forward Pass)

(b) Computing LS and LF (the Backward Pass)

Source: Adapted from Joseph Horowitz, "A Simplified Approach to CPM Planning," *Plant Engineering* (October 18, 1983), pp. 136-139.

Figure 4.8: Precedence Diagram Showing Alternative Logic in Planning/Scheduling of Effort

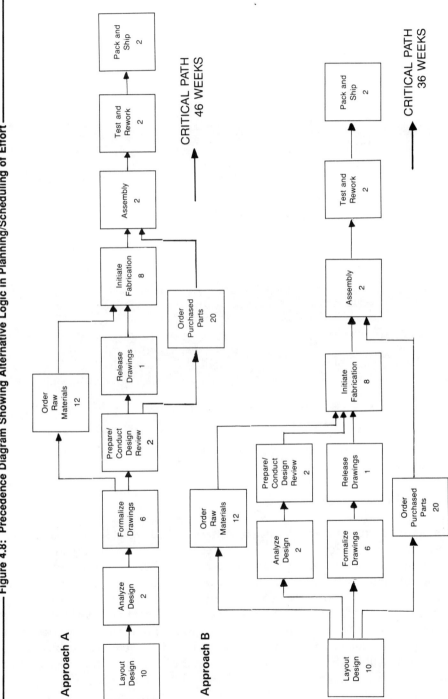

Approach A

Layout Design 10 → Analyze Design 2 → Formalize Drawings 6 → Prepare/Conduct Design Review 2 → Release Drawings 1 → Initiate Fabrication 8 → Assembly 2 → Test and Rework 2 → Pack and Ship 2

Order Raw Materials 12

Order Purchased Parts 20

CRITICAL PATH 46 WEEKS

Approach B

Layout Design 10 → Analyze Design 2 → Prepare/Conduct Design Review 2 → Initiate Fabrication 8 → Assembly 2 → Test and Rework 2 → Pack and Ship 2

Order Raw Materials 12

Formalize Drawings 6 → Release Drawings 1

Order Purchased Parts 20

CRITICAL PATH 36 WEEKS

Figure 4.9: Effect of Project Duration on Total Project Costs

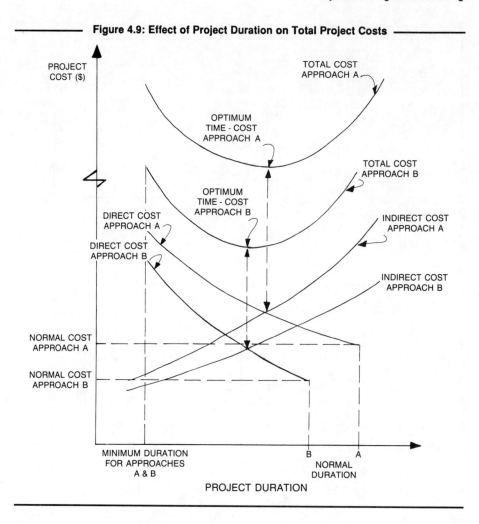

The Critical Path and Costs

Since the critical path of a network refers to the longest sequence of activities within the developed network, it correspondingly dictates the overall duration of the effort and directly influences its cost. The slippage of any activity along this path will extend the project duration and will invariably affect costs. Conversely, project acceleration can only be achieved by successfully shortening the period of performance of activities along the critical path. Since schedule and costs are intimately related, project duration can be shortened through the acceleration of time, granting financial incentives, or increasing personnel. Although direct costs on the project will typically increase, indirect costs such as interest and other expenses will generally tend to decrease as project duration is compressed (Figure 4.9). The total cost of the project, that is, the sum of direct and indirect costs, will typically assume a U-shaped curve, suggesting the existence of an optimum overall cost schedule combination. This combination will be greatly influenced by the general quality of project planning and scheduling (see Figure 4.8). Generation of these curves is now practical considering the widespread availability of computers and requisite software.

It is quite possible to evolve plans and networks with multiple critical paths, which correspondingly increase both schedule and financial risk. More often than not, the number of critical paths can be reduced through replanning the effort and/or reassessing the periods of performance assigned to each of the activities. In practice, time estimates often tend to be padded; a critical path could be easily eliminated through a reevaluation and a more realistic projection of the periods of performance associated with various activities. Whenever possible, a project should not embody more than one critical path. It should be noted that the critical path seldom remains constant during a project and tends to change based on how effectively the plan is executed.

The implementation of network-based techniques requires planning and finesse in accomplishing the following tasks:

- Securing the support and backing of management
- Training key personnel in the network methodology
- Applying the technique to efforts that meet accepted criteria and definitions of the project
- Involving key personnel in its evolution and overall integration
- Developing realistic schedules with the support of the participants
- Making sure that the technique is used by the project team as a working document
- Concentrating and working on the critical paths by reviewing and updating plans frequently

4.3 Estimating the Cost and Budgeting the Effort

(a) Basic Methods

The accuracy of cost estimates as well as the ability to evaluate them effectively will be influenced by the type of work breakdown structure and the amount of information furnished to the various organizations and individuals having responsibility for the cost-estimating effort. Since costs are generally dictated by the approach taken to a given effort as well as its projected period of performance, collective costs will also be a reflection not only of *what* is being planned and scheduled, as specified by the WBS, but also of *how* it is being planned and scheduled, as discussed in the preceding section.

Normally, cost estimating tends to be a broad-based grass-roots effort triggered by the project office, which issues a formal request for cost estimates based upon a statement of work (SOW), applicable specifications, a prelimi-

——————————— Table 4.3: Cost Estimate For Developing a Module Tester ———————————

| Work Breakdown Structure | | Costs | | | |
Module Tester	Personnel*	Facility	Material & Other	Total

1.0 Develop design concepts
   1.1 Select key design features
   1.2 Evaluate final design, including
       human factors criteria
	$8,000	$2,000	$3,000	$13,000

2.0 Develop work prints for build-up
   2.1 Review for any revisions
   2.2 Final prints
	5,000	500	1,000	6,500

3.0 Fabricate model of tester
   3.1 Develop final configuration
   3.2 Evaluate from user
       point of view
	2,000	—	150	2,150

4.0 Construct functional prototype
     of tester
   4.1 Complete check-out of design
   4.2 Test hardware on tester
       4.2.1 Evaluate test results
	6,000	500	1,000	7,500

5.0 Calibrate system
   5.1 Check out accuracy with
       established standards
	200	—	50	250

6.0 Release tester to inspection for production line use	20	—	—	20
Total costs	$21,220	$3,000	$5,200	$29,420

*Different labor categories are usually indicated.

nary master schedule, a WBS along with ground rules, assumptions, and other special instructions. In response to this request, each participating organization or individual will generally evolve an estimate including personnel requirements by labor category, material, and other direct charges, like travel, computer time, and/or reproduction, in accordance with the indicated master plan and schedule prepared by the project office. Such an input could have the format shown in Table 4.3. Customarily, justification or appropriate backup are included as part of this package which, once completed, is transmitted to a central processing function for summation. This function can verify and apply the appropriate labor and overhead rates, compute general and administrative costs, and add the appropriate fee or profit in the case of proposals being prepared for submission to a customer. As cost estimates are collected, the proposal manager may or may not elect to review and negotiate these costs with each of the areas involved. Based on such reviews or negotiations, the proposal manager may elect to cut costs, leave costs unchanged, or add a contingency or management reserve.

In principle, this process for estimating costs is fairly simple and straightforward; in practice, however, a variety of factors may complicate the effort. First, budgets may be developed or adjusted based on management "feel" or "bogies." Under such conditions, the resulting budgets are typically either highly overstated or grossly inadequate. These practices are counterproductive as they ultimately lead to a lack of commitment and effort to control costs and budgets on the part of the participants. Second, cost inputs may be inflated at the operating level in anticipation of cuts by the proposal manager or higher levels of management during the evaluation cycle. Inflated cost estimates often reflect an already highly pessimistic grass-roots estimate of what it takes to accomplish a given task. Under competitive conditions, management's expectation of such cost-estimating practices may lead it to cut a great deal more from a quote than may be minimally required to do the job. This can result in serious problems, particularly in cases of underestimates based on errors of the type discussed below. Such a negative situation can be ferreted out if a sound WBS exists and time is taken to evaluate costs in concert with a developed plan and schedule. Third, personnel requirements at the operating level may often be based on an extrapolation of historical costs including an excessive reliance upon past experience rather than rigorous analysis of the requirements and peculiarities of the specific project at hand. Direct project comparisons based on cost are inherently dangerous for a variety of reasons including (a) subtle technical or other differences; (b) overall economic instabilities and uncertainties; (c) changes in labor, overhead rates, and general and administrative costs; (d) variations in the available or requisite mix or complement of human and physical resources; and (e) external factors like rapid rates of obsolescence and phaseout of certain types of parts, changes in supplier base, and so on.[18, 19]

It should be noted that budgets in and of themselves control nothing,[20] but should be considered as yet another means of quantitatively describing the objectives of a project, in this case, the anticipated costs.

(b) Advanced Cost-Estimating Techniques

The traditional or grass-roots cost-estimating technique, although widely used, has some inherent drawbacks, particularly on larger efforts. Such drawbacks include the following: (1) The technique is susceptible to human error. (2) It is a time-consuming, often cumbersome, process. (3) It is an expensive exercise since it usually involves fairly senior technical, scientific, and other personnel. (4) It is an inflexible framework as it is not amenable to cost-effective iteration of design approaches and project costs.

These factors are of substantial significance, particularly where frequent preparation of budgetary estimates or firm quotations are part of the normal course of doing business.

As an alternative or supplement to the traditional estimating method, there are some extremely powerful parametric cost-estimating tools that are now available. The RCA programmed review of information for costing and evaluation (PRICE), which can be used in the financial scoping and planning of the effort across the various stages (or phases) of the product life cycle, is such a tool.[21]

The PRICE program is an aggregation of cost-estimating and evaluation models, including auxiliary programs that relate through mathematical expressions a host of input variables to cost. Sets of these input variables uniquely define the hardware for the purpose of cost modeling so that output costs are determined strictly on the basis of the mathematical equations. It is adaptable to most types of projects, although the primary use to date is believed to have been in the areas of electromechanics and electro-optics. It can be applied to the entire spectrum of hardware acquisition problems ranging from development through production and modification and can include a variety of costs such as project management, documentation, and sustaining engineering. Among PRICE's primary applications, aside from bid no-bid decisions, proposal preparation, and submittal are the following:[22]

- Long-range planning
- Cross-checking of design concepts
- Design-to-cost trade-off analyses
- Design-to-unit-production-cost analyses
- "Should" cost analyses
- Estimates of cost to complete
- Procurement planning
- Life-cycle cost analysis

The basic parameters that represent the hardware to be costed and which are ultimately stored in computer files include the following:[23]

- Quantity of hardware
- Development, production, procurement, modification, integration, and testing schedules including all associated lead times
- Hardware characteristics such as size, weight, and packaging density
- Type and manufacturing complexity of structural, mechanical, and electronic portions of the hardware
- Extent of new design and complexity of engineering development
- Fabrication processes to be used in production
- Hardware yield expectations
- Environmental and other specifications

Once the data are entered into the computer, the cost-estimating process proceeds along the lines of a dialogue between the model and the user. The model requires calibration or fine tuning; that is, it must first be adapted to the general type of hardware to be produced or updated to new situations. This process involves running the model in reverse, namely, whereby historical costs are used as inputs by way of generating typical complexity factors as outputs. The process relies upon the availability and integrity of past cost data or case histories. In the course of such calibration or fine tuning, users can adapt the model to the particular type of accounting method used by the company. Depending upon the situation, this overall process of adaptation of the model may take about a month to set up for a given product line. Furthermore, the data files created before the model run can be made to represent various systems or subsystems comprised of many distinct subassemblies that may be readily correlated with the WBS. Among the more interesting applications of such parametric models are these:[24]

- Calculation of complexity factors from any cost data base
- Calculation of design geometries from target costs
- Calculation of manufacturing complexities of non homogenous assemblies
- Various sensitivity analyses
- Calculation of field reliability
- Measurement of the cost impact or effect of reliability improvement programs

Some users have reported projection accuracies for the use of the PRICE model of the order of 1% of actuals. Somewhere around 10% should be realistically and consistently attainable; this is certainly within the range of a best-run traditional cost-estimating effort.

Unquestionably, a costing model such as PRICE is extremely powerful and can afford project management a great deal of capability and flexibility in at least four general areas of prevailing concern: (1) rapid and cost-effective response to customer inquiries as well as evolving market conditions, (2) validation of design approaches and project cost estimates, (3) cost and risk reduction efforts especially as part of the development of a greater degree of competitiveness, and (4) monitoring, iterating, and controlling the effort to attain specified cost objectives.

4.4 The Project Plan

After the various planning and scheduling activities discussed in Sections 4.2 and 4.3 have been completed, the results can be summarized in a project plan. Such a plan is valuable as a reference for the project manager and other involved parties during the course of carrying out the project. Typical ingredients of a project plan are as follows:

- Major goals and objectives
- Statement of work
- Detailed system requirements
- Organizational structure:
    How project fits into the company organization
    How Project is organized internally
- Work breakdown structure (including work packages)
- Task bar charts (GANTT charts) and milestones
- Overall project schedules
- Work flowcharts (CPM, PERT, or PDM)

- Allocation of resources: dollars, personnel, facilities, material, travel, documentation, computer use, and so on
- Engineering work orders (EWOs)
- Planned personnel use versus time
- Reporting and review procedures
- Cost control procedures

The project plan allows the PM to integrate and review all the essential elements of the project so that compatibility of the various aspects of the effort can be readily assessed and interface or other problems identified. The project manager must continually update the project plan to provide for changes in scope or direction of the plan and changes in the allocation of resources.[25]

4.5 Organizing and Initiating the Effort

The subject of organizing and staffing the project was generally discussed in Chapter 3. There we described the various types of project organizations that are presently being used and provided the organizational context in which they are found. In addition, the staffing and organizational relationships that can strengthen the capability of the project manager were identified and discussed.

In this section we present some of the problems that the project manager encounters, especially the constraints under which he must operate in organizing and staffing the project. For example, planning the organization does not necessarily imply the freedom to restructure the overall organization to suit his perception of the project's requirements. In fact, the project manager may have little to say about the position (level) the project will occupy in the organization, the type of internal organization of the project (weak matrix, strong matrix, or pure project), and the selection of the individuals for the project. These decisions will depend on the size of the project, the existing organizational mode of the company, and the general manner (culture) in which projects of that type and scope are usually handled. Organizing should be viewed form a broader perspective as including some aspects of staffing, such as a voice in selecting personnel by way of defining personnel requirements, delineating project responsibility relationships, documentation requirements, information flow, forms, procedures, and an overall control system for the project effort.

There are a number of areas that the project manager typically needs to consider, organize, and control. The following is a checklist of such items:[26]

- Personnel requirements and qualifications (who, when, how many and for how long)
- Project and funds status reporting (what, who, how, and how often)
- Make or buy decisions and procedures (who, what, how, when, why)

- Associate or subcontractor monitoring and control (who, what, how, and how often)
- Project configuration management/change control (what, when, who, how)
- Problem review and resolution procedures (when, what, who, how)
- Subdelegation of accountability (financial and technical)
- Customer interface and marketing activities (establish and define extent of project manager's participation)
- Project quality requirements and disposition of deficiencies/discrepancies (what, when, who, how)

All established companies have on file specific job descriptions and publish a host of company procedures, policies, and practices covering operations. The project manager or aspirant to such a position must become intimately familiar with these to be able to successfully work with and through the company system. Often these procedures, policies and practices are adaptable to a wide range of efforts, which means that the project manager not only has the latitude but also the responsibility to specify and enforce their use. The linear responsibility chart of the type shown in Figure 3.11 can be an effective tool in organizing, communicating, and coordinating a host of requirements and activities on a given effort and should be used whenever appropriate.

Once the organizational framework and staffing has been set and all the detailed planning activities have been completed and "blessed" by higher management, the project can proceed with full-scale implementation. The stage for execution of the project has been set, as the three important criteria of performance (described by the WBS and work packages), cost (budget), and schedule (based on network analysis) have been defined.

Launching the project is usually accomplished by issuing documents authorizing the expenditure of funds to carry out the work. The name given these authorizations varies form company to company; some common designations are work authorization, engineering work orders, and work release. In essence, they are brief statements of the work to be done, what groups will do the work, and how much money will be allocated for the particular work segment or package. An example of a work order for a technical job is shown in Figure 4.10. This standard form serves as a go-ahead, authorizing the responsible leader or principal investigator to assign work and accumulate expenses in accordance with the funding allocated. Note the table of milestones and the graph showing estimated cumulative expenditures plotted against time and milestones. This allows the project manager to closely monitor both the financial and the schedule performance of the effort during the year. As expenses are incurred, accumulated actual costs can be plotted and compared with the estimated values for that time period. The attainment of scheduled milestones can also be examined to verify the status of the work accomplished. This will be discussed more fully in the next chapter.

————————— Figure 4.10: Sample Engineering Work Order —————————

Group	Engineering Hours	
Advanced structures	811	hours
Materials	1,000	
Test	300	
Illustrations	100	
Manufacturing	210	
Total Hours	**2,421**	**hours**
Total Engineering Labor	**$35,500**	

Other Costs	Dollars
Materials	$21,500
Travel	1,500
Subcontract	10,000
Consultant	1,500
Total other costs	**$34,500**

Title: High Temperature Materials
Reference: Program 618 — High-Temperature
                              Furnace Development
EWO No. 618-592
Product Line: High-Temperature Furnaces
Project Leader: J. Smith, Ext. 4095
Research Manager: G. Jones, Ext. 3508
Date: 12-15-79
Total Budget: $70,000
Work to be completed by: 12-31-80

All charges to this EWO must be authorized by the Project leader.

1.0 Objectives
  1.1 To investigate the thermal and mechanical properties of advanced high-temperature materials.
  1.2 To relate the thermal and mechanical properties of these new materials to their method of fabrication and chemical composition.
  1.3 To design and test samples of these materials fabricated into components of a furnace structure.

2.0 Technical Approach
  2.1 Subject new materials to increasingly high temperatures ranging up to 1500 degrees F for various lengths of time and test mechanical properties after exposure. Note dimensional changes.
  2.2 Investigate correlation of thermal properties with method of fabrication and chemical composition.
  2.3 Fabricate most promising materials into components of a furnace structure and test at furnace temperatures.

3.0 Facilities and capital equipment
Existing facilities at high-temperature laboratory are adequate.

4.0 Milestones
  4.1 Test all materials before thermal treatment   March 15
  4.2 Expose materials to thermal treatment   June 10
  4.3 Test materials after thermal treatment   August 10
  4.4 Fabricate promising materials   October 1
  4.5 Test new components   December 30

5.0 Estimated Expenditures vs. Time

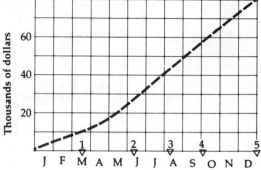

Source: S.E.Stephanou, *Management: Technology, Innovation & Engineering* (Malibu, Calif.: Daniel Spencer, 1981), p. 51.

——————Questions and Topics for Discussion——————

1. How can a buy-in dictated by top management complicate the effectiveness of a PM in his planning and execution of a project? What can a PM do to alleviate such a situation?

2. What are the important techniques that can be used in project planning? List and discuss each briefly.

3. Show by an example how a work breakdown structure (WBS) can be used in planning a hypothetical project. How can the WBS be integrated into the organizational structure?

4. If a network analysis method is required by the customer for tracking a project, how would you decide whether to use PERT, CPM, or PDM? Give reasons for your choice.

5. Why is the consideration of float times important in planning the project?

6. A rule of thumb proposed by some observers of public-sector projects is that the project will probably overrun in time at least 30%. Explain the reasons for this.

7. Develop the cost of a hypothetical small project using the general technique illustrated in Table 4.3.

8. Prepare a task bar chart for starting a university bookstore. The space and housing for the bookstore has already been provided by the university. Also, draw a chart showing anticipated expenditures and milestones. (Estimate cost and activity times.)

9. Use a network technique instead of a task bar chart for problem 8 above and account for any differences observed.

10. Discuss the following statement, "Outputs of the various functions, rather than functions as such, are and should be the primary focus of project management's concern." (More, specifically, discuss implications relative to WBS, project monitoring and control.)

————————————— References —————————————

1. George A. Steiner, *Strategic Planning* (New York: Free Press, 1979).

2. Arthur A. Thompson, Jr., and A.J. Stickland III, *Strategy Formulation and Implementation* (Dallas: Business Publications, 1980), p. 8.

3.   Steiner, *Strategic Planning*.

4.   Robert B. Youker, "The Trouble with Government Management," *Government Executive* (January 1973.)

5.   DOD and NASA Guide: PERT/COST System Design (Washington, D.C. Office of the Secretary of Defense and National Aeronautics and Space Administration, 1972).

6.   Department of Defense MIL-STD-881.

7.   Hughes Aircraft Company, *Cost Information Manual,* (December 1983), p. 5.

8.   S. R. Goodman and J. S. Reece, *Controller's Handbook* (Homewood, Ill.: Dow Jones-Irwin, 1978), pp. 1106-1111.

9.   Goodman and Reece, *Controller's Handbook,* Dow Jones—Irwin, 1978

10. Charles T. Horngren, *Accounting For Management Control,* 2nd ed. (Englewood Cliffs, N.J.: Prentice-Hall, 1970), pp. 3-6.

11. Joseph Horowitz, *Critical Path Scheduling,* 2nd ed. (New York: Ronald Press, 1967).

12. R. Archibald and R. Villoria, *Network Based Management Systems PERT/CPM* (New York: John Wiley, 1975).

13. J. O'Brien, *Scheduling Handbook* (New York: McGraw-Hill, 1971), p. 6.

14. Joseph Horowitz, "A Simplified Approach to CPM Planning," *Plant Engineering* (October 18, 1973), pp. 136-149.

15. B. V. Dean, *Operations Research in Research & Development* (New York: John Wiley, 1963), p. 269.

16. W. H. Middendorf, *Engineering Design* (Boston: Allyn * Bacon, 1969), p. 113.

17. Clifford F. Gray, E*ssentials of Project Management* (Princeton, N.J.: Petrocelli Books, 1981), p. 52.

18. Robert R. Rothberg, *Corporate Strategy and Product Innovation,* (New York: Free Press, 1976), p. 456.

19. Steiner, *Strategic Planning,* p. 218.

20. *Ibid.*

21. RCA, "PRICE Parametric Cost Models," RCA PRICE Systems, Bldg. 204-1, Cherry Hill, N.J. 08358.

22. *Ibid.,* p. 5-6.

23. *Ibid.,* p. 6.

24. *Ibid.,* p. 9.

25   L. C. Stuckenbruck, ed., *The Implementation of Project Management: The Professional's Handbook* (Reading, Mass.: Addison-Wesley, 1981), p. 147.

26. C. J. Middleton, "How to Set Up a Project Organization," *Harvard Business Review* (March-April 1967).

—————————— Chapter 5 ——————————

Project Monitoring and Control

5.1 Introduction

As the outgrowth of the typical planning process, objectives and goals are established, work is structured, schedules are developed, and budgets for each of the activities are defined. Monitoring involves the observation and evaluation of performance relative to the plan during the execution stages of the project. When monitoring shows variations from expectations, action is initiated to improve the situation. This is the essence of the control function. To exercise such measurement and subsequent action, the required information must be assembled, processed (if necessary) into an appropriate format, and made available to the project manager in a timely manner by the project manager's information system (PMIS).* To supplement the PMIS there must be adequate oral and written communication to report progress, discuss special problems, and interface with groups with whom coordination is needed.

In addition to the constant communication and information flow among the project manager, his peers, staff, and personnel performing the detailed work, the project manager must be in constant communication with management and the customer to implement any policy changes that are dictated by the decision makers. Since the project is usually goal-oriented with definite objectives, any policy or other change would not generally affect the ultimate

---

* To the extent that the PM's attention is focused on major deviations from the plan, it can be said that the PMIS uses management by exception. However, the degree of variation in performance that is allowed is a function of the specific activity, circumstances, and the perception of the PM and the customer as to what is acceptable.

goals of the project but rather their method of achievement. There is always a possibility, however, that an out-of-scope change can be induced and in fact such changes commonly occur. A key responsibility of the PM is to continually monitor the project for out-of-scope efforts so that adjustments in schedule, cost, or performance requirements can be formally incorporated into the statement of work if appropriate.

Frequent oral communication is needed both on an informal and on a formal basis in order for problems to be quickly recognized and the full resources available to the project manager brought to bear on their solution. Formalized oral communication can consist of weekly reports or staff meetings where each supervisor reports on the status of his portion of the work and brings up any problems. An effective technique used by project managers is to assign "action items" to involved and knowledgeable individuals to be carried out, or at least initiated, in the ensuing week. These action items are based on recommendations and conclusions arrived at during open discussion at the staff meeting. In addition to the staff meetings, there should be regularly scheduled meetings of the groups working on the subsystems and components developments or complex problem solutions Staff meetings at the project manager's level can include a number of subsystem and component development groups that frequently cross disciplinary and organizational lines. The project manager or a member of his staff may also call special meetings to solve problems that require immediate attention and that involve different functional groups. As a result, individuals may be assigned to ad hoc committees or task forces, an effective means of attacking problems when time is short.

If vendors or subcontractors are used, the project manager or his staff must meet with subcontractor personnel to monitor performance. These meetings must be held often enough so that subcontractor and vendor accomplishments are commensurate with the achievement of project milestones and cost goals. * Changes of direction, suggested improvements, general evaluation, and critiquing of subcontractor efforts can be accomplished at such meetings. Supplier control is a key to the success of many projects.

5.2 Project Management Information System (PMIS)

Performance (quantity and quality of the work), cost, and schedule are the essential elements that must be monitored and controlled by the project manager. This requires a well-organized communication system that can rapidly disclose the status of each activity. Any report on status of these elements must tie them together in a meaningful manner. A major activity may be on schedule and within cost but may be failing in performance. Similarly, a project may be overspent as of a certain date but ahead in meeting milestones.

---

* The high rates of change, rapid obsolescence, in supplier turnover and shortages are particularly acute problems in dealing with vendors and high-technology industries such as electronics and computer software.

In order to provide the project manager and the involved functional groups with the information needed to carry out the project effectively, the PMIS should include some or all of the following:

- Financial reports (usually computerized)
- Updated network plans (showing changes or slippages)
- Performance/cost/time (P/C/T) graphs including variance reports ("earned value")
- Progress reports
- Subcontractor or vendor performance status
- Special problem reports
- Results of meetings (including project and system design reviews)

With this information, the project manager can continually obtain readings on the following vital questions:

1. How is the project proceeding according to time? Will it be completed on schedule?
2. Are accumulated costs consistent with accomplishment? Will there be sufficient funds to complete the project?
3. What is the quality of the performance? Is it adequate to justify the requirements or specifications that have been set forth in the contract or agreement?
4. What technical problems are being experienced and what progress is being made in affecting solutions?

5.3 Financial Reports

An effective system for day-to-day and item-by-item recording of expenditures is necessary for appropriate control of project costs. This must include all direct costs* chargeable to the project and should be summarized weekly, biweekly, or monthly for review by the responsible work package or task supervisor, the project manager, or the PM's deputy. In many companies this is done by members of a financial control group or an administrative assistant under a head of finance. Such a group can collect, process, and distribute all the financial reports for a number of projects. If the project is large enough, it may have its own administration and finance group.

Unless the project is very small, the tallies of expenditures are classified according to type (engineering labor, materials, computer costs and so on).

---

* Direct costs are costs that can be directly attributed to the project such as engineering labor, materials, computer use and programming, consultants, documentation, travel, and so on. Indirect or overhead costs refer to general expenses that are incurred by a number of projects and other operations of the company such as secretarial costs, utilities, services, and the salaries of middle and upper management. Often general and administrative (G&A) and general costs are listed separately from indirect costs.

Figure 5.1: Schedule and Activity/Event Report

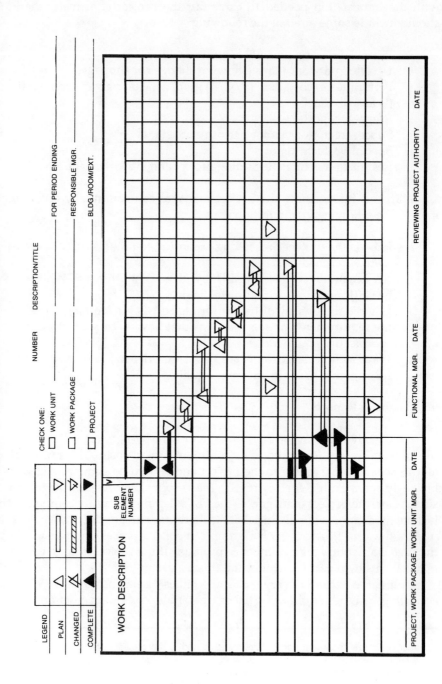

Figure 5.2: P/C/T Graph Showing Project
Expenditures Plotted Against Time and Milestones

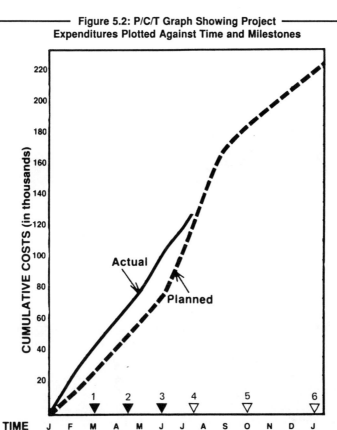

Milestones   **Date**
1. Completion of preliminary design   March 1
2. Completion of final design   April 15
3. Experimental model fabricated   June 1
4. Testing of experimental model completed   July 10
5. Pilot plant completed   Oct. 1
6. Pilot plant operated successfully for 3 months   Jan. 1

▼ Indicates milestone has been met.

Source: S.E. Stephanou, *Management: Technology, Innovation & Engineering* (Malibu, Calif.: Daniel Spencer, 1981), p. 47.

The computer output displays for each important element of the WBS such items as how much money was spent during the reporting period for the various categories of expenditures; the total accumulated expenditures for the various work packages, dollars remaining, and percentage of original funds expended; and personnel loading and name tab runs.

Timely computer printouts allow for close financial control so that the project manager can have time to reallocate resources or take corrective measures such as reducing personnel, decreasing material costs, eliminating marginal tasks or tests, and the like. Promptly processing and issuing the computer output also helps to identify errors in charging false charging, and overcharging so that action can be taken before there is an excessive drain of project funds. The use of a financial group can be of considerable value to project manager in performing a variety of tasks related to the cost accounting function, including maintaining cost records, updating network charts, calculating new completion times, and keeping track of subcontractor expenditures.

5.4 Application of Planning Tools

Planning the WBS in terms of work packages, network-based programs, activity reports, and milestones is extremely effective in subsequent tracking of activities with respect to schedule and performance. Network analysis programs are preferred because of their adaptability to computerization and the fact that they show relationships among many tasks. For briefings to higher management and the customer, for small, simple, projects and work packages, activity reports (actually a form of task bar charts) like that in Figure 5.1 can show schedule status of tasks or subtasks and changes.

As the project progresses, network and activity charts and milestone tables can be updated. For small projects this can be done manually; for large projects new estimated completion dates of activities are fed into the computer and slippages for dependent activities, new float times, as well as the new completion date for the whole project, are calculated.

5.5 Performance/Cost/Time/Graphs

From the data of the financial reports and the updating of the activity charts, several plots can be developed that graphically depict the status of the project at a particular point in time. For example, for a given task or work package, a curve of estimated or planned expenditures versus time can be compared with actual expenditures (Figure 5.2). Milestones can be indicated on the graph so that work accomplished can be roughly related to expenditures to date.

Another type of plot shows the percentage of work completed for a given work package versus the percentage of work planned (Figure 5.3).* Similar plots can be drawn for the project as a whole. It should be noted that whether an activity or project is in trouble depends not only on the difference between the actual and planned costs but also on the milestones that have or have not been met. The performance measurement technique discussed later in this chapter uses similar charts along with calculations to determine quantitatively the difference (variances) between actual and planned or estimated costs and schedule.

---

* For high technology developments, the accuracy of this type of plot can be questioned since it is often difficult to assess exactly how far along a technical development has progressed. The performing engineers or scientist tend to give themselves the benefit of the doubt, usually indicating a higher percentage of completion that is actually the case. The use of milestones (as shown in Figure 5.3) along with such a graph can alleviate this difficulty.

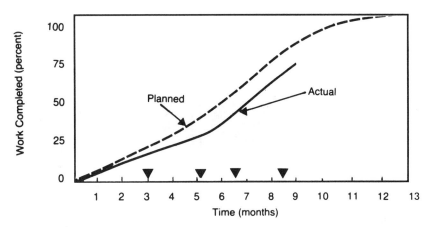

Figure 5.3: Graph Showing Percentage of Work Accomplished Versus Percentage of Work Planned

Source: S.E, Stephanou, *Management: Technology, Innovation & Engineering* (Malibu, Calif.: Daniel Spencer, 1981), p. 208.

5.6 Cross-Correlation Versus Integration of Key Parameters

Cross-correlation of the plan, schedule, and budget of a given task does not necessarily constitute integration of the task's performance, cost, and schedule parameters, but it is the first and essential step toward such integration Figure 5.4). The process of integration involves these parameters in such a manner as to enable management to assess whether accomplishment is commensurate with budget expenditures at any given point in time. Accomplishment in this context means *the attainment of specific technical objectives in concert with the pre-established plan and the pre-specified schedule.* This is the basis of the concept of "earned value."

In Figure 5.5(a) and (b) a customary cost/time graph and an activity task bar chart are shown as output for the project manager's review. They represent a status report for a particular work package up to the end of the third period of time. The actual status of the work package is problematic despite the cross-correlation of cost and accomplishment. Some may view the status of the effort with considerable alarm on the basis of the financial report, which indicates a budget overrun. Others may argue that on the whole the effort appears to be running ahead of schedule and the budget correspondingly reflects the accelerated pace of the effort. Still others, confused or uncertain, may well adopt a wait and see attitude toward the effort until a more definitive trend evolves, at which time it is likely that any possible corrective action would have been preempted by events. Conclusions based upon such status reports may be questionable based upon the following considerations:

First, in evaluating the reports, it must be determined whether the planned rate of expenditure was evolved on the basis of past experience and "feel," as is frequently done, or on the basis of the time-phased summation of the costs

Figure 5.4: Cross Correlation and Integration of Plans, Schedules, Work Packages and Organization

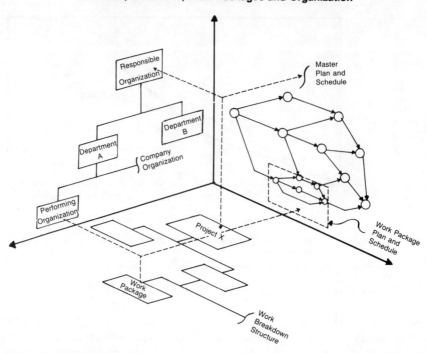

associated with each of the work elements scheduled. If any planned rate of expenditure is indeed arbitrary, then any comparisons of actual versus planned costs are clearly specious considering the lack of a sound baseline.

Second, actual costs incurred may or may not be consistent with either the cost of the work scheduled or the "worth" of the work actually performed for the period of time under review. This suggests that costs incurred must be gauged not only against the cost of work scheduled but also against the cost of the work performed if true accomplishment is to be properly evaluated. This would provide a more realistic assessment of the schedule and cost status of the effort in progress.

Third, the various elements of the work package are generally not equal in value. Since they tend to be in different stages of completion as of any given period of time, the actual worth of the work performed must be based upon the sum total of the relative worth of the individual elements — a combination of their percentages of completion and cost.

Misinterpreting the type of reports shown in Figure 5.5(a) and (b) can mean failure to provide the degree of visibility and control needed for the timely identification, sound interpretation, and consequent action to keep the project on schedule and at appropriate performance level. The situation can be remedied by concurrent determination of the aforementioned costs, namely (a) actual costs incurred in the performance of the effort, (b) scheduled or

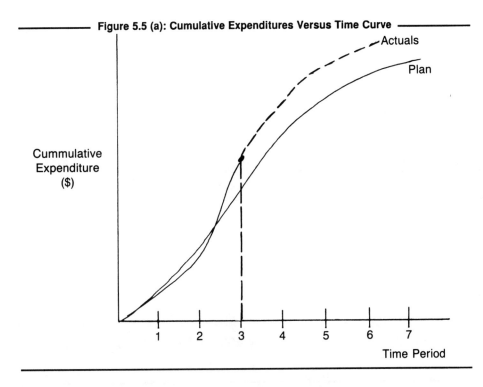

Figure 5.5 (a): Cumulative Expenditures Versus Time Curve

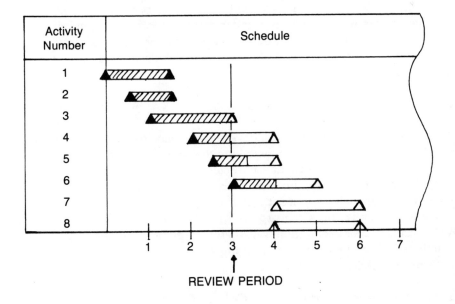

Figure 5.5 (b): Activity Task Bar Chart

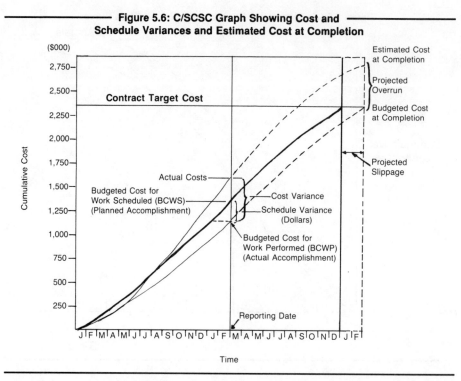

Figure 5.6: C/SCSC Graph Showing Cost and Schedule Variances and Estimated Cost at Completion

baseline costs developed at the outset of the effort, and (c) allowable (or earned) costs based on the sum total of the product of cost and percentage of completion associated with each of the elements in the work package.

This approach to monitoring and reporting costs and schedules, commonly known as the performance measurement method, is an effective way to integrate performance cost, and schedule. The details of its use are discussed in the following section.

5.7 Performance Measurement Techniques

To better track large contracts, government agencies such as DOD, NASA, and DOE have implemented a technique that in principle can quantitatively measure project performance at a particular point in the life of a project. In DOD contracting the technique is called cost/schedule control systems criteria (C/SCSC), whereas in DOE it is the performance measurement system (PMS); they are essentially the same procedure. These methods are based on the WBS, accurate cost accounting, and network planning data—data that are assimilated in the process of monitoring and control. C/SCSC is typical of performance measurement methods.

(a) Cost/Schedule Control Systems Criteria (C/SCSC)

C/SCSC is usually developed on a work package basis using the following criteria:

- The actual cost of work performed (ACWP), which is determined on the basis of the data provided by the organization's cost accounting and information systems
- The budgeted cost of work scheduled (BCWS) or baseline cost determined by the costs of scheduled accomplishments
- The budgeted cost of work performed (BCWP) or earned value—the actual work of effort completed as of a specific point in time

At any point in time, cost and schedule variances for a work package may be established on the basis of these costs and in line with the following equations:

Cost variance	=	BCWP - ACWP
Percent cost variance	=	(Cost variance/BCWP) x 100
Schedule variance	=	BCWP - BCWS
Percent schedule variance*	=	(Schedule variance/BCWS) x 100
ACWP and remaining funds	=	Target cost (TC)
ACWP + cost to complete	=	Estimated cost at completion (EAC)

For each of the periodic reviews, an attempt is made to project the estimated cost at completion (EAC). On the basis of these estimates, cost and schedule variance at completion can be forecast as shown in Figure 5.6.

The predisposition toward this method of monitoring and control may be significantly influenced by whether one views it from the perspective of a customer or of a supplier. Unquestionably, it can be an extremely effective tool in monitoring and controlling the effort. However, it can also be quite time consuming to implement and cumbersome as well as costly to maintain. Its use should be carefully evaluated and selectively implemented as there may be other more suitable alternatives. It may be that the real value of C/SCSC lies not so much in the added visibility and control it affords as in the greater degree of thoroughness in planning required and the added higher-management attention generally given projects upon which C/SCSC is imposed.

There are some potential weaknesses of C/SCSC that should be recognized to assure the most effective use of this method.[1]

---

* Some companies in non-government-related work use a modification of this technique where cost variance and percentage of cost variance are the same as described above but scheduled variance is calculated differently:

Schedule variance	=	[Schedule time to reach milestone] - actual time
Percentage of schedule variance	=	$\frac{\text{Schedule variance}}{\text{Schedule time}} \times 100$

In such use schedule variance is expressed in units of time rather than in dollars.

First, since estimates of the percentage of completion tend to be subjective and sometimes ill founded, assessments of completion status can frequently mask potentially serious problems. As an example, consider the situation where all but one of the engineering drawings are released to manufacturing as of their scheduled due date. Although the periodic status report may reflect a completion status of 99% for the technical data package preparation and therefore gives little basis for alarm, consider the impact if the unreleased drawing as of the due date were to be associated with one of the longest lead or pacing items on the entire project. This example illustrates a long-recognized and serious flaw of the percentage of completion reporting technique. Aside from being subjective, this parameter focuses attention on past accomplishments rather than on current or projected requirements for the successful execution of effort.

Second, the technique relies generally on key personnel for continual updates of the extent of accomplishment and the projected cost at completion. Since key participants on a project tend to be very busy and preoccupied with the technical aspects of the effort, they are not normally inclined to invest a great deal of personal time and effort in a recurring administrative exercise. Consequently, the quality of the results reported may not only be questionable but also variable depending on the organizational gamesmanship and politics involved.

Third, since various indices of accomplishment are usually based on updates or projections that may vary considerably from one reporting period to another, they can be of questionable accuracy in assessing the true standing or effectiveness of corrective action.

Despite these potential shortcomings, C/SCSC can be an extremely powerful and effective technique in the monitoring and control of a project. Of course its effectiveness can be significantly influenced by the extent of management support and the degree of participant commitment, cooperation and support. A final consideration in the use of C/SCSC is its cost, which varies according to the size and the contract. For small contracts the cost of such close control could become an appreciable and unacceptable percentage of the total contract.

(b) Accomplishment Cost Procedure (ACP)

C/SCSC is not the only approach to the integration and evaluation of progress in achieving performance, cost, and schedule objectives.* The accomplishment cost procedure (ACP) offers a simper, more practical, powerful,

---

* For DOD projects there is a general misconception that Department of Defense Instruction DODI 7000.2, which imposes the requirement for C/SCSC on certain classes of projects/ programs, also dictates methodology and format. That is not the case. DODI 7000.2 states specifically that the instruction is *not to be "construed as requiring the use of any single system of specific method of management control or evaluation of performance"* [italics ours], (DOD Instruction 7000.2 Enclosure 1, 1977).

Figure 5.7: The Accomplishment Cost Procedure (ACP) Reporting Technique

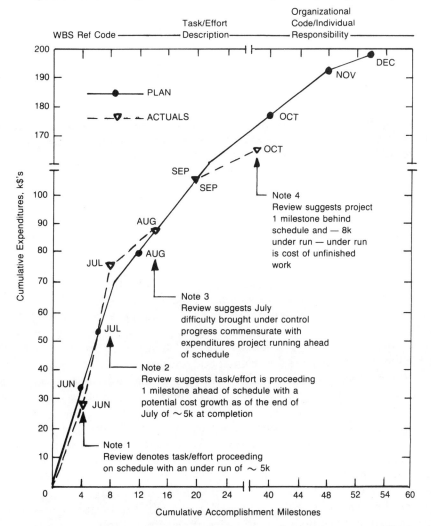

and cost-effective technique for relating and monitoring the elusive relationship between the resources budgeted and the work accomplished.[2] Because of its adaptability to either the customer's management or user requirements and its ease of implementation, it can be an effective tool for a broad range of efforts.

ACP presents costs based on scheduled accomplishments, rather than as a function of time. To determine the progress of an individual effort with respect to cost, the cost/progress relationship planned is compared with the cost/progress relationship attained. The status of both of these elements of information is presented at the same time, using data generated at the outset of the program as a basis for the evaluation of subsequently accumulating periodic actuals. Figure 5.7 shows the general reporting technique, which is easily implemented at any desired level of the WBS. This approach to cost and progress monitoring, reporting, and control offers several advantages over the usual technique of data collection and presentation. Among these advantages are the following:[3]

The first advantage is simplicity and ease of understanding. The format of ACP (Figure 5.7) allows the direct correlation of costs with schedule accomplishment and an immediate assessment of the difference between the planned and the actual performance at any given level of the WBS.

Second is a greater degree of objectivity, visibility, and control of operational performance. Accomplishment is typically gauged only in terms of discrete units completed. This should not represent a problem of distorting if the planning is sufficiently detailed and costs are programmed on the basis of this assumption at the outset. Also, this reporting procedure permits early detection of errors in planning or difficulties in execution along with the implementation of timely corrective action based on the degree of deviation of actuals from the plan and observation of the trends of actuals.

The third advantage is an inherently greater degree of accuracy. Inasmuch as cost is equated with progress, the accumulating costs on a WBS effort are related to something quantifiable, measurable with consistency and comparable to a fixed frame of reference. Scope changes are programmed into ACP in the same manner as the original budgets and schedules. Projections of the cost to complete an element of the WBS are available on an ongoing basis and are only associated with periodic budget updating, as may be required by added scope.

The final advantage concerns user orientation and cost effectiveness. Summary tasks are invariably planned, scheduled, estimated, and performed by the functional elements of the organization. Programming and maintenance of this report does not require either large staffs or computer availability.

The ACP cost and schedule reporting technique permits personnel responsible for tasks to use the reports as an objective indicator of their own actual performance compared with stated projections. Problems and responsibility are thus clearly isolated and easily pin pointed for all appropriate levels of management in ample time to bring about corrective action.

5.8 Design Reviews and Project Audits

During the development of all types of systems, whether hardware, software, operational, or social, there should be periodic reviews of designs, drawings, plans, mock-ups, models, and the like. Such reviews can be an effective technique for monitoring and controlling technical effort. Persons outside the project — the customer and higher management—and key personnel engaged in the project are invited to examine all of its aspects and comment on the adequacy of the engineering effort, design, models, cost to date, plans, data, and so on. Comments can also include perceived flaws, omissions, or possible improvements in the design and procedures.

Design reviews can be called by the project manager, the supervisor in charge of the design effort, or the customer and may be regularly scheduled or carried out at key milestone dates. The best time for such reviews depends on the system being developed. For hardware systems, the completion of preliminary design, final design, mock-ups, experimental or manufacturing prototype, and pilot plants are appropriated times. The results can affect design changes at an early stage to preclude serious errors before fully committing resources to subsequent phases of the project. Failure to correct errors can result in wasteful and unrecoverable expense. In fact, projects sometimes can and should be stopped where technical, economic, or other difficulties cause an insurmountable impasse. In such cases it is best to discontinue the project at the early stages of the system development process as costs are minimal then but rise rapidly as the product development goes from the research to the hardware, prototype, and pilot plant stage (Figure 2.10).

Project audits are similar to design reviews as they provide an independent appraisal of the project status at a specified point in time and can determine whether the organization is likely to successfully complete the project.[4] They can serve as a catalytic tool for the project manager, since they foster self-appraisal, bring in outside critiquing and evaluation from qualified experts, stimulate total program thinking, and furnish higher management with additional input for appraisal.

The particular time for the audit and the composition of the audit team are usually determined by higher management or the customer. Audits are most productive when carried out in the earlier phases of a large project, say in the first year. The size of the audit team is customarily not more than 10 and its composition includes generalists as well as specialists. The audit's value will depend on the quality of the audit team.

The scope of the audit can be narrow or it can cover all aspects of the project operation including organization, functional support and relationships, project plan, work statement, quality control, policies and procedures, cost control, and subcontractor support.

Audits can be also carried out by an outside management consultant firm, although this tends to be more costly and time consuming since outsiders have to become familiar with the details of the project, its mode of operation, and the principal personnel.* The success of an outside audit team depends on the degree of support it receives from higher management and the project team. The usual approach is to initiate the audit by conducting audit interviews, starting with the higher levels of the organization and working downward. A report summarizes the findings and makes recommendations; this is accompanied by a briefing to top management or the responsible project manager and functional managers.

---

*However, the independent nature of an outside audit team can be a definite advantage.

5.9 Reports and Documentation

Variance analysis reports, special problem reports, updated network plans and task bar charts, P/C/T graphs, and milestone status and financial reports have already been mentioned as part of the PMIS. In addition, there may be weekly, monthly, bimonthly, or quarterly reports depending on the size and complexity of the project. The format varies according to the type of project and is usually decided on by the project manager and his staff, although it may be dictated by the customer or contracting organization. A typical progress report includes an introductory or background section, a section describing details of what has been accomplished during the reporting period, a summary of accomplishments, and finally a section stating what is planned for the ensuring period. There is also a section or a separate volume giving financial details of the expenditures during the reporting period. Because the work of the project is frequently a one-time activity, the final report assumes particular significance. It usually describes what was accomplished during the last reporting period and summarizes the work of the whole project.

In technical efforts where there are no hardware or software deliverables, the reports are the end products of the project. Feasibility studies testing programs, and product evaluations are in this category. A company engaged in such projects may have a publications group whose responsibility is to finalize all project reports. Their responsibilities include the report format, grammar, illustrations, and the like. Such a group might also handle proposals, bulletins, handbooks, and other printed matter necessary for the functioning of a project-oriented company.

5.10 Problems in Planning, Monitoring, and Control

(a) Effect of the Organizational Culture

Many reasons have been advanced to account for the success attained by the Japanese in the marketplace. Among these is that the Japanese characteristically delay implementation and expend a great deal of effort in achieving consensus on the course of action to be taken at the macro and micro levels or the organization. It has been argued that in the process both the quality of the front-end planning and the extent of the people commitment to the planning are of significant benefit to the undertaking. By contrast, the typical American attitude is to forge ahead with implementation as rapidly as possible to attain efficiencies considered necessary to "fast track" action.[5] The end result is that more often than not, planning and people commitment suffer. Symptomatic of this tendency are the following:

- False starts and high rates or rework
- High rates of change in part prompted by mistakes and errors
- Chronic delays or schedule slippages
- Confusion and a loss of enthusiasm and motivation

- Parochialism and lessening of mutual respect among participants
- "In-place" retirement on the part of some, turnover or departures in the case of others

These symptoms are much more prevalent in industry than is generally believed or management is willing to acknowledge. The literature and industry have emphasized trying to "do it right." The problem is, however, that this slogan means different things to different people. Doing it right the first time requires that objectives and general expectations be properly reflected and linked through the consistent and realistic formulation of the statement of work (SOW), including technical, cost, and schedule parameters during the planning and programming stages of the effort. As an example, imposing such a slogan on an assembly-line employee as a means of improving the quality of work is useless if the employee is given a highly complex assembly planning package that defies the average employee's ability to "do it right" the first time through. Similarly, despite its best intentions, the assembly planning department may be limited in its approach by the type of design that engineering has released to manufacturing. Engineering, however, can hardly be faulted if its recommendation to include a design production study phase is ignored, its cost estimates are trimmed, and the proposed schedules compressed to fit marketing, program office, higher-management, or customer constraints and expectations.

Clearly, the general tone of a project will be greatly influenced by the quality of front-end or baseline planning and structuring. The benefits of proactive planning and structuring can be expected to yield high rates of return in the areas of product competitiveness, higher quality, lower cost and risk , and higher degree of profitability. The net effects of proactive planning and structuring have been contrasted to the current and more traditional reactive approach in the graph in Figure 5.8. The conclusion is that effective monitoring and control is ultimately a function of the time and money expended on the planning and programming of a project.

(b) Impediments to Success

There are a number of factors that can impede the planning, scheduling, and control of projects. These factors include the following:

- Unavoidable human errors of commission and omission that manifest themselves in a wide variety of forms.
- Prevailing resistance to changes in methods, procedures, or practices, which tends to be particularly debilitating within a dynamic environment like that of a project.
- Reluctance to commit to an iterative effort that is time consuming and costly, despite its ultimate value.
- The tendency to go through the motions of complying with the requirements of planning, scheduling, and control rather than ac-

—— Figure 5.8: Effects of Proactive Versus Reactive Management on Cost/Schedule ——

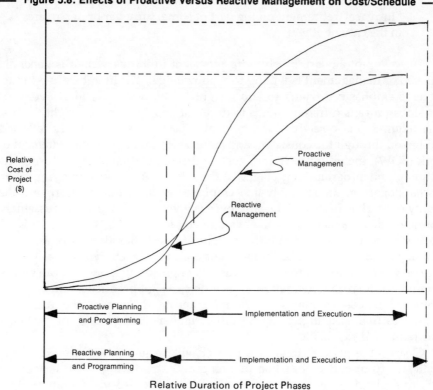

Relative Duration of Project Phases

Source: Adapted from Mark S. Caspe and Saburo Tamura, "Making Productivity Soar – Secret Ingredient for Blending American and Japanese Management Technology," *Project Management Quarterly*, (September 1982), p. 37. Project Management Institute, P.O. Box 43, Drexel Hill, PA 19026.

tually applying such efforts. Doing can be much easier, faster and satisfying than thinking and planning.

- Skepticism about the ultimate value of planning conditioned by the frequent ineffectiveness of past half-hearted efforts.
- Inappropriateness of selected tools and applied techniques stemming from expedience or a lack of experience on the part of the project manager or the participants.
- Inadequate communication about specific intent including scope, interfaces, description of desired end product, and hierarchy of trade-offs.
- Disagreement about the preferred approach, generally prompted by varying perceptions of the relative importance of the various elements or aspects of the effort. This is typically a result of differences among experts and often results in a lack of broad-based acceptance and commitment by the team.
- Lack of acceptance and commitment based on limited participation in the development of requirements, plans, schedules, and

control system in situations where these functions have been highly centralized.

- Perceived infringement and loss of control over one's prevailing activity patterns or output standards.
- Fear of failure. Nothing exposes errors or potential failures more than thorough planning. Planning unfortunately can be used as a whipping tool rather than as a basis for requisite corrective action.

Even successful organizations tend to be susceptible to the deleterious effects of one or more of these factors. The difference between successful and less successful organizations and individuals generally lies in how aware they are of these factors and how they deal with them.

These impediments to effective planning and control tend to be largely organic or people oriented. The mechanical aspects of planning and control, important in their own right, assume even greater importance since they can either amplify or mitigate the prevailing negative influences of organic factors. As the first step in the road to successful project planning, scheduling, and control project managers should try to decrease antiplanning biases. This is not easy, but knowledge of the business and an understanding of the job to be done can be of significant usefulness although not completely preemptive. Even more important to the project manager is an understanding of people and a high degree of creativity and imagination in the setting up and execution of the effort. This subject is considered further in Chapter 9.

———Questions and Topics for Discussion———

1. How can "management by exception" be applied in project management?

2. What should be included in a PMIS? How would you decide who should receive the information and to what extent?

3. Why is earned value of major importance in the control of complex projects with many work packages?

4. What should a financial report for a project include?

5. What are the pros and cons of having a separate financial control group monitoring expenditures and reporting to project managers rather than having designated individuals within each project monitor expenditures?

6. Why is the punctuality of financial reports so important in monitoring the project, and what can be the consequence of a time lag of one month or more?

7. Why is it important in regularly scheduled planning or review meetings

to (a) issue an agenda before the meeting, (b) resolve questions and problems to the maximum extent possible, (c) assign action items with names of responsible individual and due dates, and (d) take and distribute minutes?

8. How is the WBS valuable in project monitoring and control?

9. List advantages and disadvantages of the C/SCSC performance measurement method.

10. Why is the accomplishment cost procedure (ACP) a simpler,more practical and cost-effective technique than C/SCSC?

11. How can project audits be helpful in evaluating the status and modifying the direction of a project?

12. Enumerate and discuss four key problems in the planning, monitoring, and controlling of projects.

13. You are designated as the project manager on an effort that is overrun and behind schedule. Team morale is very poor. Discuss (in detail) what you would do immediately upon assuming responsibility and over the near term to turn the project around.

———————————— References ————————————

1. Ellery B. Block, "Accomplishment/Cost: Better Project Control," *Harvard Business Review* (May-June 1971).

2. *Ibid.*

3. *Ibid.*

4. K.O. Chilstrom, "Project Management Audits" in D.I. Cleland and W.R. King, eds. *Project Management Handbook* (New York: Van Nostrand Rheinhold, 1983), p. 465.

5. Mark S. Caspe and Saburo Tamura, "Making Productivity Soar — Secrete Ingredient for Blending American and Japanese Technology," *Project Management Quarterly* (September 1982), p. 37.

6. George A. Steiner, *Strategic Planning* (New York: Free Press, 1979), pp. 44-47, 95-101.

--------------------------------- Chapter 6 ---------------------------------
Risk Analysis And Management

6.1 Framework For Decision Making
    (a)   Decision Making Under Certainty
    (b)   Decision Making Under Risk and Uncertainty
    (c)   Decision Making Under Conflict
    (d)   Expected Monetary Value
    (e)   Expected Utility
         (1) Utility Function
         (2) Practicality of Utility Curves
6.2 Decision Trees
6.3 Risk Analysis: The Natural Fallout of Sound Planning
    (a)   Pert Revisited
    (b)   Risk Analysis Using Monte Carlo Simulation
    (c)   Risk Reduction and Management
6.4 Risk Analysis: Advanced Network Based Techniques
    (a)   The General Approach
    (b)   A Structured Approach
         (1) Network Optimization
         (2) Stochastic Decision Models
6.5 Summary

6.1 Framework For Decision Making

We are frequently called upon to make a decision given two or more alternative courses of action. Our decision making process is often complicated, if not impeded, by the range of possible *consequences* or outcomes that may be attendant to each of the alternatives identified. The range of potential consequences is invariably the result of intervening events over which the decision maker normally has no control These intervening and uncontrollable *events* (or factors) are typically referred to as *states of nature*. The consequence of a decision, therefore, is as much a function of the alternative selected as it is of the "states of nature" (or intervening factors) that ultimately occur. Consider the following illustration: DINKO Inc. is a manufacturer of Christmas novelty items. Two of DINKO's major distributors place an order in September for the entire production run of ten thousand widgets. Both distributors work on "consignment". Namely, whatever cannot be sold is returned to the manufacturer. If the demand for the product is high, both distributor A and B will move at least nine thousand units. If demand is low, A would move at least sixty five hundred and B would move at least seventy five hundred. Distributors A and B are at opposite ends of the state. The problem is illustrated in Table 6-1.

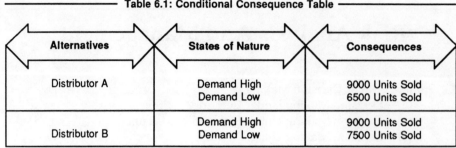

Table 6.1: Conditional Consequence Table

Alternatives	States of Nature	Consequences
Distributor A	Demand High Demand Low	9000 Units Sold 6500 Units Sold
Distributor B	Demand High Demand Low	9000 Units Sold 7500 Units Sold

Clearly, DINKO management has the option of one of two alternative courses of action. Specifically, consignment of widgets to either distributor A or B. The consequences of the decision can be gauged in terms of the number of widgets likely to be sold or, alternatively, returned to DINKO after the holidays. The consequences not only depend upon the alternative selected but also on the "state of nature" that may occur, that is, either high or low demand. Table 6.1 may, therefore, be referred to as a *conditional consequence table.*

Parenthetically, it should be observed that although the problem gives rise to a total of four possible consequences, two of these are numerically identical based on the problem's formulation. The net result is that, in this case, there are only three unique consequences.

As noted earlier, decision makers do not have control over states of nature. They often have little, if any, knowledge or true understanding of the underlying factors which affect or control the states of nature.* This makes it difficult to determine with certainty the exact consequences of selected courses of action and thus the selection of the most desirable consequence. Based upon the preceding and depending upon the kind and extent of knowledge available about the particular "state of nature", the decision maker generally faces one of four general decision conditions. These include:[1]

- Certainty
- Risk
- Uncertainty
- Conflict

Each of them is addressed in the ensuing discussion.

(a) Decision Making Under Certainty

Under conditions of certainty, the decision maker has at his disposal complete information relative to the prevailing state(s) of nature. To illustrate, consider the case of an individual seeking to invest a sum of money for a

---

* Ignoring for the moment that demand may be affected by price and that decision makers thus may have *some* control.

given period of time. Among the alternatives available to him are investments in a bank savings account, a credit union shares account and a mutual fund money market account. Assuming his objective is to maximize profit, the investor can easily compute the consequences of each alternative given the true states of nature known with certainty. In this case, he would use the (known) interest rate paid by each of the institutions to calculate his profit and select the most desirable consequence.

To be sure, not all decision making under certainty is this trivial. Solutions quite often can be very involved and may rely on various applied calculus and linear programming techniques. The reader is referred to any number of fine texts on operations research. Our primary interests in this chapter are in the areas of risk, uncertainty and conflict.

(b) Decision Making Under Risk and Uncertainty

All of us, at one time or other, have made a decision on the basis of the "likelihood", "chance", "odds", "prospects" or "probability" of the occurrence of some event. Most of us have a good intuitive feel for what is meant by "high likelihood", "fair chance", "good odds", "poor prospects", or "reasonable probability". Generally speaking, such characterizations are derived form one of two sources:

- Judgement based on past experience under similar conditions. In effect, implicit reliance on the existence of a frequency distribution that describes occurrences of the state of nature. Judgement, however, may be influenced by recollections, misinterpretation of data, one's current beliefs or degree of confidence in the occurrence of the event in question. In view of the preceding, resulting characterizations tend to reflect an *intuitive and highly subjective* assessment of the chances or "probability" of occurrence.
- Expectations evolved on the basis of the application of a validated methodology, describing outcomes of a repetitively random, process consisting of a series of trials solely governed by "chance". In effect, explicit reliance on a frequency distribution of the states of nature *objectively* ascertainable under relatively standardized, formal and well documented conditions.

Whether determined subjectively or objectively, the probability of occurrence of any event (i.e. state of nature) lies between strict "impossibility" at one end of the spectrum and absolute "certainty" at the other. The continuum of possibilities is usually quantified and represented on a scale of 0 to 1. On this scale the value of 0 represents impossibility and 1 a certainty. Thus, a fifty/fifty chance (or probability) of occurrence would have a value of .50 on this scale, *regardless of this underlying approach to its quantification.* A decision as to whether a fifty/fifty chance represents an acceptable level of *risk*, under a given set of circumstances, would clearly depend upon previously *established* decision criteria.

The words *"risk"* and *"uncertainty"* are frequently used synonymously. There *is* a difference and this difference tends to arise out of the context in which these words are used. In probability and decision theory, the decision maker is said to be facing "risk" in cases in which the event (or state of nature) under consideration has a probability distribution. Absent the probability distribution, the decision maker faces uncertainty. We are reminded of an often used tongue-in-cheek definition of risk and uncertainty that tends to illustrate the significance of the preceding. It has been suggested that one faces risk upon sitting down at a poker table, knowing full well the odds associated with the various hands and the game in general. When one sits down at the poker table recognizing that the deck may have been "loaded", and still elects to play, he faces uncertainty.

The frequent synonymous use of "risk" and "uncertainty", stems from the latter's use in both a narrow and broad sense. The use of uncertainty in the narrow sense is reflected in the above discussion. In a broad sense, uncertainty refers to a situation in which the true state of nature is either completely unknown, or, partially known such as in the case of decision making under risk. In this context, we use probability as a way of measuring uncertainty.

Consider the following as an example of decision making under conditions of risk. The investor of section 6.1.1 is considering setting aside five thousand dollars into a particularly aggressive mutual fund. The investment newsletter to which he subscribes suggests that the fund will appreciate 25 percent if the stock rises but might loose 15 percent if the market retreats. His broker friend estimates that there is a 60 percent probability that the market will rise over the short term and, hence, a 40 percent chance that it may decline. Since our investor can be assured a return of 525 dollars over the time frame of interest from his credit union, he is attempting to evaluate the best course of action. The problem is summarized in Table 6.2.

As previously noted, the consequence of a decision is as much a function of the alternative selected as a function of the state of nature that ultimately prevails. In our example, the investor is faced with two alternatives:

Table 6.2: Payoff Table

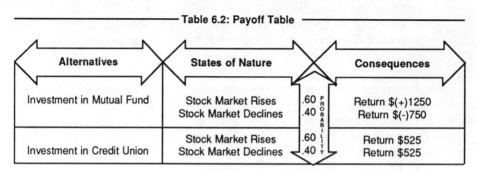

Alternatives	States of Nature		Consequences
Investment in Mutual Fund	Stock Market Rises	.60	Return $(+)1250
	Stock Market Declines	.40	Return $(-)750
Investment in Credit Union	Stock Market Rises	.60	Return $525
	Stock Market Declines	.40	Return $525

(1) Invest the five thousand dollars in the mutual fund, or,
(2) Invest the five thousand dollars in the credit union.

The mutual fund alternative has two possible states of nature:

(1) Stock market rises over the short term
(2) Stock market retreats over the short term

Whereas the investor does not know the true state of nature for this alternative, he does know the probability of occurrence of each of the states of nature. In the credit union alternative, the investor has complete information as to the prevailing state of nature and can determine the consequence of this alternative with certainty. The consequence of investing in the credit union is a return of 525 dollars, regardless of whether or not the market goes up or down.

Clearly, if the investor wants to be *assured* of a minimum return of 525 dollars he should invest in the credit union. If he were to do otherwise, he would be exposing himself to a 40 percent probability of losing 750 dollars. On the other hand, if the investor were searching for a course of action that might lead to the *highest* possible return, he might be inclined to pursue the mutual fund alternative. As may be seen from Table 6.2, there is a 60 percent probability that this action may result in a profit of 1250 dollars. This type of a table is often referred to as a *conditional payoff table*, or, simply, *payoff table*. It is an explicit basis for taking into account the combination of monetary consequences and probabilities involved in decision making. This is discussed further in section (d).

In practice, it is not only desirable but important to determine the probability of occurrence of an event (or events) with a high degree of objectivity, precision and certainty. This falls within the realm of *statistical inference*. Probability theory attempts to convert subjective assessments into more supportable and precise determinations of the likely outcome of events (or states of nature) of interest. Mathematical definitions, procedures and techniques involved can be quite abstract, very complex and often highly specialized. They are clearly beyond the scope of this text. The reader is presumed to have some background in statistics and probability theory and is being provided with Appendix J for reference.

(c) Decision Making Under Conflict

In many practical situations, a specific course of action is often considered or selected in response to competitive reactions or counter actions. As an example, take the case in which two products are competing for the major share of a localized market. An advertising campaign is being considered that would cost a fair amount of money. Company A's management is evaluating options and their reasoning proceeds as follows:

- We're currently realizing about $500 K on the sale of the product.
- If the competition proceeds with it and we do not, we stand to drop off to about $350 K.

- If both of us proceed with advertising campaigns, our increased prices will offset sales and will result in a bottom line of about $450 K.

The situation may clearly present a dilemma for company A's (and/or B's) management. The consequences of their decision will not only depend upon the course of action they select but the competition's response as well. In this case, two conditional payoff tables could be constructed; one from A's perspective, the other from B's perspective. This general type of problem is addressed by way of *game theory* techniques. Examples of these are discussed in subsequent sections of this chapter.

(d) Expected Monetary Value (EMV)

It may appear from sections 6.1(b) and 6.1(c), that a decision maker is in a position more akin to gambling than deliberate and conscious decision making. In effect, having to gamble "on" or "against" the exact state of nature or the actions of the competition. In a sense this is true. Neither the actions of the competition nor the exact state of nature likely to prevail can be determined, *a priori*, with certainty. The decision maker, therefore, is selecting a course of action hoping that it will result in the most desirable of consequences, but, realizing that there is a chance that it may not.[2]

The EMV criterion involves the explicit consideration of the combination of monetary consequences and their associated probabilities. Specifically, *the EMV for an act is computed by multiplying the monetary consequence associated with each state of nature by its probability of occurrence and summing up all by products.* To illustrate the methodology, consider the example of section 6.1.2. The EMV of the mutual fund alternative would be computed as follows:

EMV = 1250 (0.6) - 750 (0.4) = 450 dollars

It must be noted that EMV represents a weighted, average, result that can be expected and attained only over the long run. It is based upon the expectation of a recurring decision process as noted in the following example.

DINKO Inc., estimates that the combination of marketing and bidding expense averages out at 6 percent of gross sales. The company is considering pursuing a $500,000 job. Historically, the company wins 55 percent of jobs this size and realizes a gross profit of 15 percent. Management is evaluating the advisability of the continued pursuit of jobs this size.

Marketing/Bidding Expense:	$500,000 x .06 = $30,000
Projected Gross Profit:	$500,000 x .15 - $75,000
Net (Potential) Profit:	$ 75,000 - $30,000 = $45,000
Net (Potential) Loss:	$ 30,000

EMV = ($45,000)(.55) + (-$30,000)(.45) = $11,250

If the decision to pursue this type of a job were to be made just this once, clearly, an EMV expected profit of $11,250 would never materialize. The company would either win the job and make a net profit of $45,000 or lose the job and post a "loss" of $30,000. If, however, the company were to continue to pursue jobs of this size and general type, over time, the actual average profit would approach a theoretically expected profit of $11,250. On that basis alone, pursuing the business would clearly be preferable to the alternative of conceding it to the competition by no bidding (EMV = 0). The underlying question, however, is whether management would consider an average expected profit of $11,250 an adequate "reward" for tying up company resources on jobs of this size and general type.

(e) Expected Utility

As noted above, DINKO Inc. was in the process of considering the desirability of the on-going, long term, pursuit of jobs in the range of $500 K. On that basis EMV had tangible significance. Many business and personal decisions, however, involve *non*-recurring situations. Under such conditions EMV may not necessarily be a valid or sound decision making criterion.

To illustrate, assume that KINKO Inc. is assessing a unique opportunity that may require commitment of $50,000 for a possible net profit of $150,000. KINKO is a small, fledgling business. It's line of credit has been exhausted and the $50,000 represents all of the currently available working capital. The probability of a win is estimated at fifty percent and the EMV was calculated as follows:

EMV = $150,000 x .5 - $50,000 x .5 = $50,000

In spite of the above EMV (*), KINKO management elects not to pursue the opportunity. Whereas both the amount of probability of profit would have been tempting under ordinary circumstances, the probability of loss, *at this time*, would have carried with it the most dire of consequences.

In the above case, the attitude towards risk, rather than EMV, determined and dictated KINKO's course of action. Clearly, then, in situations in which "aversion to" or "preference for" risk play a dominant role, EMV may not be a valid guide for decision making under uncertainty. In this context, the words "preference" and "utility" are often used interchangeably. *More specifically, "utility" is a measure of "preference"* as described in section (e.1). It should be noted that "utility" is also used in economic theory but has an altogether different meaning. In economics, generally speaking, "utility" refers to the "satisfaction" which consumers derive from the consumption of goods and services.[3]

---

* Note that it is larger than the consequence of the act of doing nothing.

(e. 1) Utility Function

Consider the case faced by BINKO Inc. The cost of submitting a particular proposal is estimated at $50,000. The return, net of bid costs, is projected at $150,000. At one end of the spectrum BINKO stands to *lose* $50,000, at the other it stands to *gain* $150,000.

Let us gauge the "preference" for these outcomes on a relative scale of 0 to 1. On this scale, the "preference" (or *utility index*) for a loss of $50,000 would be assigned the value of 0 and the gain of $150,000 the value of 1. Given a probability of a win at 50 percent, we could calculate the *expected utility* of this opportunity in the same way as we calculated EMV:

Expected Utility = 1 x .5 + 0 x .5 = 0.5

We could associate this utility index with the effort's EMV. This, however, would not be correct. We need a more comprehensive and objective tie in between the utility index and monetary consequences to reflect the overall, prevailing, (company) situation *and the decision maker's attitude towards risk*. In other words, the assessment of utility for a monetary consequence must be distinguished from the actual situation under consideration. This will become clearer from the following.

Assume for a moment, that six months earlier, BINKO had won a contract that was expected to yield a net profit of $50,000 and cost $10,000 to prepare. Further assume that the probability of a win at the time was estimated at 50 percent. BINKO ran into some difficulties and is currently discussing a possible release form its contractual obligation. All things considered, management is willing to pay up to a maximum of $25,000 dollars to obtain a release from the contract. *In other words, the current utility of (-) $25,000 is equal to the previously expected utility of this effort.* Stated yet in another way, this is a point of "indifference" as to whether to continue with the contract or disburse $25,000 to get out from under the obligation.[4] Mathematically, this can be shown as:

$$U(X)_A = P \times U(X)_H + (1-P) \times U(X)_L$$

where:

$U(X)$ =   The utility associated with X dollars

P =   Probability of receiving X_H dollars

$(1-P)$ =   Probability of receiving X_L dollars

In the case under consideration, the BINKO situation could be represented as follows:

U(-$25,000) = U($50,000) + U(-$10,000) or
U(-$25,000) = 1 x .5 + 0 x .5 = 0.5

Note that we now have three points on a curve which is generally indicative of BINKO's financial position along with its inclination to gamble on the latest proposal. These points include:

Utility Index	Monetary Consequence
1.00	$150,000
.50	- $25,000
0	- $50,000

Additional money-utility points can be developed by similar reference to other situations, as long as the decision maker's asset position remains constant. The resulting curve is known as a utility function in Figure 6.1.1. These functions tend to be either "risk averse" or "risk prone". The function is "risk averse" if the decision marker requires high probability of payoff. In effect, a premium is placed on loss avoidance. A curve is "risk-prone" if, generally speaking, the reverse tends to be true.

————————————— Figure 6.1.1: Utility Curve (Risk Averse) —————————————

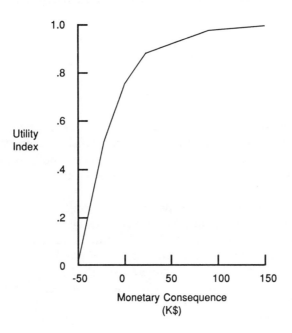

(e. 2) Practicality Of Utility Curves

Utility curves lend some objectivity to the decision making process, however, their validity and practicality tends to be constrained by:

- A decision maker's general attitude towards risk which often differs from that of other decision makers involved.

- A certain amount of conditioning that results from a previously successful or an unfortunate transaction.

- The "ebb and flow" of working capital/assets and hence the "general state of the company and/or economy".

- The priorities and preferences of management that may subjectively discount differences between alternatives, even though in terms of "utility" they may in fact be the same.

Although useful, utility curves are thus neither consistent nor stable even when dealing with relatively short periods of time. As Hertz points out, there is no simple, consistent, way of integrating all of the above considerations into a single "corporate utility curve". The real strength of utility curves lies in helping to identify and deal with very risky decisions. That is, decisions so risky that "ordinary calculations of profit expectation do not provide straight-forward answers".[5]

Most decisions, therefore, tend to be made on the basis of a combination of:

- Expected Monetary Value (EMV) and
- Pertinent non-EMV considerations

6.2 Decision Trees

A decision tree provides an easy method of accounting for all of the alternatives and associated states of nature and a means of simplifying the decision making process. The use of decision trees is based on a natural extension of our previous discussions of decision making under risk, uncertainty and conflict.

Even relatively simple situations may present a multiplicity of alternatives and possible outcomes that lead to varying consequences. Research has shown that there is an inability on the part of the human mind to cope with more than about 7 aspects or facets of a problem. This has been attributed to a condition sometimes referred to as a "cognitive overload."

Let's pick up the DINKO Inc. example of section 6.1 (d) and assume that as management debates the bid/no bid question on that job (project x), a second opportunity presents itself.[6] This second opportunity (project Y) involves a job estimated at about one million dollars. Historically, seventy percent of jobs that size are won and the gross profit averages 13.5 percent. Based on the latter, consider the growth in the range of possibilities and consequences faced by management in the sequence of evolution.

In the original scenario, there were two alternatives. The first to bid project X, the second to no bid project X as shown in figure 6.2.1(a). Bidding project X would involve the expenditure of $30,000. No costs would be incurred as a result of a no bid decision. One of two outcomes would result from a decision to bid. A win would translate into a net profit of $45,000; a loss would cost the company $30,000. The probabilities associated with each of the preceding were .55 and .45 respectively. By computing the EMV for the "bid" decision, the decision diagram could be simplified as shown in figure 6.2.1(b) and a decision would be made based on pre-established decision criteria.

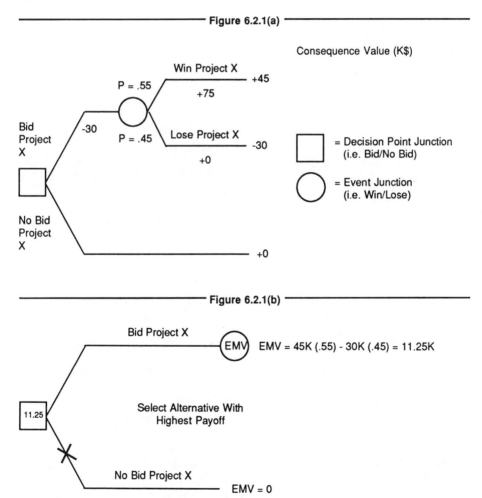

Figure 6.2.1(a)

Consequence Value (K$)

Win Project X
P = .55   +45
+75

Bid Project X   -30
P = .45   Lose Project X   -30
+0

☐ = Decision Point Junction (i.e. Bid/No Bid)

○ = Event Junction (i.e. Win/Lose)

No Bid Project X
+0

Figure 6.2.1(b)

Bid Project X
EMV   EMV = 45K (.55) - 30K (.45) = 11.25K

11.25
Select Alternative With Highest Payoff

No Bid Project X
EMV = 0

Now, let us consider the effect of Project Y on the overall situation. Whether project X proposal is won or lost, one of two alternatives are still open to DINKO management. These are either to bid or no bid project Y as shown in figure 6.2.2. If project X is won and a decision to no bid project Y is made, the gain or monetary consequence would amount to $45,000. If, on the other hand, upon winning project X a decision is made to bid project Y, one of two possible consequences would result. In the event project Y was won, the total gain would amount to $120,000. In the event project Y was lost, the net result would be a loss of $15,000. The probability of winning Y is given as 0.70 and hence that of losing Y is 0.30. Figure 6.2.2 shows all of the other possible consequences. The reader is encouraged to follow through the balance of figure 6.2.2 to ascertain its completeness. From the above, it may be seen that even the simplest of situations can lead to considerable sprouting of "branches" of the decision tree.

────────────────────────── **Figure 6.2.2** ──────────────────────────

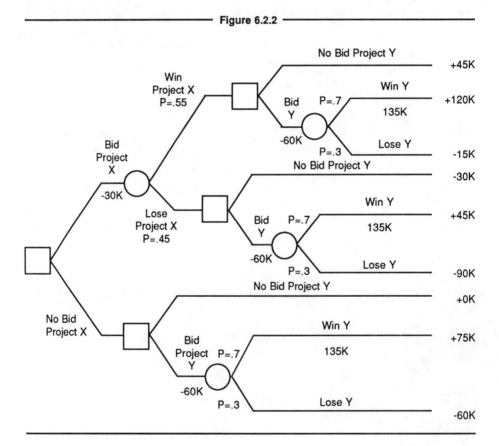

The determination of the preferred course of action proceeds from right to left through a process of progressive "roll back" or "fold back". First, the EMV is calculated from the end of the tree to the event node. This is accomplished, as shown in figure 6.2.1(b), by multiplying the value of each outcome by the probability of its occurrence and then summing the products. Second, at the decision node, the stage is assigned a value based on the highest (previously) established EMV. The stage is then considered as if it were the end of the decision tree and the process repeated until the basic fork (or original question) is reached. Using figure 6.2.2 as the starting point, the process is illustrated through figures 6.2.3(a), (b) and (c). Analysis suggests that Project X should be "bid"; if Project X is won, Project Y should be "bid".

————————————————— **Figure 6.2.3(a)** —————————————————

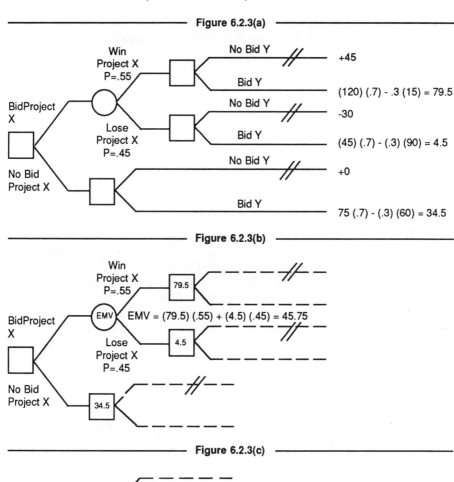

————————————————— **Figure 6.2.3(b)** —————————————————

————————————————— **Figure 6.2.3(c)** —————————————————

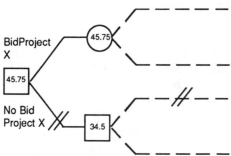

Decision tree analysis is adaptable to a wide range of questions and issues within virtually any field. The more unusual (if not interesting) applications involve military operations, intelligence and political analysis.[7]

6.3 Risk Analysis: The Natural Fallout Of Sound Planning

Webster's dictionary defines risk as exposure to "the chance of injury, damage or loss". In the business environment, many factors contribute to such exposure. As discussed in other sections of this book, customer needs, competitive conditions and pressures, performance requirements as well as other dictates collectively influence the feasibility, approach, cost, schedule and hence the profitability of a given effort. In many cases uncontrollable or unexpected factors (e.g. weather, economy, suppliers, etc) intervene and exacerbate problems faced by management. Overall these factors can lead to the pursuit of unrealistic goals and expectations which are frequently fueled by business dictates *and compounded by problems involving unanticipated interactions between the variables themselves.* The range of possible outcomes, indicated trade offs and required priorities, which characteristically vary over the effort's life cycle, are thus often obscured. *Timely corrective action and probability of success can thus be severely impaired from the very outset.*

As discussed in Chapter 11, organizations understandably focus and rely heavily on their existing products, processes, properties, policies, procedures and precedents. This internal orientation invariably influences the approach to an effort, its design, including the selection, allocation, utilization, scheduling and control of human and physical resources. In the process, technical, cost, schedule and other factors are directly affected from the start.

Inconsistencies between external demands and dictates and internal capabilities and expectations are often addressed and accounted for on the basis of empirical adjustments, "revised cut off rates", three level estimates or similar management techniques which are subject to serious limitations.[8]

Empirical Adjustments:

- Cut down on the likelihood of making a *bad* investment but also spoil the chances of making a good one. Adjustments are *not based on uncertainty but rather biases* which far too often lack a sound basis given the specific uniqueness of issues under immediate consideration.

- Do not provide decision makers with an explicit basis for evaluating return in relation to the odds of achieving specified goals and targets either from the outset or on an on going basis.

- Do not give a clear picture for comparing the probability of possible results, goals and targets among suggested or competing alternatives. Specifically, *they do not provide any indications whether pessimistic expectations are more likely than optimistic ones, or whether average results are more likely then extreme ones.*

In this section we present practical means of overcoming some of these problems by capitalizing on the front end investment in network based planning and scheduling (see Chapter 4).

6.3 (a) Pert Revisited

The application of PERT embodies certain frequently overlooked assumptions. An awareness of these is essential to its use as risk analysis tool.

First, while it is clearly most appropriate in situations in which the duration of activities is subject to random (chance) variations, the specified time estimates are seldom the by-product of an implied statistical sampling process. The three level time estimate suggests that an activity has been repeated numerous times and under the same general conditions; this, in fact, may not be the case. The very nature of the effort under consideration may be such that no data exists to support the estimates other than one's *experience and judgement*. The implied distribution is thus purely *hypothetical* and hence the frequent by-product of either undue optimism or pessimism.

Parenthetically, it is for this reason that, historically, the Beta distribution* has been accepted as a mathematical model for the expected activity duration times.[9]:

$$T_{exp} = (T_{opt} + 4T + T_{pess}) / 6$$

This equation is the same as that given in Chapter 4. It should be noted that, originally, the standard deviation (and variance) were approximated by the expression:

$$\text{Standard Deviation} = \sqrt{(\text{Variance})} = (T_{pess} - T_{opt})/6$$

This was based on a definition of *Tpess* and *Topt* as being the 0 and 100 percentile values of the performance time distribution. Intuitively, one may be lead to conclude the preceding to be unrealistic on at least two counts:

- Since estimates are primarily based on past experience and judgement, such "end values" would be extremely difficult to estimate as they would have never been experienced.

- Estimates should not be based on events so infrequent as to no longer be thought of in terms of "ordinary" chance events (or variables).

---

* A distribution contained within a finite interval

It has been suggested that 5 and 95 percentile definitions of *Tpess* and *Topt* would be more practical and realistic. Moder and Rodgers have shown that the difference (Tpess - Topt) is on an average about 3.2 standard deviations for distributions including the Beta, Normal, Exponential, Rectangular and Triangular.[10] In line with the preceding, an alternate approximation of the standard deviation (variance) has been proposed and is given by:[11]

$$\text{Standard Deviation} = \sqrt{\text{Variance}} = (T_{pess} - T_{opt}) / (3.2)$$

The values of standard deviations (variances) used in the subsequent discussion are based upon this equation (rather than the previously given rough estimate of 1/6 the distribution's range).

Second, it is well established that conventional PERT analysis will lead to *optimistically biased* estimates of early completion of events and/or network. The sources of errors in PERT have been the object of extensive study by a number or researches.[12,13] An excellent overview and treatment of this overall subject is presented by Moder and Phillips.[14]

In general, the bias arises since non-critical paths (and their variances) are ignored in the "forward pass" leading to the establishment of project duration. By way of illustration, consider the simplified examples of Figure 6.3.1. (a) and (b).

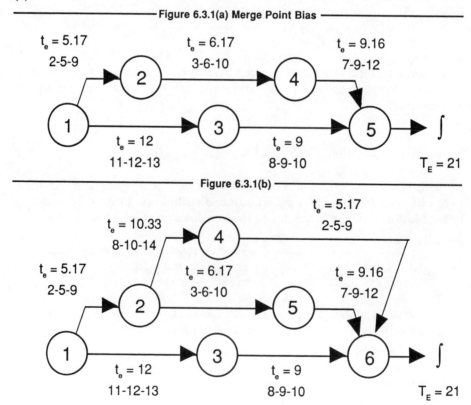

——————————— Figure 6.3.1(a) Merge Point Bias ———————————

——————————— Figure 6.3.1(b) ———————————

Using standard PERT methodology, the critical path in Figure 6.3.1(a) includes activities 1,3,5. This stems from the identification of the path with the longest total expected duration through the network. Once the critical path has been established, the standard deviation is based on the Central Limit Theorem and computed taking into consideration variances of activities along the critical path:

$$\text{(Standard Deviation)}_{\text{Project}} = \sqrt{(2/3.2)^2 + (2/3.2)^2}$$

The expected project duration (T_E) is thus said to be equal to:

$$T_{E_{1,3,5}} = 21 \ (+/-) \ 0.884$$

Note, however, that the identification of the critical path, as based on the "forward pass", did not take into consideration the impact of the variances associated with *sub-critical* activities. Although the expected duration of sub-critical path 1,2,4,5 is somewhat shorter than that of path 1,3,5, the probability that the overall project's duration may exceed expectations could be significant. This stems from the variability (or degree of uncertainty) associated with the expected completion times of activities along path 1,2,4,5. The expected duration of this path falls in the range of

$$T_{E_{1,2,4,5}} = 20.5 \ (+/-) \ 3.466$$

The above points to the existence of an optimistic bias considering the range of realizations of random activity durations that may actually occur. A similar built-in bias can be observed in the example of Figure 6.3.1(b). Note, however, that in the latter case the expected duration of either of the sub-critical paths could exceed the expected duration for the overall project.

It has been shown that under certain conditions, actual duration times can run as much as 50 percent higher than PERT estimates.[15] "Merge point bias", as the condition is known, has been shown to increase as (1) the number of merging activities increases, (2) their expected duration *and/or* completion times grow closer together and (3) time variances increase.[16]

One of the weaknesses of conventional PERT analysis has been a conditioned expectation and reliance on the existence of a unique critical path. In practice, such reliance may prove costly in terms of missed schedules, budgets and the general loss of confidence as discussed below.

6.3(b) Risk Analysis Using Monte Carlo Simulation

As noted earlier, an activity's time variance is a measure of the extent of uncertainty associated with its completion time. The larger the variance, the greater the degree of (implied) uncertainty. Given the mathematical relationship between variance and the standard deviation of a distribution, the extent of uncertainty associated with an activity can be quantified in terms of the probability of meeting a specific schedule. Clearly, the actual completion schedule will reflect a specific realization from the range of (chance) possibilities associated with each activity. Considering the preceding, any number of unique critical paths are possible through the network based on the combination of actual realizations that ultimately occur. These, however, can be anticipated. A *random assignment* of completion times to each of the activities, within the range of possibilities associated with each, will yield a solution reflecting *a specific* realization of project activity duration times from among those possible. Repeated end-to-end computer simulations of possible project outcomes, through the assignment of random completion times to the activities, would thus yield:

- A mean project completion time distribution and hence a less biased assessment of the probability of meeting schedules of interest.

- A "criticality index" for all of the activities in the network based on the frequency of their appearance on the critical path (e.g. a ratio of the number of times an activity appears on the critical path to the total number of simulations run).

The latter is especially useful and important for two reasons:

- The amount of slack time associated with an activity is *not* necessarily an indication of the relative importance of the activity to the project's overall success.

- Typically, management tends to focus attention on activities with little or no slack time (critical path) at the expense of those which reflect a high degree of uncertainty with respect to completion times.

Depending on the network, sub-critical activities can have higher "criticality indices" than *some* of the activities on the critical path identified through conventional methods. Criticality indices provide an objective means of prioritizing managerial attention based on the degree of uncertainty associated with each project task.

Computer simulations can provide management with a much greater degree of a priori visibility and pro active control over the effort. It is a relatively simple matter to modify or develop software to accept an estimated time range fo reach of the activities and then proceed to select random values of T_{cpt}, T_{mean}, T_{pes}, within that range, on successive end-to-end simulations of the project. Several hundred realizations of the entire project could thus be performed within a matter of seconds at a touch of a keyboard. A similar approach, involving the appropriate summation of all costs, can be used to develop a mean project cost distribution curve. The combination of the mean time and cost distribution curves shown in Figure 6.3.2(a) and (b) can then be plotted to arrive at a "risk envelope" of the type shown in Figure 6.3.2(c). Such envelopes can be very useful in comparing expected results with the probability of achieving desired combination of cost/schedule goals and targets.

6.3(c) Risk Reduction and Management

As is frequently pointed out, no tool or technique is a substitute for managerial insight, experience and judgement. This is especially true in the area of risk analysis.

Monte Carlo simulations can be a powerful tool in quantifying the extent of risk along with some of the key contributors to the level of risk faced by management. A great deal of insight may be gained from an examination and study of risk envelopes in combination with activity "criticality indices" and the proposed approach to the execution of the effort. Ultimately, however, steps may have to be taken or a decision made relative to the containment and/or reduction of the level of risk associated with a particular undertaking. The following is a generalized discussion of a practical approach to some of

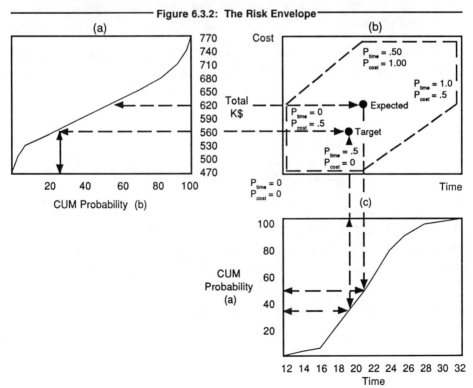

Figure 6.3.2: The Risk Envelope

the challenges faced by management in this area.

Generally, risks lend themselves to suppression and/or management through one or more distinct strategies. Typically, these include:[17]

- *Risk Assumption*: Based on inclusion of contingencies commensurate with cost/impact/benefit considerations.

- *Risk Reduction*: Through analysis and planning of the effort including the re-allocation and dedication of key resources.

- *Transfer/Substitution*: Taking unknown or high risk elements and substituting for them known or lower risk elements. Transferring risk, for example, may be accomplished through make or buy decisions; sometimes contractual provisions/arrangements.

- *Avoidance*: Analytical exploration or actual testing of proposed or alternative methods/approaches to implementation or execution of a particular task.

- *Hedging*: Concurrent or parallel pursuit of two or more methods or approaches that differ as to the extent of risk exposure. It should be noted that such pursuit need not necessarily be taken to a logical conclusion. The secondary effort(s) can be suspended once the weakness or threats posed by the primary approach are under control.

Thorough risk analysis and management generally requires an iterative blending of experience and judgement with computer based simulations and analyses. It tends to be *a selective process of adjustment of aspirations to the attainable, expectations to the acceptable and results to the desirable.* Figure 6.3.3 illus-

———————————— **Figure 6.3.3: A Risk Analysis Model** ————————————

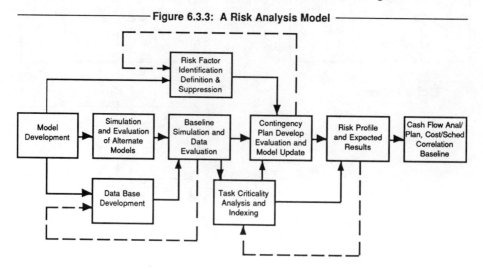

trates a possible approach to this overall process.

A key issue in risk analysis involves the weighing of the probability of occurrence against the consequences of failure. This suggests a need for the pre-establishment of targets, goals and/or acceptable thresholds. Once these have been established, risk analysis need not be a long and tedious effort providing it is systematized. Ancillary (tailor made) questionnaires or check lists of the type shown in figure 6.3.4 can be extremely helpful in organizing the effort, crystallizing the issues and expediting the output. They are intended for use in combination with the general process described in Figure 6.3.3. Given the proliferation of personal computers and the cost/benefits attendant to the performance of such analyses, there is little justification for not investing the added time and effort as a matter of organizational policy on projects of significance to the enterprise.

─────────────── Figure 6.3.4: Risk Analysis Check List ───────────────

Act. Nodes	Orig. Time Est.	Crit. Index	Type	Factor	Aspect	Strategy	Possible Measure	New Time Est.
				• Design • • •	• New Process • • •	• Assume • Reduce • Transfer/ • Substitute • Avoid • Hedge	• Add Time/$$$ • Use Proven Process/Chge. Make-Buy • Proof Tests • Pursue Two Methods	4-6
7-8	6-8	.75	• Technical •	•				
				• Safety • •	• Personnel • •	• Assume • Reduce • Transfer/ • Substitute • Avoid • Hedge	• Build In Redundancy • Automate • Work Around	6-9
12-13	10-12	.60	• Environment	•				
				• Schedule • •	• Tight • • •	• Assume • Reduce • Transfer/ • Substitute • Avoid • Hedge	• Add O/T $$$ • Planning/ Reallocation Key Resources • Explore Alt. Methods	7-10
16-17	8-12	.70	• Management	•				

6.4 Risk Analysis: Advanced Network Based Techniques

Network diagrams can be adapted to the solution of problems involving complex series of decisions. Both theoretical and applied interest in network diagrams has grown. It stems from advances and innovations in computational methods which allow solution of a wide range of problems heretofore unapproachable by other methods.

Decision network application and development requires skill and experience. Practical considerations limit our objective to the promotion of an awareness of these techniques. Our primary intent, therefore, is to serve as a catalyst for the further, independent, study of these powerful tools.

In general, CPM/PERT like network diagrams can provide a graphical accounting of alternatives and consequences involved in a wide variety of decision problems. In such problems, paths through the network are the equivalent of operating plans or decisions that control or influence the simulated "system". A good synthesis of both traditional and more recent techniques in network modelling and analysis is presented by Jensen and Barnes.[18]

6.4(a) The General Approach

Consider the following relatively simple "transportation" (or "allocation") problem by way of illustrating the general approach. Variations of this classic problem appear in nearly all books on operations research.

Binko Inc. is a manufacturer of a consumer product made out of plastic. It obtains raw materials from two major sources. The materials are shipped to four plants, strategically located throughout the country, for fabrication and assembly. The completed product is then shipped to four major distribution points. The cost of raw materials, inclusive of shipping, from each of the sources to each of Binko's plants is given in Table 6.4.1. The cost of fabrication, assembly and shipping from each of the plants to each of the distribution points is given in Table 6.4.2. Binko is seeking an optimum combination of allocations of raw materials and the completed product among its plants and

Table 6.4.1				
From \ To	P1	P2	P3	P4
S1	2.0	2.2	2.6	2.4
S2	2.6	2.0	2.4	2.4

Table 6.4.2				
From \ To	D1	D2	D3	D4
P1	6	6	7	5
P2	6	5	12	9
P3	6	4	12	6
P4	10	7	6	7

distribution centers respectively.

The problem is illustrated in Figure 6.4.1. Nodes S1 and S2 represent the sources of raw materials. Nodes P1 through P4 Binko's plants and D1 through D4 the distribution centers. Arrows are used to represent the alternatives at each stage of the decision process. As can be seen in Figure 6.4.1, several combinations of material and finished product flows are possible.

Starting at node S1, raw materials can be dispatched to any one or a combination of four plants for end item fabrication and assembly. Similarly, the finished product can be shipped to any one or a combination of distribution points. The same is true using S2 as the starting point in evaluating

———————————————— **Figure 6.4.1** ————————————————

	BEST SOLN	SECOND BEST	THIRD BEST
	S1-P1-D1 ($8.0) S2-P2-D1 ($8.0)	S1-P2-D1 ($8.2)	S2-P3-D1 ($8.4)
	S2-P3-D2 ($6.4)	S1-P3-D2 ($6.6)	S2-P2-D2 ($7.0)
	S1-P4-D3 ($8.4) S2-P4-D3 ($8.4)	S1-P1-D3 ($9.0)	S2-P3-D3 ($10.4)
	S1-P1-D4 ($7.0)	S1-P4-D4 ($7.4) S2-P4-D4 ($7.4)	S2-P1-D4 ($7.6)

available options.

Clearly, material could also be shipped from both S1 and S2 to several combinations of plants and distribution centers.

A majority of decision problems involve some type of an "optimization" process. That is, either the minimizing or maximizing of a variable such as cost or profit. Given a network representation of alternatives, states and consequences of acts, it may be intuitively obvious that the optimum decision could be arrived at on the basis of the expected path value through the network. More specifically, the minimum cost approach could be established on the basis of a sequence of actions and associated (cost) consequences yielding the lowest total path value through a network. Alternatively, maximizing profit would involve the identification of a sequence of actions and associated (profit) consequences with the highest path value through some other network. In the Binko problem, the consequence of each act is presented in Figure 6.4.1 in terms of cost incurred.

It must be noted that decision networks *need not* necessarily either start or end with a single "state". *Singular starting and end points are unique to CPM/ PERT and are strictly associated with slack/float time calculations. In addition, actions starting and ending with the same node are allowed in decision networks. That is not the case in CPM/PERT.*

Given the cost data and the network formulation of the above problem, the best *solutions* to Binko's problem are easily identifiable. Specifically, we could identify not only the best sequence of flows to a distribution point, but, the second and third best solutions as well. Lowest (cost) path values can be tabulated manually or using a computer.

Generally speaking, development of decision networks is not any more difficult than development of network based project plans. It requires skill, some experience and a familiarity with the overall problem at hand. The latter typically leads to the identification of key issues from which an integrated pattern can be developed.

Applications of decision networks are virtually unlimited. Among the more common are:

- A variety of production problems including capacity planning, scheduling, routing and stock control.

- Resource planning, budgeting and allocation including evolution of equipment replacement strategies/policy.

- General "traffic" and transportation problems.

- Product development and marketing strategy problems.

In more general terms, this technique is applicable to a host of scientific, social and economic problems.

6.4(b) A Structured Approach

An excellent treatment of a technique that combines the power of dynamic modelling with the simplicity of CPM/PERT is provided by Hastings and Mello.[19] The treatment is application oriented and covers both *deterministic and probabilistic* networks. The technique is similar to decision tree analyses yet seemingly more compact and powerful. In addition, the approach is more defined and structured than that presented above. It is discussed in the following sections based on its conceptual proximity to the material already covered in this chapter.

In decision networks, circles can be used to represent states of the system and arrows to represent actions. More specifically, a circle represents a condition or configuration of the system. An arrow is used to connect two adjacent states of the simulated system. Each action involves a "return" of some type at the given state. The "return" can be defined in terms of any variable of interest such as time, cost, profit, market share, yield, output, consumption, etc. The following example should illustrate the convention and general approach to the formulation of a typical problem.

Assume that DINKO, Inc. manufactures expensive special purpose automated test equipment. The rate of demand for this equipment is non-uniform over time. To maintain some semblance of continuity of production and hence cost effectiveness, the test equipment as manufactured under a company funded inventory account. As the equipment is sold from inventory, stock is periodically replenished. Currently, 10 test sets are available in the inventory. Five of these are to be delivered in the next two months. A decision is to be made as to whether to commit an additional 5, 10 or 15 sets to production.

A *section* of the decision network corresponding to the scenario is shown in Figure 6.4.2. Ignore how the current situation was reached and the subsequent considerations that may be involved in arriving at an actual decision. The purpose, as noted earlier, is to illustrate the general convention and formulation of a problem.

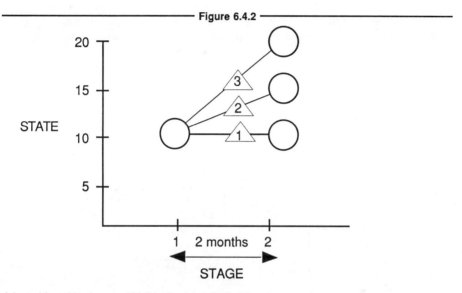

Figure 6.4.2

Adapted from Hastings and Mello, "Decision Analysis", p.4

The current state or configuration of the system can be defined in terms of existing inventory level. Three mutually exclusive actions are available at this state. The actions are thus numbered as shown in Figure 6.4.2. The effect of any one of these actions is to shift the "system" to a new (or adjacent) state. Depending on the decision, the state of the system, or, in this case the inventory level, would be altered as illustrated in Figure 6.4.2. The shift (or action) is accompanied by a "return" of some type. As noted, a return can be defined in terms of any variable of interest. In this case, assume the return to be the cost of production associated with each of the alternatives.

The "stage" of the system, heretofore undefined, is a variable that measures progress in time or, alternatively, measures the transition of the system in terms of some type of achievement or accomplishment in other suitable units. In the example at hand, time is used to account for *progress* or record *transitions* of the *system*.

Stage identification is an aid in the analysis of decision problems and not a necessity. This decision analysis tool can be applied to any type of a network problem. It does not require a "stagewise structure" as long as no sequence of actions can lead back to a state already experienced.[20]

6.4.(b.1) Network Optimization

Let's take a short cut. Specifically, assume that a decision network has been successfully developed for a problem of interest and that it is shown in Figure 6.4.3. Given the returns in Figure 6.4.3, optimization is achieved using "forward" and "backward" passes in a manner somewhat analogous to that used in CPM/PERT. The backward pass is performed first to establish either the shortest or longest paths through the network. In the process optimum actions are identified. The forward pass is performed next. It links optimal actions and thus establishes the optimum *sequence* of actions or the optimum path.[21]

The backward pass is initiated by assigning a value of 0 to the terminal node (or state) of the network. As we proceed from right to left, the value of adjacent nodes is calculated by adding return values to the value of the termi-

───────────── **Figure 6.4.3** ─────────────

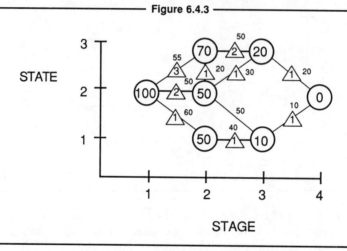

nal node. Nodes at coordinates (3,1) and (3,3) would thus have values of 10 and 20 respectively. At junction nodes such as (2,2), the value of the node depends on the type of solution desired. In minimum path value problems, the value of the junction node would be the smaller of the sums of adjacent node and corresponding return values. For a minimum path problem, node (2,2) has a value of 50. For a maximum path value problem, the node value is 60. The calculations are repeated until the initial stage is reached. In Figure 6.4.3, the minimum path value (or minimum cost) is 100. As the backward pass is performed, the optimum action at each state is identified as that involving the *best immediate choice*. This means that at nodes (3,1) and (3,3) available choices are optimum, by definition, as they are the only ones available or possible. At (2,2) action 1 is optimal; the same is true at (2,3) and so on. Optimal actions identified during the backward pass are marked with a hash mark in Figure 6.4.4(a).

The *forward* pass starts at the initial state (1,2) and proceeds left to right.

At each state the optimizing action is selected and identified with double hash marks. For instance, at (1,2) the optimizing action is number 2. At (2,2) it is action number 1 and so on as shown in Figure 6.4.4(b).

——————————————— Figure 6.4.4 (a) ———————————————

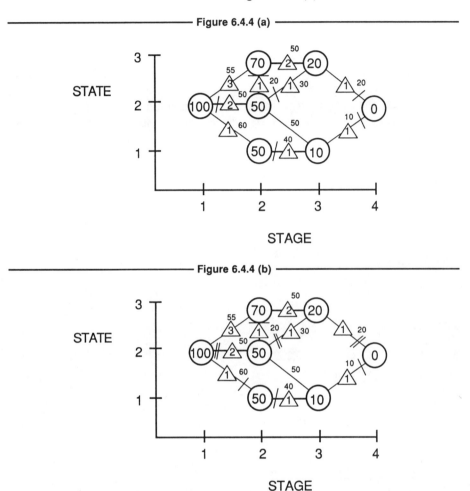

STATE

STAGE

——————————————— Figure 6.4.4 (b) ———————————————

STATE

STAGE

The above discussions were based on an unstated premise. Namely, that future states or configurations of the system were independent of *how* current states or configurations were reached. In more technical terms, it was assumed that the system possessed the *Markov property*. No special significance need be attributed to this fact at this time other than to note that nearly all analytical techniques in management are based on this assumption. Furthermore, note that preceding discussions centered on *deterministic systems with the Markov property*. Deterministic in the sense that transitions between system states (or configurations) were known with certainty. The following discussion covers stochastic networks with the Markov property.

6.4.2.2 Stochastic Decision Models

Stochastic networks are networks in which the transitions between system states or configurations are probablistic. Schematically and analytically these networks have a great deal in common with decision trees. To illustrate this point consider the problem of section 6.1.3. Assume that profit figures cited do not take into consideration the cost of advertising.

Let's address the problem from the perspective of company A's management. The state of the system is subject to change whether management elects to (1) institute the advertising campaign or (2) maintain the status quo.

Assuming company A proceeds with the advertising campaign, the "system" will transition to one of two possible states. This is shown in Figure 6.4.5(a) by a transition symbol of the type used in decision tree diagrams to indicate a decision point. The state to which the system transitions will effectively be the by-product of a decision over which company A has no control. Specifically, company B's decision relative to advertising. Company A's subjective assessment of the probability of transition to a given state is shown in Figure 6.4.5(a) next to each of the transition arrows. The value of end states is expressed in terms of the anticipated profit. A return of (-)100K is associated with the cost of advertising.

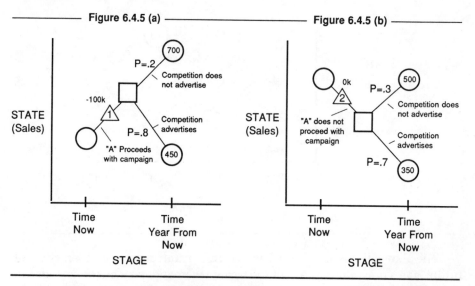

Figure 6.4.5 (a) ———————————— Figure 6.4.5 (b)

Figure 6.4.5(b) shows possible system transitions given company A's decision not to advertise. The return associated with this decision, transition probabilities involved and end state values are shown as before. Figure 6.4.6 shows the integrated formulation of the overall problem under consideration.

In this particular case, depending on one's perspective, Figure 6.4.6 could be said to represent a decision tree or decision network with multiple end states. Recall, based on section 6.4.1, that *decision networks are not constrained to singular end points* as in the case of CPM/PERT. *In addition, it must be recognized that in a decision tree only one path can exist between any pair of nodes. Although not shown here, this is not necessarily the case in decision networks.* A generalized example is shown in figure 6.4.7 illustrating the preceding.

In computing path values, the weighted average of adjacent states is entered into the transition symbol. The previously described general procedure is then followed to identify the maximum or minimum mean total return. The maximum mean total return for the problem at hand is included in figure 6.4.6. The reader is encouraged to review the *minimum* path solution of Figure 6.4.7.

─────────────────────── **Figure 6.4.6** ───────────────────────

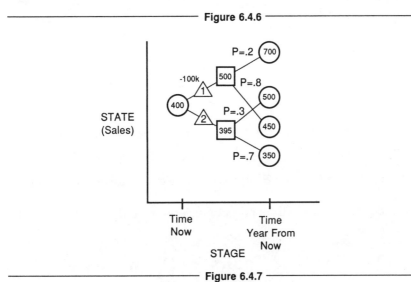

─────────────────────── **Figure 6.4.7** ───────────────────────

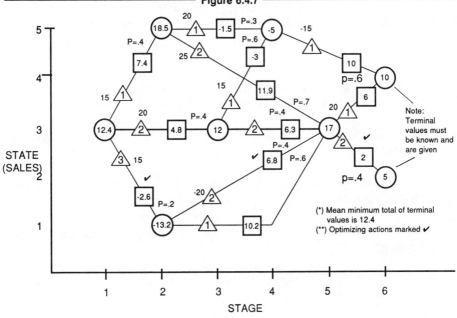

Decision networks offer a more flexible, compact and powerful alternative to decision tree analyses. They lend themselves to a variety of applications including, for instance, complex problems where steady state or limiting solutions need to be found. A detailed discussion of the approach and specified techniques involved in the solution of such problems is clearly beyond the scope of this text. The conceptual background provided is intended as a basis for further independent study or as a basis for the solicitation of support from those with backgrounds in computer science, operations research and programming.

6.5 Summary

As stated and supported in other sections of this text, the relatively high proportion of project "failures" is not so much due to complexity. The application of tools and techniques discussed may vary on a case by case basis. However, their rigorous application is critical, in combination with other management tools, to the identification of errors and omissions, technical problems and contingent responses, cost drivers and preferred solutions. In effect, directly or indirectly they are the key to:

- Improved *competitiveness* in an increasingly competitive climate

- *Profitable execution* in a dynamic and uncertain environment.

———— Questions and Topics for Discussion ————

1. Define and discuss the difference between risk and uncertainty.

2. Define EMV and use an example to illustrate the concept.

3. Define a "utility function;" Draw two utility curves representative of what may be considered as risk averse and risk prone curves.

4. Name three risk reduction/management strategies. Define and give an example of each.

5. Develop your own risk reduction model as an alternative to the one presented in Figure 6.3.3. Explain/support your model.

6. An activity has a large variance. What are you likely to conclude from the preceding?

7. PERT/CPM network diagrams must start and end with a single activity/event. This is not the case when network diagrams are adapted to the solution of problems involving a series of complex decision. Why?

8. Define "probabilistic," "deterministic," "Markov property" and "stochastic network."

9. Risk analysis and management may involve considerable time, effort and expense; when would you call for such an effort on a proposed project — list specific guidelines/criteria.

10. Where and/or under what conditions would you consider developing "contingency plans."

11. The typical if not obvious economic tradeoff may involve the cost of planning versus the cost of errors. Discuss how these could be quantified for the purpose of arriving at the optimum level of planning.

——————————— **References** ———————————

1. Park J. Ewart, Professor Emeritus, Administrative Statistics Lecture Notes. The Graduate School of Business Administration, University of Southern California, Los Angeles, CA 1970 (unpublished).

2. Ibid.

3. Richard H. Leftwich, *"The Price System and Resource Allocation"*, Dryden Press Inc., 1970 p. 56.

4. David B. Hertz, "Incorporating Risk in Capital Expenditure Analysis", in: S.R. Goodman and J.S.Reece, *"Controller's Handbook"*, Dow Jones-Irwin, Homewood, Illinois, 1978 p. 416-426.

5. Ibid.

6. Similar examples and/or versions of this problem appear throughout literature given their practical appeal and ease of understanding. A more involved version of this problem appears in the "Handbook for Decision Analysis", prepared under the sponsorship of the Defense Advanced Research Projects Agency and the Office of Naval Research. A similar treatment of this problem also appears in: "Compressed Air Magazine", Ingersoll-Rand Company, Volume 86, Number 6, June 1981, p 14-17.

7. Ibid.

8. Hertz.

9. Charles E. Clark, "The PERT model for the distribution of an Activity Time", *Operations Research*, Vol No 3, May-June 1962, pp 405-406.

10. J. J. Moder and E.G. Rodgers, "Judgement Estimates of the Moments of PERT Type Distributions", *Management Science*, Vol 15, No 2, October 1968.

11. J. J. Moder and C.R. Phillips, "Project Management with CPM and Pert", Van Norstraud Reinhold, New York, 1970, p 285.

12. K.R. MacCrimmon and C.A. Ryavec, "An Analytical Study of the PERT Assumptions", *Operations Research*, Vol. 12, No. 1 January-February 1964, pp 16-37.

13. W.R. King and T.A. Wilson, "Subjective Time Estimates in Critical Path Planning - A preliminary Analysis", *Management Science,* Vol 13, No 5, January 1967, pp 307-320.

14. Ibid.

15. A.R. Klingel, "Bias in PERT Project Completion Time Calculations for a Real Network", *Management Science,* Vol 13, No 4, December 1966 pp 194-201.

16. Moder and Phillips p 304.

17. Daniel D. Roman, "Managing Projects: A Systems Approach"; Elsevier Science Publishing Co. Inc., New York, 1986 p 250.

18. Paul A. Jensen and J. Wesley Barnes, "Network Flow Programming", John Wiley and Sons, Inc., New York, 1980.

19. N.A.J. Hastings and J.M.C. Mello, "Decision Networks", John Wiley and Sons, New York, 1978.

20. Ibid p. 5.

21. Ibid p. 6.

Part Three

Getting The Most Out Of People And The Organization

————————————— Chapter 7 —————————————
Making Project Management Work

7.1 Attributes of a Successful Project Manager
7.2 Factors That Make for Project Success
7.3 Upgrading Knowledge and Skills

7.1 Attributes of a Successful Project Manager

In simplest terms, the project manager's responsibility is to "produce results." As an acronym, these words define the primary functions and essential attributes of an effective project manager:

PM Functions	PM Attributes
Planning	Realistic
Reiterating	Energetic
Organizing	Self-Confident
Delegating	Unpretentious
Understanding	Listener
Communicating	Trustworthy
Evaluating	Systematic

It is the proper blending of these functions and attributes in the performance and behavior of the PM that is critical to making project management viable. Managers typically reflect their personal attributes in the functions they are called on to perform. For example, in the area of planning and scheduling, PM's realism affects not only the inherent soundness of the master plans and schedules but also the degree of commitment which they are likely to be afforded by the project team. An effective manager must strike a balance between what is feasible and what is not, what is likely to stress the organization positively versus what is likely to cause distress within the organization and among the project participants. An effective manager accepts the project as a dynamic undertaking requiring continual scrutiny and reiteration to keep on target and typically responds to this challenge with seemingly boundless enthusiasm and capacity for work. He tends to be self-assured, not only in what he knows, but also in what he is, and consequently he is not likely to allow his weaknesses to stand in the way of the best organization of personnel or the best implementation and interpretation of procedures and information flow. These "bests" more frequently occur when the project manager is capable of being a contributing member of the team as opposed to cases in which he is constrained either by training, ability or experience, to fulfilling a primarily ceremonial or pontifical function. The combination of personality and competence plays a significant role in a manager's self-image, feeling of security, and self-worth and correspondingly has a major impact on the nature and quality of interaction in the delegation of work.

Unquestionably, among the most important attributes of a manager is an ability to listen and assimilate the thoughts, ideas, suggestions, and feelings of others. Such an ability leads to a greater sensitivity, understanding, appreciation and tolerance for the peculiarities and the ambiguities of the business, effort, situations and people involved. These attributes, coupled with high personal and professional ethical standards and a strong sense of fairness and equity, are essential to developing trust and respect among the participants and effective communication. All these qualities are essential ingredients in the systematic evaluation and control of the project effort so that the desired goals and objectives are achieved. As a result, effective project management does not lend itself to rules of thumb or a cookbook approach. It is rather an art form that generally needs to be learned and refined through a great deal of study and experience.

In a study by N.E. Thornberg and J.R. Weintraub of more than 100 project managers in a cross section of eight high-technology firms, five core dimensions were identified as necessary for effective project manager performance:[1]

- Oral communication
- Influencing skills (leadership)
- Intellectual capabilities
- Ability to handle stress
- Work skills

Communication skills were particularly important because of the large percentage of the manager's time spent in oral communication, either face to face or by phone, monitoring, evaluating, controlling, and reporting. There was direct correlation between the ability to communicate and project performance. Effective managers were found to be good listeners, articulate, concise, straightforward, and astute in reading messages, both verbal and nonverbal. They were particularly skilled in evaluating problem situations, determining key components, and making decisions that solved or at least alleviated the problem.[2]

The study further showed that a high level of influencing skill is a key characteristic of the effective project manager. He must be able to convince company personnel (who may not be directly within his authority) to perform for the good of the project. He uses his power of persuasion and ability to negotiate in order to accomplish project goals; cooperation is most frequently solicited rather than forced.[3]

Thornberg and Weintraub found that successful project managers were capable of processing (that is, taking and sorting out) large quantities of information and making accurate analyses and evaluations. They took into account the "big picture" as well as the details. Furthermore, they were able to tolerate a high level of stress and ambiguity, were efficient managers of their own personal time, possessed a generous supply of stamina and energy, and had an innate capability for depersonalizing and defusing conflict. Delegation, follow-up, the willingness to take risks when necessary, and accurate identification of trade-offs are essential to the PM's management style.

7.2 Factors That Make for Project Success

For project management to succeed, the organizational climate must be generally receptive. Certainly, a classical functional organization upon which a matrix project operation has been forcibly imposed may not be the ideal spawning ground for a successful project. In such situations the PM is in a precarious position from the outset and the probability of his being successful is appreciably diminished. The problem of identifying situations where project management can be successful has been described in detail by various authors, notably by L.C. Stuckenbruck in his handbook, *The Implementation of Project Management*.[4] Project management is *not* a panacea for the management of all multiple efforts and special tasks. Therefore the success of a project manager in carrying out a project, whether it is set up as a pure project or in a matrix context, depends on the attitude toward and experience of the organization with projects and management's view of the particular project.

Although some projects meet system requirements and specifications are completed on time and within budget, they are frequently perceived as failures. Conversely, some projects that fail to meet the constraints of time and budget are nevertheless perceived as successful. This was the subject of a NASA-sponsored study by B.N. Baker and colleagues titled *Determinants of Project Success*.[5] The results of this study of some 650 nonaerospace and aerospace projects* indicated the following requirements for the "perceived" success of a project:

> If the project meets the technical performance specifications and/or mission to be performed, and if there is a high level of satisfaction concerning the project outcome among: key people in the parent organization, in the client organization, on the project team and key users or clientele of the project effort, the project is considered an overall success.[6]

The significance of this study is that schedule and cost performance can be secondary factors in judging whether a project is a success or failure. Meeting the technical performance or mission requirement is of greater importance to both customer and vendor than the project being on schedule and on cost. Overruns in cost and schedule can be serious, however if technical and/or operational goals are met the project can still be perceived as a success. This should be kept in mind by PMs who are overzealous in maintaining cost and

---

* About 80% of the projects selected for study were nonaerospace and 20% were aerospace-type projects.

schedule performance to the point of neglecting completeness and quality of technical and operational accomplishment. The study further showed that "being close to the customer," as emphasized by T.J. Peters and R.H. Waterman, Jr., in the best seller, *In Search of Excellence*,[7] is just as important in project management as it is in other operations of successful companies. It is vital to the sucess of a project that it is seen as a success by the customer. It remains for the PM to discern from conversations with the customer and his management their criteria for project success. (See Section 4.1(a).)

Another significant but not unexpected finding of the study was that effective project planning is absolutely essential to success. Half of the variables associated with perceived project failure could have been avoided by better planning (see Section 5.10(a)).

7.3 Upgrading Knowledge and Skills

The project manager in today's rapidly changing environment must maintain currency in technical and management skills that can optimize his performance. Some key areas in which he must be knowledgeable are the elements and approach to long-range planning, productivity improvement techniques, conflict management, and the legal aspects of project management, in addition to those basic aspects discussed in Chapters 1 to 6 of this text. (There are a number of current management journals and texts cited as references in this book that can supply updating information to the ambitious PM.) Also, he should become versed in the pertinent ancillary subjects that can be critically important in either the execution of the project or the operation and use of the product or system that results. Several such subject areas are briefly outlined in the appendices.

Last but not least, is the level of skill and understanding of computer use that a PM must possess. He should become familiar with computers and then applications especially within the project environment. Ideally, he should develop a working knowledge of the use of personal computers so that he and his people can fully exploit this rapidly developing tool for carrying out many of the exercises and calculations required in the project planning, administration, monitoring, and control process.

———— Questions and Topics for Discussion ————

1. Why is the persuasive power of the PM so important in carrying out his functions, more so than a manager in the functional organization of a company?

2. How can charisma be important to a PM in carrying out a difficult technical project?

3. What are some of the problems that can be precipitated by a PM who des not have effective communication skills?

4. Given that stress in unavoidable for the PM and his team, what are the positive and negatives aspects of such stress?

5. What are the important factors that make for project success? Enumerate and discuss briefly.

6. T.J. Peters and R.H. Waterman, Jr., in their best seller, *In Search of Excellence*, stress the importance of being close to the customer. Why is this particularly important for the PM and how can he accomplish this?

7. Should a PM learn computer programming? Discuss pros and cons.

8. Detail an action plan you would follow if you were an engineer seriously interested in upgrading yourself to a project manager.

——————————— References ———————————

1. N.E. Thornberg and J.R. Weintraub, "The Project Manager: What it Takes to Be a Good One." *Project Management Quarterly*, Vol. 14, No.1 (March 1983), p. 73.

2. *Ibid.*, p. 74.

3. *Ibid.*

4. L.C. Stuckenbruck, *The Implementation of Project Management* (Reading, Mass: Addison-Wesley, 1981).

5. B.N. Baker, D.C. Murphy, and D. Fisher, *Determinants of Project Success*, National Aeronautics and Space Administration, NGR-22-03-028, September 15, 1974, p. 669.

6. B.N. Baker, D.C. Murphy, and D. Fisher, "Factors Affecting Project Success," in D.I. Cleland and W.R. King, eds. *Project Management Handbook* (New York: Van Nostrand Rheinhold, 1983), pp. 670-671.

7. T.J. Peters and R.H. Waterman, Jr., *In Search of Excellence* (New York: Harper & Row, 1982).

8. B.N. Baker *et al.*, *Factors Affecting Project Success*, p. 678.

—————————————— Chapter 8 ——————————————
Conflict Management

In the complex world of project management where there are many interfaces and more than the usual amount of organizational complexity, conflict is inevitable. It has been claimed, and in some cases perhaps rightly so, that conflict is healthy since it stimulates competition, provides a challenging environment, and results in overall enhancement of individual and organizational performance. Many companies tend to avoid the project structure because of the fear that they will not be able to handle the conflict that will ensue.[1]

Before discussing the specific sources, types, and methods of coping with conflict in project management, let us examine the anatomy of interpersonal conflict—this is considered by many to be at the root of and part of all types of conflict.

8.1 The Anatomy of Interpersonal Conflict

The diversity in our sociocultural and economic backgrounds, values, individual personalities, education, life experiences and environment aggregate into a self image replete with a unique and complex blending of needs, perspectives, interests, priorities, attitudes and motivations. These in turn are instrumental in fostering within each of us conscious as well as subconscious standards of rational and acceptable behavior by which we tend to gauge and interpret those of others. We are, for instance, very quick in spotting inconsistencies in the behavioral patterns of others, yet are seldom, if ever, as quick, critical or judgmental in the assessment and evaluation of our own behavior. We often perceive deviations on the part of other people from our own concepts and relative standards of proper and acceptable behavior as threats, impediments, encumbrances and even irritants.

Our reactions to other people, whether conscious or subliminal, are a rational to us as other people's reactions and responses tend to be towards us given their perception of the nature and extent of our deviation from their own standards of rational and acceptable behavior. Nothing mandates that responses be either conscious, overt, valid, logical, immediate or understandable either to the participants themselves or any of the observers involved. In

Table 8.1: Analysis of Project/Functional Group Conflicts

Factor	Typical Functional System Response	Typical Project System Response	Source of Conflict
Scarcity of resources	Allocate use of all available resources across enterprise	Compete and use all available resources on project	Schedules/ priorities
Rate of change	Plan for future business needs	Focus on current business issues	Priorities/ schedules
Complexity	Develop and sustain needed expertise	Commit existing expertise	Personnel/ technical issues
Cost and risk	Diversify efforts to reduce overall risk	Concentrate on effort to reduce risk	Cost/profit/ technical issues

effect, interpersonal conflict, of some type or another, is both ubiquitous and pervasive wherever people live, work, learn, or play.[2]

8.2 Sources and Types of Conflict

(a) Sources of Conflict

Considering the approach to and process of project organization, the types of individuals generally involved, and the typical modes of operation, it is not surprising that the formation of a project invariably creates an environment for conflict. Among the considerations which promote conflict is the existence of two independent yet interlocking organizational systems—the functional and project systems—each of which has its own unique response to the four characteristic factors that prompt the need for project formation: complexity, rate of change, cost and risk, and scarcity of resources. Table 8.1 summarizes the general response of the functional and project organizations to each of these factors and notes the source of the conflict that generally results.

The primary sources of conflict on projects and their relative intensities during the various phases of the project's life cycle have been extensively investigated by Thamhain and Wilemon.[3] The results of their survey of 100 project managers showed that conflicts occurred primarily in the following areas:

- Schedules
- Priorities
- Manpower
- Technical issues
- Administration
- Personalities
- Cost

During the project formation and build-up phases, conflicts over priorities had the greatest intensity. During the main project and end of project phases, schedule conflict was greatest, whereas the intensity of personality conflicts remained essentially the same during all phases of the project life. The high intensity of conflict over schedules was attributed to the cumulative effect of project performance and personnel problems. Further, most managers chose the technique of confrontation for conflict resolution. The use of compromise and smoothing were second choices and used almost equally. Techniques for resolving conflicts are discussed later in this chapter. Finally, the investigators found that the negative effects of conflicts were faulty decision making, lengthy delays over unimportant issues, and disintegration of the team's effort.

Wilemon[4] and Wilemon and Cicero[5] found that the following conditions tended to initiate, amplify, and sustain the occurrence of conflicts:

- A generally unconventional reporting relationship between the project organization and management and among the project participants. Neither reporting relationship is constrained by the traditional format and highly structured chain of command and lines of communications.

- The temporary nature of the project organization, which promotes divided interests, allegiances, motivations, objectives, and goals among the participants and frequently diverts commitments, priorities and emphasis.

- In the matrix structure, the lack of direct or line authority on the part of the project manager in dealing with personnel and personnel matters. Project managers often fail to accept the fact that their authority generally lies in the realm of ideas rather than in command.

- The relative technical and managerial strengths and "balance" of the project manager. Balance is critical in sustaining the project manager's overall credibility, function as a mediator, and primary role as an integrator.

- Ambiguity in requirements, objectives, standards, procedures, roles, responsibilities, and interrelationships. This can be significantly influenced by the thoroughness of the front-end planning and iteration in the course of executing the project.

- Personal ambitions and biases along with a number of often imponderable personal and impersonal factors that result in typecasting people as either "in" or "out." This often prompts confrontation based upon assessment of people's relative status and "assailabilty" within the organization.

- Higher-management policies, indecisiveness, and hence lack of effective backing of the project or its management. Often higher-management tends to be divided on the merits of a particular direction and consequently of a specific undertaking. In such cases the project manager can find himself with little tangible support, a situation that is invariably recognized by the overall organizational constituency and hence contributes to conflict.

(b) Types of Conflict

Conflict within goal-oriented organizations can generally be described as technical, political, or personal. Conflict over technical issues is almost unavoidable by virtue of the nature of projects, the organizations, and personnel required to carry them out. Projects characteristically require a multidisciplinary approach to the resolution of diverse issues, and therein lies the basis for task-oriented conflict. Even within a specific engineering discipline, the solution to a given problem requires the art of compromise. The potential for conflict is amplified by the differences in training, experience,and perspectives among the project participants in their approach to the solution of problems. Technical conflict, however, is not always negative. Within the proper environment and under the proper conditions, conflict can be an effective stimulant to the exchange of innovative ideas. How effective such conflict will be is largely influenced by the actions of the project manager, especially his diplomacy in dealing with the project team and the organization at large. His failure to integrate the multidisciplinary team can not only inhibit the efficient execution of the effort but can also precipitate the more dysfunctional types of conflict.

The sources of political conflict are many and varied. They can include personal aspirations and biases, self-protection, cronyism, quid pro quos, expedience along with any number of other often imponderable considerations. Since political conflict is no less pervasive in private industry than it is in the public sector, it cannot be ignored. Perhaps the most realistic approach to dealing with political conflict is to become sensitized to it as a major force that should be inhibited or defused at every opportunity. The dysfunctional effects of political conflict can generally be lessened but not completely eliminated by the project manager through thoroughness of front-end planning. Escalation of problems encountered in the course of project planning, programming and execution to higher management for resolution invariably fuels political conflict and promotes suboptimal solution of problems. In general, the intensity of political conflict is a function not only of the role assumed by the project manager but his effectiveness in structuring and administering the execution of the given effort through his interaction with the project participants. Mismanagement of conflict, whether technical or political, can degenerate into intense personal conflict, perhaps the most debilitating of the three types of conflict.

Interpersonal conflict, however, is insidious and seems always to occur regardless of the presence of technical or political conflict. It can be prompted and intensified by any number of quiescent and imponderable factors which can be triggered, for example, by the mismanagement of situations in which individual feelings and emotions are strained and allowed to run out of control. It may not be possible for personal interactions to be totally devoid of conflict; however, it is the intensity of the conflict that ultimately matters in efforts to sustain a productive working relationship. A project manager thus needs to develop, on the basis of past experience or continued observation, an awareness of the residual or potential personality conflict among project participants and its likely impact upon the effort. In extreme cases, restructuring of the organization or even changes in the staffing of the project may be necessary.

8.3 Beneficial Versus Dysfunctional Aspects of Conflict

The effect of conflict upon an organization tends to be much like that of adrenalin upon the human body. Just as a certain amount of adrenalin energizes and sustains the body in times of exertion and stress, a certain amount of conflict within an organization challenges and stimulates it to perform. However, just as an over production of adrenalin can lead to tachycardia and severe cardiac distress, an excess of conflict can be similarly debilitating to the organization. Conflict is therefore not necessarily bad or good. Its ultimate effect depends upon the dosage. In proper doses, conflict stimulates individual psyches, prods egos, and fuels a healthy competitive spirit that can be used to advantage in promoting greater participant involvement and the generation, exchange and pursuit of innovative ideas and solutions to the problems at hand.

An overdose of conflict has the opposite effect upon the organization. Among the negative ways it can manifest itself are the following:[6]

- Factions and coalitions may form within the organization that extend and complicate the decision-making process and invariably result in suboptimal problem solving and decision making about performance, cost, or schedule parameters.

- Excessive and somewhat specious documentation symptomatic of burgeoning animosities may result from a combination of aggressive and defensive behavioral patterns.

- Delay and ultimate distortion of the underlying issues may occur with the passage of time.

- The involved individuals may redirect their interest, energies, and commitment and, in extreme cases, search for alternative employment within or outside the company.

Conflict can lead not only to the paralysis of the project organization but, also to its effective disintegration. Few competent individuals, dedicated to their professions and committed to their careers, are either inclined or compelled to tolerate mismanaged conflict, given the intense competition for talent in the marketplace. This is generally appreciated by corporate management. The ability to manage conflict is thus not only of operational importance but also should be viewed as practically important to those seeking advancement up the managerial ladder.

8.4 Essential Considerations in Managing Conflict

The first practical difficulty in managing conflict is determining what kind and how much conflict can be tolerated within the project organization, given the variable nature of problems, objectiveness, environmental conditions and individuals involved. The line of demarcation between beneficial and dysfunctional conflict is neither consistent nor sufficiently recognizable to allow for its effective exploitation even by seasoned managers much less by the neophyte thrust into the project environment. All of us have varying degrees of tolerance in dealing with stressful situations; what may be stressful to one is not stressful to another. Since conflict can cause stress, how long conflict can be allowed to continue is a moot point. It is difficult to measure the extent to which conflict can provide a positive driving force upon the organization. Conflict may thus be impractical as a management tool for all except those with highly developed skills in the management of human resources (discussed later in this chapter.)

The second practical difficulty in the management of conflict is in choosing an approach by which conflict is to be sustained and controlled by the manager. As a general rule, channeling conflict along positive lines requires the management of its nature, level,and intensity.

First, to the extent possible, conflict should be kept task oriented. Our approach to efforts is often influenced by our personal interests, inclinations, preferences and even organizational politics. A manager must strive to make allowances for these factors and control them through a clear definition of the problem, project objectives, extensive preparation, an open mind, observation and control of interactions through a relentless pursuit of facts and exchange of information among the participants.

Second, the secret to keeping conflict task oriented is predicated upon the manager's ability to confine conflict to the working level by searching out viable, acceptable alternatives to the problems of concern to the participants and keeping open channels of communication. Effective communication among participants generally precludes escalation of problems to levels of management at which solutions tend to be based on expediency or political considerations rather than on technical merits. The project manager should recognize that there are generally one or more acceptable approaches to the solution of nearly all problems.

Third, the intensity of conflicts can affect its nature, the level of manage-

——————————————— Table 8.2: Conflict Management ———————————————

Conflict Factors	Conflict Management Skills	Suggestions for Conflict Management
Nature	Observation	**Keep task oriented and impersonal** • Through thorough participative front-end planning (i.e., homework) • By supressing extreme demands, stands, inflammatory language, and ambiguities • By reiterating objectives to keep ends in mind and team on target • By monitoring the interaction and keeping an eye out for an equal balance between questions/answers versus comments/reactions
Level	Communication	**Keep it at working level** • Listen for bottom-line message as well as feelings; reflect understanding • Search out and distinguish facts from feelings • Do not judge, interpret, moralize, advise, joke, interrupt, ridicule, explain or command • Deal with facts but consider and, to the extent possible, accommodate feelings • Emphasize joint benefits while keeping in mind basic differences
Intensity	Negotiation	**Keep it under control** • Plan time, place, agenda, and participants • Seek clarifications and eliminate the likelihood of confusion • Verify all assertions • Collaborate so both can win; seek agreement on principles and generalities to suport through documentation, defer details for future agreement • Search out and provide immediate emotional gratification on secondary issues in exchange for primary longer-range gains

ment involvement, and the primary focus in its adjudication. This means that the focus and hence the solution can be unrelated to the underlying cause of conflict. Disagreements among participants that are allowed to escalate can easily transform productive task-oriented conflict into a debilitating personality conflict. Managing the intensity of conflict is not merely a function of the effectiveness of the communication process; it is equally a function of the effectiveness of the negotiation skills of the project manager.

The effective management of conflict is contingent upon acquiring the skills of understanding (by observation) the true nature of the conflict, communication with the involved parties, and negotiation.

8.5 Successful Management of Conflict

Table 8.2 presents the parallelism between conflict factors and required skills along with suggestions for positively maintaining and controlling conflict. In addition to these conflict management techniques are a number of approaches that have been presented for dealing with conflict.[7,8,9,10]

Figure 8.1: Alternative Strategies for Conflict Management

Avoidance/ Withdrawl	Defusion/ Postponement	Containment/ Compromise/ Smoothing	Confrontation/ Negotiation

Four of these approaches are shown in Figure 8.1 as a continuum of available options. In a dynamic, multivariate environment, no single approach can be relied on. A project manager must develop a repertoire of behavioral skills and the judgement of when such skills are called for. The ability to manage conflict is as much a function of the individual's acquired knowledge as his judgement and experience in dealing with people. As the folk song "The Gambler" advises, you have to know how to play the game, that is, when to make a move, when to withdraw, and when to hold your ground. Each of the approaches can be a winning strategy or a losing one depending on the problem, the requirements, aggregation of people, circumstances, timing, and managerial attributes.

Avoidance or withdrawal typically entails retreat from a possible conflict situation. Although clearly such an approach seldom, if ever, resolves a problem, it may under certain circumstances be the most expeditious approach to some types of conflict. As Stimac points out, "If your head and your gut augur disaster, then run."[11] It is sometimes far better to withdraw than to aggravate a situation by muddling through because of lack of skill or knowledge or because of other equally compelling considerations.

Defusion through postponement also has positive as well as negative aspects. Certainly, there is merit in postponing confrontation in cases where emotions seriously threaten to take over a situation or have done so. Time tends to promote healing, but time also tends to distort people's recollections and perceptions of facts and issues. Suppression of conflict by postponement often promotes its resurgence in other forms and as part of other issues, generally at unpredictable and inopportune times.

Smoothing or compromising involves a search for solutions that afford some degree of satisfaction to all of the parties at odds. This may be brought about by emphasizing areas of agreement while playing down and progressively reconciling areas of disagreement. The danger in this approach is one of suboptimal problem solving while trying to please "all of the people all of the time." Still, it is often preferable to either avoidance or postponement, both of which fail to come to grips with problems that are immediate and pressing.

Most experts agree that confrontation is the most desirable of all of the available approaches to conflict management. This approach involves attacking disagreements directly in a problem-solving mode to induce the affected parties to work out their disagreements. It is undoubtedly the most positive and potentially productive of all approaches since it can furnish solutions to the issues in question that all affected parties can live with.[12]

Figure 8.2: Linear Responsibility Chart

	Center Director	Marketing Manager	Proposal Manager	Contracts Manager	Accounting Manager	Project Manager	Task Leader(s)
Establish business objectives.	1	3		4			
Identifying business opportunities	2	1					
Decision to seek specific technical work.	1	3	4	4		4	
Prepare technical proposal	2	4	1				
Prepare cost proposal.	2	4	4	1	3		
Accept customer's contract	5	5	5	1	4		
Appoint project manager.	1					3	
Prepare technical plans	2					1	4
Organize technical team	2					1	3
Supervise technical work.						2	1
Submit technical reports	4					1	4
Submit cost invoices				2	1	3	
Deliver final end products	5			5	5	1	4
Submit final invoice	5			2	1	3	
Close the contract.	3	4		1	5		

Code:

1 actual responsibility   4 may be consulted
2 general supervision   5 must be notified
3 must be consulted

Source: J.R. Wells, research paper, "Institute of Safety & Systems Management," University of Southern California, 1979.

A final method of conflict resolution when an impasse has been reached is to call for a decision by higher management. This is a method that should be used seldom and only under special circumstances when lower-level managers cannot resolve their problems. Such a situation could develop, say, where a functional manager and a project manager have need for a company resource such as a facility or personnel during the same time frame. In matters of who has jurisdiction and where responsibility lie, the use of a linear responsibility chart can be very helpful (Figure 8.2).

In general, the preceding suggestions are geared to the confrontation (negotiation) or problem-solving approach in the resolution of conflict. The ultimate choice of a specific strategy should be dictated by the nature, circumstances, and timing of a situation as assessed through careful analysis and mature judgement.

Since conflict is not a characteristic of organizational behavior peculiar only to projects, management literature is replete with approaches for resolving conflicts. Kast and Rosenzweig list a set of approaches that are similar to those discussed here: withdrawal, smoothing, compromise, and forcing.[13]

Organizational behavior specialists use still other closely related conflict-handling modes, for example, competing, collaborating, compromising, avoiding, accommodating.[14,15,16]

——— **Questions and Topics for Discussion** ———

1. What are possible sources of conflict in relationships between (a) project managers and functional managers, (b) a project manager and other project managers, (c) project management and administration, (d) project management and the customer, and (e) a project manager and a subcontractor?

2. What is meant by the term *dysfunctional behavior*? How can it be mitigated?

3. Describe the various types of conflict in a project and their possible results.

4. Give examples of how the presence of conflict in a project organization can be a positive force or a negative force.

5. Why is some conflict in an organization inevitable?

6. What issues or areas of involvement of project management can be expected to be primary sources of conflict?

7. What are the pros and cons of resorting to higher management to resolve a conflict between a project manager and a functional manager?

8. How should a project manager deal with organizational politics?

9. Why is it important for the project manager to defuse interpersonal conflict within his project?

10. What are ways by which a project manager can resolve a bitter interpersonal conflict within his project?

11. A key engineer working on your project in a matrix-type organization is not fully responsive to your requests and seems disinterested in his work assignment. What would you do to improve the situation?

———————————— **References** ————————————

1. Harold Kerzner, *Project Management: A Systems Approach to Planning, Scheduling, and Controlling* (New York: Van Nostrand Rheinhold, 1979), p. 247.

2. Michele Stimac, "Strategies for Resolving Conflict: their Functional and Dysfunctional Sides," *Personnel* (November-December 1982), p. 37.

3. Hans J. Thamhain and David L. Wilemon, "Conflict Management in Project Life Cycles," *Sloan Management Review* (Spring 1975), pp. 31-50.

4. David L. Wilemon, "Project Management and Its Conflicts," *Chemtech* (September 1972).

5. David L. Wilemon and John P. Cicero, "The Project Manager—Anomalies and Ambiguities," *Academy of Management Journal* (September 1970).

6. Wilemon, "Project Management and Its Conflicts," p. 42.

7. R.A. Cosier and T.L. Ruble, "Research on Conflict—Handling Behavior—An Experimental Approach," *Academy of Management Journal*, Vol. 24, No. 4, (1981), pp. 816-831.

8. J. Sullivan et al. "The Relationship Between Conflict Resolution Approaches & Trust—A Cross-Cultural Study," *Academy of Management Journal*, Vol. 24, No. 4, (1981), pp. 803-815.

9. Daryl G. Milton and Betty Lilligren-Milton, *Management Clout* (Englewood Cliffs, N.J.: Prentice-Hall, 1980).

10. George M. Prince "Creative Meetings Through Power Sharing," *Harvard Business Review* (July-August 1972).

11. Stimac, "Strategies for Resolving Conflict," p. 42.

12. Kerzner, *Project Management*, p. 268.

13. F.E. Kast and J.E. Rosenzweig, *Organization and Management* (New York, N.Y.: McGraw-Hill 1974), p. 594.

14. R.M. Steers, *Introduction to Organizational Behavior* (Santa Monica, Calif.: Goodyear, 1981), pp. 220-230.

15. Norman B. Sigband, *Communication for Management* (Glenview, Ill.: Scott, Foresman, 1969).

16. David R. Hampton, Charles E. Summer and Ross A. Webber, *Organizational Behavior and the Practice of Management* (Glenview, Ill.: Scott, Foresman, 1968).

———————————— Chapter 9 ————————————
Improving Productivity

9.1 Introduction

The sagging economy, prompted in part by the erosion of this country's competitive position in the international marketplace, has made productivity* a household word and a source of widespread concern. The disturbing trend in American productivity is shown in Figure 9.1. An unlikely coalition has emerged between informed management, professionals, and labor placing the blame for this condition squarely on the shoulders of American management.

A poll by the American Institute of Industrial Engineers revealed that 51% of the engineering professionals and 64% of the labor representatives surveyed attributed low productivity to management concentration on short-term profits at the expense of long-range goals.[1] This has been further reinforced by Judson's findings in a survey of 195 corporations representative of 36 industries, in which approximately 60% of the 236 senior managers polled felt

---

* Although the subject of productivity is treated here in a general manner, it has special applicability to project management and systems development, including projects whose aim is to improve design, development, and manufacturing capabilities.

—————————— **Figure 9.1: Inflation Versus U.S. Productivity Growth** ——————————

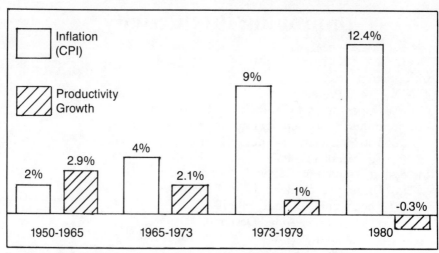

Source: T. Murrin, "Why Industrial Productivity Is As Important As Military Arms," *Government Executive*, Vol. 13, No. 10 (October 1981), p. 39. ©1981.

that the problem of low productivity was generally the fault of management.[2] Overall, management's track record in this area has been very poor. Of the companies surveyed one-quarter had no data on productivity and one-third had actually experienced a decline in productivity once the data had been corrected for inflation.[3]

As in the case of Mark Twain's observation about the weather, the subject has elicited a lot of talk but little in terms of substantive action. The reason stems from its overall complexity and the interaction of the issues involved. A good portion of it also stems from the diverging perspectives on the proper vesting of responsibility for productivity. Top management tends to view it as the responsibility of operating management, whereas the latter typically considers it to be a top management initiative that has not been given either proper attention or adequate backing. Compounding the problem are very narrow definitions of productivity and varying perceptions as to the constituent considerations, including approaches that should be taken toward improving productivity.

Increased productivity is an effort in which all levels of management must have a role. It is a key consideration in successful project management and system development in a turbulent market and is of paramount importance to an improvement in the national economy.

9.2 The Essence of Productivity

Productivity deals with the overall aspect of organizational efficiency and effectiveness as generally viewed in terms of the ratio of the value of outputs to the sum total of applied inputs over a given period of time.* Organizational outputs are typically tangible and measurable in the form of products and services. Organizational inputs, however, are usually not as clearly definable as they consist of a combination of tangible and intangible elements.

Clearly, tangible inputs include such elements as capital, facilities, equipment, and labor required for the generation of the desired outputs. The magnitude and extent of these requirements, including their effective and efficient utilization particularly in technologically intensive industries, are generally strongly driven by the ideas, talent, motivation and commitment of the corporate constituency to a given course of action. These intangible elements are the critical ingredients in the process of innovation typically involving the generation of ideas and their successful conversion into products. John W. Kendrick has estimated that a full 40% of America's growth in productivity over the last half century must be attributed to innovation compared with 15% due to increases in the amount of capital used by each worker.[4] Ginzberg and Vojta explain it as follows: "it is the expansion of knowledge, skills, imagination, ideas and insights of working people that creates the margins from which physical capital is accumulated, leading from productive investments to the further accumulation of capital."[5]

9.3 General Impediments to Productivity Improvement

Galbraith points out that in our technologically evolving, progressively more complex and competitive environment, there has been an increasing tendency for the individual to sustain the organization rather than as in years past to have the organization sustain the individual.[6] This is often a difficult proposition for management to fully accept for a number of reasons.

First, much of the difficulty stems from the higher rate of evolution of technology in relation to the managerial rate of assimilation of technological change across the range of disciplines that typify modern project management and system development. This condition has had a tendency to accelerate obsolescence even in technical management ranks and has thereby, to a large extent, usurped the superior-subordinate role which management used to enjoy in part based upon presumably greatly superior knowledge and experience. As noted by Diebold, "One difficulty in the whole history of applying technology has been that it's rare to find an entrepreneur who not only thinks about the mission of the enterprise, but who is familiar enough with the technology to know which way it's going."[7] At no time has this been more of a problem than at present, nor is it likely to become less of a problem in the future. In general, it can be said that the higher the management level, the greater the likelihood that it will be technically out of date and consequently the more likely it is to be uncomfortable with the advancing technology, as

---

* Productivity is most commonly thought of in terms of economic output (GNP with modifications) divided by the economic input in person-hours of labor. This is operationally too restrictive.

well as with its practitioners. Correspondingly, management will frequently tend to impede and delay the pursuit and timely implementation of new and innovative ideas. There is a great deal of truth to the often heard, although somewhat cynical, observation that there tend to be two basic types of people working at the forefront of technology: "those who understand what they do not manage and those who manage what they do not understand."* As Patton observed, "The sad fact is that management, rather than face up to the problem of today's industrial scene, too often seems to operate on the basis of a series of well-established myths that inhibit rather than enhance its effectiveness."[8]

The point is that the rate of technological evolution has forced a degree of intrusive parity in employer/employee relations and has promoted a need for a new climate of mutual respect, confidence, cooperation, and shared responsibility, which are essential to stimulating innovation and productivity. This can only occur at the expense of the generally entrenched traditional view of the management function and posture, which typically ascribes to centralized planning and direction as well as structured communication and control. To many, the current environment is highly unsettling, if not personally threatening, and consequently very difficult to adapt to and accept. Pascale and Athos quote an executive who expresses a generally pervasive and suppressed view in industry: "Everybody says, 'the test of a true executive [manager] is that you have men working for you who can replace you so you can move up.' That's a lot of baloney—The manager is afraid of the bright young guy coming up. Fear is always prevalent in corporate structures."[9]

Second, the frequent inability of management to relate to individual and group needs is often aggravated by the broad social, political and cultural changes of the past 20 years. The latter have led to the evolution of an apparently irreversible "psychology of entitlement," whereby the work force increasingly perceives not only a right to a job but also one conducive to self-fulfillment.[10,11] According to AT&T findings based on longitudinal studies, the profile also includes a "dispirited new generation of [younger] managers," who want "primarily an interesting job, emotional sustenance from peers...no heavy commitment to the organization." They share "pessimism about organizational rewards, little inclination to assume leadership and an equal disdain for following others" as they tend to perceive that "people in authority often earn it with time rather than ability."[12] The unfortunate implication for productivity appears to be that those who could provide technological leadership are seemingly not inclined to do so and a large body of those who presume to do so don't. The latter group often exude the spirit of the leader in the French Revolution who was overheard to say, "There go my people, I will try to find out where they are going so that I can lead them there."[13]

Whether one subscribes to the philosophy of relative modern day Calvinism as typified by the old guard, or espouses the Egalitarianism of the younger,

---

* Sometimes referred to as "Putt's law," source unknown.

"ME," generation, the fact is that there is a clear-cut disparity in values between those considered as "bosses" and those characterized as "workers" which
must be accommodated as it seriously inhibits stimulation of productivity
within our corporate world.[14] Howard and Wilson state, "Though some organizations may be willing to adjust their implied psychological contracts
with employees, resistance to substantive structure change is apt to be intense,
especially if change were to threaten traditional power and authority relationships."[15]

Under such conditions, namely, cosmetic realignments, there can be little
expectation of marked improvements in productivity considering the current
state of evolution of our socio-cultural and political environments. In addition, there is mounting recognition by those with highly marketable skills of
the ultimate economic value of their contributions and the leverage this gives
them. Even such entrepreneurs as Henry Ford and Sewell Avery had to
eventually concede, if not abdicate, to groups of men sharing specialized information required for the operation of the enterprise.[16]

Lastly, management frequently makes no attempt to relate to individual
and group needs, as the cost effectiveness of the intangible factors is not
directly quantifiable in specifically actionable terms and thus frequently fails
to attract and hold requisite management attention and priority. This is not to
say that the importance of intangible factors has not been recognized and
generally accepted by industry. An ever-increasing number of companies are
reflecting the importance of these factors in their corporate creeds. However,
commitment to these factors and execution at operating levels cannot be met
through corporate pronouncements of virtuous ends. "Institutional doctrine
is never a frank description of the practice...of the institution."[17] The unfortunate truth is that the major problem is most frequently generated at that amor-
phous level known as "upper-middle management" which causes, for some of
the aforementioned reasons, many American corporations

> "to treat individual workers as little more than hired hands. This
> practice tends to deny the validity of feelings, emotions, and loyalty
> in the work place. To deny the existence of individual feelings and
> emotions of self-worth through the exclusive use of traditional crite-
> ria, such as profit or sales, simply drives these phenomena under-
> ground. Perceptual screens that do not permit recognition of indi-
> viduals lead to a management that is out of touch with human nature.
> Reality becomes rationalized and responses to human beings become
> mechanized."[18]

This is underscored by the results of a poll conducted by a major and generally very progressive corporation in which 50% of its employees, much to the
surprise of management, either "strongly agreed" or "tended to agree" that
their company was losing touch with its employees.

The preceding are among the primary reasons why overall success in
increasing productivity has proven elusive and why, for the most part, efforts

in this area have been narrow in scope, gravitating primarily towards cost savings of some type or other in some part of the company or another. As pointed out by Judson, for many companies, productivity improvement has yet to evolve beyond a host of "separate, uncoordinated initiatives, directed at 'whatever we're hurting' at the moment—reducing scrap and rework, for example, or reducing absenteeism and accidents, tightening standards, or correcting the abuse of work breaks and lunch periods.[19] In medical parlance this is treating symptoms rather than the patient.

Few seem to have recognized and fewer yet have accepted the proposition that improvement in productivity is a long and arduous task requiring a comprehensive and coordinated effort, sound management practices, rigorous training, and conditioned acceptance of the human side of the enterprise. This lack of current recognition and acceptance stems in part from the short-term, quick-fix mentality of management that has been fostered over the past two decades by a host of frequently unanticipated political, economic, as well as technological conditions and considerations.

Abernathy attributes a major portion of our decline in competitiveness to a change in the "origin and experience base of management personnel" since the mid-fifties.[20] He points to a statistical trend during the sixties and the early seventies towards a greater population of top management positions by individuals with financial and legal backgrounds as opposed to those with production, engineering, or scientific backgrounds as in earlier years. This trend has generally promoted the proliferation and entrenchment of a formal and financially based management control philosophy that frequently lacks appreciation for the potential of technology. A case in point cited by Abernathy is the electronics firm that in the early 1970s concluded upon completion of its formal market research effort that pocket calculators held no market potential. It is not surprising that we increasingly see ourselves as "becoming a nation based on fear: fear of taking risk, fear of change, and fear of being sued."[21]

In view of this management bias, it is not surprising that more than 75% of the executives surveyed by Judson indicated that their company's commitment to the objective of improving productivity was typically restricted to a time frame of a year or less.[22] On such a time scale these efforts are highly unlikely to yield positive, long-lasting results and may well prove disappointing in view of the "go for it" philosophy of implementation which has been characteristic of the approach to the application of management concepts. Robinson alludes to this tendency in his assessment of the problems associated with the implementation of quality circles when he observes:

> "Oh no," I thought to myself, "here we go again." I had seen my friend flit from fad to fad over the years with the same unerring results. Nothing! He had tried every new management idea that came down the pike in the last 20 years. He had been enamored with PERT, MBO, GRID, sensitivity training, team building, zero defects, and others at one time or another. One always knew about what was

"in" at any time because he was trying it in his organization. Yet, here we were, years later, still looking for the magic wand that would solve all his and his organization's problems. My only real surprise was that it had taken him so long to discover this latest activity.[23]

Is Total Quality Management (TQM) yet another such craze? As a result of the above, the questions can be asked: "What, if not all of the above, does productivity improvement embody?" "What, then, does the optimum approach to the productivity improvement involve?

9.4 Preconditions to Productivity Improvement

(a) The Management Planning Factor

There are two basic preconditions to effecting an improvement in productivity. The first is management planning. There is a dictum of management that states that superior, even flawless, execution is fruitless if the plans are faulty. Productivity improvement is contingent upon the implementation of explicit plans which must be consistent with and supportive of the organization's overall long-range business interests. These plans and interests must be congruent with the projected direction of the evolving technology and market place by way of assuring the inherent soundness of pursuits in terms of their prospects of marketability. This consideration is of fundamental importance as it goes to the core of the ultimate efficiency and effectiveness of utilization of committed resources. In other words, *commitment of company resources to ill-chosen pursuits cannot be conducive to improvements in organizational productivity.**

Sound product-line planning should generally lead to increased demand and should thus provide the required stimulus along with the best rationale for the replacement and addition of equipment to increase output. The latter is among the most critical factors requiring management attention today. The pursuit of innovation, however, has not been accompanied by a commensurate concentration on updating the means of production. This is evident from the rate of investment in the United States today, which runs at approximately 10% of the GNP. By comparison, Germany expends 15% and Japan 20%.[24]

When confined to manufacturing, the data historically depict an even greater lag (Table 9.1). As a consequence, the average age of industrial equipment in this country has crept up to the 23-year level compared with the 9-year average that experts consider optimum. Even the U.S. government is struggling to reduce the average age of its machinery to 18 years.[25] This situation has been prompted in large part by an accounting process "originally designed for an agrarian economy, characterized by manual labor and static technology and used as a short-term model for the purpose of measuring management performance during a single year."[26] As Avard and colleagues

---

* This lack of organization productivity can occur even though personnel are innovative and productive within the framework of a poorly chosen pursuit.

Table 9.1: Investment and Productivity in the U.S. and Other Industrial Nations, 1960-1976

Country	Percent Increase in Productivity Manufacturing	Investment as Percentage of GNP
Japan	9.0	31.3
Germany	5.9	25.2
Netherlands	6.4	23.7
Belgium	6.5	20.5
Italy	5.9	21.0
France	5.7	22.2
Canada	3.8	21.6
United Kingdom	3.3	17.5
United States	2.2	14.2

Source: Lawrence A. Skantze, "Productivity: Making It Good Enough, Fast Enough, Soon Enough," *Program Manager*, Vol. 10, No. 6 (November-December 1981), p. 11.

---

point out "The effect of advances in technology is to render capital assets obsolete many years before they can be expected to wear out."[27] Such conditions often make replacement difficult to justify to an accounting mentality. Tax laws in our country have not helped matters. In terms of first-year allowable depreciation, the United States is reportedly in fifth place behind Japan, the United Kingdom, Canada, and Switzerland.

The Economic Recovery Tax Act of 1981 (ERTA) gave considerable relief and incentive to industry to update and replace assets. This provided for greatly accelerated write-offs for investments in plant and equipment acquired as of 1981 and beyond, regardless of whether the acquired assets were new or used. In addition, it gave significant tax credits from the time the assets were placed in service, except for real property. All this greatly increased the desirability of modernization and replacement based on accounting methods typically used for their evaluation.

The second and somewhat questionable aspect of ERTA, however, was that it provided a 25% tax credit for certain R&D expenditures regardless of whether they were funded internally or contracted outside the organization. Since the major portion of the R&D expense consists of wages and salaries of personnel engaged in the more creative and speculative pursuits, it may be argued that this provision was a disincentive to the rigorous review and reassessment of the soundness and yield of the corporate longer-range product-line planning and R&D efforts. The approximate level of waste is addressed in Section 12.1(b).

As the saying goes, however, the government giveth and the government taketh away. As of this writing the dust is yet to settle on the Tax Reform Act of 1986. One thing appears certain: The repeal of investment tax relief laws, increased tax complexities and the threat of budget balancing tax increases do not bode well for "high tech." As technical corrections to the Tax Reform Act of 1986 continue to be hammered out by Congress and the IRS, watered down versions of various tax credits could still provide big perks for the alert or-

Table 9.2 Achievement of Productivity

Productivity			
Requires	**Implies**	**Commands**	**Yields**
Skill	Training Experience	Performance Quality	Effectiveness
Will	Understanding Motivation	Awareness Drive Perseverence	Efficiency

ganization. Such technical corrections, however, must close down "counter-productive" loop holes and abuses. Investment in the corporation must be based as much on economic grounds as on favorable tax breaks.

(b) The Human Factor

The second precondition to productivity improvement stems from a corollary to the management dictum presented earlier, namely, that superior, even flawless, planning will be greatly impeded and significantly degraded by a lack of broad-based commitment to its execution. The quest for increased productivity requires a two-pronged effort by management. Traditionally, management focus and preoccupation has been with the best available concentration of skill, implying a need for a composite of experience and training in the pursuit of performance and quality. As shown in Table 9.2, these efforts are inherently geared toward the effective, as opposed to the efficient, accomplishment of goals. Creativity, innovation, and commitment to a course of action, however, require the type of willingness on the part of the work force that comes from a combination of knowledge of what is expected and, more important, a belief that it is worthwhile. The latter suggests a need for motivation, commands greater awareness, drive, and perseverance, and results in a greater degree of organizational efficiency in the pursuit of goals. Management posture towards employees is critically important from the standpoint of its overall effect on attitudes and actions.

9.5 Increasing Productivity Through Automation

(A) Driving Forces for Automation

The combination of management's preoccupation with the near term, labor's escalating demands, and the evolution of a psychology of entitlement have contributed to a disastrous erosion of productivity in the United States by comparison to the rest of the industrialized world. By several accounts, the average Japanese automobile worker outproduces his American counterpart by a factor of 2 to 1 while drawing one-half of his hourly wage.[28,29] The overall picture is not better in other industries. Much has been made of the attitudinal differences between the workers in the two countries, which no doubt abound, but this does not completely account for such large differences.

Unquestionably, significant gains in productivity could be achieved in this country through a combination of modernization and greater automation of its means of production. Surveys suggest that labor, engineering professionals, and management agree on the need to spend more on modern equipment and facilities by margins well in excess of 70%.[30,31] Whether this will result in positive, across-the-board action remains to be seen as there is still a considerable amount of resistance to longer-range financial commitments and union insistence on the preservation of a highly labor-intensive approach to production. It has been reported, for instance, that as of 1979 there were a total of 35,000 industrial robots installed worldwide. Japan accounted for 30,000 of the total, Western Europe for 3,000, and the United States for the balance, 2,000. There can consequently by little question as to one of the main causes of the difference of 30% in the productivity growth rate between Japan and the U.S. in the time interval between 1975 and 1979. There appears, however, to be some disparity in the total number of industrial robots in the world— Japan's robot population has been estimated between 14,200 in 1981 [32] to more than 90,000 as of 1982.[33]

In spite of resistance to automation its rate will undoubtedly increase in the future. There are several reasons for this.

First, the progressively insurmountable advantages of automation in the areas of cost, uniformity throughput, safety and operational flexibility when viewed against the growing complexity and stringency of technological requirements. It has been estimated that use of robots in industry costs less than a third of the cost of labor. It has been projected that if General Motors had the number of robots in 1982 that it planned to have by 1990, it would have been realizing annual savings of three-quarters of a billion dollars.[34]*

Second, the increasing scarcity of a skilled and stable labor base vis-a-vis the increasing demand for high-technology products coupled with projected shortages of entry-level personnel. According to a National Tooling and Machining Association study, at least 2,000 additional journeymen machinists are currently needed in the aerospace industry alone. Congress has expressed concern over declining emphasis on science and mathematics beyond the ninth grade among students and its negative impact upon a society growing progressively more dependant on science and technology.†

Third, the growing advocacy for automation is prompted by an increased transfusion of the "computer generation" into the managerial ranks formerly populated mostly by the "slide-rule generation."

Fourth, the mounting recognition of the need to train (or retrain) for the higher level of skill demanded by the current projected job market.

---

* It was estimated that GM had approximately 300 industrial robots as of 1982. By 1990 it has been set that this number should equal 14,000.

† This was noted as early as 1981. See: *Staff Report of the Committee on Science and Technology*, U.S. House of Representatives, 97th Congress, 1st Session (June 1981), pp. 189-190.

Finally, the dwindling influence and hold of the union movement on the worker. Since 1947 nonagrarian labor force unionization has declined from 34% to about 24% at the present time.[35] Even attempts at unionization of the fastest growing sector of the economy, namely, governmental and office workers, is not likely to restore the unions to their former preeminence owing to restrictive legislation on strikes.

The inevitability of automation is perhaps best summarized in the words of James Baker of General Electric: "Any manufacturing operation of any size that is not actively pursuing productivity enhancing automation measures is on death row. It is a factory—and a business with no future."[36] In terms of choices faced by U.S. business, Baker points out the stark realty: "automation, emigration or evaporation."[37]

(b) The Potential of Automation

Scenarios depicting the future extent of industrial automation are appearing with increasing frequency in a number of trade and professional journals. Among the more interesting and prophetic was that of Eugene Merchant. At a meeting of the American Association of Engineering Societies in May 1982, he provided a technological vignette, which can be summarized as follows:[38]

Product design through final assembly and inspection in the near future will take place through a process of interactive communication between people and computers. People will provide the creative work and the design concept, whereas the computer will provide storage, standardized information for carrying out design calculations, producibility improvements, and a host of other activities including the following:

- Production planning and scheduling of the type of equipment and processes, sequence of operations, operation conditions, and so on

- Set-up, tool selection, material handling, part fabrication, transfer and unit assembly

- Process self-monitoring, process optimization, part inspection, and rework or replacement as required

- Machine and equipment self-diagnoses and repair as needed and appropriate

These functions are shown schematically in Figure 9.2 and are similar in concept to General Electric's view of the automated factory in Figure 9.3. The inference in such accounts, is one of futurism which frequently does not do justice to the potential level of automation currently possible or considered imminent based upon the fast paced developments in this area as, for instance, in the fields of Computer-Aided Design (CAD) and Computer-Aided

—————————— Figure 9.2: A View of the Automated Factory ——————————

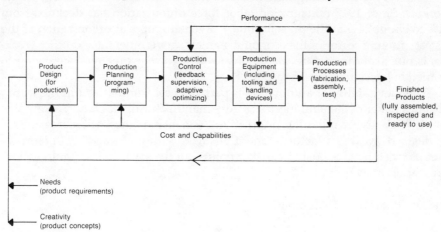

Source: "The Automated Factory: Technology Paves the Way to Improved Productivity,"
Compressed Air, (September 1982), p. 8.

Manufacturing (CAM). This technology, aside from being characterized by explosive development, is so new that only a relatively small number of individuals in an equally small segment of the academic and industrial communities are familiar with it. To place the current status of CAD/CAM in proper perspective, along with their potential for productivity improvement, each is briefly addressed in the following sections.

Computer-Aided Design (CAD)

An increasing number of companies are either phasing in or expanding CAD/CAM capabilities within their organizations. A CAD system is typically built around a microcomputer with an interactive graphics terminal and peripherals such as plotters and printers that enable the engineer to perform a variety of design functions in one of several engineering disciplines based upon mathematical modeling techniques. The terminal is generally used to develop a geometric model of a part descriptive of its general size and shape, which in turn can be added to the geometric data base and used not only in subsequent design efforts but also as input for numerically controlled (NC) machinery. The net effect of this capability is that a host of geometrically similar parts can be produced at a later date at a fraction of the time and cost. This capability also extends to tooling and fixturing. CAD systems typically offer engineering the capability of calculating and iterating a host of design characteristics and parameters such as area, volume, weight, center of gravity, and stresses based on loading conditions and profiles, all virtually at a touch of the computer keyboard.

Recent advances in solid modeling and an explosive proliferation in the availability of software have greatly expanded capabilities in the CAD area

Figure 9.3: The GE Automated Factory Concept

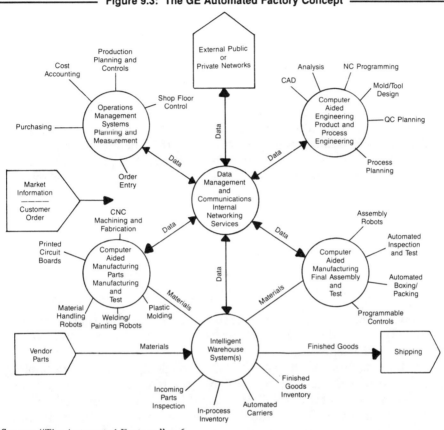

Source: "The Automated Factory," p. 6.

and have provided the basis for the integration of CAD with CAM. These advances in modeling currently make it possible to perform an analysis of a range of very complex motions that heretofore have required lengthy and cumbersome solutions. In addition, specialized simulation software is currently available that in some cases makes it unnecessary to engage in costly and time-consuming prototype development. Today the engineer can manipulate and optimize the design at the computer terminal in an ever-increasing number of areas as well as generate all of the necessary flowcharts, logic diagrams, engineering drawings, and illustrations at the push of a button. International Harvester, for instance, completed the design effort on a new diesel engine a while back, a year ahead of schedule and at an estimated savings of 33% in overall hours of labor (inclusive of design, drafting, analysis, checking, and project management) required by traditional methods. Their experience suggests that in the areas of design and drafting, savings by comparison to conventional methods range from 3 to 1 to as high as 30 to 1 depending upon the size and complexity of the parts.[39]

The current state of the art in CAD has the potential of extending engineering influence and control far beyond the engineering office and deeply into the previously exclusive domain of the manufacturing organization. The geometric data base previously discussed can be used, for example, to program numerically controlled machines through user prompting at the design terminal. A number of turnkey CAD/CAM systems, some of which have been specifically designed with smaller companies in mind, currently incorporate capabilities described as follows:*

> In a typical system, the terminal screen displays a menu from which the user selects the machine to cut the part. Then another menu appears that allows the user to select cutter size, type of material, feeds and speeds, material thicknesses, and a clearance plane above which the tool must rise when not cutting. Next, the screen displays the geometric model on which the user defines machining operations for the periphery of the part, cutouts, pockets, or holes. User-defined machining operations such as rough cuts, finish cuts, and scribing are indicated on the screen by various types of lines such as solid, dashed, or phantom. From these input data software in the system automatically generates NC instructions to machine the part.[40]

There are currently CAD/CAM systems on the market offering voice input (command) as an option. One such system can reportedly handle a vocabulary in excess of 250 phrases.

The limiting factor in the use of CAD no longer appears to be technology per se as much as the relative cost and availability of the software, although even the availability of the "solid" software is becoming less of a limitation as competition intensifies and the number of sources increase.[†] The main thrust in software development is currently to extend the geometric data base to the more generalized and arbitrary geometries. Even in this area a major breakthrough seems to have been made by General Electric's introduction of its "System Design" software package, which reportedly allows for the easy modeling of complex, arbitrary geometries through a process analogous to the sculpturing of clay.

Computer-Aided Manufacturing (CAM)

A number of rather sophisticated computer-based manufacturing systems are available and in use today in industry. Computer control has been extended to such areas as production planning and control, material handling, flexible machining, process control, testing, and quality assurance. For the

---

* Some such systems are available for well under $100,000.

† Daratech Associates of Cambridge, Mass., has published a directory of 44 suppliers of CAD/CAM systems. There are, in addition, at this time at least two dozen sources for state-of-the-art, "solid" model software.

most part, however, these systems tend to operate in functionally independent or compartmentalized modes based upon: (1) the general variability and to some extent uncertainty inherent in the manufacturing process and (2) a prevailing lack of interfacing standards within the computer industry which up until now have inhibited intercommunication between devices from different manufacturers.

If the recent developments in electronics and particularly computer technology are omitted, the evolutionary pattern of automated machinery and equipment has been primarily oriented in the direction of "hard" automation, that is, automation in specific and well-defined areas involving large and continuing production runs. This was fostered as much by the above noted factors as by economic issues which in some cases today are a legacy constituting one of the impediments to a considerable amount of potentially warranted modernization. The Ford Motor Company is a case in point. One of its most highly automated facilities included a plant that had been designed and implemented for the production of eight-cylinder engines. When marketing conditions forced Ford to shift to six-cylinder engines, Ford found it necessary to close down the plant as the extent and cost conversion proved to be far too great.[41]

Technological advances over the past decade, as in electro-optics, robotics, and most notably the microprocessor and microcomputer areas, are currently able to decrease some of the variability and uncertainty in manufacturing. These advances, in combination with a trend within the computer industry to resolve the problem of intercommunication between devices through the establishment of a protocol to permit data exchanges in large computer networks, are paving the way for the rapid automation and integration of the manufacturing function.

Space limitations do not allow for a complete review of the state of the art of CAD/CAM. Rather, we want to emphasize the significant role that computers already play in many areas of manufacturing and their potential for productivity improvement.

Production Planning and Control

Production planning and control systems are of fundamental importance in CAM. A number of such systems are currently available that, despite being functionally independent, offer the capability of eliminating years of tedious, error-prone, recurring effort. In this section we review a typical production planning and control system to illustrate not only the capability of some of the systems currently in place but also their relative proximity to the evolution of a fully integrated CAD/CAM capability.

In some of the larger, more complex manufacturing operations, the production planning and control system integrates the functions of several computer-based systems as shown in Figure 9.4. These may be subdivided into the following categories:

- A grouping of several independently operated function systems

Figure 9.4: Production Control System

Simplified sequence of operation in which the input data are translated weekly into the material requirements plan and related action documents

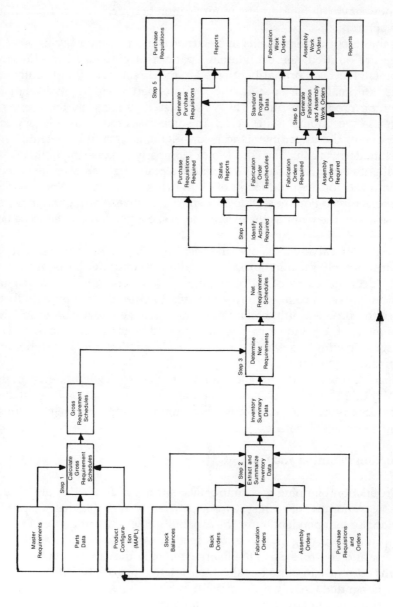

Source: Hughes Aircraft Co., "Production Control at Hughes, El Segundo," February 1977, p. 25.

that provide daily operating (control) information and inputs to the so called material requirement planning (MRP) system.

- The MRP system proper, which performs the time-phased prioritization of requirements based on actual orders or forecasts. This system has received considerable attention and is gaining extensive use in many segments of the industrial community.[42]

- Usually some type of a capacity requirements planning (CRP) system that extracts MRP information for the purpose of giving management visibility to enhance the use of available capacity.

The general advantages of such systems are an improved mix and reduced inventory level throughout the production cycle, reduced purchasing and operating costs, and general improvement in overall resource use. These systems are especially important to management involved with production as well as to projects including production improvements.

In the system shown in Figure 9.4, the master requirements file contains deliverable quantities and due dates for all of the end items and required spares along with information on their "sold" positions. This file also contains the bill of materials, serial numbers, project codes, cost accounts, and "make" departments. Aside from the master requirements file, the overall system generally maintains two other information files: the parts data file and the product configuration file. Gross requirements and schedules are determined form this overall information for each of the end items at every level of the product's indenture through a process often referred to as level-by-level netting, shown in simplified form in Figure 9.5.

The second step in the process is generally to determine what requirements have been satisfied and which parts and assemblies are on hand or on order. This is summarized in a suitable format required for the subsequent netting of requirements. Based on net requirements at all of the levels of indenture, the computer undertakes to identify the requisite actions to reconcile actuals with plans. In cases where purchases are indicated, the system can print out the necessary requisition or orders including typical information such as the following:

- Project name/number
- Cost account
- Part number
- Required quantity (including attrition)
- Need dates
- Affected department
- Delivery instructions
- Storage instructions
- Requester name
- Approving authority

Generally, similar action is triggered in cases requiring additional fabrication

Figure 9.5: Assembly Lead Time Set Back (Derivation of Need Dates)

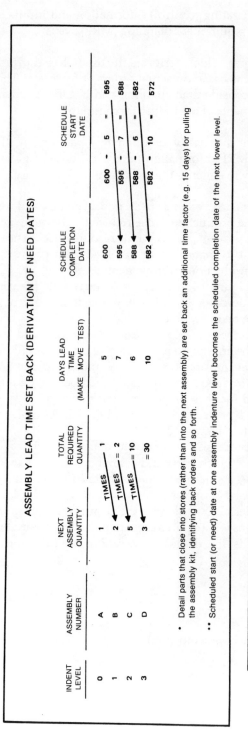

ASSEMBLY LEAD TIME SET BACK (DERIVATION OF NEED DATES)

INDENT LEVEL	ASSEMBLY NUMBER	NEXT ASSEMBLY QUANTITY	TOTAL REQUIRED QUANTITY	DAYS LEAD TIME (MAKE MOVE TEST)	SCHEDULE COMPLETION DATE	SCHEDULE START DATE
0	A	1	1	5	600	600 - 5 = 595
1	B	2	= 2	7	595	595 - 7 = 588
2	C	5	= 10	6	588	588 - 6 = 582
3	D	3	= 30	10	582	582 - 10 = 572

• Detail parts that close into stores (rather than into the next assembly) are set back an additional time factor (e.g. 15 days) for pulling the assembly kit, identifying back orders and so forth.

** Scheduled start (or need) date at one assembly indenture level becomes the scheduled completion date of the next lower level.

NET REQUIREMENT PREVIOUS LEVEL × NET ASSY QUANTITY - GROSS REQUIREMENT (LESS QUANTITY IN NEXT ASSY) + BACK ORDERS - STOCK - OPEN ORDERS = NET REQUIREMENT

Source: Hughes Aircraft Co., "Production Control at Hughes, El Segundo," February 1977, p. 29.

and assembly.

This type of production planning and control system is typically supported by a network of on-line data collection devices or "transactors" interspersed throughout the working areas, which in combination with similarly interspersed CRT terminals are used to furnish input-output information and updates as required.

The capacity requirements planning system generally compares the projected shop loads with available capacities and will schedule release fabrication work orders, taking into consideration running time and performance standards as well as move-and-wait time factors on an operation by operation basis. Some production planning and control systems can thus provide the framework for a considerable amount of simulation of the effects of different solutions to day-to-day problems encountered in production. Depending upon the system, such planning and control can be projected as far as two years ahead and give invaluable assistance in multiproject or program management functions. This level of capability is a key building block in the overall CAD/CAM integration efforts depicted in Figures 9.2 and 9.3.

The Production Effort

Batch production, involving relatively small quantities of a large number of different parts, characterizes by far the major portion of the total manufacturing effort in the United States today. In general, automation of such efforts requires very sophisticated programming and complex feedback, which is now realizable and becoming progressively more economical owing to the revolutionary advances in micro- and minicomputers.

A variety of machines currently on the market incorporate a wide range of features such as multiple program storage, which allows random programs to be called by part or by tape number, tool status interrogation and replacement, electronic or electro-optical devices for process inspection, palletized material handling and transfer, as well as a number of other features. Some of these machines have been appropriately referred to as "manufacturing centers" as they effectively furnish a basis for the establishment of a factory within a factory.

In concert with these developments, considerable interest and attention is being focused on so called group technology (GT) or cell manufacturing (CM). This embodies the concept of arranging equipment in specialized cells according to the particular family of parts to be manufactured rather than the more traditional approach based on generic grouping of available machinery and equipment. In view of the significant advances in the state of the art of manufacturing machinery and equipment as well as allied areas such as robotics, proponents of GT or CM argue that considerable advantages could be derived from the latter including the following:[43]

- Reduced tooling and part handling requirements
- Lower set-up times and scrap rates and generally improved ma-

—————————————— **Table 9.3: Potential Benefits of Group Technology** ——————————————

```
•  Reduced new part designs . . . . . . . . . . . . . . . . . 3 to 10%
•  Increased engineering productivity . . . . . . . . . . . Up to 50%
•  Reduced N/C programming . . . . . . . . . . . . . . . Up to 83%
•  Reduced set-up time . . . . . . . . . . . . . . . . . . . . .20 to 30%
•  Reduced tooling expense. . . . . . . . . . . . . . . . . .25 to 40%
•  Work-in-process reduction . . . . . . . . . . . . . . . . .25 to 40%
•  Lead time reduction . . . . . . . . . . . . . . . . . . . . Up to 80%
•  Material handling . . . . . . . . . . . . . . . . . . . . Unquantified*

*Primarily owing to difficulty in quantifying such efforts
with consistency.
```

Source: R.J. Levulis, "Group Technology—State of the Art in the United States," National Institute for Management Research, Computers in Manufacturing Conference, July 1981.

chine utilization
  • Lower inventory acquisition and in-process carrying costs
  • Shorter production lead times

Expected quantifiable benefits among current users are presented in Table 9.3.

Implementation of group technology or cell manufacturing is a major step that few companies in our country have undertaken at this time. It is, however, quite actively being pursued by the Japanese. Some concerns that have caused resistance to GT/CM may be summarized as follows:[44]

  • The mechanics, cost, and impact of the disruption necessary to achieve the rerouting to support the new layout
  • Obsolescence of cells based on product changes, at least in cases where older machinery and equipment are used
  • Decline in machine/equipment use through dissolution of existing banks and dedication to various part families
  • Need to incur additional expense in the form of upgrading or expansion of the asset base

Group technology is an exceptionally powerful concept that cannot be dismissed lightly and may well find a wide range of possible applications in may areas of the industrial community. It has been estimated that 20 to 30% of Japan's total output is the by-product of automated factories or GT; both are currently being heavily subsidized by the Ministry of International Trade and Industry.[45] It is certainly an issue worthy of consideration for many companies as part of a comprehensive strategic planning and productivity improvement effort.

Other key issues in the overall automation of the manufacturing process are material identification and coding, transport, storage, and retrieval. Even here, accumulating technology has considerable potential for productivity improvement and lends further impetus to the advancement of computer-inte-

Figure 9.6: Distribution of Robots by Application

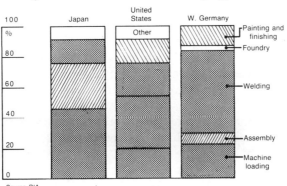

Source RIA

Source: "Science and Technology – The Next Step in Factory Automation," *The Economist* (London, England, December 19, 1981), p. 79.

grated manufacturing (CIM). Bar code readers and other electro-optical devices are currently used for a variety of inspection and sorting tasks.

A number of general purpose material-handling robots are now available. One such robot has a 10-foot diameter operating envelope consisting of a 5-axis, servo-controlled, point to point, fully-jointed arm capable of lifting about 50 pounds. It can be programmed with a hand-held device or a terminal and features a wide range of control options including a decision-tree operating mode. The use of robotics by application is shown in Figure 9.6. These advances in technology are representative of the "push-pull" taking place in the overall effort to automate the factory.

In some cases progress has been truly remarkable: "the Fujitsu Fanuc plant in Japan, for example, uses robots to make robots; during the third shift, all lights are turned off because no workers are present. The Japanese are also far along toward completion of a plant that will run with no blue-collar workers at all."[46] The latter is not as farfetched as it may seem since the Fujitsu Fanuc's flexible production system includes 16 robots that function 24 hours a day unattended.[47] It should also be noted that the preceding were headlines approximately a decade ago.

It has become increasingly apparent that the potential benefits from CAD/CAM technology are much too great to be allowed to run their course towards eventual integration or to be ignored until such a time as the prospects of full integration are a practical reality. This situation has been recognized through the formation of a nonprofit consortium of more than 100 firms in 1972 for the specific purpose of advancing and exchanging information in the area of applied computer technology.[48] It is also being recognized by an increasing number of governments that are funding their own independent efforts ad advancing this technology. In the United States the effort is being spearheaded by the Air Force's $100 million integrated CAM program initiated in 1978.[49]

Fulfilling the promise of CAD/CAM productivity-enhancing efforts requires commitment to its implementation according to a carefully structured program that includes the following logical steps:

1. Assessment of the full potential of CAD/CAM in concert with the evolution of the corporate strategic plan. Such an assessment requires a systems approach to the evolution of a total manufacturing concept of the future rather than the mere evaluation of the equipment.

2. General quantification of anticipated benefits in line with the range of options likely to unfold as part of the implementation of the strategic plan. According to Gold, CAD/CAM is a "special kind of technology whose adoption requires a broader level of analysis than that applied to the purchase of equipment and facilities."[50]

3. Planning of human resources reaccommodation.

4. Development of an internal CAD/CAM advocacy particularly at the top echelons of management.

5. Selection and commitment of a broad based, and experienced team under strong leadership to the tasks of planning, implementing, and measuring possible as well as actual productivity improvements of CAD/CAM.

Automation of Management

In many cases the emphasis on the implementation of labor-saving automation has diverted attention not only from the potential for automation in the managerial function itself but also from the amount that already exists. More than 25 years ago, a correlation was postulated between the manager's organizational level and the extent to which his activities encompass a variety of programmed and nonprogrammed, structured and nonstructured, and routine as well as nonroutine elements.[51] It was predicted that by the mid 1980s we would be experiencing a declining middle-management population as a number of middle-management decisions requiring experienced judgment would yield to automation based on advances in operations research and applied computer technology. The extent of automation over the years in each of the main areas within the general domain of middle management, including finance, production, information, and personnel, bear out these projections. This trend will most likely accelerate in the future. As pointed out by Allen E. Puckett, former chairman of the board and CEO of Hughes Aircraft Co.:

> ...rather than a role as a tool, the digital data-processing system is becoming the backbone or the framework around which we will plan, organize, and operate in most of our business and industrial functions. The organization of the data-processing system and in particular of its software—the hierarchy in the system of automation handling—will determine the organization of our people and the way they work together...[52]

We have noted that the fast pace in the development of computer-integrated manufacturing (CIM) is inexorably tied to the development of a hierarchy of computers needed to integrate a host of managerial functions and manufacturing operations. A major milestone in this development will have to include the resolution of communication interface problems, which should provide the impetus for revolutionary advances in the software area. It is out of such a pattern—and in line with Simon's forecasts of the future beyond 1985—that highly selective trial-and-error search programs should evolve, using various rules of thumb to "guide the selection of solutions; by abstracting from the problem and solving first the abstracted problem; by using analogy; by reasoning in terms of means and ends, goals and subgoals; by adjusting aspirations to the attainable."[53] To some this may seem a farfetched fantasy, but such a project was effectively undertaken in Japan during the summer of 1982 with the backing of the Ministry of International Trade and Industry (MITI) and the involvement of Japan's most prestigious research laboratories. The objective of the 10-year project is to build what has been referred to as the fifth-generation computer or, effectively, a human-level artificial intelligence.[54] The approach is to build a system with an associative memory through "parallel processing," enabling the computer to subdivide the problem into parts and work on several at once. It has been suggested that hardware holds the key to such breakthroughs in the form of logic chips with processing power 10 times faster than that of current chips. *(See discussion of VHSIC technology in Chapter 12.) Whether the Japanese succeed in this effort within their designated time scale is not important; what is important is that such an effort has been undertaken and the fallout technology likely to be generated.

Certainly the above is far beyond the level of technology which will bring a much greater degree of automation in the management function than that experienced to date. The trend toward management streamlining through progressive automation may have an overall beneficial effect on employer/employee relations, partly because of mounting recognition on the part of management that they too are potentially expendable employees. Out of such recognition should stem a much greater degree of appreciation and concern for the plight and needs of employees more imminently threatened by automation and a reformulation of the future role and function of management.

(c) The Impact and Mandate of Automation

Many experts agree that full automation of the means of production is highly unlikely even in cases where this may be theoretically possible. Two rather compelling arguments have been advanced for this. The first is that the incremental complexity and cost of bringing a manufacturing organization to the level of total automation would never prove economically attractive or desirable. The second is that we as a society would never be willing to pay the price of the social and political upheavals that would accompany a widespread degree of automation approaching this level, even if it were proven practical. Still, there appears to be a general consensus that between 70 to 80%

of current manufacturing positions will likely be lost to automation by the end of this century. The picture tends to be equally grim when viewed from the perspective of the general office worker. Ultimately, we face a situation where as many jobs will be lost for want of automation as may be lost because of automation. The prevailing view is that unemployment will generally be the by-product of waning demand rather than of technological change.[55]

The prospects of automation tend to be seductive, especially if isolated and viewed within the framework of the advantages to be gained in one's own company. Infusion of a progressively greater degree of automation within a given company or industry should lead to improved competitiveness and greater output. However, wholesale automation to the degree projected and possible in the future would result in bulk displacements of the work force, which unless offset by the creation of new jobs through advancements in technology will ultimately lead to reduced demand and lower output. Overall, as pointed out by Le Quement, "the capacity to create jobs closely depends on the state of the trade balance of a robotized system. It is in deficit in most European countries and results in a great deal of difficulty being encountered in trying to reduce the effects of unemployment on redundant workers.[56] Generally therein lies what Kahn has referred to as the "Faustian Bargain" with technology:

> For, as we remember, Faust (in Goethe's play) bought magical (that is, secular) knowledge and powers that he was compelled to use and then perforce he had to proceed to the next experience, the next project—or be forever damned. And that illustration provides a good analogy with some formulations of the current predicament. We do agree that mankind is involved in a process that probably cannot voluntarily and safely be stopped, or prematurely slowed down significantly, even if there are good arguments for doing so. But we maintain that on the balance and with some exceptions, the arguments are heavily against deliberate policies to halt or slow down the basic long-term technological trend, even if it could be done with safety. Indeed, we would prefer to accelerate some aspects of this trend, while being prudent and generally watchful in order to prevent or reduce the impact of the baneful possibilities.[57]

Automation raises a host of complex, interrelated issues that are touched on only briefly here. Among the most significant are (a) the vesting of responsibility for the rehabilitation of technologically displaced persons (TDPs), (b) the optimum rate of automation and realism in the extent of rehabilitation and accommodation of TDPS, and (c) the managerial implications during the transition states in the area of interpersonal relations.

Projections suggest that the required rehabilitation of TDPs will be extensive as well as expensive. Because of this a number of views have been advanced on the proper vesting of the responsibility and initiative for the action needed. This problem deserves closer scrutiny and attention.

Whether corporate management is inclined to accept the lead in this matter or not, it is clearly being called upon to uphold a higher standard of social consciousness and accountability than perhaps at any other time in the history of industrial development in this country. A significant part of the problem stems from the evolving social, political, and cultural climate over which the corporate sector may in fact have limited control. Another aspect of the problem is the growing reliance of the corporate world on incentives, concessions, and bailouts, not only from the public sector, but from its own employees as well.* In many cases this reliance is symptomatic of a lack of creative initiative prompted by a host of shortsighted policies and rigid practices that in some instances have brought even giants like Lockheed and Chrysler to the brink of relative extinction. It is in part the solicitation and acceptance of such incentives, concessions and bailouts that tend to restrict the range and relative absoluteness of managerial prerogatives and in the process mandates a higher level of social consciousness and accountability.

It is certainly true at the very top of the corporate ladder there appears to be a very high degree of social consciousness and accountability among management. Edward N. Cole, former president of General Motors Corporation, once wrote:

> The big challenge to American business—as I see it—is to carefully evaluate the constantly changing expressions of public and national goals. Then we must modify our own objectives and programs to meet—as far as possible within the realm of economics and technological feasibility—the new demands of the society we serve.[58]

It is also unfortunately true, however, that this level of social consciousness accountability tends to dissipate within the corporate world at successively lower levels of management in favor of a preoccupation with the production of goods and services at prices consumers are willing to pay. Such narrowness of corporate purpose and perceived managerial function is no longer realistic or viable. As Patton noted, we should be concerned about the education available to future business leaders. "What is badly needed is a curriculum that deals with hard business skills, such as leadership abilities, decision making, business ethics, and management skills that are such a vital part of everyday work world."[59]

Broad-based public and employee support for the reindustrialization of the United States is not likely to be sustained if the main result of desperately needed automation translates into widespread unemployment. Rapid developments that make old jobs obsolete are already driving unions to work for contract guarantees for retraining TDPs.[60] Management must take the initiative, be it at the micro or macro level, in implementing rehabilitation and reabsorption of TDPs into the industrial system as part of any concentrated

---

* Most notable examples include the automobile and airline industries.

effort at automation. Management must do this, if not out of a sense of social responsibility, then out of self-interest and expediency. However, such an initiative cannot be sustained without government and union support. Such an initiative was reportedly undertaken at one of GM's plants in California after its closure.

There is evidence of mounting concern within the work force over management's apparent insensitivity to this overall general area. Many employees are resisting and indeed refusing to joining the computer revolution at a significant cost to the organization as they tend to perceive far too many dangers as compared to prospects of opportunities.[61,62,63] The amount of tangible commitment to the aforementioned programs and actions as perceived by the employees will affect not only employee attitudes and actions but also the rate and level of productivity improvement ultimately attained.

Clearly, science and technology are powerful economic and political tools. The rate of automation is not likely to be dictated by the preferences of the various segments of the work force or individual companies but rather by the evolving norms of the world's industrial community based on a variety of national interests. U.S. business appears to be embattled in this area for want of a governmental agency to orchestrate and coordinate a policy of economic growth through technological development as is the case in other developed countries. Although the rate of automation is not likely to be dictated by the preferences of the work force, it will be strongly influenced by management's approach to automation considering issues of survival and overall national interest. The approach to the rehabilitation and accommodation of the TDPs must consequently be driven in the general direction of the imbalance likely to be created by automation if the transition to automation is to be successfully negotiated. Specifically, most projections suggest a complex trend in the creation and displacement of jobs. Concern is being expressed into primary areas: First, the considerable growth anticipated as a result of innovation is highly unlikely to generate a commensurate demand for unskilled and semiskilled positions. It is in fact anticipated that innovation will promote a progressively higher demand for those with paraprofessional and professional skills, creating a potentially significant imbalance in employment. Second, history shows that surplus labor created by innovation is very seldom absorbed into the new positions that it creates. This appears to be especially true in the absence of commitment of the private sector to the rehabilitation of the displaced labor force.

It should be apparent that management must assume a much more active role in the rehabilitation and accommodation of TDPs. Management's inclination to assume such an initiative largely accounts for the greater employee acceptance of automation and the higher productivity growth rates in foreign countries. In France, for instance, Citroën is already implementing a computerized career management system, including 100,000 files, whose objective is to establish a state of equilibrium among the aspirations and potential of the employee, the current and projected requirements of the company, and the conditions of the outside market.[64] The system can reportedly accommodate a considerable degree of variability in these parameters and incorporates enough methodological rigor to enable assessment of impact at any point in time.

Any program of TDP rehabilitation/(re)accommodation should take into consideration and reflect such variables as:

- Size and resources of the firm
- Nature or type of products involved
- Employee inventory and profile
- Long-range plans and requirements of the organization
- Existing apprentice, vocational, and other employee development programs sponsored by the firm along with their consistency with the aforementioned
- Rate at which redundant labor can be phased out through a process of natural attrition (turnover, retirement, and so on)
- Feasibility or advisability of some type of economic "reparation" program
- Degree of anticipated union cooperation and involvement in the overall effort
- Prevailing governmental programs and incentives

9.6 Computer-Aided Acquisition and Logistic Support (CALS)

In September of 1985, as part of an effort to improve quality *and productivity* within DOD, Deputy Secretary of Defense William H. Taft set the goal of acquiring all technical data in digital—rather than paper—form for weapon systems entering production by 1990 and beyond. By August of 1988, a major step had been taken towards routine contractual implementation. This was accomplished through the issuance of MIL-STD-1840A and supporting military specifications covering national and international standards for digital data delivery and access. As of that time, Deputy Secretary Taft decreed that all plans for new weapon systems and related major equipment items include use of CALS standards. More specifically, he decreed that various DOD components begin planning and programming the automated receipt, storage, distribution and use of digital weapon system technical information as of the earliest possible date on a case by case basis.

It has been estimated that up to eighty percent of the "end item's" reliability and maintainability (R&M) characteristics are determined during its conceptual design phase. Furthermore, that about thirty percent of a product's life cycle cost is directly traceable to its R&M attributes.

Experience has shown that "stand alone," post conceptual design phase, reliability and maintainability efforts have a very limited impact on the overall design effort. The CALS initiative is thus, in part, intended as a means of:

- Accelerating the integration of R&M design tools into contractor's CAD/CAE systems

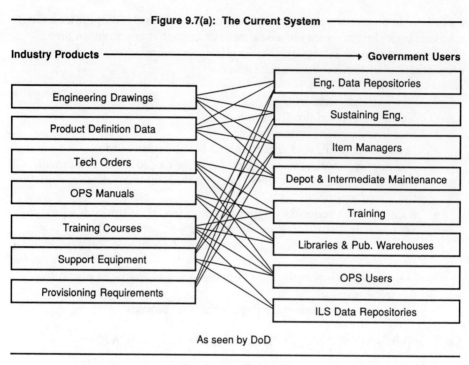

Figure 9.7(a): The Current System

As seen by DoD

- Automating and improving the contractor's process of generating and updating information
- Speeding up the dissemination, evaluation, and integration of technical information between all interested parties
- Cutting down of paper, reproduction and maintenance/storage costs
- Improving Configuration Management
- Developing and providing more consistent training methods and procedures
- Increasing system supportability and mission readiness

The current system as seen by DOD is shown in Figure 9.7(a). The target (CALS) system as envisioned by DOD is shown in Figure 9.7(b).

9.7 Increasing Individual and Organizational Productivity

The key to employee productivity improvement is deeply rooted in theories of human behavior and motivation. Some of the more dominant are summarized in Table 9.4. The findings associated with these theories are consistent with respect to the impact of the individual's overall personal and intellectual attributes, the effect of job-related environmental factors, and the importance of management in productivity improvement.

Although popularized by contemporary management and business literature and generally espoused by the managerial community, the effective ap-

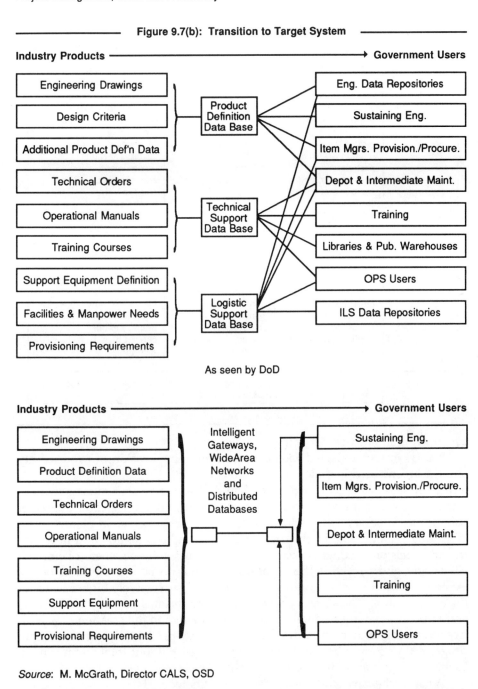

Figure 9.7(b): Transition to Target System

As seen by DoD

Source: M. McGrath, Director CALS, OSD

plication of these concepts and theories has been inhibited by the frequently slow, selective and limited effort and the difficult task of creative implementation given the framework of change-resistant conditions and constraints often

Table 9.4: Concepts of Human Behavior and Motivation in an Organizational Environment

	Argyris	Drucker	Hertzberg
Major Principle or Assumption Regarding Worker Motivation	Draws significantly on Maslow's work. Suggests that the primary management function is to *reduce* the degree of submissiveness, passivity, dependency, and frustration of the employee.	Stresses managerial focus on results rather than activities with an underlying emphasis on motivation and managerial self-control.	Mere absence of dissatisfiers (hygiene factors) does not promote a motivated work force. Motivation must be fostered through achievement, advancement, responsibility, and so on.
	Lickert	**Maslow**	**McGregor**
	Promote team work and employee needs by creating a friendly and supportive environment as opposed to threatening or punitive one.	A hierarchy of human needs governs attitudes and actions. Motivation dependent upon stimulation and gratification of social esteem and self-actualization needs of employees.	Create opportunities, release potential, remove obstacles, encourage growth. (Theory Y only realistic and valid premise in our current high-technology environment.)

Basic problem in each case is one of balancing individual/group needs versus requirements and philosophy of the organization

encountered in practice.

This is in part reflected today in the continuing erosion of productivity and the accompanying dialogue on the most effective means of reversing this trend. A significant part of the problem appears to be that management is reluctant to commit itself to changes that would portend a greater degree of subordinate involvement, participation, and control, such as in planning, establishing standards and performance criteria, implementation and task control and decision making. Resistance to the expanded involvement of employees at any given level of the organization tends to be symptomatic of the existence of such resistance at one or more of the successively higher levels of the organization. The above consequently often dictates policies, procedures, and structure that are frequently counterproductive to the creation of a positive, enriching, and rewarding environment. A productivity improvement program thus cannot be effectively implemented without total commitment, backing and guidance starting at the highest levels of management.

A comprehensive study of productivity initiated by Hughes Aircraft Company in 1973 involving 59 aerospace and consumer product companies, governmental and educational institutions, more than 2,000 R&D managers and senior technical personnel, and 28 nationally prominent consultants has been the broadest and most authoritative effort on this subject to date. The conclusions reached by this study dispel many frequently held and constraining myths about productivity, among them the following:[65]

- The myth that productivity correlates positively with I.Q.
- The myth that productivity correlates positively with excellence of education, grades, or course work taken after graduation
- The myth that productivity correlates with age
- The myth that technological obsolescence is an undeniable function of age
- The myth that stress adversely affects productivity (noting that there is a very significant difference between "stress" and "distress" within the work environment)

The study points out that overall productivity is heavily dependent upon the top 5% of the organizational staff who deal primarily with innovative ideas, critical judgment, and major decisions and who through their ideas and actions affect the productivity of the entire organization.[66]

To some this may prove somewhat surprising and will hopefully provide the stimulus for a certain degree of introspection. For the most part, upper levels of management have been conditioned into recognizing the importance of first level supervision in the area of worker motivation seemingly to the point of a disproportional reliance upon the latter and its own apparent disassociation with this function. This may stem from a strict interpretation of the results of the Hawthorne experiments conducted in the mid-twenties at the Hawthorne plant of Western Electric Company, which conclusively indicated that worker morale and motivation, as influenced by supervision, have a significant impact on production output. From this a priority with respect to the need for motivational training seems to have been erroneously inputted. Qualitative observations suggest that even in organizations that encourage their employees in the development of interpersonal skills through various human relations programs, such programs are typically geared to and populated by managerial aspirants or junior-level managers. By contrast few organizations appear to focus on the need to update and upgrade the skills of higher levels of management through any type of a structured review and periodic upgrading program. The preceding is cited by way of underscoring the modularized and often disjointed approach to productivity improvement in industry observed by other authors as well.

An effective effort in productivity improvements requires a systems approach to dealing with individual needs, managerial functions, and organizational structure. This means (a) defining the problem in terms of objectives, needs, goals, and resources; (b) analyzing existing subsystems, their interrelationships, criteria for success, and constraints; (c) synthesizing in the form of procedural and structural innovation and redesign; and (d) verifying through implementation, measurement, or qualitative assessment.

(a) The Productive Individual

Aside from being better informed and educated, today's work force has a markedly different value system, outlook and work attitude compared with that of its counterpart of some 25 years ago. Although the above is increasingly recognized, its extent and impact is yet to be fully appreciated and consciously reflected in the day-to-day operations of many organizations. The latter stems not so much from any conflicting observations as much as from the impedance created by diverging interpretations as to the the nature and extent of impact relative to a general preference for the status quo. According to prevailing characterizations, today's (particularly younger) qualified business and professional employees are profiled as:[67,68,69,70,71]

- Being highly independent and unwilling to devote years to the corporation in anticipation of some future reward. Many aspire to start their own businesses as they view loyalty to the corporation as a "misfortune" suffered by their parents.

- Enjoy a diversified life-style in contrast to the more traditional, dedicated quest for the trappings of power and symbols of success. Money, as an example, is primarily sought after as a necessary evil to the sustenance of a definitive life-style including a host of leisure activities, vocational and avocational interests.

- Demonstrate a strong need for challenge and personal job satisfaction without a necessarily commensurate inclination to work hard, most definitely not when the latter is prompted by "fire fighting" or "crisis" management.

- Generally self-assured, confident, sensitized to the preeminence of individual values and social needs, and highly intolerant of ineptness in management.

Depending upon one's predisposition, these could be considered either positive or negative attributes. Ultimately, the issue is moot as productivity improvement is critically dependent upon the enlistment and integration of the full range of skills and talents of the profiled employees. This is unlikely to be attained in organizations with bureaucratic tendencies or with a propensity to view the employment they provide not only as the full extent of their social responsibility but also as a quid pro quo for an all-out employee commitment to the pursuit of corporate sales and profit objectives. Factors contributing to counter-productivity and frequently characterizing such organizations include the following:[72]

- Overinflated organizational structure
- Poor psychological environment
- Lack of people orientation in management
- Misemployment/underemployment
- Ineffective structuring of assignments

- Lack of effective performance appraisal and feedback
- Ineffective reward system promoting a disparity between individual productivity and compensation
- Lack of equitable parallel promotional opportunities along managerial and technical ladders
- Lack of equity in operations
- Operational/procedural overcomplexity
- Excessive organizational politics and gamesmanship

In effect, it is the organization that through the sum total of its policies and practices can transform a qualified individual into either a productive or non-productive employee. The making of a productive individual is largely a function of management's sensitivity, understanding, and creative accommodation of the attitudes and motivations of individual employees through:

- Reformulation of the statement of purpose and objectives in socially more palatable terms and tangible deeds, thereby rejuvenating a sense of direction, heightened internal expectations and operating standards.

- Organizational design conducive to the stimulation of entrepreneurial spirit, prospects of growth, visibility, and meaningful advancement. Implicit in such design is a requirement to provide for: parallel paths of advancement, elimination of "red tape" and the restructuring of the individual's work content to include, in part, logical subdivisions of the effort. This in turn suggests a need in some cases for appropriate realignments, reassignments, or even restaffing as a solution to misemployment and underemployment.

- Promotion of a greater degree of individual participation in the planning and formulation of the work content, autonomy in its execution, and communication about the evaluation and appraisal of results. It has been long understood that participation results in a vesting of interest and correspondingly a much greater degree of commitment to success.

- Gradual and progressive streamlining and repopulation of managerial positions, as required, with current and well-rounded individuals capable of challenging and motivating a brighter, better-rounded, and more skeptical constituency (as opposed to "super techs," "bean counters," "senior statesmen" and/or plain "politicians").

- Establishment of a very high degree of equity in all areas, at all levels and in all facets of the organization and its operations. The sense of equity within the work force is seldom served for instance by situations wherein at the upper echelons of the organization a host of visible "perks" prevail, while near the base of the corporate pyramid employees are either reluctant to accept promotions into supervisory positions or seek downgrading into hourly positions as they tend to perceive their economic well being clearly tied into the unions.

- More timely, comprehensive and realistic correlation of compensation with contributions and accomplishment. There seem to be recurring policies and practices in industry tending to inhibit a greater degree of innovation and productivity that apparently stem from a prevailing misperception and often time convenient distortion of the value of money as a motivator.* These policies and practices include the following:

    1. A ritualistic and often highly subjective approach to periodic employee compensation reviews and adjustments which invariably neither reflect changes in the cost of living nor account for individual merit. As a result, such reviews and adjustments neither tend to be all that rewarding nor reinforcing. More often than not, their net positive impact tends to be so insignificant as to foster an eventual sense of exploitation even among the best-adjusted employees.†

    2. An apparent imperviousness to the corrosive effect of salary "compression" on the vitality, expectations, and motivations of the more senior employees. Compression as used here means a disparity created and promoted by disproportional rates of increase in the salaries of entry- and junior-level personnel compared with those of the more senior and experienced employees. This underlying devaluation of the worth of age and experience fosters a self-fulfilling prophecy among the incumbent employees that partly accounts for the waning loyalty observed in younger employees.

---

* Hertzberg suggests that the mere suppression of dissatisfiers is not likely to promote a motivated work force. As an example, a lack of dissatisfaction with salary is not likely to motivate an individual. This is often misinterpreted by industry to mean that money is not a motivator.

† Consider the fact that many top corporate executives have compensation packages, including bonuses, worth millions of dollars, that are not always tired into performance of the organization. Many collect such compensation even when their corporations post losses.

3. A frequent lack of substantive employee participation or reward in cost, product improvement and innovation ideas of financial benefit to the organization. Tokenism in this area, justified or not, is unquestionably one of the significant reasons why large corporations, despite often heavy expenditures of R&D funds, have accounted for only a small proportion of major inventions in this century.[73] This is perhaps also why the United States has experienced a pronounced negative trend over the past decade in the total number of patents issued. Very simply, the average employee has little if any incentive to innovate.

As noted earlier in Table 9.2 employee productivity is as much a function of *skill* as it is a matter of *will* influenced by the prevailing conditions, perceptions, needs and desires. The re-awakening of the will of the American worker is a pressing priority and should be considered among the primary functions of top management today for, as we have seen, the great majority of the issues raised tend to fall outside the day-to-day operating management's purview.

(b) The Productive Manager

In many circles management still appears to be perceptually aligned with ownership to the point of indistinguishable association. Some of this stems from historical considerations that the unions have tacitly exploited and that management has not effectively dispelled through many of its policies and practices. The latter is reinforced by management's implausible accountability to what the work force sees as an absentee ownership consisting primarily of flitting money manipulators with a transient, strictly pecuniary interest. The above accounts for the frequent and general unwillingness of the work force to subordinate anything even remotely connected to its interests to such ownership and the prevailing tendency on the part of management to hammer at worker productivity and measurement at the expense of closer, more critical and overt scrutiny of performance within its own ranks. As Patton noted, "Too many companies make a big issue of measuring a $7-an-hour machine operator's output but often ignore any standards of accountability for a $75,000-a-year executive who is responsible for the performance of hundreds of machine operators."[74] This condition has understandably prompted many to view "industrial democracy" as a more sophisticated method of pressuring workers toward greater productivity rather than as a means of redistribution power.[75,76]

Managerial productivity is much too often either taken for granted or, worse, effectively sidestepped. A great deal of this can be attributed to Adam Smith's philosophy, which permeates the corporate environment today and tends to reflect the view that he who owns or for that matter controls both the capital and the profits has every right to manage as he sees fit. Although this may be theoretically true it is practically unrealistic in today's sociotechnical, political, and cultural environment. Two other factors contribute to the lack of attention to managerial productivity: (1) a reluctance to channel productivity improvement efforts in the direction of any corrective policies that are perceived to substantively dilute centralized control and authority or any other traditional trappings of managerial elitism, and (2) a reluctance to undertake corrective action on the basis of anything other than purely quantitative assessment and evaluation which tends to be difficult in the case of longer-range, more creative, abstract or nonroutine activities. These factors are the root causes of homeostasis in industry today.

We must recognize that a manager is also an employee whose response is governed by his own general needs, expectations, and aspirations, which are frequently much more intense than those normally distributed with the work force. This suggests a need to stimulate and cultivate management with high personal standards, collaborative spirit, infectious enthusiasm, drive, and perseverance to serve as role models to others. This is an essential priming function to the enhancement of overall organizational productivity. These desirable attributes can only be fostered through an attack on organizational counterproductivity factors (see preceding section). Once the proper environment is structured, there are a number of managerial practices in the areas of work assignments and day-to-day interaction that can enhance subordinate productivity and are applicable regardless of the organizational level. Some of these practices are as follows:[77]

- Establish high personal and organizational performance and evaluation standards.
- Determine objectives with a high degree of specificity based upon knowledge of the technology, market, competition, and resources.
- Delegate authority, responsibility, decision-making control, and accountability as far down the organization as possible.
- Apply work elimination, simplification, and standardization techniques whenever appropriate.
- Encourage innovation and invest in the future. Support use of latest technological aids.
- Look for preventive rather than corrective action.
- Do not overemphasize or shortchange any individual or part of organization. Be fair.
- Be alert for and correct counterproductive factors.
- Provide employees with necessary information and resources to do the job effectively.
- Keep assignments from being overspecified by focusing on end results rather than activities.
- Make schedules tight but realistic.
- Assign work in line with employee capabilities and interest but do not deny people a chance to learn and grow.
- Strive for equity in work-load distribution and try to rotate, change,

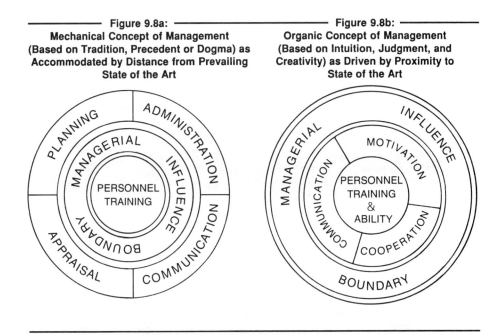

Figure 9.8a:
Mechanical Concept of Management
(Based on Tradition, Precedent or Dogma) as
Accommodated by Distance from Prevailing
State of the Art

Figure 9.8b:
Organic Concept of Management
(Based on Intuition, Judgment, and
Creativity) as Driven by Proximity to
State of the Art

or expand employee assignments periodically.
- Define assignments, roles, responsibilities, and interfaces clearly.

The classic centralized, and mechanical approach to management (Figure 9.8a) is unlikely to yield a significant improvement in productivity especially in the high technology areas. As an alternative (Figure 9.8b), the organic approach to management has been advanced. It embodies as its precepts *communication, motivation,* and *collaboration* which are deemed to be more in line with the dictates of current technological complexity and evolved expectations of the work force.[78,79,80] These precepts suggest the need for more innovative approaches to dealing with people especially in the areas of planning and control. Some of the more effective techniques have been summarized as follows:[81]

Planning
- Involve affected individuals and organizations.
- Ensure realism of cost, schedule, and performance parameters.
- Define all pertinent trade-offs.
- Simulate various courses of action through analysis of interdependencies.
- Develop contingency plans inclusive of specific trigger points.
- Communicate objectives and requirements clearly and effectively.
- Avoid overplanning.
- Assign/define responsibilities/accountability.
- Make full use of computers.

Control

 - Involve users in control system design.
 - Keep controls reasonable and focus on most critical operations with greatest impact.
 - Be leary of "squeaking-wheels" and the tendency to focus attention in proportion to insistence or advocacy rather than importance.
 - Apply controls carefully and review them regularly along with effort.
 - Hold responsible individuals accountable.
 - Evaluate corrective actions carefully before implementation (the cure may be worse than the malady).

In line with the preceding, it should be noted that the productivity enhancing concepts approaches and suggestions delineated thus far reflect the practical embodiment of the major theories of motivation summarized in Table 9.4.

The effective enhancement of productivity thus largely depends on the degree of managerial understanding and tailored, creative, and *on-going* operational commitment to and application of industrial psychology. Productivity improvement techniques inevitably embody the broader and generally more difficult problem of employee motivation and leadership. Overall this is a challenge to which managers regardless of level have not met effectively.

(c) The Productive Organization

In the often quoted words of Lewis Carroll, Alice asked the Cheshire Cat, "Would you please tell me which way I ought to go from here?" To which the cat replied, "That depends on where you want to get to." There is an obvious parallel between Alice's quandary and an organizational search for the road to greater productivity. Both require a specific answer to the question of "where you want to get to." The answer implies that an organization must undertake and sustain a strategic planning effort, which in turn suggests that organizational productivity is an integral part of strategic planning rather than a series of independent cost-saving initiatives as it is often made out to be.

Performance evaluation and measurement–in a specific direction and on an on-going basis–is a central part of the strategic planning effort. In general, however, the more complex the undertaking, the less likely that it can be quantitatively measured and, correspondingly, the more sensitive its quality becomes to a broader-based, albeit quasiqualitative and recurring effort. The extent to which working levels are actually involved in such planning and rewarded in the attainment of desired pursuits will greatly influence the quality of planning and should materially affect the development of a more productive organization. The productive organization will be highly susceptible to the successive integration of inputs whose quality will be shaped by upper-level policies and practices and the imposed organizational structure. These typically constitute in mathematical parlance a first-order effect on productivity over which working levels have little if any direct influence. The impact of lower levels of management in productivity improvement, although significant, tends to be higher order and cannot be a substitute for macro-level realignments (see section 9.6a).

The following prerequisites are necessary for making a more productive organization:

- Treatment of productivity as an integral part of the assessment stage of strategic planning
- Recognition of key, distinct roles in productivity improvement of all levels of management
- Retraining all levels of management to accept the more contemporary view of its function and its impact on the attitudes, motivations, and actions of the work force
- Continuing organizational reevaluation, reassessment, and readjustment in line with results obtained through the strategic planning effort

(d) The Role of Government

Considering current national and international trends, it has become apparent that the role of government in this country must be adjusted beyond that of merely correcting "market imperfections."[82] Among the questions that immediately arise are the nature, direction, and extent of governmental sponsorship of economic activity and its impact upon the free enterprise system and our personal freedoms. For the most part, the fears of an assault on free enterprise have been specious and self-servicing, promulgated by special interest groups who have been responsible for a mass of often inconsistent and ultimately counter-productive legislation. Business apparently finds little inconsistency, for instance, in promoting the concept of free trade while seeking protection from the government in the perpetuation of management and labor philosophies that have been widely recognized by the public to yield ostensibly inferior, more expensive products that are generally non-responsive to the needs and desires of the marketplace.* Although business is quick to promote the strengths and merits of the free enterprise system in opposition to government intervention, it tends to rely upon government initiatives to sustain the system through a variety of bailouts, guarantees, and incentives. In the aftermath of the generally resulting quid pro quo legislation, business tends to bemoan and rationalize its woes to a host of ill-applied, if not ill-conceived, social economic programs that invariably serve special interests, fuel unralistic expectations, and promote lack of differentiation between superior and infe-

---

* As an example consider legislation passed by Congress Requiring a high proportion of American-made parts in the very popular Japanese car imports.

rior performance at the expense of the longer-range interests of the nation and society as a whole.[83,84]

The answers to the question of governmental involvement are by no means simple. In fact, they tend to be so complex as to generally defy analysis because of the perceived number of uncertainty of some of the variables and their interactive effects. This often inhibits corrective action notwithstanding the influence of special interests. There appears to be, however, a consensus of sorts about certain governmental initiatives that should markedly stimulate national productivity. They include the following:

- Formulation of an agency along the lines of the Japanese MITI to orchestrate technological development for economic growth
- Revision of our archaic patent and copyright laws
- Stimulation of the transfer of government sponsored R&D into the private sector in a more effective and rapid manner
- Tax incentives geared to reinudstiralization
- Incentives for participation in savings and thrift programs

——— Questions and Topics for Discussion ———

1. Give two definitions of productivity.

2. There has been ongoing discussion in the literature about what level of management is most responsible for productivity improvements in industry. At what level(s) should responsibility for productivity improvement be placed and why?

3. What are some common impediments to productivity?

4. Discuss the significance of Putt's law. How can the dilemma of Putt's law be resolved?

5. Outline a specific program for increasing productivity in the organization in which you work.

6. How does the accounting process, which depends upon an annual review with emphasis on profit, inhibit the improvement of productivity?

7. What are the forces that are presently driving industry toward automation?

8. What is CAD/CAM and how can it play an important role in the improvement of productivity?

9. What is meant by the statement that "as many jobs will be lost for want of

automation as many be lost because of automation?"

10. What are key factors that affect employee productivity in a large company?

11. What is the most deleterious effect of salary "compression?"

12. How can government actions have an effect on industrial productivity?

13. There has been much written about Japanese productivity vis-á-vis American productivity. What role do differences in Japanese and American culture play in such a comparison?

14. What actions can a project manager take to improve the productivity of the personnel on his project?

15. What will be the effect of automation on employment in the near future? In the distant future?

16. Industrial and economic experts commenting on the international scene say that what is needed in underdeveloped countries is labor-intensive rather than automated industries. Do you agree? Discuss.

17. T.H. Peters and I.J. Waterman, Jr., in their best seller *In Search of Excellence* refer to company culture as being of utmost importance in the productivity of individuals. Explain.

—————————— References ——————————

1. L. Boulden, "An Emerging Coalition for Productivity," *Production Engineering* (December 1981).
2. Arnold S. Judson, "The Awkward Truth about Productivity," *Harvard Business Review* (September-October 1982), p. 93.
3. *Ibid.*
4. Steven Avard, Vladi Cotto, and Martin Davidson, "Technological Innovation – Key to Productivity," *Research Management* (July 1982), p. 40.
5. Eli Ginzberg and George Vojta, "The Service Sector of the U.S. Economy," *Scientific American* (March 1981).
6. J.K. Galbraith, "The Entrepreneur and the Technostructure," in *The New Industrial State* (Boston: Houghton Mifflin, 1967), pp.86-87.
7. "Automation Thirty Years Later – A Conversation with John Diebold," *Administrative Management* (October 1982), pp. 24-27; 63-65.
8. John A. Patton, " Managers and Productivity...No One to Blame but Themselves," *Management Review* (October 1982), p. 15.
9. Richard Pascale and Anthony Athos, *The Art of Japanese Management*, (New York: Warner Books, 1982), p. 248.
10. Arne L. Kalleberg, "Postwar Trends and Future Prospects," *Business Horizons* (July-August 1982), p. 79.
11. Ann Howard and James Wilson, "Leadership in a Declining Work Ethic," *California Management Review* (Summer 1982), p. 42.

12. *Ibid.*
13. Quoted by President John F. Kennedy; source unknown.
14. Bong Gon Shin and Elliot Zashin, "Management and the New Egalitarianism: McGuire Revisited," *California Management Review* (Summer 1982), pp. 5-12.
15. Howard and Wilson, "Leadership in a Declining Work Ethic," p. 44.
16. J.K. Galbraith, p. 87.
17. Thurman Arnold, "The Folklore of Capitalism," in Ernest Dale, ed., *Management Theory and Practice* (New York: McGraw-Hill, 1965), p. 81.
18. Shin and Zashin, "Management and the New Egalitarianism," p. 11.
19. Judson, "The Awkward Truth About Productivity," p. 94.
20. William J. Abernathy, "Competitive Decline in U.S. Innovation: The Management Factor," *Research Management* (September 1982), p. 39.
21. Patton, "Managers and Productivity," p. 16.
22. Judson, "The Awkward Truth About Productivity," p. 94.
23. Daniel G. Robinson, "Quality Circles – Are They Good for the American System," *Program-Manager*, (January-February 1982).
24. W.S. Brower, "CAM, Where Is It Going in the 80's?" National Institute for Management Research, Computers in Manufacturing Conference, Los Angeles, California, July 1981.
25. L. C. Hackmack and B.I. Hackmack, "Replace That Machine," *Production Engineering* (August 1982), pp. 32-34.
26. Avard et al, "Technological Innovation – Key to Productivity," p. 40.
27. *Ibid.*
28. Abernathy, "Competitive Decline in U.S. Innovation," p. 38.
29. Brower, "CAM, Where Is It Going in the 80's?" p. 10.
30. Boulden, "An Engineering Coalition for Productivity," p. 27.
31. Judson, "The Awkward Truth About Productivity," p. 93.
32. Arthur Gerstenfeld and Paul Berger, "A Model for Economic and Social Evaluation of Industrial Robots," *Proceedings of the 12th International Symposium on Industrial Robots*, 6th International Conference on Industrial Robot Technology, Paris, June 1982, p. 346.
33. Y. Hasegawa and N. Sugimoto, "Industrial Safety and Robots," *Proceedings of the 12th International Symposium on Industrial Robots*, 6th International Conference on Industrial Robot Technology, Paris, June 1982, p. 13.
34. "Robots Pay for Themselves Quickly," *Machine Design* (March 11, 1982). Projection credited to Joseph Engleberger, considered to be the "father" of industrial robotics, President of Unimation, Inc., and Consolidated Controls Corp.
35. Kalleberg, "Postwar Trends and Future Prospects," p. 79.
36. Gerstenfeld and Berger, "A Model for Economic and Social Evaluation of Industrial Robots," p. 346.
37. Richard T. Dann, "Getting Set for Automated Manufacturing," *Machine Design* (November 11, 1982).
38. "The Automated Factory: Technology Paves the Way to Improved Productivity," *Compressed Air* (September 1982).
39. J.K. Krouse, "Software for Mechanical Design," *Machine Design* (October 7,1 982), pp. 42-48.
40. *Ibid.*
41. B. Gold, "CAM Sets New Rules for Production," *Harvard Business Review* (November-December 1982), pp. 88-94.
42. A comprehensive compilation of more than 70 sources and descriptive software is given in Richard Bourke, "Surveying the Software, A Compilation of Available Systems and Their Vendors," *Datamation* (October 1980).
43. Raymond J. Levulis, "Group Technology – State of the Art in the United States," National Institute for Management Research, Computers in Manufacturing Conference, July 1981.
44. *Ibid.*
45. John K. Krouse, "Automated Factories: The Ultimate Union of CAD and CAM," *Machine Design* (November 26, 1981), pp. 57-60.
46. Gold, "CAM Sets New Rules for Production," p. 91.
47. J. Le Quement, ":The Social and Economic Stakes in International Competition in the Robotics Industry," *Proceedings of the 12th International Symposium on Industrial Robots*, 6th International Conference on Robot Technology, Paris, June 1982, p. 17.

48. Krouse, ":Automated Factories."
49. *Ibid.*
50. Gold, "CAM Sets New Rules for Production," p. 88.
51. H.A. Simon, "The Automation of Management," in *Management and Corporation 1985* (New York: McGraw-Hill, 1960), pp. 39-52.
52. Allen E. Puckett, "The Changing Role of Electronics," *Vectors*, Hughes Aircraft Co., June 1980.
53. Simon, "The Automation of Management," p. 42.
54. "Building a Superbrain," *Newsweek* (August 9, 1982), p. 55.
55. Gerstenfeld and Berger, "A Model for Economic and Social Evaluation of Industrial Robots," p. 346.
56. Le Quement, "The Social and Economic Stakes in International Competition in the Robotics Industry," p. 17.
57. Herman Kahn, *The Next 200 Years* (New York: Hudson Institute/William Morrow, 1976), pp. 165-165.
58. Quoted in George Steiner, "Comprehensive Managerial Planning," in E.R. McLean and J.V. Soden, eds., *Strategic Planning MIS* (New York: Wiley/Interscience, 1977), p. 36.
59. Patton, "Managers and Productivity," p. 16.
60. *U.S. News and World Report*, March 14, 1983, p. 12. Communication Workers of America, for instance, were stressing retraining and a job guarantees as part of their contract negotiations with AT&T.
61. Craig Brod, "Managing Technostress: Optimizing the Use of Computer Technology," *Personnel Journal* (October 1982).
62. *Los Angeles Times*, November 19, 1982. James T. Yenckel, "Office Workers Eyeing Computers."
63. Brandt Allen, "An Unmanaged Computer System Can Stop You Dead," *Harvard Business Review* (November-December 1982), pp. 77-87
64. Annie Beretti, "Robotics: A New Career Opportunity for Technicians in Industry," *Proceedings of the 12th International Symposium of Industrial Robots*, 6th International Conference on Robot Technology, Paris, June 1982.
65. Robert M. Ranftl, *R&D Productivity*, 2nd ed., (Hughes Aircraft Co., Culver City, Calif. June 1978).
66. Robert M. Ranftl, "R&D Productivity," *Chemtech*, Vol. 2 (November 1980), pp. 661-669.
67. Gwen Kinkead, "On a Fast Track to the Good Life," *Fortune* (April 7, 1980), pp. 74-84.
68. Howard and Wilson, "Leadership in a Declining Work Ethic."
69. Gail Sheehy, " Introducing the Postponing Generation," *Esquire* (October 1979), pp. 25-33.
70. "Why Success Isn't What It Used to Be," *US News and World Report* (July 30, 1979), p. 48.
71. "Technology and the Workplace – Changing Values of the MBA," *Technology Review* (June/July 1978), p. 78.
72. Adapted from: R&D Productivity, 2nd ed., pp. 4-5. Copyright © 1978, R.M. Ranftl, P. O. Box 49892, Los Angeles, CA 90049.
73. Avard et al, "Technological Innovation – Key to Productivity," p. 40. Avard et al cite several sources indicating that only one in four or five major inventions can be attributed to major corporations and their laboratories. For the most part, major inventions are primarily the by-product of independent inventors and to a lesser extent small firms (started by ex-employees of large companies) and universities.
74. Patton, "Managers and Productivity – No One to Blame but Themselves," p. 15.
75. Howard and Wilson, "Leadership in a Declining Work Ethic."
76. Christopher Lash, *The Culture of Narcissism: American Life in an Age of Diminishing Expectations* (New York: W.W. Norton, 1978).
77. Adapted from: R&D Productivity, 2nd ed. pp. 50-51; 78-79. Copyright © 1978, R.M. Ranftl, P. O. Box 49892, Los Angeles, CA 90049.
78. David L. Wilemon and John P. Cicero, "The Project Manager – Anomalies and Ambiguities," *Academy of Management Journal* (September 1970).
79. David L. Wilemon, "Project Management and Its Conflicts: A View from Apollo," *Chemtech* (September 1972).
80. A.W. Gutenberg and E. Richman, *Dynamics of Management* (Scranton, Pa.: International Textbook), p. 126.
81. Adapted from: R&D Productivity, 2nd ed., pp. 14-15; 34-35. Copyright ©1978, R.M. Ranftl, P. O. Box 49892, Los Angeles, CA 90049.

82. "Survey of Science and Technology Issues – Present and Future." *Staff Report of the Committee on Science and Technology*, U. S. House of Representatives, 97th Congress, 1st Session (June 1981).
83. Kahn, *The Next 200 Years*.
84. "The Man from MITI speaks his Mind," *Fortune* (October 4, 1982), pp. 91-96.

Legal and Ethical Aspects
of (Project/Program) Management

——————————— Chapter 10 ———————————

Legal Aspects of Project Management

10.1 Introduction
10.2 Contractual Requirements
     (a) Mutual Assent
     (b) Competent Parties
     (c) Valid Consideration
     (d) Lawful Object/Purpose
     (e) Clear-Cut Terms and Form Prescribed by Law
     (f) Principles in Government Contracting
10.3 Basic Types of Contracts
     (a) The Variety of Contracts
     (b) Firm Fixed-Price (FFP) Contracts
     (c) Fixed-Price Incentive Fee (FPIF) Contracts
     (d) Cost Plus Fixed-Fee (CPFF) Contracts
     (e) Cost Plus Incentive Fee (CPIF) Contracts
     (f) Other Contractual Arrangements
     (g) Contract Negotiations
10.4 Common Contractual Problems and Issues
     (a) Statements of Work/Specifications
     (b) Disputes and Remedies
     (c) Warranties
     (d) Contract Modification
10.5 Patents, Trade Secrets, and Licensing
     (a) Basics and Requirements for Patentability
     (b) Patent Licensing
     (c) Trade Secrets
     (d) Patents and Trade Secrets in Government Contracting
     (e) Patent Reforms and Changes
10.6 Products Liability
10.7 Government Law and Policies
     (a) Keystone Labor Relations Legislation
     (b) Environmental Laws and Safety Regulations
     (c) Procurement Integrity
     (d) Other Laws

10.1 Introduction

A great many of the project manager's functions, responsibilities and actions have legal implications that can have a significant impact upon the outcome of the project and the financial outlays of the company. Although virtually all companies either retain or maintain legal staffs, the project manager must be sufficiently well informed about the legal aspects of his job to be in a position to protect the best interest of the enterprise through cooperation with the legal staff, particularly in interactions with subcontractors, the customer, technical and engineering personnel, and labor. This is an area that has been overlooked in most writings on project management, yet it can be a key element especially in the success of project-oriented organizations. In this chapter some of the legal matters that a project manager can become involved with are discussed, namely:

- Contractual requirements and negotiations
- Patents and Licensing
- Trade secrets
- Products liability*
- Labor laws and policies
- Industrial/environmental laws and regulations

Our purpose is to introduce the reader to basic practices, procedures, potential problems, and terminology; for exact legal interpretations and supplementary information there are excellent texts[1,2] available as well as large number of specific cases recounted in the extensive literature of law.† The material is not intended to replace the services of an attorney but to help the project manager avoid legal difficulties where possible and provide the necessary support to the legal staff when it is needed.

10.2 Contractual Requirements

Although many companies carry out their own in-house projects for the development of new products and processes, a number of companies are involved in performing projects for other companies or government agencies. In such instances it becomes necessary to develop a working agreement that is legally sound and mutually acceptable to both parties. An agreement (contract) binds each of the parties to do something or perhaps even to refrain from doing something. As part of such an agreement, each of the parties acquires a legally enforceable right to fulfillment of the promises made by the other at law or in equity.†† Specifically, this means that courts may award damages as compensation for losses sustained by a party in breach of contract by another or others. Furthermore, in cases in which adequate financial remedies may not be available at law, the courts may order "specific performance,"

---

* *Products Liability* is a "term of art" and is the strict legal term that is used when referring to this type of litigation.

† "Contract Administration," Vol. 1, Thomas Smith and John. A. McCann, eds., AFIT, School of Systems and Logistics, Wright Patterson AFB, Ohio.

†† There are four basic types of law: Constitutional, statute, common law, and equity. For definitions of these various types, see R.C. Vaughn, *Legal Aspects of Engineering*, 3rd ed. (Dubuque, Iowa: Kendall/Hunt, 1977), pp. 8-14, or any basic book on law.

which has the effect of enforcing the contract in equity under the threat of a contempt of court penalty.

Contracts may be either oral or written. An oral contract can constitute just as binding a commitment as a written contract. As a practical matter, however, agreements of any importance should always be and generally are reduced to writing. It is important to note that a contract may also be created by implication based upon the conduct of one party toward another (this is discussed later). In more general terms, for a contract to be valid and enforceable by and between the parties, it must embody certain key elements including (a) mutual assent as consisting of an offer and its acceptance, or a "meeting of the minds" (between) (b) competent parties (based on) (c) valid consideration (for a) (d) lawful purpose or object (in) (e) clear-cut terms and in some cases forms prescribed by law. In the absence of any one of these elements, a contract will not exist and hence will not be enforceable in a court of law.

(a) Mutual Assent

An offer constitutes a proposal to enter into a contract with the offeree (buyer), generally, but not necessarily, in response to the offeror's solicitation of an expression of interest on the part of offeror (seller). There are no legal requirements for proposal form or its degree of formality; however, a valid offer must embody three basic elements: (1) It must reflect the presence of contractual intent. (2) It must be communicated to the offeree. (3) It must be certain and definitive in its terms and conditions. When an offer meets these criteria, the offeror effectively creates and provides the offeree with the power of acceptance of a legally binding agreement.

Since in industry most proposals (or offers) are generally submitted in response to an offeror's specifications (technical data package or requirements), the offeree must take great care in the preparation of the solicitation to assure its feasibility, completeness, accuracy, and clarity. Any voids, inaccuracies, or ambiguities that may be subsequently discovered can be construed to the detriment of the party responsible for their existence and could invalidate the offer or the agreement. Care should be exercised in the evaluation of certain "proposals" (for instance, advertisements), as they may constitute nothing more than an invitation to do business rather than a legally binding offer. Just as in the case of the presentation of offers, there are certain ground rules that govern the proper acceptance of offers. In general:

- An offer can only be accepted by the offeree.
- Except for unilateral contracts, acceptance must be communicated to the offeror and be in compliance with the terms and conditions identical to those prescribed by the offer. In the case of unilateral contracts, acceptance is affected through performance of the act for which a promise was offered.
- Acceptance must be absolute and unconditional.
- Silence or inaction can only be construed as acceptance in special

circumstances that dictate that the offeree speak up or take overt action.

A counter-offer has the same effect as a rejection of the offer. Normally, a written acceptance becomes effective as of the time and place of its dispatch, providing the transmittal is properly addressed and stamped. However, the revocation of offers or their rejection do not become effective until they are received. It is standard practice to specify a reasonable time limitation on the validity of an offer including the mode, time, and place of acceptance.

Mutual assent, sometimes referred to as a "meeting of the minds," is thus deemed to exist when an offer has been made and accepted by the parties in accordance with the general ground rules just described. The term *meeting of the minds*, however, is often misconstrued and assumed to relate to a personal account of the mental state of each of the parties and their intent to contract as of the time of the agreement. It is important to note that such is not the case. The courts will typically evaluate and rule on the existence of mutual assent on the basis of an objective assessment of overall representations, dialogue, and actions of the parties during the course of doing business, since it is highly improbable that parties literally agreed on all aspects of the agreement reached. Usually, the intent to contract is not so much at issue as are the rights and duties of each of the parties to the contract. Taking time and being careful in reaching a "meeting of the minds" is thus extremely important since it scopes and defines the extent of the contractual commitment and consequently bears directly on the cost, schedule, and performance parameters for which a project manager is responsible.

(b) Competent Parties

The lack of legal capacity to contract on the part of minors, the insane, and intoxicated is well recognized. A contract entered into with such parties is voidable and should be considered one that for all intents and purposes does not exist. Care must be exercised in business dealings with any entities, be they individuals (consultants), partnerships, joint ventures, and even representatives of corporations. The capacity of a corporation to contract is limited to the areas of operations described in its articles of incorporation as well as by statutes of the state in which it is incorporated. In cases where corporations exceed their powers in the court of contracting, resulting contracts will typically be nonbinding to the extent that neither party has performed. If, however, either party has performed fully, this so-called *ultra vires* contract will not be voided or interfered with by the law. As a finer point, corporations are restricted to contracting only in their full, legally chartered name; thus any contraction or modification of the name, unintentional or otherwise, could raise the question of competency and lead to the invalidations of a contract.

Whereas a partner or joint venturer may enter his organization into an enforceable agreement without the consent of his associates, such an agreement may prove binding upon the organization only to the extent that it falls within the organizations' stated purpose and scope of activities. As a result it is possible to effect an agreement that may not be binding on the organization as a whole but merely binding on an individual with limited authority and liability. The key point is that capacity and authority to contract tend to be separate and distinct issues. They are governed by the state in which the entity was organized and that in which it does business.

Quite often a relationship is developed between two parties based on an express or implied agreement whereby one of the parties is authorized to represent and act for another. The party authorized to represent and act on behalf of another is known as an agent, whereas the party being represented is known as the principal. With very few exceptions, which in themselves do not lend to delegation, such as voting, an agent can perform all such lawful acts that are within the scope of his authority as the principal could perform himself. An agent differs from an employee, in that he is generally hired for the expressed purpose of representing his principal in dealings that can often have a binding effect on the principal's legal status. This is an area that typically causes many problems in contracting insofar as many employees such as project managers, engineers, inspectors, and others can make statements or act in a manner that may convey the impression to third parties that they are acting with authority on behalf of the principal. In so doing, they may effectively legally bind their employers even though they may not have intended or been authorized to do so. A contract negotiator for a company does have this authority.

The condition of agency can be created in several ways:

- Appointment, verbal or written, whereby the purpose and intent of the agency is communicated and accepted
- Conduct, whereby acts of the individual are condoned by the principal such as by not disvowing them in words or deeds
- An after-the-fact approval or ratification of the actions of an unauthorized individual as being the principal's own
- Operation of the law, which frequently involves a court order to correct a social problem.

The authority of agents falls into one of three categories:

- Express authority: namely, that communicated by the principal in word or deed
- Implied authority: typically, incidental authority required to execute express authority
- Apparent authority: authority stemming from such conduct of a principal as to lead a third party to a reasonable conclusion that an agency exists

As a result of these legal considerations, it is apparent that in dealing with customers and contractors, individual actions, particularly those of the project manager, can have a profound impact on the effort and the organization. In government contracts, for instance, such problems tend to be precluded, as key individuals authorized to represent or act on behalf of the government and the contractor are invariably identified in the contractual document. Normally, a clause is included that stipulates that if the contractor proceeds on the basis of requests or direction from individuals or representatives other than those identified in the contractual document, the contractor shall be doing so at his own risk and shall not be relieved of any of his contractual duties and obligations thereby.

(c) Valid Consideration

Consideration is something voluntarily promised, given, or done in exchange for a reciprocal and valuable commitment by another party or other parties. There are at least five key considerations in determining whether valid consideration exists. First and foremost, there must be some form of bargain and exchange. In other words, a contract will not exist to the extent that the commitments were strictly one sided such as in the case of individual A promising to do or give something to individual B. Second, voluntary performance without actual awareness or knowledge of the existence of the offer is not consideration. More specifically, there must be an *a priori* intent to bargain and exchange between the parties. Third, the obligation undertaken by each of the parties to the agreement cannot be one that either party is already legally obligated to perform. Fourth, a moral duty is typically insufficient consideration in support of a contract. Finally, the adequacy or apparent fairness of the consideration is legally irrelevant as long as there is some semblance of value in the exchange. The concept of valid consideration involves many legal intricacies that frequently have to be reviewed with and addressed by competent legal counsel depending upon the particulars of the case.

(d) Lawful Object/Purpose

A contract entered into in violation of the law is, of course, legally void and unenforceable. The contract, however, need not be patently illicit or tortious* to be unenforceable. Contracts tending to obstruct justice, violate fiduciary (special trust) responsibilities (public or private), circumvent or impede public policies and regulations may prove equally void and unenforceable in part or as a whole. As an example, California statute provides that a tenant upon reasonable notice and subsequent inaction on the part of the landlord may effect certain repairs and deduct the cost of such repairs from the rental payments due the landlord. A clause that has been and is still included in many of the rental and lease agreements used by landlords states that the tenant upon execution of the agreement agrees to waive all of his

---

* A tort is an offense against an individual, in the form of injury to his person or property rights "not arising in contract" (Vaughn, *Legal Aspects of Engineering*, 3rd ed., p. 28). *Black's Law Dictionary* defines it as "a private or civil wrong or injury. A wrong independent of contract."

rights provided in the applicable sections of the Civil Code. It should be noted that the statute specifically states that "any agreement by a lessee waiving or modifying his right...under this section...shall be void as contrary to public policy..."* If this clause were enforced by the landlord, it could be used by an informed tenant to invalidate the agreement. However, virtually all contracts contain at least two standard recitations to preclude the invalidation of the entire contract on the grounds of unlawful purpose or object, by either party or other parties, based on current or subsequently passed legislation. Typically, as part of all agreements contracting parties will seek to protect their interest by concurring (a) to abide by and be in compliance of all prevailing local, municipal, state, and federal laws and regulations in the course of fulfillment of their contractual obligations and (b) to invalidate only such specific clauses of the contract or parts thereof as may be affected and rendered unenforceable by the prevailing laws and regulations, rather than the entire contract.

(e) Clear-Cut Terms and Form Prescribed by Law

The courts apply various rules in the interpretation of contracts in cases of conflict or ambiguity. Some standard clauses that are often spelled out in contractual documents involving projects to reduce the prospect of conflict or ambiguity of the type that would require judicial ruling are the following:[3]

- Changes (for example, in engineering)
- Excusable delays
- Allowable costs
- Inspection and correction of defects
- Subcontracting
- Termination
- Default (failure to perform)
- Disputes
- Customer-furnished property or facilities
- Patents and copyrights
- Overtime and staff premiums

It is significant that in dealings with government agencies, certain of these clauses (commonly referred to as "boilerplate") are an automatic part of every contract by operation of the law. Exclusion of such clauses will not invalidate the contract since they are typically considered to be in full force and effect as if spelled out in their entirety.

Clarity is essential to the enforceability of a contract. If a contract is overburdened with terms to the point that its purpose is obscured, the contract will fall under its own weight. Since the statute of frauds is in force in nearly all states, certain classes of contracts must be in writing to be enforce-

---

* California Civil Code, 1942:1.

able, the prime example being contracts involving sale of real property.

To a considerably lesser degree than in contracts with government agencies, standard clauses are also attached to contracts drawn up by commercial companies in their negotiations for projects. Such clauses represent standard policies required by the (offeror) company that must be adhered to by any other company (offeree) performing the work. It is essential that the project manager as well as the contract negotiator understand and are in agreement with the boilerplate clauses of the contract.

(f) Principles in Government Contracting

With some significant exceptions, the same general principles apply in contracting with the government as with the private sector. The exceptions typically evolve from the concept of "sovereign immunity" and the "exigencies of public policy." Some of the more significant of these exceptions are summarized here:

1. The validity of contracts including all rights and obligations thereunder are governed by applicable federal laws and not state laws as in the private sector. Whereas the government has consented by statute to being sued on contractual claims, it has consented to such actions only after exhausting available administrative remedies.

2. The government acting in its sovereign capacity cannot be held liable for damages resulting from its general as well as public acts. The contractor's nonperformance under such circumstances is excused.

3. A public agent ultimately receives his authority form statutes that are public records and are thus presumed to be known by all persons. Correspondingly, neither the doctrine of apparent authority nor that or estoppel have the same force in government contracting as in the private sector. *Estoppel* refers to a legal technique in the commercial world that can hold a person liable for injuries resulting form innocent misstatements and actions or the failure to make so-called affirmative actions in correcting misconceptions that may arise therefrom. Whereas the courts have reaffirmed that the government is subject to commercial laws, those contracting with the government cannot seek protection under the doctrine of apparent authority, as they would within the commercial environment, because of these reasons. Since all persons are presumed to know the law, government agents must not only be authorized to act but also must do so within the scope of their authority before the government can be held liable.

Figure 10.1: Types of Government Contracts

Contract Variations / Contract Types	Fixed Fee	Incentive Fee
Fixed Cost	Firm Fixed Price (FFP)	Fixed Price Incentive Fee (FPIF)
Cost Reimbursement	Cost Plus Fixed Fee (CPFF)	Cost Plus Incentive Fee (CPIF)

4. As noted above and affirmed by the courts of claims, certain clauses including clauses based on executive orders, even when omitted from the contract, will be deemed included by operation of the law.

5. Finally, subcontractors are not considered parties to the agreement between the government and the prime contractor. This lack of privity of contract between the subcontractor and the government precludes the former from appealing disputes to the contracting officer in concert with established administrative remedies. The prime contractor, however, may bring an appeal on behalf of his subcontractors.

Anyone contemplating contracting with the government should become intimately familiar with the Federal Acquisition Regulations (FAR) in effect at the time.* FAR effectively supersedes the Defense Acquisition Regulations (DAR) and its precursor the Armed Services Procurement Regulations (ASPR).

10.3 Basic Types of Contracts

(a) The Variety of Contracts

Although there are many classifications of contracts depending on the particular contract characteristic to be emphasized, for the purposes of project management there are two general types: fixed and cost reimbursable. These classification are based on compensation arrangements rather than underlying differences in the intent, form, or structure of contracts and are applicable in both the private and the public sector. In private use where only commercial firms are involved, procurement actions are not subject to the extensive rules and regulations that must be strictly adhered to when dealing with a govern-

---

* Government documents are changed and updated periodically, sometimes with surprising frequency (every two to three years or with a change of administration).

ment agency.

Two variations of each of these two main types of contracts are possible to account for the nature of the effort and provide for a fair allocation of the attendant risk between the buyer and the seller. These variations typically affect or in the case of government contracts, specifically involve the net profit or fee to be earned by the supplier. Each type of contract can be let on the basis of a fixed or incentive fee option. It is thus possible to have at least four distinct classes of contracts as shown in Figure 10.1.

In government contracting there are further variations on each of the categories. These include the following:

- Fixed-price contracts with an economic price adjustment clause to protect the supplier at times of economic uncertainty against major fluctuations in the cost of labor and materials

- Fixed-price incentive contracts with successive targets (FPIS) to cover situations in which contract price cannot be established with the desired degree of certainty at the outset but can be negotiated during the contractual period of performance

- Fixed-price redeterminable contracts (FPR), either on a prospective (FDRP) basis through the negotiation of a series of FFP contracts or retroactively (FPRR) through the establishment of a ceiling price and subsequent audits.

- Cost plus award fee (CPAF) where part of the fee may be fixed and the balance established based on a range of contractor performance factors such as adherence to schedule, cost effectiveness, quality, and the like.

There are further variations of project contracts that cover special situations and are beyond the scope of this text. Those likely to be involved with government projects should become familiar with the specifics of these types of contracts; others may find them of potential interest as a basis for more innovative, risk-limiting contracting options and practices.[4]

(b) Firm Fixed-Price (FFP) Contracts

On a firm fixed-price contract, the supplier assumes and bears the full risk of cost, schedule, and technical performance requirements. In effect, he guarantees full performance on the contract usually until such time as the product or service has been delivered to and *accepted* by the customer. Government contracting practices require that costs be identified, supported, and segregated from the proposed profit. In the private sector, proposals are evaluated on the basis of the acceptability of the bottom line figure.

There are a number of factors that typically influence the desirability and

——— Figure 10.2: Fixed-Price Incentive Fee (FPIF) Contract: Schedule Incentive ———

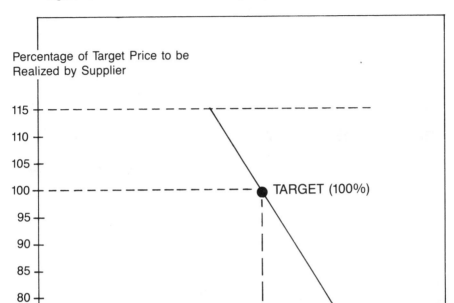

Percentage of Target Price to be
Realized by Supplier

TARGET (100%)

Delivery Schedule as Percentage of Target

Notes: 1. If delivery date occurs after the target date, the profit of the supplier decreases.
2. If delivery date precedes the target date, the supplier receives a larger profit.

practicality of this form of contracting from the standpoint of both the buyer and the seller. The most obvious is the availability of complete and definitive specifications. Even if these are available, buyer and seller should consider the suitability of this type of contract in the light of a number of other factors:

- The certainty (or uncertainty) of costs over extended periods or during times of economic instability.

- The feasibility, time, and cost effectiveness of developing complete and definitive specifications.

- The likelihood and anticipated extent of competition for the contemplated effort on a firm fixed-price basis given such factors as (a) availability of and interest on the part of reputable and qualified suppliers; (b) overall risk and rewards given the value of the contemplated effort, specificity of the statement of work, potential follows-on, other opportunities, and so on; (c) existence of a sound historical data base for cost estimating proposes; and (d) the customer's formulation of the statement of work inclusive of all requirements and specifications. As a general rule, when the latter suggest the "how" rather than describe the "what," the buyer should recognize the possibility that competition may be severely curtailed because of the seller's perception of a lack of fit or assumption that the solicitation is perfunctory and effectively aimed at circumventing company or governmental procurement policies.

(c) Fixed-Price Incentive Fee (FPIF) Contracts

Incentive contracts, whether fixed or cost reimbursable, are designed to stimulate supplier performance through appeal to the supplier's profit motive. Financial rewards are offered to contractors up to a prescribed ceiling to improve the negotiated cost, delivery schedule, performance criteria, quality, or degree of reliability. The most common incentives involve cost or delivery schedule. An incentive pattern is established to reward contractor performance in excess of the preagreed-on goal (or target) or to penalize him for performance below those expectations (Figure 10.2). Ideally, the target should expose each party to a fair and equitable risk, which suggests from a buyer's perspective that the supplier should have about a 50/50 chance of attaining the established goal or target.

The reward or penalty feature of incentive contracting as applied to overrunning or underrunning cost can be implemented in a number of different ways. A common method involves what is called the "sharing ratio." In the sharing ratio method, both parties agree in advance how an overrun or underrun will be shared. For example, if a sharing ratio of 80/20 is decided upon, 80% of any overrun is paid for by the government agency and 20% by the contractor; if there is an underrun (and this does not occur very often) the contractor will be paid 20 cents on every dollar saved. In terms of incentive contracting, FFP could be considered as having a 0/100 sharing ratio, whereas CPFF has a 100/0 sharing ratio. An example of an FPIF contract showing the use of sharing ratio is presented in Figure 10.3.

(d) Cost Plus Fixed-Fee (CPFF) Contracts

As the name suggests, the bulk of the risk on cost reimbursement-type contracts is borne by the buyer. Ordinarily, one or more compelling reasons will exist before a buyer will assume the bulk of the risk for a contracted effort. Among the more obvious reasons for contracting and effort on a cost reimbursement basis would be if it involves research and development. However, the fact that an effort may be labeled as or include R&D in and of itself is not a sufficiently compelling reason for the seller to expect or for the buyer to consider a cost reimbursement contract. Factors that favor the selection of this type of a contract include (a) an inability to define or describe the required scope of work with certainty, (b) the unavailability of a full and compete data

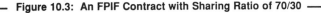

Figure 10.3: An FPIF Contract with Sharing Ratio of 70/30

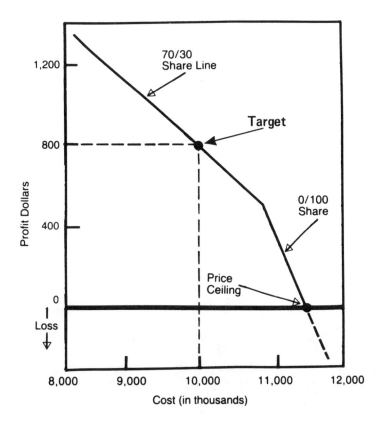

Source: Incentive Contracting Guide, Department of Defense and National Aeronautics and
Space Administration, October 1969, p. 24.

package, more specifically, detailed product specificiations, (c) concurrency or
overlap with related efforts likely to promote a high rate of change in requirements and specifications, (d) inability to price the effort with any degree of
accuracy, and (e) ultimately, reluctance of key suppliers to take the contract on
any other basis due to any number of qualitative or quantitative reasons.

The fee on cost reimbursement efforts is fixed based on the best estimates
of the projected cost of a particular effort. In dealings with the government,
allowable and reasonable costs are well established and documented; in the
private sector these costs, including descriptors such as "usual and customary," may have to be defined and negotiated.*

---

* Customary fees for CPFF-type contracting with government agencies range from 5-15% of the
target cost. If costs exceed target costs, the profit dollars remain the same.

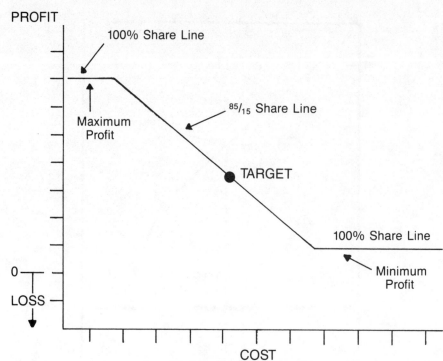

Figure 10.4: Typical Cost Plus Incentive Fee (CPIF) Arrangement

Notes: 1. Above target cost buyer pays 85% of overrun and seller pays 15% of overrun.
2. Below target cost buyer saves 85% of underrun and seller earns 15% of underrun.

(e) Cost Plus Incentive Fee (CPIF) Contracts

There has been a common misconception, perhaps arising from frequent criticism of governmental procurement policies, that a CPFF contract is a supplier's nirvana. The fact is that such contracts are frequently not as attractive to suppliers as is generally believed. An argument often advanced is that CPFF suppliers are adequately rewarded for their efforts considering that they do not incur any risks. A distinction, however, must he made between the relative fairness (or adequacy) of reward and the generally harsher dictates of economic survival. The ability to service and prosper within the marketplace is inextricably tied to an organization's willingness to assume risks as well as the extent of its risk-taking behavior. In government contracting, the CPIF contract is in part a recognition of the fact that CPFF contracts in some cases do not offer suppliers sufficient motivation to undertake a specific project or put forth superior efforts. Since about 1962, financial incentives in cost reimbursement-type contracts have proven effective in motivating the seller to the ultimate benefit of the buyer. Figure 10.4 shows the relationship between profit and contract cost for a CPIF-type contract with a share ratio agreement.

(f) Other Contractual Arrangements

There are sometimes special situations that call for types of contracts other than those just described. The basic ordering agreement is such a contract. This type of legal arrangement is similar to a retainer as the contractor must be available to perform various tasks on an as-needed basis with quick response. The tasks when required are authorized by a letter and the lengthy formal process of contract negotiation every time work is to be done is avoided. The basic ordering agreement contains ceilings of price and time and usually describes the general types of tasks to be performed.

A similar type of contract is the commonly used time and materials (T&M) contract. It provides for the reimbursement of costs (including fees) for labor and materials in the performance of work of a repetitive nature over a specified period of time. It can be used for such jobs as testing, equipment repair, overhaul, maintenance, and certain kinds of R&D projects where some degree of flexibility is desired. A ceiling price is usually designated but this is kept flexible in the event that the workload exceeds what was originally anticipated.

(g) Contract Negotiations

The actual negotiation of the contractual agreement between the buyer and the seller of the project is usually carried out by a skilled contract negotiator who may or may not be a lawyer. However, the project manager must be prepared to supply the necessary information and backup material to support the contract negotiator in obtaining the most favorable terms for the company. Debatable items during the negotiation can include costs, subcontracting, schedule, and even technical requirements and specifications. Of these the most important is usually cost, which in government contracts and to a lesser extent in private industry can include deliberations on:

- burden rates — overhead, G&A, material burden, redline items
- categories of labor (mix)
- labor rates — midpoints
- other direct costs such as subcontracts, materials, purchased parts, travel, reproduction, computer time, and consultants
- learning curves
- profits and fees

The project manager may be required to be present and take part in the negotiations by supplying detailed information on a variety of matters relating to the conduct of the project. In carrying out such an assignment, he must be prepared with the necessary data usually in chart form for backup if needed.

Contract negotiations as carried out in complex systems procurement is rightfully claimed to be an art requiring a variety of sophisticated skills. The role of the project manager is a supportive one; that is, he must be knowledgeable and available to participate and contribute in a positive way to the formation of an agreement that optimizes the position of his company.

10.4 Common Contractual Problems and Issues

(a) Statement of Work/Specifications

Contractual disputes most frequently arise because of disagreements about some aspect of the scope of work defined in the statement of work or accompanying specifications and agreed upon by both buyer and the seller. In general these disagreements are prompted by voids, inaccuracies, and ambiguities in the statements of work and/or specifications or conditions that sometimes extend beyond these issues and to a question of the ultimate attainability of the desired end. Mistakes stemming from mutually unknown, preexisting causes will excuse performance and preempt the contractual obligation. However, situations that arise in practice are seldom clear cut.

For the most part, obvious voids, inaccuracies, ambiguities, or other difficulties tend to be resolved amicably through changes and equitable adjustments to the contract. The less obvious difficulties particularly those that become cumbersome or tend to inhibit performance, may not lend themselves as easily to routine reconciliation and are often contested on the ground of *practical impossibility*, which provides for an excusable default on a contract. In the 1932 restatement of contracts, Sections 454-469, practical impossibility as evolved by the courts has been defined as "not only strict impossibility but impracticality because of extreme and unreasonable difficulty, expense, injury or loss involved." This is further supported by the Uniform Commercial Code (UCC), which defines practical impossibility as something "not possible within the basic objectives contemplated by the parties as evidenced by the contract and the surrounding circumstances" (UCC 2-615). This is consistent with a general rule governing contract interpretation whereby the contract must be read as a whole and that meaning must be given where possible to every word, phase, provision, and diagram as indicated in the section on mutual assent. A considerable amount of case law has evolved in recent years that has further qualified the theory of practical impossibility and extends the conditions under which it can be invoked for the purpose of an excusable default.

Because of these possibilities, individuals (including project managers) involved in the generation, review, or approval of contractual specifications and statements of work should be aware of the following general rules and principles:

1. Faulty specifications can and will frequently be used to allege practical impossibility. However, to use this allegation in the successful assertion of an excusable default, the supplier must not have abandoned the effort.

2. As part of a successful defense, the supplier must have demonstrated an attempt at using all reasonable alternatives.

3. Even total loss of anticipated profits cannot constitute grounds for the assertion of practical impossibility. However, if under commonly accepted business practices it can be shown that there is no feasible way of accomplishing the effort within contractual funding, the supplier may be in a position to invoke commercial impracticability as a basis for an excusable default. In more general terms, there must be a gross inconsistency between the negotiated funding and that necessary for the completion of the effort.

4. When a contractor undertakes an R&D-type effort with full knowledge of the inherent risks, he is unlikely to be relieved of his "follies" in the event of default. This situation can easily arise, for instance, when a supplier proposes substitute specifications that are ultimately incorporated into the contractual document without any reproposed modifications or actual changes before the execution of the agreement by the parties (*Hol-Gar Manufacturing vs. United States*, 11 CCF, 80,438). As in everything, there are possible exceptions. In *Helene Curtis Inc. vs. United States* (9 CCF, 71,922) there appears to be a precedent suggesting that a buyer, in cases in which he possesses superior knowledge, although not a fiduciary toward his supplier, "can no more betray a contractor into a ruinous course of action by silence than by the written or spoken word."

5. A supplier may in some instances avoid default or perhaps even obtain an equitable adjustment (usually in cost or schedule) based on contractual changes to the extent that specifications called for an effort beyond the state of the art as of the contract date.

Contract termination need not necessarily be occasioned by default of either party. The nature of work to be performed, for instance, may suggest that contractual termination may prove desirable or necessary at some point in time. In such cases the prospects of reserving the right of termination for convenience should be considered. Such a provision tends to be standard in government contracts.

In summary, technical specifications and statements of work should be considered key documents that require careful review and thorough discussion among technical, management, and legal personnel before being issued to avoid future disputes.

(b) Disputes and Remedies

The so-called technical disappointments discussed in the preceding section are not the only grounds on which a contract may be terminated. Generally speaking, extenuating circumstances including vital misrepresentations or serious mutual mistakes and nonperformance of either party in accordance with the contractual document, inclusive of all provisions of the statement of work, specifications, terms and conditions, and so on, are sufficient grounds for contract termination by default. There are, of course, mitigating circumstances, typically beyond the control of the parties, that will excuse the nonperformance of either party. Such circumstances include acts of God (earthquake, flood, windstorm, fire, and the like), government actions, public enemies, labor shortages, and strikes. These are generally spelled out in all contracts.

In a breach of contract, the aggrieved party may pursue a number of alternatives depending on the circumstances. The aggrieved party may elect to seek either temporary or permanent restraining orders or injunctions to compel compliance with the terms of the contract. In cases in which financial remedies may be inappropriate or inadequate, such as those involving property rights, the courts may order specific performance by way of enforcing the agreement in equity under a threat of contempt of court. Given a material breach of the contract, a supplier may, for instance, seek recision of the contract along with possible restitution to a position equivalent to what he would have had if the contract had never been consummated. Typically, restitution under such conditions involves the recovery of costs and expenses incurred by the aggrieved party in conjunction with the performance of the contract. In such cases, *time* tends to be *of the essence*, meaning that the aggrieved party must press his claim promptly upon becoming aware of the pertinent facts.

Normally, contracts embody a liquidated damages clause in an attempt to fix fair and reasonable compensation for any anticipated losses in the event of a breach of contract or termination for convenience. Such damages may not bear any direct relationship to damages ultimately sustained and at times may be either substantially above or below those actually incurred. As a rule, disparities between projections and actuals will not invalidate the liquidated damages provision providing it was based upon *fairness, reasonableness, and uncertainty*. Section 2-718(1) of the Uniform Commercial Code specifically states that a provision establishing "unreasonably large" liquidated damages as penalties shall be deemed void. What constitutes "unreasonably large" liquidated damages would obviously be contestable depending on the circumstances.

Typically, liquidated damages cannot be claimed under the following conditions: (a) when "substantial completion" of the effort has taken place as measured by the reasonableness of its competition given the intended purpose, (b) when excusable delays are involved, (c) or when bilateral (or collateral) delays have taken place.

A liquidated damages clause can furnish immediate relief without the need of having to engage in lengthy and costly litigation. Whether or not an aggrieved party elects to abrogate the agreement in the case of a breach of contract, such a party may bring a suit to recover damages from the offending party. It should be noted, however, that total damages cannot always be fixed or proven with absolute certainty. Often they embody speculative elements such as "lost profits," which may be difficult to prove. In addition, an aggrieved party has an obligation to mitigate damages and may often have to continue performing despite losses, which may further complicate the issues.

Recognizing that disputes and some of the available remedies could cripple critical procurements such as those for national defense, means have been evolved to work through disagreements while assuring the continuity of the effort. In cases where an acceptable and equitable agreement cannot be reached with the contracting officer, an administrative resolution may be sought through the Armed Service Board of Contract Appeals (ASBCA). In many respects this is equivalent to submitting to arbitration in the commercial sector. Other remedies available to a contractor are a request for relief from the General Accounting Office; a request for relief under Public Law 85-804 in cases involving amendments without consideration, correction of mistakes and ambiguities, or formalization of informal commitments; and as a final resort and upon exhaustion of all administrative remedies, a lawsuit filed in federal court.

Everything considered, given the invariably costly and lengthy nature of litigation as well as its somewhat uncertain outcome, the prospects of litigation should always be avoided where possible through cooperation with qualified legal counsel.

(c) Warranties

The effect of warranties is to protect buyers of goods and services from defects that may appear following acceptance. Specifically, warranties commit the seller to the repair, rework, or replacement of defective or unsatisfactory goods or services. They generally start at the time of delivery and run for a specified period of time. Although warranty protection generally ceases after this period, the supplier's liability in cases of injury or death caused by the product may not cease (see Section 10.6, Products Liability). Warranties apply to specifications and performance or the so-called fitness of purpose and are covered under the Uniform Commercial Code, which has been adopted in whole or in part by most states.* Section 2-313 through 2-315 of the code describe two distinct types of warranties: the express and the implied.

Express Warranties

Express warranties may be created by the seller in any one of several ways:

- Through seller's affirmation of facts or promises about the general nature, character, or quality of the goods or services to be provided, which becomes a part of the basis of the bargain between buyer and seller

---

* With respect to warranties, the Uniform Commercial Code is not completely uniform as the wording used in each state may vary somewhat. For further information on this subject see W.L. Prosser, J.W. Wade, and V.E. Schwartz, Torts, Cases & Materials, 7th ed. (Mineala, N.Y.: Foundation Press, 1982), pp. 754-756.

- Through any of seller's descriptions leading to a bargain between the buyer and seller predicated upon the goods or services complying with the descriptions

- Through the use of any samples or models by the seller in effecting a bargain with the buyer predicated upon the goods or services conforming to the samples or models

- By advertising*

It is therefore not necessary for the seller to either intend or formally guarantee the nature, character, or quality of goods or services to establish an expressed warranty. There are several different types of (express) warranties or guarantees:

- The hardware guarantee whereby the seller assumes the responsibility to correct any failures or defect over a prespecified period of time or operation. Such guarantees may include or be restricted to the correction of deficiencies in design, materials, or workmanship that are detected in the early stages of operation causing the specific item to perform below advertised or agreed-upon specifications.

- The supply guarantee in which the seller assumes the responsibility to replace or rework items based on defects in materials or workmanship that may be discovered within a specified period of time.

- The service guarantee under which the seller assumes responsibility for his services for a specified period of time and agrees to reperform defective services that may be required.

The type, duration, and extent of the guarantee will be influenced by a great many variables:

- Type of product and its use
- Susceptibility to failure and quality assurance provisions
- Ability to isolate flaws or defects at time of acceptance or delivery
- Past history
- Nature and extent of required logistics support
- Projected useful life
- Industry norms and competitive pressures
- Overall cost (usually the driving factor)

---

* See N. Baxter, Ford Motor Co., 12 P 2d 409; *Randy Knitwear vs. American Cyanamid*, 181, N.E. 2d 399.

Implied Warranties

Implied warranties as covered in Sections 2-314 and 2-315 of the Uniform Commercial Code provide that goods sold must be *merchantable* as well as fit *for the purpose* for which they are intended.

The concept of merchantability requires that the goods sold must (a) be fit for the ordinary purpose for which they have been intended and are to be used; (b) be adequately packaged and labeled and conform to the representations made on the packaging or labels; and (c) be reasonably consistent with respect to the type, quality, and quantity of units that constitute its specific class of goods.

The UCC further amplifies fitness of purpose. It specifies that if the buyer at the time of contracting relies upon the seller's knowledge and judgment in selling or providing suitable goods for a purpose known to the seller, than an implied warranty is created by the seller of fitness for the use intended. This does not apply if the buyer avails himself of the opportunity to examine the goods as thoroughly as he wishes to or declines to do so. Implied warranties can be modified or excluded by the seller providing that he specifically and clearly communicates his qualifications or exceptions to the buyer.* Aside from defining conditions under which implied warranties arise, the UCC also prescribes general remedies for their breach. Since the subject of warranties tends to be highly technical and complex, problems involving warranties require careful consideration and extensive scrutiny by the project manager with the assistance of legal counsel.

(d) Contract Modifications

Often during the course of a procurement process, requirements change and there is a need to alter the procured article in some manner. Therefore, most contracts contain clauses that make it possible to alter contract provisions. In the case of government contracts, these changes can be made by mutual agreement between the contractor and the government or the government can unilaterally direct a change through the contracting officer. The two methods of modifying a contract are by a change order (unilateral change) or by a supplemental agreement (bilateral change).

Change Orders

Change orders are usually issued by the contracting officer. To expedite the change, a contractor may be ordered to proceed verbally but a written order must follow. A change order cannot be issued if the requested change modifies the scope of the work effort; once the change order is issued, an

---

* However, there can be exceptions and complications such as (a) *Henninger vs. Bloomfield Motors*, 161 A 2d 69; (b) *Delta Airlines vs. McDonnell Douglas Corp.*, 503 Ff 2d 239; and (c) UCC 2-302, 2-316, 2-719 (3).

equitable adjustment in cost must be negotiated. The negotiation must be conducted in the same manner as any other contract modification. Finally, a change order cannot be issued after completion of a contract since this would lengthen the contract and change its scope.

Supplemental Agreements

Supplemental agreements are bilateral in nature as the government and the contractor mutually agree on a change before it is implemented in the contract. Since supplemental agreements are not required to be within the established scope of the contract, the contractor and the government may alter the basic ground rules of the contract. The cost of the changes must be negotiated and agreed on in advance of contractual implementation of the new work effort.

10.5 Patents, Trade Secrets, and Licensing

Because of the potential major monetary and competitive value of patents and trade secrets, it is essential that a project manager involved in the development of new processes, products, and systems have a knowledge of the law and procedures concerning patents and trade secrets. He should be able to recognize situations where potential patents can arise and know the appropriate procedures to follow. He should also be able to recognize trade secrets when they develop in the course of carrying out a project and be aware of their proprietary nature and need for protection.

(a) Basis and Requirements for Patentability

A patent is a legally recognized and enforceable property right for the exclusive use, manufacture, or sale of an invention by its inventor (or his heirs or assignees) for a limited period of time that is granted by the government. Article 1, Section 8 of the United States Constitution specifically addresses this property right by stating that Congress shall have the power "to promote the progress of science and the useful arts, by securing for limited times to authors and inventors the exclusive right to their respective writings and discoveries." In the United States, exclusive control of the invention is granted for a period of 17 years, after and in consideration of which the right to free and unrestricted use passes to the general public. To obtain protection in other countries, the inventor must file an application according to the laws of each country in which protection is sought, generally within a period of the year of the date of the United States grant. The period of protection in other countries varies from 10 to 20 years. Clearly, patent law in this country and others has been structured with the intent of stimulating technological growth and industrial development by motivating the individual through the prospect of financial gain. Patents may be granted to one or more individuals for *new* and *useful* processes, machines, manufacturing techniques, and materials, including improvements that are not obvious to one skilled in the particular art. The inventors in turn may license, sell, or assign their patent rights to a company or the government. It is common practice for employees to enter into an agreement with the employer whereby their creative inputs are routinely assigned to the company. A sample of such an agreement is shown in Figure 10.5.

A patent award is *not* a guarantee of the assertability of the inventor's claims. The assertion of patent rights can be extremely complex, lengthy, costly, frustrating, and ultimately an uncertain undertaking. At least 50% of the patents that are challenged in court are found to be invalid. Often the best way to protect an invention or a key discovery is by not disclosing it through a patent application but rather by safeguarding it, as long as possible, in the form of proprietary data or information. This in fact has been the trend in industry. Proprietary data or trade secrets are protected under common law; for example, an employee is barred from disclosing such information to his new employer or other third parties. Many organizations issue stitched, ledger-type record books with consecutively numbered pages to their technical personnel in which they are required to record their daily work product, not only for subsequent referral, but also as a form of insurance to the company.* Such records are of critical importance for verifying invention claims, particularly if there is subsequent litigation.

(b) Patent Licensing

Companies can circumvent patents in a number of ways other than by directly challenging by infringement. Infringement can turn out to be quite costly and is not recommended except where the patent infringed upon is on shaky ground – that is, the claims are weak and not well substantiated, either as to content or true novelty. One common way that companies get around a patent is to have their engineers or scientists develop a comparable device, product, or process that produces the same effect but is not identical to the item described in the patent. For example, the water bumper that has been used on automobiles for cushioning impacts and crashes and is patented can be replaced by bumpers that ride on pistons capable of absorbing shocks or other devices. The automobile companies have preferred to develop their own techniques for reducing this hazard rather than pay royalties or licensing fees. Sometimes portions but not all of several claims of a patent will be used as a basis for a new device. The idea is to design around a patent and develop a comparable product that performs the required tasks but does not infringe on the original patent.

There are numerous advantages and some disadvantages in trying to design around a patent, but before initiating such efforts serious consideration should be given to obtaining a patent license. Very often licenses may be

---

* The notebooks must be countersigned and dated by someone else "skilled in the art," usually a supervisor or lead engineer.

―――――――――――― **Figure 10.5: Employee Agreement: Invention and Data** ――――――――――――

In consideration of my employment by the ABC Co. or by any of its subsidiaries, affiliates, or successor entitles (hereinafter referred to as the "Company"), I agree as follows:

1.   During the period of my employment I shall discharge such duties as may be assigned to me by the Company and shall exercise my inventive faculties for and one behalf of the Company to the best of my ability and shall not engage in any other employment or any other activity that conflicts with or impairs my obligations as an employee of the Company.

2.   I understand that the Company engages in engineering, design, research, development and consultation and that the Company does accumulate, and from its customers does receive, confidential information which is not published or otherwise in the public domain. I shall at all times during the period of my employment and at all times thereafter hold in confidence for the use and benefit of the Company all such confidential information acquired by me from either the Company or its customers relating to the Company's or its customers' products, processes or business, including, but not limited to, its or their instructions, departmental procedures, circular letters, inter-organization forms, notes, records, curves, drafts, tracings, calculations, techniques, formulae, drawings, apparatus, and all other data in any way concerning the business of the Company or its customers. During and subsequent to my employment by the Company I shall not disclose or use (except in the course of my employment by the Company and pursuant to the rules of the Company) any such information described in this paragraph.

3.   On termination of my employment with the Company I shall return to the Company all originals, copies or duplicates of any and all papers, documents, models, samples or other matters relating to the business of the Company and I shall not retain a copy, draft, duplicate, representation, or extract thereof.

4.   I shall not disclose to the Company or its customers, or permit the Company or its customers to use, any confidential information or material belonging to others.

5.   All inventions, discoveries, developments and improvements (whether patentable or not) made or conceived by me, solely or jointly with others, during my employment with the Company, which pertain to the products, processes or business of the Company, or which result from or are suggested by or otherwise arise out of my work, are the sole property of the Company. I shall keep complete records of such inventions, discoveries, developments and improvements and shall promptly and fully disclose and assign them to the Company.

6.   At the Company's expense, I shall execute such assignments, patent applications and other documents and do such other things as may be deemed necessary or proper by the Company to enable the Company to perfect its title and obtain patents on such inventions, discoveries, developments and improvements during the period of my employment and for one year thereafter.

7.   Attached is a list and brief description of all inventions, discoveries, developments and improvements made or conceived by me prior to my employment with the Company on which no patent application has yet been filed. Should any question arise as to whether an invention, discovery, development of improvement was made or conceived during my employment by the Company, all such items not on this list shall be presumed to belong to the Company.

8.   This agreement shall be governed by the law of the State of California.

Dated ....Employee ....
Witness ....

Source: S.E. Stephanou, *Management: Technology, Innovation & Engineering* (Malibu, Calif.: Daniel Spencer, 1981), p. 74.

obtained with little effort at low cost and with attractive terms and conditions.

There are a number of sound business reasons for seeking as well as granting patent licenses. Among the most common reasons for seeking a licensing agreement are the following:[5]

- A desire to avoid the hassle and expense associated with resolving patent infringements
- A need to diversify one's product line, expand business prospects, and promote growth
- An interest in improving the design, producibility, or quality of existing products
- An effort to reduce R&D expense and delays or the prospect of injecting a greater degree of flexibility into the R&D program
- An interest in mitigating the uncertainty and risks in the development of alternative technologies

The patent owner, however may have a number of equally compelling reasons for granting a license, notwithstanding the hassle, expense, and uncertainty in resolving infringements through legal channels:[6]

- The prospect of potentially significant income without the need for an appreciable investment
- The possibility of stimulating demand and broader market acceptance through a combination of greater availability and selection of suppliers
- The desire to capitalize on the by-products or spin-offs of one's R&D program without the need for a corresponding commitment and tie-up of resources on efforts outside the mainstream of one's primary business interests
- The potential for making an advantageous agreement with a source or supplier of materials, goods, or services of importance to the continued success of one's operations

There are a number of critical issues in licensing that require careful consideration, review, and clarification by both the licensor and the licensee in line with their individual objectives and expectations:[7]

- The exact scope of the license grant (is it for manufacture, sale, or both)
- The degree of exclusivity of the grant
- The validity of the patent and the prospects of infringement as well as litigation
- The base and the rate on which royalties are to be computed
- The inclusion of the requisite know-how and proprietary data by the licensor
- The licensee's right to sublicense or sue infringers

- The specific rights of each party to any improvements made to the patent (for example, the right of the licensor to relicense improvements made by licensee to third parties)
- The abatement or escape provisions in the event conditions change to seriously affect the value of the patent

Perhaps the most fundamental issue from the licensee's viewpoint is the ultimate usefulness and projected life cycle of the technology being acquired or licensed. Both sides in these transactions tend to assume that the market for the technology will keep on growing and that each party will be in a position to exploit it without undue interference from the other. A key issue in these transactions is the establishment of the price to be paid for the license. There are no hard and fast rules in this area other than perhaps that the price paid for the license should not exceed the cost of designing around the patent and the cost of the inconvenience of this. Licensing agreements are often the by-products of intense negotiations. The common denominator in all of these agreements must be a fair and reasonable bilateral economic advantage, which generally can be forged from the various conflicting interests.

(c) Trade Secrets

Many companies rely on trade secrets to protect their technical processes and products. By keeping certain types of information secret, the company can often maintain an advantage over existing or would-be competition. For reasons of cost and immediate as well as long-range protection, the company may elect not to patent the process or know-how. Know-how refers to special procedures a company uses in making a product or conducting an operation that are not patented but are necessary and valuable in obtaining the desired end product. The composition of electroplating baths and the sequence of procedures used for electroplating are examples of such know-how. Other examples are the ingredients and preparation techniques for Coca-Cola syrup and wine-making procedures. Companies sometimes prefer to keep a manufacturing process secret rather than attempt to patent it and allow it to become known, especially if it is questionable whether the process or procedure is really patentable.

Trade secrets have legal status and are protected by common law. For example, if an employee leaves a company and is employed by a competitive company, he cannot disclose valuable know-how or trade secrets to the new employer that were revealed to him in confidence by the previous employer. There have been numerous lawsuits where key employees have done just that. In some states the illegal disclosure of trade secrets is classed as fraud and employees can be fined or even jailed for such activities.[8] Customer lists, suppliers' identities, equipment, and plant layouts cannot be patented, yet they can be important in the conduct of a business and therefore are candidates for protection as trade secrets. Along with trade secrets has come industrial spying. With the present high mobility of personnel and a decreased commitment of employees to the companies that employ them, disclosure of trade secrets has become a serious problem for management. Signing an initial agreement (Figure 10.5) diminishes but does not eliminate the problems. Ultimately, there is the matter of the court's interpretation of the specific facts for a particular alleged theft of proprietary information.

(d) Patents and Trade Secrets in Government Contracts

Since government agencies sponsor a major amount of R&D (Chapter 2), their patent policies have a significant effect on the patent rights of companies with whom they do business. There are two dramatically opposite positions on patent ownership; one is that the government agency obtains the title and the other that the contractor retains the title.[9] Unfortunately, all government agencies do not operate under a uniform patent policy. The Department of Defense (DOD) requires royalty-free use and can withhold publication of the patent for as long as security conditions require; companies are usually allowed to retain commercial rights. Other agencies take title to the invention and ownership as if they were companies. If carrying out the contract includes the invention and first reduction to practice of a new concept, the government agency obtains title and royalty-free use of the invention. This has been a source of considerable disagreement and negotiation between companies and government agencies. For example, what about patents developed by a subcontractor working for the prime contractor, where the patents are an extension or part of work that the subcontractor has been financing from his own company funds? Such problems have brought about extensive litigation. Because of these possible complications, some companies will try to do as much preliminary work on a new concept (using company funds) as is necessary to establish a patent position before using the new concept in the execution of a government contract. Then they can rightfully claim that the invention was conceived and reduced to practice before the contract was granted.*

The DOD practice of withholding publication of patents that have security implications can be troublesome for companies, since the invention may become obsolete by the time the patent can be issued. DOD may not allow the company to apply for foreign patents or to sell the product to a foreign government without agency approval. The State Department has withheld the sale of certain high-technology products (such as special purpose computers) to the Soviet Union and other communist countries.

The question of know-how and trade secrets is also a legal matter that must be addressed in contractual relations with government agencies or other companies. Some government agencies allow the purchase of trade secret data from contractors in return for reasonable compensation. Companies do not normally like to disclose know-how, even for a price, but it is sometimes necessary in order that the company can bid on government contracts. The

---

* A recent bill passed through Congress allows companies to retain patent rights on inventions conceived under federal research contracts (see Section 10.5e).

company may be asked to turn over manufacturing drawings and procedures, detailed design specifications and drawings of equipment, and the like. When so doing, the company may leave out key bits of information not immediately discernible to the uninitiated but necessary for the system development.

An additional problem of government contracts and patents is the view taken by Public Citizen, Inc., a nonprofit organization headed by Ralph Nader, that granting patents by a government agency to a private company is unconstitutional.[10] It can be logically argued that companies should not be allowed to privately profit from products or processes developed from the expenditure of public funds. The counterargument is that if the technology is not going to be further developed or used, it is justifiable to give it to a company that will proceed with its development and use by the public, which then benefits.

(e) Patent Reforms and Changes

Since its inception in 1790, and particularly during the last decade, the U.S. patent system has come under considerable criticism. Recent criticisms have been centered around several key issues:[11]

1. The large percentage of patents that have been found to be invalid when tested in court (ranging from 50 to 70%)
2. The concern of antitrust forces in the government that the monopoly aspect of patents is being taken advantage of by companies, to the detriment of the public
3. The large number of patents (estimated to be about 50%) presently being granted to foreign applicants
4. The arbitrary limit of 17 years, which is too long a period for the monopolistic condition to persist
5. The large number of patents that go into litigation

In response to these and other criticisms, various bills have been introduced into Congress to modify the patent law. One of these, SB 2255, addressed the monopolistic aspect and provided more stringent requirements for both the inventor and the corporation. For example, the bill called for the corporation (to whom the patent is assigned) and the inventor to disclose the best mode for carrying out the invention. Companies have argued that this could involve trade secrets and furthermore that inventor and officers of the company might not agree on the best mode.[12] Although the bill had its good points, critics contend that it would have jeopardized this country's leadership in technology. They also stated that the attempt to transform the patent law into an antitrust vehicle would make it more difficult, time consuming, and costly to obtain patent protection. Individual inventors and small business people would suffer most from the expensive and protracted litigation that could result. It could encourage greater reliance on trade secrets and add to the cost of using the patent system, to the overall detriment of the public.

A more recent bill compels government agencies to favor private retention of patent rights on inventions conceived under federal research contracts.[13] It grants large companies as well as small companies and universities patent rights for the bulk of federally funded R&D contracts, grants, and cooperative agreements. This bill will have considerable impact on the technical spin-offs from government-sponsored projects. Contractors performing work for a federal agency will have unimpeded capability to commercialize any product or process that result from project technical effort. The only exception to this would be technology or new systems that have national security implications.

10.6 Products Liability

Products liability has been defined as the liability "imposed upon a manufacturer or other seller for personal injury, death, property damage and/or commercial loss arising with respect to a product or service provided by it."[14] It has been estimated that some 20 million Americans are injured annually by consumer products used in and around the house exclusive of food, drugs, cosmetics, insecticides, cigarettes, flammable fabrics and certain other commodities.[15]

Products liability has become by far the most litigated part of tort law, most claims being settled out of court by some kind of financial compensation to the plaintiff. It is generally agreed that litigation in this area has not only reached epidemic proportions but that it has also had a tremendous impact on research, development, screening, introduction, and support of new products into the marketplace. Many argue that products liability lawsuits tend to be indefensible. Most certainly, the time and cost of deploying and supporting a company's products today threaten a large number of smaller companies with extinction, given the combination of skyrocketing products liability insurance premiums and multimillion dollar judgments. *McPherson vs. Buick Motor Company** (1916) is often cited as a landmark case that replaced the doctrine of *caveat emptor* (buyer beware) with the practice of *caveat vendor* (seller beware). In this case the plaintiff brought suit against the Buick Motor Company on the grounds of severe injuries sustained due to the collapse of a wooden wheel in the course of operating the vehicle. Buick argued that inasmuch as the wheel had been procured from a qualified and reputable supplier, the supplier and not the company should be held liable. The appellate court ruled that a manufacturer engaged in the making and selling of product likely to be dangerous in normal use, if it is made negligently, must take care in its manufacture even to the extent of inspecting component parts manufactured by a supplier. More recently, there have been the highly publicized cases of the DC-10 midair explosion, the Ford Pinto and the Firestone 500 tires.

There are three accepted theories today on the basis of which a products liability lawsuit may be filed.

---

* Law Reference III N.E. 1050. Another landmark case that is said to have opened the field of products liability is *Greenman vs. Yuba Power Products* (377 P2 897)

Breach of Warranties. Breach of warranty can be defined as a breach of either an express or implied representation of the nature, character, or quality of the product sold. Express warranties arise out of specific affirmations or promises made by the manufacturer, whereas implied warranties evolve out of the operation of law and are covered under the Uniform Commercial Code. The latter specifies that products sold must be fit for the general purpose for which they have been intended and for which they are to be used. These types of warranties are distinct and separate. A breach of warranty as a basis for legal action has been described as a "freak borne of the illicit intercourse of tort and contracts."[16]

Negligence. According to *Black's Law Dictionary*, negligence is "the omission to do something which a reasonable man, guided by those ordinary considerations which ordinarily regulate human affairs, would do, or the doing of something that a reasonable and prudent man would not do."[17] In effect, negligence is deemed to exist in cases in which harm can be foreseen and is not prevented. It should be noted that the concept of "reasonable man" is difficult to define, although there has been a tendency by the courts to interpret it as being a person of average intelligence, health, and ability. This gives the courts a wide range of interpretations. Negligence in the course of manufacture and assembly is also typically very difficult to prove. It is for this reason that products are more often and increasingly attacked on the basis of strict liability.

Strict Liability. The doctrine of strict liability has been adopted by the courts through changes in section 402a and 402b of the Restatement of Torts 2d by the mid-sixties.[18] In strict liability cases, neither warranty nor negligence are at issue but rather whether the product is "defective" so that it is unreasonably dangerous within the bounds of its intended purpose.* A major problem in this area has been defining a defective product. Legal decisions reflect varying interpretations of the word. Included are definitions that suggest an embodiment of unreasonably dangerous design, imperfections in manufacturing, and the even more conceptually difficult tenet of the imbalance between the foreseeability of injury in relation to its seriousness.[19]

Dudley et al[20] cite a number of specific factors on the basis of which verdicts have been rendered for the plaintiff in product liability cases brought against the manufacturer. These factors have included:

- Defective design
- Negligent manufacture
- Inadequacy of warnings
- Defects in purchased materials
- Negligent assembly
- Inadequate test and inspection

---

* In California the words "unreasonably dangerous" are rejected, the rationale being that this puts the test back into negligence which Justice Traymor specifically rejected in the Greenman case.

- Defective packaging
- Misrepresentation in labeling
- Incomplete instructions about use, installation, or maintenance
  Several defenses have been suggested and used in products liability cases[21]
- Modification of the product subsequent to delivery
- Unintended as well as unforeseeable use of the product
- Use of product with full knowledge of the existence of defects or danger with the consequent assumption of risk (or contributory negligence) on the part of the plaintiff
- Disregard of warnings including failure to follow instructions
- Abuse of the product

Although many of these defenses have been cleverly and successfully used in product liability cases, many experts nonetheless feel that products liability is becoming increasingly indefensible.[22,23] Among the reasons cited are the following:

1. Contributory negligence* as measured by the reasonable man concept is generally difficult to define. Aside from that, some jurisdictions are reluctant to recognize contributory negligence, especially when it involves dictating the use or maintenance of someone's personal property, whereas others do not recognize contributory negligence in toto.

2. The assumption-of-risk defense is often not available to a manufacturer in cases involving employees injured by a product used in conjunction with his employment.

3. In some jurisdictions, California being one, the plaintiff does not have the burden of proving the unreasonably dangerous nature of the product and that a defect caused the injury.

4. Certain disclaimers and warnings by the manufacturer have been suggested as evidence that designing around the problem would have been a more reasonable and prudent approach than putting the user on notice.

5. The Illinois Supreme Court decision stating that state-of-the-art evidence is totally irrelevant in all strict liability cases suggests the absolute liability of manufacturers.

6. The *Ault vs. International Harvester Co.* case found that certain

---

*If used as a term of art most states have done away with the term *contributory negligence* in favor of *comparative negligence*.

product modifications and changes can be introduced as a basis for demonstrating the existence of defects.

7. The statue of limitations typically runs from the date of the injury and not the date of manufacture of the product, exposing manufacturers to unreasonably long periods of time (this issue, however, has been addressed by a number of legislatures).

A great deal of the difficulty in products liability arises from the fact that most of the law in this area has been the product of court-made or common law rather than law determined by the legislative process. The issues are consequently often subtle and the laws tend to be in a continual state of evolution. Nowhere is this more evident than in the area of warnings. The courts have determined, for instance, that use of such words as *danger, flammable,* or *toxic* in and of themselves do not constitute warning by a manufacturer of the existence of a hazard. The courts have effectively decreed that manufacturers must warn of the danger, specify the severity of the risk, and delineate the consequences of not following the prescribed use. There are more than 50 evolving products liability laws just pertaining to warning labels.[24]

Products liability prevention requires the coordinated efforts of all of the major functional departments within the company including general management, marketing, engineering, quality assurance, manufacturing and purchasing, field service, and general counsel. There are a host of activities within each of these areas that should be audited to markedly reduce the prospects and extent of exposure to products liability. Detailed checklists have been prepared by Corley and Brown[25] and Shankula[26] for each of the preceding functional areas.

In more general terms, there are a number of fundamental criteria and duties imposed upon all manufacturers with which the reader should become familiar. These reflect minimum requirements to decrease the prospects and extent of exposure to products liability claims and focus on the front end of product research, design, and development. Dudley and Heldack suggest that before all such efforts, products should be screened according to the following:[27]

- Extent of need, usefulness, or desirability of product
- Availability of safer substitutes
- Probability and severity of injury
- Clarity or obviousness of danger
- Public awareness and perception of danger, especially vis á vis similar or other established products
- Likely effect of instructions and warnings in avoiding injuries
- Potential for reducing or eliminating danger without adverse impact on usefulness or economics
- Expected and projected users

In the course of design and development, Dudley and Heldack point to the following minimum requirements and duties imposed upon the manufacturers:[28]

- Reduction or elimination of hazards through design
- Incorporation of safeguards and interlocks for hazards that cannot be eliminated through design
- Identification of hazards residual to the incorporation of safeguards and interlocks
- Delineation of proper procedures and instructions on the use and maintenance of the product to minimize risk

Products liability mitigation is a complex effort that should not be undertaken without the guidance of a competent and experienced legal counsel. The project manager must give serious consideration to potential liability problems of a new product or system, particularly in the design phase. (See Section 14.2)

10.7 Government Laws and Policies

(a) Keystone Labor Relations Legislation

Labor relations can have considerable impact on the cost and general operation of a large project. Formalized relations must be set up between major unions and the company so that labor rates are relatively firm and in accord with union and government regulations. When contracts are negotiated, the position of the union is to obtain an optimum salary/wage and benefit package for its members. The company and the project manager must maintain this package at a level where competitive position is not sacrificed.

In carrying out government contracts, there are a number of federal laws that must be adhered to by firms doing business with government agencies. Most of these laws come under the jurisdiction of the Department of Labor and have to do with minimum wages, benefits, and work conditions. Some of these are as follows:[29]

Davis-Bacon Act – (40 USC 276, a-1 to a-5)
Walsh-Healy Act – (41 USC 35-45)
Contract Work House and Safety Standard Act – (40 USC 328-332)
Fair Labor Standards Act – (29 USC 201-19)
Equal Employment Opportunity Act – (EO 11246)
(including affirmative action) – (EO 11375)
Employment of handicapped – (29 US 793)

In addition to federal laws, individual states have their own legislation on fair employment practices. The essence of these laws is that there cannot be employment discrimination on the basis of race, color, religion, sex, or national origin. Furthermore, employers as well as labor organizations and employment agencies cannot discriminate against any individual in "compensation, terms, conditions, or privileges of employment," in recruiting, referring, hiring, or classifying.[30]

Employment Harassment and Discrimination

With an increasing number of lawsuits brought by employees charging harassment and discrimination, the project manager must be careful to avoid generating problems in this complex area of human relations.

Employers have long recognized their obligation to provide their employees with an environment free of sexual, racial, ethnic, or religious discrimination and harassment. An increasing number of companies accept this responsibility as an imperative dictated not only by moral and legal considerations but also by their quest for greater employee productivity.

Seemingly, problems in this area do not originate, nor are they as prevalent, on "mahogany row" as they are within the lower layers of the corporate infrastructure. This perhaps stems from the association of discrimination with hiring and promotion practices, the responsibility for which is centralized more in middle management. Many employees fail to recognize a personal responsibility in this area and the fact that any form of employee harassment – sexual, racial, ethnic, or religious – regardless of its source, constitutes discrimination and amounts to unlawful behavior. It is important to realize that harassment and hence discrimination can include many forms.[31]

- Unsolicited and unwelcome sexual advances, requests, commentary, or physical conduct of a sexual nature, explicit or implicit, regardless of whether they are made a term or condition of employment or a basis of subsequent employment decisions

- Derogatory or defamatory remarks or slurs about gender or any racial, ethnic, or religious group

- Display or circulation of any materials derogatory of either gender or any racial, ethnic, or religious group

Discrimination has occurred if the company allows these actions to either interfere with an individual's work performance or create an intimidating, hostile, or offensive environment. It is the responsiblity of the individual involved, his supervisor, and the company itself to initiate immediate, appropriate action to correct such situation. A project manager must be perceptive in recognizing such situations and assume that responsibility of correcting those they may fall within his purview.

Obligations Toward the Handicapped and Disabled

Most people and organizations that provide employment to the handi-

capped or disabled concur on two key issues: (1) Overwhelmingly, handicapped people seek nothing more than a chance to "make it or break it" on
their own.[32] (2) Handicapped people as a group are typically conscientious,
committed, and hardworking employees. Despite these attributes, the handicapped continue to experience difficulties in obtaining employment even in
cases in which their handicap has no direct bearing upon their ability to perform a specific function.

Under the terms of section 503 of the Rehabilitation Act of 1973 and 402 of
the Vietnam Veterans Readjustment Assistance Act of 1974, any employer
doing business with the federal government in an amount of $2,500 or more
has an "affirmative obligation" to hire the handicapped. These acts further
require employers to provide reasonable accommodation and to ensure non-
discrimination of handicapped/disabled individuals in the matter of promotions. Whether or not an organization falls within the category covered by
federal or state laws, the project manager should recognize that hiring the
handicapped and disabled has proven time and again to be "good business."

(b) Environmental Laws and Safety Regulations

As part of its responsibility to protect the public, government has enacted
laws dealing with safety in the workplace, working conditions, and environmental effects of the plant or business operation. Such legislation includes

- Occupational Safety and Health Act (29 USC 651-758)
- Clean Air and Water Act (42 USC 1857)
- Recycled Material Act (P-L 94-580)

Through the Occupational Safety and Health Act (OSHA), the federal government has set requirements and guidelines for working conditions in almost
every industry. These guidelines include safety and health standards that the
company (including the project manager) is legally bound to adhere to. The
requirements are very specific and cover a wide area, ranging from specifying
the thickness of a worker's hard hat to the maximum decibel noise level in a
plant. Management cannot plead innocent because of ignorance of OSHA's
standards; if the company is found guilty, it can face a stiff fine and be excluded from government contracts.

Today management must be certain it is not in violation of any environmental laws. The Clean Air and Clean Water Acts are constantly being monitored by government agencies. A repeated violation of standards can bring
action suits in the civil courts, large fines, and possible loss of future contracts.
It is much more cost effective for management to go through the initial expense of reducing pollutants than face the costly litigation process. Adverse
publicity about environmental violations and the possibility of a production
stoppage until the problem is rectified may lead to a negative image in the
consumer's mind and a possible breach of contract.

It is the duty of the project manager to become aware of any safety or environmental hazard that can arise as a result of the work of the project. A knowledgeable and alert project manager can avoid or reduce such hazards by ensuring that proper procedures are followed within his project and by all functional groups involved. This can only be effective, though, with the cooperation of all parties from highest management to functional manager through all subordinate levels.

(c) Procurement Integrity

On July 16, 1989, a far reaching law known as the "Procurement Integrity" law went into effect. This law applies to all government contracts, including modifications of such contracts, regardless of their dollar value. The law covers *the conduct of both Government Employees and Contractors including the latter's employees once procurement has begun*. Prohibitions include:

- Offers of Employment (i.e. discussing, soliciting or accepting an offer of future employment or business opportunity).
- Seeking or receiving gratuities or anything of value.
- Unauthorized exchange of "source selection information" or proprietary information."

Source Selection Information (SSI) is considered to be information "the disclosure of which to a competing contractor would jeopardize the integrity or successful completion of the procurement..." This information may include:

- Listing of offerors and prices
- Listings of bidders prior to bid opening
- Source selection and technical evaluation plans
- Technical evaluations or competing proposals
- Competitive range determinations
- Source selection board recommendations, reports and evaluations

Proprietary Information (PI) is any information so marked and can include cost and pricing data, technical data etc.

Procurement is generally considered to have started at the earliest date of the list of specific identifiable actions noted included:

- Requirements computation at inventory control point
- Publication of R&D sources sought
- Development of Acquisition plan
- Development of purchase request
- Development of SOW/Specifications
- Publication of Agency's intent to develop or acquire supplies

In cases in which contracts exceed $100,000 additional obligations are imposed and *apply to agents, consultants and representatives of the company*. The law provides that:

- A company must certify to the government that no violations have occurred
- Certain employees "personally and substantially involved" in the procurement (*e.g. Project/Program Managers) must certify to the company that no violations have occurred
- Stiff criminal penalties may also apply for false certifications

Individuals are certifying that they are familiar with the procurement integrity requirements, that they will comply with such requirements and that they will immediately report any violation *or possible violation. The unique aspect of this law is that it requires a good faith inquiry of the other party regarding whether information is/was proprietary or source selection information.* Furthermore, one must ask "appropriate" Government officials if the inquiry is of no value.

Penalties which can be imposed upon the company for violating this law include:

- Cancellation of solicitation/termination of contract for default
- Suspension or debarment
- Denial of contract profit
- Civil fine up to one million dollars
- Criminal prosecution and fines

Similarly, the individual employee can be subject to:

- Civil fine up to $100,000
- Criminal prosecution with fines and up to a 5 year prison term
- Prosecution of other various other laws

This is a very important and far reaching law with which everyone doing business with the government, either directly or indirectly, should become intimately familiar. This law was temporarily placed in abeyance subsequent to its enactment. It is a reflection of a trend toward greater employee accountability, in part, based on past corporate indiscretions.

(d) Other Laws

Other legislation that can affect a major project, particularly if it is for a government agency involve the following:

- Small business (15 USC 63-647(1))
- Minority Business (15 USC 631-647 (1))
- Products of Blind and Handicapped (41 USC 46)
- Labor Surplus Area (PL 95-89)

- Disabled and Vietnam Veterans (38 USC 2012)
- Women Business Enterprise (EO 12138)
- Buy American Act (41 USC 10a-b)
- Gratuities (10 USC 2207)

The requirements for abiding by these laws are usually set forth in the boilerplate clauses of an RFP and must be adhered to in letting subcontracts, hiring personnel, and other related matters. As noted in Section 10.2(f), some of these clauses, even when omitted from the boilerplate will be deemed included by operation of law.

———— Questions and Topics for Discussion ————

1. What are the principal requirements of a valid contract?

2. Describe the important aspects of an agent/principal relationship. Why should a project manager by very much aware of this relationship in discussions with the customer?

3. What is meant by the term *boilerplate* as it pertains to RFPs and proposals? How is it involved in project contract negotiations?

4. What are some legitimate reasons why a vendor could fail to perform? give some reasons that would not be valid for failure to perform.

5. Name some common causes of disputes in carrying out projects for a customer. How can disputes be generally avoided?

6. What are the two general clauses of contracts that government agencies use? How can these be modified to provide incentives for performance, schedule, and costs?

7. From the inception of a complex system to its final implementation and use, the type of contract used by a government agency varies according to the different phases of the systems acquisition process. Explain with an example what type of contract is usually associated with each of the systems development phases. Assume that you are the contracting officer in the government agency.

8. Assume the following scenario: A contract with a customer has been won by your company and the company negotiator has asked you to accompany him to the contract negotiations. How can you support your company's contract negotiator?

9. Government agencies are identical in some aspects of their patent policies but are significantly different in others. Give some examples and indicate similarities and differences.

10. What are the differences between applied and express warranties?

11. Why would a company choose to keep a process a trade secret rather than apply for a patent?

12. What are the pros and cons of licensing a new product or process compared with proceeding to develop your own competitive product or process?

13. It has been stated many times that government projects have multiple objectives, whereas project in the private sector are usually directed toward increasing company profits. Explain this statement.

14. What are some of the reasons why the probability of overrun in government contracts is so high?

15. What should a project manager who is involved in projects having considerable technical content know about patents?

16. Name the key elements of a preemployment agreement.

17. What precautions can a company take to protect its trade secrets and know-how?

18. Discuss some of the problems that arise in the setting up a DTC/LCC contract.

19. Give an example of a project where the project manager's knowledge of products liability would be of considerable importance. Why and how would it be important?

References
---

1. R.C. Vaughn, *Legal Aspects of Engineering*, 3rd ed. (Dubuque, Iowa: Kendall/Hunt, 1977).
2. C.W. Durham and R.D. Young, *Contracts*, Specifications and Law for Engineers, 3rd ed. (New York: McGraw-Hill, 1979).
3. V.G. Hajek, *Management of Engineering Projects* (New York: McGraw-Hill, 1977), pp. 86-97.
4. W. H. Riemer, *Handbook of Government Contract Administration* (Englewood Cliffs, N.J. Prentice-Hall, 1968).
5. Enid Baird Lovell, "Licensing: Reasons, Royalties, Dangers," in Robert R. Rothberg, ed. *Corporate Strategy and Product Innovation* (New York: Free Press, 1976), pp. 106-120.

6. *Ibid.*
7. *Ibid.*
8. "Legal Aspects of Management, Legal Preparation of Technical Developments," *Pulp and Paper* (April 1975), pp. 102-104.
9. Riemer, *Handbook of Government Contract Administration.*
10. K. Johnson, "Defense Patent Rights Policy Challenged." *Aviation Week and Space Technology* (March 18, 1974), p. 58.
11. A.R. Whale, "The Patent Reform Bill – The Con Side," *Research Management* (May 1977), pp. 16-19.
12. *Ibid., pp. 12-15*
13. P. Mann, "Draft Patent Bill Favors Private Rights," *Aviation Week and Space Technology* (October 17, 1983). This bill has since been passed by Congress.
14. R.H. Dudley and J.H. Heldack, "PLP Planning in a Multi-National Corporation," *Proceedings of the American Society for Quality Control. Product Liability Prevention*, Washington, D.C. (1980), p. 1.
15. A.B. Mundel, "Product Liability Prevention," *Proceedings of the American Society for Quality Control, Product Liability Prevention*, Washington D.C. (1980), p. iii.
16. J.J. Kircher, "Product Liability – Current State of the Law," *Proceedings of the American Society for Quality Control, Product Liability Prevention* (1978), pp. 1-9. This remark attributed to William Prosser, "The Fall of the Citadel," *50 Minn. L. Rev..*, 791,800 (1966).
17. *Black's Law Dictionary*, 4th ed. (St. Paul, Minn.: The Publisher's Editorial Staff, West Publishing Co., 1968), p. 1184.
18. J. J. Scanlon, "Preparing the Expert and the Case for Trial,"*Proceedings of the American Society for Quality Control, Product Liability Prevention* (1979), pp. 13-14.
19. Mann, "Draft Patent Bill Favors Private Rights."
20. Dudley and Heldack, "PLP Planning in a Multi-National Corporation," p. 3.
21. Mann, "Draft Patent Bill Favors Private Rights."
22. Mel Furman, "Defending Product Liability Litigation," *Proceedings of the American Society for Quality Control, Product Liability Prevention* (1978), pp. 25-28.
23. Robert L. Zink, "The Punishing of Progress," *Proceedings of the American Society for Quality Control, Product Liability Prevention* (1978), pp. 39-44.'
24. Milan Ruzicka, "Liability Based on Warnings," *Proceedings of the American Society for Quality Control, Product Liability Prevention* (1979).
25. George Corley and Francis Brown, "Auditing – A Product Liability Prevention Tool," *Proceedings of the American Society for Quality Control, Product Liability Prevention* (1978), pp. 45-56.
26. Robert E. Shankula, "Preventing the Cause of Claim," *Proceedings of the American Society for Quality Control, Product Liability Prevention* (1979), p. 19.
27. Dudley and Heldack, "PLP Planning in a Multi-National Corporation."
28. *Ibid.*
29. S.S. Sherman, *Government Procurement Management* (Gaitherberg. Md.: Wordcrafters, 1981), p. 279.
30. *Fair Employment Practices*, Bureau of National Affairs, No. 415, (February 1981), p. F-1.
31. Hughes Aircraft Co. (EDSG) Human Resources, *Update*, Vol. 1, No. 5, (Fall. 1983), pp. 2-3.
32. *Ibid.*

—————————— **Chapter 11** ——————————

ETHICS

11.1   Introduction

In a prize winning essay on ethics, Sir Adrian Cadbury* wrote:

"It is, of course foolhardy to write about ethics at all, because you lay yourself open to the charge of taking up a position of moral superiority, of failing to practice what you preach, or both."[1]

In some respects what may be even worse is that you lay yourself open to the prospect of a great deal of professional criticism. Our primary objective is, as was Sir Cadbury's, to acknowledge and stimulate a discussion of the role that ethics plays in our lives. We have attempted to do so based on an

---

* Sir Cadbury is the Chairman of Cadbury Schweppes PLC

encapsulation of relevant literature that spans decades of research, study and observation by a number of writers and authors.

As anyone in government, business or industry will agree, most ethical problems and decisions involve:[2]

- Extended and uncertain consequences
- Multiple alternatives and mixed outcomes
- Personal implications

All of us have a concept of "reality" based on our own organization and evolving perceptions of the complex world around us. They form the basis of our beliefs and hence the basis for our actions. All of us tend to cling to "what is" and, therefore, "what should be", frequently in the light of evidence to the contrary, as it is part of the stability we seek to achieve in our lives.

Ultimately, in government as in business and industry, a discussion of ethics generally reduces to an issue of the balance between social and economic performance. This explains, at least in part, the sharply differing views and frequently intense disagreements over questions of ethics especially in business, industry and government.

This Chapter essentially divided into three parts. The first part scopes the magnitude of our current moral and ethical predicament along with its impact. The second part *attempts* to provide a rationalization and a perspective as to the underlying causes of some relevance to our current environment. It is intended to set the stage for centuries worth of deliberations over questions of ethics and morality against the backdrop of more contemporary business and management issues. The third part presents some of the more important "belief systems" along with a basis for the analysis of ethical problems.

11.2 The Current Predicament

No single issue permeates our lives more or currently seems to command greater attention than *ethics*. The most consistently suggested reason for the latter appears to be the loss of anonymity due to an explosion of sophisticated technology and its applications. The rapid expansion of computer based exchange of information in our world of "full disclosure", "freedom of information" and other similar laws and public policies, in combination with the watchfulness of the media, has placed literally everyone under the scrutiny of a microscope.[3,4]

Questionable practices along with outright wrongdoing in nearly all sectors of our society have aroused public indignation and refocused attention on a need to reexamine our *values*. Reportedly ninety percent of the Fortune 500 firms have emplaced ethical codes along with nearly half of all other companies.[5] Interest in applied ethics seems to be at an all time high with some 11,000 courses currently being offered by colleges and universities throughout the country.[6]

While, unquestionably, a great deal of decency still exists throughout our society, the extent of duplicity and corruption found in academia, business, government, the professions, organized religion and sports abounds and is seemingly unparalleled in our history. Consider a number of recent and well publicized lapses in legally and generally acceptable standards of behavior in each of the above sections:[7]

- Student cheating and falsification of research by faculty at *several* prestigious universities.
- Numerous stockbrokerage scandals involving account "churning,"* insider trading, bank fraud including a variety of bank scams.
- Bribery and payoff of elected officials and government employees through illegal campaign contributions, "consulting" fees, grossly inflated "speaking honorariums," gifts and gratuities.
- Performance of questionable or unnecessary services based on conflicts of interest, collusion and kickbacks.
- Outrageous claims, demands and conduct on the part of sanctimonious ministers that neither serve nor honor God by their actions.
- Substance abuse, recruiting violations, point shaving and intentional infliction of injuries in sporting events.

John F. Akers, Chairman of the Board of IBM, citing the above in "Ethics and Competitiveness-Putting First Things First" writes:

"I do not say the sky is falling here in the United States...We do face ethical and competitive problems, to be sure."[8]

Seemingly, many view the above as an aggregation of isolated examples of individuals and organizations failing to live up to the generally accepted standards of our society. Consider, however, the broader problem of erosion of ethical standards explicit in the statistics provided in the source material from which the above examples are drawn:[9,10]

- One in four among us frequently lies to his/her spouse and members of their *own* family.
- One out of every three among us alters his/her educational credentials or other employment qualifications in some way.
- One in three among us cheats on his/her income taxes.
- One in three with an expense account pads his/her account.
- One in about three among us takes time off from work on the *pretense* of illness.
- One out of approximately every three among us feel that under certain circumstances *it is justified to steal* from the employer.

---

* Excessive trading of an investor's portfolio to maximize brokerage fees/commissions and generally disastrous consequences to the investor.

- One in three actually misappropriates supplies, small tools, mer-
chandize and/or other company property.

Experts estimate that white-collar crime stands at a minimum of 200 billion dollars a year. During 1984, criminal acts played a part in half of more
than 100 bank and savings and loan failures.[11] American workers reportedly
"steal" at least 160 billion dollars a year by arriving to work late, leaving early
and misusing time on the job.[12] Between 1971 and 1980, *at least* 2690 corporations of various sizes were *convicted* of federal criminal offenses. Out of the
500 largest corporations, 115 during this period of time were convicted of *at least
one major federal crime* or arranged to pay civil penalties for serious misbehav-
ior.[13,14] It appears there was no abatement to this trend through the 1980's as
the government pursued waves of illegal and unethical activity involving defense procurement fraud, money laundering, insider trading and a host of
other cases According to consumer advocates, corporate crime costs the nation as much as 200 billion a year in terms of corruption of government officials
and tax evasion; poisoned air, land and water. Price fixing alone has been
estimated to cost the American consumer some 60 billion dollars a year.[15] In
1985, federal income tax evasion was estimated at 100 billion dollars.[15a] As if all
of this were not enough, tens of thousands live outside of the "system", effectively at other people's "expense," as part of a nationwide underground
economy totalling as much as 500 billion dollars a year.[16] With our trade deficits hovering at or near 170 billion annually, we are challenging Brazil and
Mexico for the top debtor nation slot in the world. Seemingly, it would be
counter-productive for us to attempt to "sugar coat" our current predicament.
The drag and implications for our economy and society are clearly staggering.
We certainly do not wish to appear "prophets of doom," however, it seems
that a parallel could be drawn between the current situation and that which
prevailed aboard the Titanic: "The band played on as the stewards kept
rearranging the deck chairs." J. Irwin Miller, noted business leader, statesman
and humanitarian, observes: "We used to have problems to solve. Now we
have disasters to prevent."[16a]

As our culture becomes more sensate*, it appears to be giving rise to
distorted value systems. Researchers throughout the country have observed
and reported the emergence of *informal value systems* which accommodate some
forms of unethical behavior. Such behavior, as an example, is condoned on
the basis of:

- Perceptions of the degree of pervasiveness of the practice.
- Circumstances and/or reasons involved.

While many would still consider theft of company property morally and
ethically repugnant, they may not necessarily find the misuse of company
time, telephone and pilferage of office supplies objectionable. In a pluralistic

---

* That is increasingly empirical, secular, pragmatic, narcissistic, manipulative and contractual.

society, this tends to evolve from the perceived pervasiveness of such practices – the "everybody is doing it, therefore it's OK" syndrome. As has been pointed out, the mere perception of pervasiveness helps damage and erode our ethical standards.

Complexity and high rates of change have prompted specialization and a growing reliance on specialists. In many, if not all, segments of our society some have developed the perspective that a "layman" (or citizen) cannot possibly understand or appreciate the "intricacies" of the issues involved and, thus, should not be "confused" or "concerned" with issues beyond his "grasp". Many are taking the view that as long as *their* intent or motive is "good," the action is justified regardless of ultimate consequences. This often results in the withholding of important information and encourages dissemination of outright falsehoods by both individuals and/or institutions. Other unethical behavior becomes easier to rationalize in line with prevailing measures of success in an increasingly sensate culture.

The above situation has not been lost on foreign observers of our culture. A KGB training manual states:

> "The average American seriously regards money as the only thing which can insure his personal freedom and independence and make it possible for him to satisfy his material and spiritual needs. This typical American attitude toward money creates indifference to the means by which it is obtained..."[17]

Given the aforementioned statistics, the ultimate question is what accounts for such a disparity in ethical standards (system of beliefs) and what contributes to the seemingly broad based breakdown in morality (standards of behavior). Seemingly, this requires an attempt at discussion if not analysis.

11.3 Questions of Ethics

Depending on one's predilections, the current predicament could be ascribed to any number of reasons. These range from the simple to the very complex based on an interaction of a host of evolving philosophical, socio-cultural, political and economic factors. The latter are the very elements that make "ethics" such a complex and controversial issue today.

As stated in the introduction, our objective in the following discussion is not to attempt to provide answers to age old questions but to attempt to provide a perspective of some relevance to the current environment; to set the stage for centuries worth of deliberations over questions of ethics and morality against the backdrop of more contemporary business and management issues.

Much has been written and attributed to the Vietnam experience. Not all of our problems can be laid at the doorstep of this experience but it is certainly true that it has had very profound and far reaching effects on our society.

As discontent grew over the use of U.S. political and military power during the late to mid-sixties, it evolved into an attack on those perceived to be responsible and most likely to benefit from the exercise of such power. The values, perceptions, inclinations and priorities of an entire generation of Americans underwent *radical* transformation. During this period of time, absenteeism and turnover doubled and tripled respectively. By the end of the decade some viewed the "Protestant Ethic" as a *bad religion and a superstition* that served to sanctify violence and exploitation.[18] In just three years spanning the late sixties and the early seventies, the percentage of college seniors espousing the belief that hard work would pay off dropped from 68 to 38 percent.[19] This in combination with the "energy crisis" placed country in the lock of a depression. More people were drawing unemployment than at any other time in the history of the nation. For many, this had a staggering impact on their personal sense of freedom and independence.

> "By 1974 America had experienced a historical dislocation. The nation's continuity with its psychological past was fractured. The cultural myths which supported and shaped American character lost their validity and became targets of ridicule and mockery."[20]

For the balance of the seventies and through the early eighties the nation steadily slipped into a deepening depression seemingly fostering a heightened sense of the "need to survive."

Numerous studies have shown that the general perceptions, outlooks and motivations of employees have not changed a great deal. As of 1985, an overwhelming 80 percent of the corporate constituency perceived *no* correlation between how hard one works and how much one is paid. Approximately 75 percent ascribed our industrial predicament to a lack of such linkage.[21] A 1985 Harris survey indicates that 76 percent of Americans feel that the "rich get richer and the poor get poorer." The same survey suggests that 65 percent feel that "people with power try to take advantage of people like yourself". Most alarming are the findings that the majority of people in both high and low income groups feel alienated by the "system" and that the number of such people is growing.

Lee Iacocca, in his autobiography, states: "*I was also greedy...I was getting soft, seduced by the good life...Of the seven deadly sins, I'm absolutely convinced that greed is the worst.*" Parenthetically, this statement predated a reportedly record, one year, 20 million dollar compensation package received by Mr. Iacocca as CEO of Chrysler*. By contrast, Ivan Boesky† once reportedly assured a commencement audience that "greed is good."

The preceding is an example of mixed signals which have had a significant impact on the general public. A number of other practices of the 1980's,

---

* A portion of it, admittedly, may have included deferred compensation. Business Week (May 1, 1989) reported that for the 3 year period ending December 31, 1988 Mr. Iacocca gave his shareholders the least of any U.S. CEO.

† A former much admired arbitrageur convicted of inside trading.

have done little to assuage the perception that unbridled greed, along with a host of other sins, continue to flourish in high places.

11.3(a) Some Negative Reinforcements

In 1983, a furor erupted as automobile industry executives rewarded themselves with bonuses totalling more than a *quarter of a billion dollars*. The bonuses constituted compensation in addition to salaries, a host of "perks" and stock option plans. The timing was especially unfortunate on at least two counts. First, these bonuses came on the heels of a decade in which the U.S. share of total world production of motor vehicles slipped from 31.7 to 19.2 percent. Second, a partial listing compiled by the Labor Department showed that 13,195 plants closed their doors between 1975 and 1982. Of this total more than 1,500 were part of the *steel, automobile, rubber and textile industries*. Between 1979 and 1984, some 12 million people lost jobs abruptly through such plant closings with as little as a day to a maximum of a week's worth of notice. This led labor leaders and officials of the Reagan administration to characterize Detroit's bonuses as *"obscene."*

Overall, approximately half of the top 100 executives surveyed nation wide at that time posted incomes of *one million dollars or more*. In addition, executive compensation in 1983 rose an average of 14.9 percent. By comparison, consumer prices rose 3.2 percent, manufacturing wages 7.2 percent and after tax corporate profits 13.5 percent. All of the above received extensive media coverage and continues to result in widespread criticism of business in general and management in particular.[22,23,24,25] Business week reported that in 1960, the CEO *on the average* drew down 41 times the average pay of a factory worker, 38 times that of a teacher and 19 times that of an engineer. By 1988, the CEO earned 93 times the pay of an average factory worker, 72 times that of a teacher and 44 times that of an engineer.[25a]

Owen Bieber, President of the UAW observed:

> *"On the one hand, they (executives) say that intense foreign competition requires sacrifice, restraint and discipline...Yet they turn around and demonstrate none of these qualities by awarding themselves more personal compensation for a year's effort than could be spent in several life-times."*[25b]

This lead *Business Week*, among many others, to question "what is reasonable" or "fair for a job well done". Economist Audrey Freedman noted:

> *"...we're not talking about gods here. We're discussing relative rewards in a society for needed work."*[25c]

This whole issue has been the subject of intense ethical debate between economists, theologians and religious leaders, politicians and labor leaders, academics as well as management. It has become more intense over time.

Paul Bernstein, formerly Dean at the Rochester Institute of Technology, notes:

"When the deep reservations (of the theologians*) are summarized, a single question about the role of profit emerges: Why should a relatively few individuals, however skillful, entertaining, or hardworking, be able to earn so much while such basic problems as hunger and disease are not fully addressed?"

J. Irwin Miller comments:

*"There is an anesthetic quality to affluence...*It is almost impossible for an affluent person to imagine not being able to earn enough money to buy food. The fact that some people have to sleep on the street because they don't have homes *is beyond reason for an affluent person."*[25e**]

On the other hand, economist Milton Friedman in his now famous treatise "The Social Responsibility of Business is to Increase Its Profits" implies that business ethics is a misnomer. He asserts that business is morally neutral and advocates a "laisser faire" approach to the market and the forces that govern it. He argues that, left alone, the market will solve every problem and right every wrong.

"If there are social responsibilities, they are the social responsibilities of individuals, not of business."[25f]

Generally speaking, he finds an ally in Professor (Peter) Drucker insofar as the latter suggests that ethics involves *"grave moral questions to be worked out in the private souls of each of us."*[25g] In effect, both Friedman and Drucker view the concept of Business Ethics as nonsense.

Leonard Silk in Business Month writes that executives are attracted by the philosophy of *"ethical egoism":* namely, the contention that an act is morally right, if and only if, it promotes self interest.

"This doctrine permits the executive to rationalize his behavior as being in the public interest as well. And encourages a flexibility that permits him to change his behavior to enhance profits without worrying about hobgoblins of consistency or principle."[25h]

In *The Changing World of the Executive,* Professor Drucker states:[26]

"Economically, these few very large executive salaries are quite unimportant. Socially, they do enormous damage. They are highly visible and highly publicized. And they are therefore taken as typical rather than as the extreme exception they are."

---

* Most notably including: Popes Leo XIII, Pius XI, John XXIII and John Paul II; Protestant Clerics Reinhold Niebuhr, Paul Tillich and William Temple; and others.
** *Emphasis ours.*

True enough, however, it is claimed that "...high rewards induce a value shift...a callous, even brutal attitude towards subordinates, contractors, etc. Very high rewards do not necessarily bring the best in us, but they do seem to bring out something new and unexpected."[27]

Greenmailing, the craze of the eighties, underscores the latter and the perception of unbridled greed in "high places". Expressing concern over this phenomenon, Harold Williams, the former Chairman of the SEC, stated:

"We are dealing with the health of the free enterprise system and all that means for the strength and prosperity of America."[28]

T. Boone Pickens, Jr., apparently undaunted by such views, reportedly chalked up *700 million dollars* in profits (within weeks) by *"losing"* his takeover bid of Gulf Oil.[29] Many felt and feel that such "rewards" for doing absolutely nothing for the economy, and, *at the expense of a great many* are absolutely appalling. Examples of other "raiders" which have been bought off by management at employee and investor expense include: Saul Steinberg (Walt Disney and Quaker State), The Bass Brothers (Texaco and Blue Bell), Rupert Mudroch (Warner Communications), Sir James Goldsmith (St Regis), Carl Icahn (Phillips Petroleum) and many others.[30,31] This has fostered the view that "those at the top" will go to any length and any expense, regardless of consequences, to perpetuate their physical, mental and emotional well being.

"When too much is at stake, either positively or negatively, customary values become distorted...when people's jobs are on the line...unthinkable becomes thinkable."[32]

Other financial manipulations, such as management buyouts, have attracted a great deal of negative attention and raise serious ethical questions. From 1979 to 1986 the value of firms going private, by way of management buyouts, jumped from 636 million dollars to approximately 41 billion dollars.[33] Management's participation on both sides of the bargaining table has come under intense criticism even when shareholders are bought out at a "premium". Clearly, the overall process is awash with opportunities and likelihood of conflict of interest, insider advantage and misappropriation of opportunities. Many thus view buyouts as a mechanism and an opportunity for "management" to become rich by transferring value from the shareholder to themselves[34]. It boils down to an issue of "It's not what I got, it's how much more are you getting in the process?" Since these transactions are typically financed by borrowing against the assets of the firm and, since the opportunities to manipulate share prices in conjunction with a buyouts are significant, many consider this a "perversion of the whole process of public financing." A former commissioner of the SEC reportedly labeled this practice *"disgraceful."*[35]

The most severe criticism of business, however, has come from those closest to the inner workings of the board rooms. Joseph Jamail, architect of Penzoil's record 10.5 billion dollar judgment against Texaco, observed:

> "There are more pompous, arrogant, self-centered, mediocre type people running corporate America who should be sent on some postal route delivering mail. I know–their judgments and misjudgments have made me rich."[36]

Such actions and testimonials shake public confidence, reconfirm smoldering suspicions among some and reinforce the perceptions among others. In the end, setting a high moral tone at the top is necessary but not sufficient; actions must speak a great deal louder than words.

11.3(b) Evolving "Bodies Corporate"

Over the years, many "eternal truths" have been born out of the reiteration of unadulterated fiction. A growing number perceives this to be the case with top management's implausible claim of accountability and unswerving commitment to stockholder interests. Over 50 years ago, Berle and Means wrote:

> *"There is no longer any certainty that a corporation will in fact be run primarily in the interest of the stockholders."*[37]

Contemporaneously, Justice Brandeis in his dissenting opinion in *Louis K. Liggett Co vs. Lee* (1933) wrote[38]:

> "Ownership has been separated from control; and this separation has removed many of the checks which formerly operated to curb the abuse of wealth and power. And, as ownership of the shares is becoming increasingly dispersed, the power which formerly accompanied ownership is becoming increasingly concentrated in the hands of a few."

In 1970, Larner[39] confirmed that the so called "Managerial Revolution" was over and that shareholders no longer had a viable role in corporate governance.[40]

In partial recognition and concession to the latter, contemporary business and management literature is now replete with references of management's accountability to *"stakeholders."* The latter group consisting of customers, employees, creditors, government regulators, shareholders and similar groups. While a number of *theoretically* plausible arguments have been advanced,[41] there does not as yet appear to be a great deal of truly *compelling practical* evidence to support such claims.*

---

* Consider as an example the actions and reactions of the insurance industry in California prior and subsequent to the passage of proposition 103 (the voter insurance initiative).

Stockholder interest has served as a basis for the corporate self absolution of a multitude of "sins" as top management continues to promote the greatest possible decoupling between corporate ownership and its control.* The actual extent of this decoupling has become apparent as part of the takeover fever. In line with this development, some have gone on to propose, devise and justify impenetrable defenses as being in the ultimate best interests of the stockholder. Proposals have included the creation of two classes of stock, the net effect of which is to vest corporate control securely in the hands of management with as little as five percent of company stock. Legislation aimed at restricting "unfriendly" takeovers, and thus potentially the legitimate rights of the stockholders, has been introduced and vetoed in some states. It is undoubtedly coincidental nonetheless interesting to note that such developments were taking place in step with the growing displeasure of pension funds with executive performance.†

The trend towards debt financing has generally relaxed pressures on profitability and increased the degree of management independence. Currently less than about five percent of corporate funds are raised through stock issues. In addition, laws relating to double taxation of dividends have encouraged the payout of dividends at rates below 50 percent of realized profits. From a shareholder viewpoint, recent takeover battles have exacerbated this general problem. They have typically prompted heavy borrowing and corporate restructuring with profound impact not only on earnings but the organization's earning capacity for many years to come. A case in point is Phillips Petroleum which has found it necessary to divest itself of about *a billion* dollars worth of assets to pay off heavy debts incurred as part of it's management's attempts to escape the clutches of T. Boone Pickens and Carl Icahn. It is highly questionable whether Phillips Petroleum's predicament can be considered a byproduct of management's active concern over the *best interests* of it's shareholders. Phillips Petroleum is not alone in this regard.

During 1984, some 78 billion dollars in *equity disappeared* and U.S. corporations went on to *assume 169 billion dollars in new debt*. Shareholders are not the only ones impacted by top management's efforts at self preservation. Heavy debts affect company credit ratings. When the corporate credit rating drops, the price of corporate bonds plummet. Under such conditions bond holders lose a lot of money.

Based on the above many believe that the stockholder has become a pas-

---

* The "metamorphosis" of the corporation has been addressed by a number of scholars and authors. Among the classic works are those of Charles C. Abbott, "The Rise of the Business Corporation" (1936); James Burnham, "The Managerial Revolution" (1941); Adolph Berle, Jr. "Power Without Property" (1959) and others.

† A Council of Institutional Investors was formed in January of 1985 to share ideas and evaluate complex merger situations. The Council was the brain child of the late Jesse Unruh, California State Treasurer. As trustee for two pension funds totalling 37.5 billion dollars, Unruh became upset by the greenmailing of Phillips, Texaco and Walt Disney which seemingly benefitted everyone involved except the two California pension funds. Among the objectives of the Council were to be attempts to head off potentially bad takeover legislation.

sive recipient of income doled out at top management's discretion. In spite of all this, the management community and its extensions still promote the idea that their primary aims and responsibilities are to maximize shareholder profits. In the words of Sir Cadbury.[42]

> "The ethical standards of a company are judged by its actions, not by pious statements of intent put out in its name."

Today's corporation is primarily a modern development "singularly independent of both the sovereign power which created it and of the men who compose it..."; it is now "curiously free of control from either direction."[43] It is, therefore, widely accepted that there is no longer control over the corporation by its "ownership" in line with the legal doctrine which brought the corporation into being. This is, in part, reinforced by the fact that:

> "The board of directors, which was supposed to supervise management and express the interests of stockholders, frequently lost the ability to control management effectively. More often than not, it was nominated and effectively controlled by top management."[44]

With mutual fund sales to American households hovering well over 100 billion dollars, critics point to a need for re-examination of the broader, more direct role and function which "fiduciary" institutions should play *on behalf of over 40 million stock holding Americans.* For all intents and purposes, *over 40 million Americans* now participating in the stock market *have nothing more than a contract right to some sum of money.* Reportedly, concentrated financial action by pension funds has generally been ruled out on the basis of existing anti-trust and feduciary laws. This situation continues to fuel the age old debate over concentration of economic and political power, the corporation's social and communal responsibilities and ethics. With respect to the latter, the majority remains highly skeptical over the corporate rush to adopt ethics codes as they perceive the latter to be:[45,46,47]

- At best, public relations posturing.
- At worst, an attempt to shift the blame for bad conduct from the company to the individual.

The public along with some members of management have expressed serious reservations over executive willingness to dig below the surface and into the full range of ethical issues facing corporate management.[48] Professor A.B. Carroll writes: "...the business landscape is cluttered with amoral as well as immoral managers."[48a]

The perception (or recognition) that management is not accountable to stockholders leads to a general discounting of stockholder interests, those of other stakeholders and a claim to a "share of the spoils." Clearly these developments have fostered a feeling among people that: "if the high and the mighty can act like that, I can, too – and the sooner I get mine, the better."[49] For some the "spoils" amount to time off on pretense of illness, to others paper, pencils and small tools, for others still padding of expense accounts, and so on.

11.3(c) Contrasting View of Society

Ideological and cultural conditioning often precludes many of us from seeing the dynamics of the work place in terms other than those involving the traditional work ethic. Namely, that work has value and is important to the employee. Specifically, that it is valuable and important based on its desirable consequences or, alternatively, as a morally or socially acceptable activity.[50,51]

Max Weber, in his classic series of essays on "The Protestant Ethic and the Spirit of Capitalism", documented a fundamental change in business ideology which occurred sometime between the Middle Ages and the Industrial Revolution. He points out that a radical break with the traditional and socially approved conduct of business took place about the time of the Protestant Reformation. As Weber saw it, the Protestant Reformation displaced the idea that innovation and initiative in business beyond the "traditionalist" norms was immoral and socially deviant behavior.

The accumulation of wealth, although often deplored for its bad consequences, became a measure of one's degree of industry and frugality. The latter were viewed not as means to salvation but as means of avoiding damnation. Based on biblical interpretations, industry and frugality became vehicles for earning God's favor. Weber supports his observations, in part, by quoting John Wesley:[52]

> "We ought not prevent people from being diligent and frugal; we must exhort all Christians to gain all they can, and to save all they can; that is, in effect, to grow rich."

The Protestant Ethic was Weber's characterization of the *spirit of economic initiative and competition* which became part of a *philosophy* of life *intimately tied to religious activity.* As Cherrington points out, the work ethic is an embodiment of a system of obligating beliefs based on the perceived moral and religious imperative of work and reflected in the entrenched precepts that "good" peopl:e[53]

- Devote their life to work regardless of the time, effort or drudgery involved.
- Have dependable and punctual attendance records.
- Take pride in work, do the job well and strive to be as productive as possible.
- Strive to advance despite and in spite of obstacles, *or ultimate success*, through hard work, thrift and wise investment.
- Display unswerving loyalty to their jobs, work groups and perhaps above all the company.

This philosophy of life was the prime mover behind the economic growth and development of early America. Things, however have changed considerably since those early days. It is often said that those that are most vociferous in bemoaning the erosion of the Protestant Ethic are least likely to apply its precepts to their own standards of conduct.

As Professor Hauserman[54] points outs, today more than 90 percent of the people employed are dependent on a wage or salary. In the late nineteenth century this number was less than fifty percent. She quotes an excerpt from the *Report of the Special Task Force to the Secretary of the HEW* that is well worth revisiting:

> "We have become a nation of employees. We are dependent upon others for our means of livelihood, and most of our people have become completely dependent upon wages. If they lose their jobs they lose every resource, except for the relief supplied by the various forms of social security. Such dependence of the mass of the people upon others for *all* of their income is something new in the world. *For our generation the substance of life is in another man's hands".*[55]

The preceding has very broad and profound implications. As Hays points out:[56]

> "...the earnings of a job are basic to *personal freedom*...a job has become *the most significant property right of our time."**

The issue of individual freedom and self determination has become the basis for the evolution of all other perceived "entitlements" of our democratic society. In effect, for many "prosperity" has evolved into a divine right, displacing the precepts of self reliance, personal initiative and the imperative of work traditionally ascribed to the Protestant Ethic.

The concept of "entitlement" has resulted in a shift in "values," growing expectations of and emphasis on "personal profit," broader *non-job* related needs, concerns and interests. Among these are family life and friends, feelings of *independence and self-determination*, community involvement, the environment, leisure life and free time. As O'Toole points out:

> "While our current managerial policies and practices were compatible with American culture...these became out of synch as a result of the turbulent social shifts. Mixed with the potent catalyst of affluence (they have) conspired to alter *the values of the nation and subtly but ineluctably change the rules under which people are willing to work hard or are committed to their jobs...*In essence managers must understand that they

---

* Emphasis ours.

are dealing *not with superficial changes in society but fundamental ones.*"[57]*

Despite revolutionary changes in the philosophy and organization of work, including significant improvements in mass-production techniques, we have experienced an erosion in productivity and competitive strength. Many analysts have taken the view that our current problems have resulted from a mismatch between the philosophy and organization of work on one hand and "economic reality" on the other.[58] Depending on one's point of view valid arguments could be made either pro-business or pro-labor.

In many respects, Kahn views this mismatch as a by product of the failures of our past success. Among the contemporary developments he cites are the following:[59]

- A relative lack of self discipline borne out of affluence and emphasis on the immediate gratification of our material wants.
- Consuming preoccupation with our physical safety, health, recreation and longevity.
- Growing secularism with an attendant loss of uplifting values, goals and ideals based on the premise that there are no absolutes except human life and the entitlement of the people.
- Imposition of impossible demands and unrealistic expectations based on anticipated governmental intervention and the promise of advances in technology.
- Promotion and evolution of an open and radically egalitarian society with no distinction between superior and inferior performance or individuals (employer/employee distinction; "entitlements?")

Christopher Lasch in the *"Culture of Narcissism"* arrives at similar conclusions with respect to our state of socio-cultural and economic evolution.[60]

Based on the preceding discussion, it is apparent that, collectively, we seem to have lost a certain sense of balance and proportion. Given the preceding, we must revert to a reexamination of the "basics," for it is the so called basics that clearly hold the key to our future growth or further decline.

11.3(d) Economic vs. Social Performance

As Steiner and Steiner point out, capitalism and democracy are *equally valid yet competing systems.* Whereas capitalism is based on economic efficiency, decentralized decision making and self-interest; the cornerstone of democracy is popular sovereignty, equality and majority rule.[61] Based on the preceding, they point to a continual process of "reconciliation" between these competing value systems. This view reflects Kondratieff's long wave economic theory which suggests that shortcomings and excesses of the capitalist system self-correct on a cyclical basis and thus keep the system from breaking down as

---

* Emphasis ours.

predicted by Karl Marx.[52*]

The above is consistent with prevailing and generally accepted view that a *balance must be sought and found between economic and social performance.*[63,64]

It is evident from numerous sources that a majority of our society does not believe that a satisfactory balance has been achieved between economic and social performance. Poll after poll continues to show that in spite of all of its faults and shortcomings, the American people strongly support our form of the free enterprise system. These findings are important insofar as they show that the American people *do not want fundamental ideological change,* rather, *they expect better functioning of the business system.*[65]

These views have been reinforced by a continuous stream of articles and reports either alleging or detailing bureaucratic bungling, "influence peddling" and corruption in both the public and private sectors; corporate irresponsibility and wrongdoing; executive greed, insensitivity and mismanagement. Sharing headlines with the above have been the plights of the homeless; the hungry and the sick; the poor and unemployed; the very young and the elderly. Such contrasting headlines have fostered the perception that, for the most part, when all is said and done, earnings take priority over human misery, alcoholism and drug abuse, divorce, suicide, etc.[66] This premise is clearly unacceptable to a great majority.

Irving Shapiro in "America's Third Revolution" writes:

> "For business there must be a correspondence between capitalism and decency...The profit motive is still endorsed – survey after survey has shown that the public has no objection to business making money – but the *allowable limits of behavior* have changed...Private gain remains a necessary condition of commerce, *but is no longer a sufficient one...The objective now should be not just to make individual companies perform better but also to make the whole system work better...*"[67†]

Social responsibility goes beyond the concept and the practice of being a "good neighbor." Tax deductible contributions of a self promoting nature such as to local charities, churches, youth groups, schools and the like may be commendable but are not an indication of social responsibility.

> *"There is no charity for charity's sake in our handling of the Company's money or in asking the Company's people to give of their time. Procter & Gamble's support of civic campaigns is now and will always be limited to what we believe represents the enlightened self-interest of the business"* - E. G. Harness, CEO.[67a]

---

* Professor Joseph Shumpeter (in: "Capitalism, Socialism and Democracy:, 3rd ed., Harper Row, New York, 1950, pp. 83-84) subsequently adopted and elaborated on the idea of economic cycles. His works along with those of Kondriatieff were set aside after World War II, when economists and politicians believed government had learned to smooth out business cycles, then rediscovered during the stagflation of the 1970's.
† Emphasis ours.

Such actions must be weighed against other common practices which have led, as an example, to the imposition of the Unitary Tax – by a number of states – to combat creative accounting practices by multinationals unwilling to pay their fair share of taxes within a given sovereignty.* The latter is an example of the very kinds of practices that bring into question the *values struc-ture* maintained by the modern corporation.**

The intensity of feelings this general issue generates is reflected in the more vituperative views that appear with greater frequency in both main-stream and the more conservative media:

> "Institutions exists for their own narrow interests, and will perpetuate themselves by whatever means they can get away with. Institutions never exist for our own sakes; but the success of institutions is de-pendent upon our believing that they exist for our own benefit...When you ask, *cui bono* ("who benefits"?), you should quickly be able to see how, 'in our trickle down' system, there are upstream hogs getting more out of the trough than you are, and that their priorities – at your expense – are dependent upon your believing that the trough is there for your benefit and, further, that you control its flow" (The Orange County Register).[68]

Few question the need for profit as the means of sustaining an economi-cally viable concern, in part, through investment in research, development, modernization of facilities and the rehabilitation of employees in select parts of the company. The problem clearly arises when profit is seen as or becomes an end in itself devoid of all other considerations. It is crucial that we recog-nize that "...if democracy is to survive, it must be generally perceived to work reasonably well for all its members, not just for selected groups. The percent-age of Americans for whom America works well is diminishing"[69a]. The cen-tral issue ultimately reduces to a question of whether prospects of short to medium range profit *maximization* to pacify flitting financial manipulators, outweighs longer range profit *optimization* in line with communal and national best interests. Consider, as an example, that several commercial as well as aerospace companies are automating their operations in surplus labor coun-tries that provide attractive tax structures largely based on the existence of labor surpluses. Prime example of such a country is Mexico with its

---

* Some multinational companies have "arranged" their books among their subsidiaries in such a manner as to shift profits to the lower-tax entities. By so doing they deny the higher tax states in which they are chartered and conduct business a fair share of the taxes to which the state is entitled. Under the Unitary Tax concept, the corporation is taxed on the basis of profits earned within as well as outside state boundaries. The tax has come under intense attack from overseas governments including Great Britain and Japan. The British adopted legislation retaliating against U.S. corporations which operate in unitary tax states which include/included: California, Alaska, Idaho, Montana, New Hampshire and North Dakota. It's debatable what's worse: The problem or the solution.

** This is another example of why many discount the concept of accountability to "stakeholders."

"maguiladoras" owned by American companies, including companies from Japan and Europe. Management spokesmen have stated: *"You can't justify automation based on the labor rates. You have to justify it in terms of quality assurance."* [69b] It's not altogether clear to us why automated assembly yields higher quality in the land of the chronically unemployed/underemployed.

Given the "good old American know-how," when thousands of employees lose jobs due to high overhead costs and plant obsolescence in Maryland, New Jersey or Southern California, it is generally due to lack of *timely and adequate* planning and reinvestment into operations and thus focus on *our people and their communities.*

Many, unfortunately, appear to have "lost faith" and are fending for themselves. *All of the preceding have had a significant impact on individual perceptions, beliefs, convictions, values, priorities and ultimately actions.* In effect they have had an effect on our ethics and sense of morality.

If, indeed, there is a solution to the current predicament, "It is imperative that our society move to recapture a concept of the individual conscience and reestablish the idea of community morality beyond the community of the "corporate society."[70] It is through such "reawakening" that society and the corporation are both likely to benefit.

11.3(e) Implications for Management

Inconsistencies abound in academia, business, industry and government. The disparity between "words" and "deeds" has had and continues to have a significant socio-cultural, political and economic fallout. Some of it is explicit in the mountain of regulations and legislation passed over the past 25-30 years covering such areas as non-discrimination, harassment, retaliation and safety on the job, the right privacy and a host of other business and political activities and practices. The balance is reflected, in part, in the statistics quoted in the introduction to this chapter. Whenever disparities arise, institutions tend to qualify, explain, minimize and rationalize them away through a host of people including human relations specialists, media experts and image makers. This general approach to both internal and external problem solving is consistent with our propensity as a highly developed communications and public relations society. *Ethnics, however, is not a challenge in communications or public relations and sloganeering.* In fact attempts at such "psychological manipulation" are increasingly seen as being unethical in and of themselves. These attempts underscore the prevailing perception that ethics generally receives a narrow and self serving interpretation focused at "wherever we're likely to be hurt the most," such as acts affecting the customer, public or employee opinions or acts contrary to company rules. This nurtures skepticism and fosters growing cynicism over the extent of commitment to the full range of ethical issues facing business, industry and government.

We must recognize that words such as *"trust," "honesty," "fairness"* and *"ethics"* in general, affect and apply to all facets of people's lives. To paraphrase what has been said by many in many different ways; eight hours of decision making dealing with the organization's relatively narrow business issues and concerns are not as irritating or demanding as the broader issues and concerns attendant to twenty four hours of citizenship. We must recognize that radical changes have occurred and are taking place in our society and that these changes will continue to have an impact on business, industry and government. Hopes have become necessities; privileges have become entitlements and prerogatives have become imperatives, in large part, due to the insensitivities of the past. There is no retrenchment. As Donald Greenbury pointed out, we are no longer in a struggle for a share of the market but our future and that of the free enterprise system. The extent to which this struggle will be impeded by restrictive legislation and overregulation will ultimately be determined by those that remain out of step and out of touch with the needs, desires and expectations of their constituencies and those of our society. If we must emulate the Japanese in our corporate life, let us not do so selectively and in a self serving manner. Let us seek out and take up, if we must, other well entrenched ideas and guiding precepts such as those of businessman/philosopher Eiichi Shibusawa that suggest that *profit maximization is commendable but only in the context of national interest.*

The focus, as Shapiro notes, must be on making the whole "system" work *better.* Judging by the senseless and unbridled greed, unadulterated waste, misappropriation and outright thievery that appears to be going on, making the system work better is not only possible but imperative. Our actions can no longer be governed by the *"expedient," "expected," "desirable" or the "smart"* thing to do given a narrow range of conditions and considerations but, rather, by *what is the right thing to do.*

Therein lies the challenge not only for management but *all* of us as members of a free and democratic society.

11.4 Ethics: A Conceptual Definition

In some respects, little has changed over the millennia. Many are still engaged in a daily struggle to survive and provide for their mates, children and family. The struggle for survival invariably involves choices and necessitates decisions. Alternative courses of action often include very difficult decisions in terms of "good" or "bad;" "right" or "wrong." As has been pointed out, these are frequently based on what exists and what is likely to happen rather than *what really matters.* [71]

Over the course of human history, a great deal of knowledge and insight has been accumulated in this area in the form of perceived duties and benefits of complying with certain prescribed, frequently "unwritten", forms of conduct in the interest of common good. Generally speaking, history teaches us that social characteristics such as discipline and self control, benevolence, loyalty, trust and mutual accommodation are critical to the proper and orderly functioning of a society. In fact, the latter are part of the one principle that is common to virtually every known ethical system. Specifically, that members of a group have *some* responsibility for the well being of other members of the group.[72] The study of these in context of *what ought to be done* under a given set of conditions defines the filed of ethics.

11.5 Philosophical Foundations

Throughout the ages, thinkers have concerned themselves with such issues as man's aims and purpose, the essence of happiness, harmony and well-being not only within oneself but in relation to one's environment. Among man's early recordings of ethical deliberations are those *formalized* by Aristotle, Naturalist theories advanced by the followers of Zeno, Hedonist and Utilitarian theories believed to have evolved from Epicurus and the Formalistic Theories reflected by Kant. An exposure to these is essential to the fuller appreciation of man's view of the issues involved in living up to the growing moral and ethical challenges that are part of our daily lives. Each of these is briefly summarized below with what most recognize and accept as Natural (or Eternal) laws.

11.5(a) Natural Law (The Golden Rule)

A majority of people believe in Natural Laws that are obvious in the state of nature and are revealed in the Holy Scriptures. Depending on one's religious persuasion the latter may include: the New Testament, the Old Testament, the Book of Mormon, the Koran, the Bhagavad-Gita or the Analects of Confucius. Each of them provides a moral standard and hence a system of beliefs (i.e. ethical standard) that supports a particular view of morality. These tend to vary from group to group and are difficult to apply to society as a whole. Consider the following example.

The most enduring of all ethical standards has been the Golden Rule: "Do unto others as you would have them do unto you." Aside from being a very prominent ethical force in most of the world's religions including: Buddhism, Christianity, Hinduism, Judaism and others, it occupies a prominent place in Greek philosophy and other systems of thought. Frequently this rule appears with some variations in phrasing. As an example, the Chinese version by Confucius reads: "What you do not want done to yourself, do not do to others."[73] Some have proposed that an extreme interpretation of the negative phrasing may suggest that one should *"not do anything"* and that the ideal state of existence may be one of permanent narcotic stupefaction.[74] As Hosmer points out: "Even the Golden Rule, that simple, elegant, sensible guide to life, can't somehow be applied universally."[75] He cites the reason as a lack of agreement among church leaders and philosophers as to the exact *provisions* of the revealed or reasoned truth. Specifically, a lack of agreement as to what tend to be acceptable rules of conduct under varying combinations of situations and personal circumstances. Some people have suggested the Judeo-Christian ethic tends to be somewhat abstract and more directly applicable to interpersonal relationships rather than worldlier and more "contemporary" issues: "Competition does not proceed through kindness but rather through self interest."[76]

Throughout history, the will of God has been *interpreted* to justify acts which today would be considered unconscionable. The general problem is further compounded by the fact that many do not follow a religion or in some cases are ignorant of the one they claim to espouse. As a result, this uncertainty over the exact provisions of the revealed truth have been the prime mover in man's struggle over the ages to establish a consistent analytical way of classifying actions as "good" or "bad;" "right" or "wrong."

11.5(b) Aristotle and the Golden Mean

Underlying Aristotle's Doctrine of the Golden Mean is the view that man's primary aim or function can be ascertained from his unique ability to apply rational principles to every day life. Given man's special gift, Aristotle concludes that a "good" man's primary function is to seek happiness and the "fullness" of life through the exercise of will, reason and the virtues:

> "The mere act of living is not peculiar to man – we find it even in the vegetable kingdom – and what we are looking for is something peculiar to him...experiencing sensations...is shared by horses, cows, and the brute creations as a whole...The function of a man is a certain form of life, namely an activity of the soul exercised in combination with a rational principle or a reasonable ground of action...The function of a good man is to exert such activity well...with the excellence proper to it."[77]

Aristotle sees virtues as being either intellectual or moral. Intellectual virtues are sought and developed independently of our frailties through education. They are used in the exercise of reason and the acquisition of knowledge, insight and wisdom. Moral virtues are acquired through training, obey reason and suggest the *means to a "good" (or desirable) end.* [78]

Given that anything to an excess (or to a deficiency) is a vice, moral virtue is defined as the middle ground (or mean) between two vices. As an example, truthfulness is the middle ground between false modesty and boastfulness; gentleness the mid-point between indifference and irascibility; honor the mean between humility and vanity, etc. In effect, the application of this doctrine involves the establishment of "balance" or "moderation" in situations or problems at hand through the exercise of reason. As an example, justice may involve balancing the gains and losses between parties to a dispute. An immoral act is consequently defined as an *immoderate* act. When one cannot hold to the mean, Aristotle advocates leaning to the side of the lesser evil (i.e.: "chose between the lesser of two evils.")[79]

The isolated performance of a "right" act does not make one "virtuous" or "ethical". According to Aristotle, one becomes "virtuous" or "ethical" when *right actions* become embedded in one's personality as habits.

In spite of the incredible range and power of Aristotle's insight, he is not without critics. Reservations which have been advanced have included the following:[80]

- His moral philosophy clearly suggest that a life devoted to social duties is less valuable than one devoted to the pursuit of knowledge (i.e. truth) and the exercise of intelligence.
- He argues that the natural order is the moral order; however, "how does one determine or establish what *natural* is?"
- Even if agreement were to reached over what is natural and therefore moral, a person is not bound to act in such ways. In other words, Aristotle's moral philosophy does not appear to bind moral knowledge with a need for moral action.

11.5(c) Naturalism

Naturalist theories are anchored in Zeno's (340-265 BC) teachings which advocate a life in harmony with nature and thus one another. Stoic philosophers, or Zeno's followers, are in basic agreement with Aristotle's teachings. They view *reason* as the highest function of man and, consequently, a life governed by reason as the highest possible good of man. In other words, evil is a failure on the part of man's reason to control his passions; virtue is the act of living in harmony with nature. In many respects, early naturalist ethics are reflected in the basic message of the old American Indian prayer that implores God to give one the strength and courage *to change the things one can, to accept those one cannot and the wisdom to recognize the difference.*

Naturalism has been assailed on two counts. *First, that it does not properly emphasize those human ideals and values that give enduring meaning and purpose to life. Second, that it often paints the forces of nature to be in direct conflict with man's highest moral and spiritual aspirations.* This has been especially true in the years following publication of Charles Darwin's *"Origin of Species"* (1859) as Thomas Henry Huxley became the symbol of fundamental conflict between nature and society.[81]

Evolutionary Naturalism

In more modern times, three names stand out as well known proponents of naturalistic ethics. They include Herbert Spencer (1820-1903), Friedrich Nietzsche (1844-1900) and Thomas Henry Huxley (1825-1895).

Some consider Spencer as the co-founder of modern evolutionary theory with Darwin; others believe that he was greatly influenced by Darwin's theory of evolution. He viewed the organized community as man's approach to adapting to the natural environment. He reasoned that since man had a much better chance of surviving as part of a society, ethics had to be based on social relationships and an evolutionary perpetuation of values necessary for the survival of society. In short, successful habits and modes of thought became permanent features of the species and the unsuccessful were ultimately to be discarded. *In that sense he perceived the ethical goal of each man as the need to help evolve the perfect society.*

Friedrich Nietzsche, on the other hand, subscribed to what he perceived to be the inevitable implications and logical consequence of Darwinism. In his "Geneology of Morals" (1887) he advances the concept of "master-slave morality" that is part of two corresponding cultures. The latter include true aristocrats (or naturally superior races of men) and the slaves (or the historically subjugated class). He rejects belief in God and immortality on the premise that "God is Dead". On that basis he suggests that *man must fend for himself.* He further asserts that sin and evil are elaborate religious contrivances of the slave culture.

According to Nietzsche, these contrivances, in combination with the concepts of democracy and equality, are insidious tactics of the salve culture intended to combat and debase the superior aristocratic class. In short, this is known as the "right equals might" ethic. It is devoid of respect for ordinary social convention and laws and thus has no legitimacy in civilized settings[82,83].

Huxley rejected Nietzche's individualism as naive. Furthermore, he viewed the claim of survival of the fittest as an absurd moral goal (e.g. consider the survival of the roach). As an agnostic, Huxley claimed that *no one has the right of assert anything without objective evidence or the right to require others to accept such unsubstantiated beliefs.*

It is interesting to note that all of these views have survived in varying extents to this day and can be observed as value systems and behavioral patterns of some individuals and groups within society at large.

11.5(d) Utilitarianism: Altruistic Hedonism

The first formal theory of ethics in this area is credited to Epicurus (342-270 BC). It asserts that pleasure and happiness are the ultimate ends insofar as they are desired by all. More specifically: pleasure and happiness are freedom from *pain in the body and trouble in the soul" as achieved through control of emotion and impulse with intelligence.* [84] *Contrary to what one may be inclined to assume, hedonists were dedicated to the simple life. A life devoid of worldly goods and the trappings of power. The latter were* **not** *considered essential elements in the pursuit of happiness, to the extent that one* **chose** *not to make them so. The ideal "Epicurian" could be defined as:*

> "The man who is wise enough to avoid cheating himself with short lived pleasures that cost too much, prudent enough to chose simple pleasures that are lasting and intelligent enough to banish all envy or ambition that troubles his soul."[85]

Whereas earlier versions of hedonism did not reflect any particular degree of social concern, later versions introduce the principle of *utility* where the essential element in ethical conduct is *an increase in the degree of happiness of the society.* As the ultimate end, one should strive to *bring the greatest degree of happiness to the largest number.* The preceding is credited to Jeremy Bentham (1748-1832) and his ablest student John Stuart Mill (1806-1873). The latter is credited with making utilitarianism less "egoistic," *Justice* (in essence equality as reflected in the greatest happiness of the greatest number) and individual *Liberty* occupy a prominent position in Mills' works.[16,17] Still later versions of utilitarianism include three important axioms of ethics advanced by Henry Sidgwick (1838-1900):[88,89]

- *Maxim of Justice:* Under similar circumstances, whatever is right for one person is right for all similar people
- *Maxim of Prudence:* Small present good is not preferable to a greater future good.
- *Maxim of Benevolence:* An individual is ethically bound to consider the good of any other individual as much as his own.

Although the utilitarian philosophy tends to be widely accepted within our society, critics cite the following general weaknesses:[90]

1. The definition of "greatest good" remains a matter of opinion.
2. There is no effective way of balancing the majority and minority rights. The infliction of immoral acts on a minority could be justified on the basis of substantial benefits to the majority.

11.5(e) Teleology vs. Deontology

Some authors classify all theories as falling into one of two general categories: Teleological or Deontological. Teleological theories judge an act by its consequences. If the consequence is *"good"* then the act is considered to have been good and the vice versa. Deontological (or formalist) theories judge an act based on motive and/or intent, regardless of the consequence(s). Consider the example that follows.

Generally speaking, a majority of people would consider bribery as unquestionably "wrong." Ask yourself, however, how you would feel about bribery if it were *successfully used* to secure the release of innocent hostages. A Teleologist would consider it "right" based on the successful outcome. A Deontologist (formalist) would consider bribery "wrong" regardless of whether the innocent hostages were released or not. Now, put yourself in the position of a "devout" teleologist *unable to predict the consequence* of the contemplated act (i.e. bribery) with certainty. What is the "right" thing to do? Seemingly, if *reason* were to prevail, the ultimate decision might be the same regardless of one's philosophical persuasion. The above reflects the general type of dilemma that may be experienced in practice.*

The Formalism of Immanuel Kant

Best known among the Deontologists (Formalists) is Immanuel Kant (1724-1804). He is responsible for a revolution in philosophical thought that, for a

---

* Consider the "Iran-Contra Affair" of a few years ago.

better part of a hundred years, has shaped the development of modern philosophy in the Western World.

Kant believes that everything in nature works according to laws; furthermore, that man as the only *rational being* has the ability to act in accordance with the conception of these laws.

> "Two things fill the mind with ever new and increasing admiration and awe, the oftener and more steadily we reflect on them: The starry heavens above me and the moral law within me."[91]

Kant believes that intuitively and *a priori* we know what is morally right and thus have but one rule to follow: The Moral Law. His categorical imperative (of duty) asks that an individual consider the consequences if everyone were to do what the individual contemplates or proposes doing.

> "Act only on that maxim whereby thou canst at the same time will that it should become a universal law" (Categorical Imperative).

> "Act as if the maxim of thy action were to become by thy will a universal law of nature" (Categorical imperative of duty).

In effect, Kant believes that *making any kind of an exception for oneself is wrong.* Regardless of how one feels about a particular situation, the categorical imperative obligates one's *will* to carry out a moral obligation. In short, *moral law must be obeyed without exception* (regardless of personal feelings or legal sanctions) *to the extent that it is within one's power to do.* Kant is leery of rules and rule makers as he perceives rules to be subject to abuse as implements of bureaucracy and tyranny. On that basis he asserts that doing the "right" thing in not nearly enough. He thus advocates *consistent and rational behavior regardless of the consequences to oneself.*

In Kant's view man's self direction, his freedom to chose and his dignity have infinite worth. In view of the preceding he believes that man belongs to the "kingdom of ends." Man is *the end,* meaning that he is never to be used as a *"means to an end" or as an "object of utility."* Man is thus never to be abused, hurt or injured.[92]

11.5(f) General Approach to Ethics Problems

It has been suggested that there are some fundamental problems with both teleological and formalist ethical systems. The former reportedly does not come to grips with the fact that some acts are plain wrong regardless of the perceived benefits or consequence(s). The latter allegedly allows the possibility of immorality by people subject to self-delusion or megalomania.

Numerous variations, combination, extensions and interpretations of these ethical theories are possible and can be found in literature. The preponderance of literature on this subject does not suggest the need for one to become a disciple of any one of these theories. Rather, it suggests a need for the systematic and orderly analysis of ethical issues on the basis of the *combination of these theories* and their *rational* application to the problem at hand. As Mantel points out, they can be used in a manner analogous to the use of various equations in engineering analyses, to test the limits or boundaries of the problem and its sensitivity to variables of interest or concern.[93] In line with the preceding, note that *"ethics* is normally used in the plural form since most people have a system of interrelated beliefs rather than single opinion."[94]

11.5(g) Ethics, The Law and Social Responsibility

Generally speaking, the law is considered to reflect the ethical standard to which a society subscribes. As social needs, beliefs and values evolve, laws require revision, clarification and (re)interpretation. Based on the preceding, laws are not an infallible guide to the prevailing sense of social responsibility as of any given point in time. In spite of this, some people believe that laws reflect a combined moral judgement of a society and thus a minimum ethical standard. In line with the preceding, they promote the view that *whatever is legal is ethical* based on the collective judgment or definition of acceptable behavior.

In a controversial article "Is Business Bluffing Ethical" subsequently followed by the book "Business As A Game" (1969), Albert Z. Carr advances the view that as long as an individual stays within the law, he may act as he pleases in the furtherance of his own interests. He asserts that since business is a game, just like poker, the rules of the game take precedence over personal moral standards.

> "...no one should think any worse of the game of business because its standards of right and wrong differ from the prevailing traditions of morality in our society."[95]

Carr views the major test of every move in business in terms of *legality* and *profit* citing, among the numerous anecdotal justifications for his position, a presumably well thought out executive view:

> "There is no obligation on him (businessman) to stop and consider who is going to get hurt. If the law says he can do it, that's all the justification he needs. There's nothing unethical about that. It's just plain business sense."[96]

Business, however, is not a game. People's lives are affected by it along with the well being of our nation as a whole. While publicly such Machiavellian*

---

*   Niccolo Machiavelli (1494-1512) in his book "The Prince" suggests that *the end justifies the means* no matter how deceitful, lawless or unscrupulous. Machiavelli admired power as an end in itself that was to be achieved without regard to moral standards. The only "sin" was to be considered a failure to achieve power (and presumably all that it entails).

views find little, if any, support, as a practical matter these views do appear to have some supporters. Between 1979 and 1984 alone, it has been estimated that some 12 million people in the U.S. lost jobs through abrupt plant closings and layoffs with as little as a *day* to a *week's* worth of notice.[97] Such business practices have come under intense criticism. Donald Greenbury, as President of the National Tooling and Machining Association, suggested that the very corporations appealing to our sense of nationalism and lobbying for protectionism are among the premier recruiters of "unskilled peasant women in other parts of the world...to peer through microscopes..." to assemble and examine the tiny nerve centers of (our) high technology.[98] At the time, Congressman Ford (D-Mich) stated: *"The reason these firms are moving away is not economic necessity but economic greed."*[99] Then Senator Quayle (R-Ind), in observing layoff and plant closure practices, noted that they were *irresponsible and callous* and went on to state that: *"If social responsibility becomes the norm, there won't be a need for legislation."* [100*]

Predating Carr by some 200 years, Adam Smith in his "Wealth of Nations" (1776) implicitly proposed that "selfish actions in the marketplace are virtuous because they contribute to the efficient use of resources and thus the "greater good" of society. On that basis, actions are considered ethical to the extent that they further financial self interest.

Although far from being a universal principle, this ethic has been the guiding philosophy behind much of the legislation of the late nineteenth century and beyond. The doctrine of "termination at will," as an example, dates back to the early stages of economic development in this country. At that time, it was thought that the freedom to contract along with the supporting concept of mutuality would amply protect the interests of both employer and employee.[102] This no longer appears to be the case.

As has been pointed out, throughout a major part of our history, *"the question of ethics was either neglected in business or was not a subject of doubt because of the popular notion that business and personal ethics existed in separate compartments."*[103] This is no longer the case.

To suggest, therefore, that the law reflects the minimal ethical standard defined by society, especially as applied to business, is to ignore the issue. An ever increasing number of people, from all walks of life, find the premise that the law reflects the minimal ethical standard of a society problematic on several counts.

First, it is noted that laws are written to prohibit and sanction acts and behavior which society finds unacceptable. In contrast to ethics, laws focus on *what must not be done rather than what ought to be done.*

Second, it has been suggested that if society finds certain acts or behavior unacceptable, then such acts or behavior can always be subject to legislation.

---

* Despite a great deal of congressional consternation, federal legislation has been passed requiring proper notification prior to plant closings. On that basis we must conclude that social responsibility has yet to become the norm. A few states also passed legislation regulating plant closings and reimbursement of tax and incentive benefits.

Arguments advanced in opposition to this view have been generally as follows:[104]

- It is difficult to influence the law in all areas of conduct and in the absence of relevant information.
- Not all people and/or organizations have equal influence or are motivated by morality.
- The socio-political process of legislation is complex, cumbersome and frequently subject to manipulation.

The above is supported, at least in part, by the fact that some of the rights or extensions of rights we may consider "inalienable" today, have only become law within approximately the last twenty five years: The right to non-discrimination based on sex, religion, age, national origin or political affiliation; the right to privacy; the right to freedom from harassment by supervisors, objection to illegal and/or unethical orders; the right to participate in outside activities; the right to safety on the job; the right to access specific information, etc.

Based on the above discussion, it should be apparent that we cannot always or exclusively rely on the law for answers to ethical problems.

11.5(h) Suggested Approaches to Ethical Analysis

The analysis and resolution of ethical questions and problems is frequently a very personal matter requiring study, *critical* thought and perhaps even considerable "soul searching." One should not look for or expect to find "quick and easy" answers. In fact any attempts at trivializing ethics should be considered unethical in and of themselves.

Basic Assumptions

All analytical efforts proceed from certain explicit or implicit assumptions. In ethics, as in other areas, it is both important and helpful to review one's basic assumptions in terms of fundamental beliefs and convictions, since they lead to the formulation of theories and their application. The following are examples of the type of *fundamental issues that require personal audit*.

- Does a human being have a purpose beyond mere existence and, if so, what is it? Similarly, does *all* human life have equal intrinsic "value" or "worth" beyond its physical or mental attributes?

- If all human beings are *"endowed by their Creator with certain unalienable Rights, (that) among these (are) Life, Liberty and the Pursuit of Happiness.–"* do human beings have certain inalienable responsibilities? Is so what are they?

- If every human being has a purpose beyond mere existence, does one have the right to interfere with another's attempts to fulfill that *basic* purpose? Alternatively, does one have the right to make another's existence (or struggle for survival) so burdensome as to preclude him from fulfilling the purpose of his existence – whatever it may be?

- If "all men are created equal" and are "endowed" by their Creator with...Liberty", how does the concept of Justice fit in terms of relative priority with respect to issues such as opportunity, pursuit of happiness, etc.?*

As may be inferred from the above, certain basic assumptions are essential to the selection and espousal of ethical principles. These in turn provide the basis for ethical analysis.

Ethical Principles vs. Ethical Rules

A number of ethical principles were presented and discussed in section 11.5(a) through 11.5(e). The espousal of one or a combination of these principles is essential to the establishment of ethical behavior. In fact, the latter is not possible without a commitment and continuing adherence to some set of general principles whether religious or secular. A number of these principles are often used for purposes of deductive analysis along the lines discussed in section 11.5(f). The usage is amplified in the following section, in part, for reasons outlined below.

The application of fundamental principles leads to the development of ethical rules. The latter are "tried precepts of reason"[105] that help promote ethical actions. Generally speaking, man's many, varied and interactive forms of associations have contributed to the evolution of complex and frequently contradictory goals, needs, interest and requirements. Under the circumstances, the application of ethical principles often precludes the formulation of and adherence to *absolute* rules. It should be intuitively obvious that *all* rules cannot possibly be made to apply to *all* people, at *all* times, in *all* places under *all* conditions and without *any* exception or deviation whatsoever. Even the application of the same principle can lead to different rules, under different circumstances, among different cultures and/or varying social conditions.[106] Consider the following.

In some foreign countries, gratuities, gifts and other forms of "financial

---

* Mortimer J. Adler ("Six Great Ideas", Collier Books, MacMillan Publishing Co, New York, 1984, p. 139) views Justice as a vehicle for the harmonious maximization of Liberty and Equality. Adler claims that the conflict is not between liberty and equality but rather between extremist components of these values (i.e. the libertarian and the egalitarian). Justice is sovereign insofar as it corrects and resolves the conflicts which can arise between equality (or inequality) and individual freedom and the exercise thereof.

accommodation", play a direct and significant role in the establishment of various business relationships and transactions. U.S. corporations operating abroad frequently retain agents to promote their business and other interests.

These agents are generally paid very high "commissions" to help "open doors," "remove road-blocks" and "grease the skids" as needed in the conduct of business. It may be reasonable to assume, on the basis of the nature of services provided and the fees these services command, that some portion of the fees paid to these agents may support either direct or indirect forms of "bribery."

While we may consider the above unethical, this may not necessarily be the case in other cultures and societies. Within certain socio-cultural and legal frameworks, the above may be justified by rules evolving from the same principle used to condemn such behavior within our society. Assuming this point is granted for purposes of illustration, *by which ethical rules should a U.S. corporation operate overseas?* More specifically, should we attempt to impose our ethical standards on other people, or, are we justified in modifying our ethical standards to the prevailing socio-cultural and legal framework within which we operate? Furthermore, to what extent would such modifications be justified? Note that even in this country some value systems would accommodate defacto bribes on the basis of the "greater good" theory, to the extent that such "bribes" would assure the continued employment of hundreds or perhaps even thousands of Americans.

The above illustrates the type of practical and troublesome ethical problem that often does not lend itself to solution by way of absolute ethical rules. While it is important to follow ethical rules, it must be recognized that rules often need extension, modification, qualification and clarification, providing there is *compelling and justifiable reason.* Because of this, several generally stated approaches have been evolved to guide ethical analysis.

The Application of Principles

The application of a structured approach to the analysis of ethical questions is based on the progressive evaluation of such questions against a select set of ethical principles. This approach is generally recommended due to a lack of agreement over the universal applicability and/or acceptability of any single system of beliefs to our society as a whole. As an example, the Utilitarian principle advocates actions aimed at the greater good of society; however, as noted previously, it may not be altogether clear:

1. What is or would constitute the "greater good" of society.
2. Who can – or is in a position to – establish that standard.
3. How the *rights* of a minority are to be balanced or protected against the wishes of a majority in cases in which opinions or a vote are the deciding factor.

Despite these apparent shortcomings, the Utilitarian approach has considerable merit and is widely accepted in principle.

Since virtually all ethical systems espouse the concept of some form of responsibility of an individual towards other members of his group, it is useful and more often necessary to *test the ethical supportability of the proposed action (or issue) against other systems of belief.* Recall that ethical rules, as based on a particular principle, may often need extension, modification, qualification and clarification given prevailing social geographic, cultural and social conditions. Based on the preceding, the ethical shortcomings attendant to a contemplated course of action (or specific issue) may thus become a great deal more apparent under the scrutiny of other ethical systems.

Some authors, based on extensive study, thought and in consultation with a variety of authoritative sources, have structured their own preferred approaches to the evaluation of ethical issues and proposed actions. These approaches invariably rely on *secular* principles. The only difference between them tend to be minor variations in the choice and sequence of application of specific principles. Based on our research we lean towards the following generally stated approach to the analysis of ethical questions and issues:

1.   Does it promote "the greatest degree of 'happiness' (i.e. benefit) to the largest number?"
2.   Is it Just? Does it account for, correct and resolve potential conflicts between Equality and Liberty?*
3.   Would it be right and just for *any other person* in a similar situation to act that way and *would you wish them to do so?*
4.   Does it follow reason and logic (or one's conscience)?
5.   Is it consistent with existing laws and the prevailing social order?

The lack of specific reference to religious principles in no way undermines the important role which such principles may play in our lives as well as in ethical conduct. Any such convictions would tend to support and enhance the more generally accepted secular approach to the analysis of ethical questions and issues outlined above.

11.5(i)   Codes of Ethics

Most business and professional societies have established codes of ethics for their memberships. In addition to these codes some societies, such as the National Society of Professional Engineers (NSPE), maintain an on going dialogue with their membership with respect to ethical issues. In the case of NSPE, this is accomplished through regularly featured case analyses that appear in the society's monthly publication.

Ethical codes can be a valuable guide and supplement to one's own sys-

---

* See: John Rawls, *A Theory of Justice*, Harvard University Press, Cambridge, Mass., 1971; also see: Mortimer J. Adler, *Six Great Ideas*, MacMillan Publishing, New York, 1984; Also note that this is consistent with John Stuart Mill's later works focusing on Justice and Liberty.

tem of beliefs in the analysis of ethical problems and issues. We have included the Ethics Codes of NSPE along with that of the Project Management Institute. They are representative of the sense of social responsibility and well being as well as personal and professional standards that other professional and business organizations expect of their memberships. We highly recommend a careful review of both of these codes in context with our previous discussion.

CODE OF ETHICS For Engineers
(National Society of Professional Engineers)

PREAMBLE

Engineering is an important and learned profession. The members of the profession recognize that their work has a direct and vital impact on the quality of life for all people. Accordingly, the services provided by engineers require honesty, impartially, fairness and equity, and must be dedicated to the protection of the public health, safety and welfare. In the practice of their profession, engineers must perform under a standard of professional behavior which requires adherence to the highest principles of ethical conduct on behalf of the public, clients, employers and the profession.

I. FUNDAMENTAL CANONS

Engineers, in the fulfillment of their professional duties, shall:
1. Hold paramount the safety, health and welfare of the public in the performance of their professional duties.
2. Perform services only in areas of their competence.
3. Issue public statements only in an objective and truthful manner.
4. Act in professional matters for each employer or client as faithful agents or trustees.
5. Avoid deceptive acts in the solicitation of professional employment.

II. RULES OF PRACTICE

I. Engineers shall hold paramount the safety, health and welfare of the public in the performance of their professional duties.
   a. Engineers shall at all times recognize that their primary obligation is to protect the safety, health, property and welfare of the public. If their professional judgment is overruled under circumstances where the safety, health, property or welfare of the public are endangered, they shall notify their employer or client and such other authority as may be appropriate.
   b. Engineers shall approve only those engineering documents which are safe for public health, property and welfare in conformity with accepted standards.

    c.   Engineers shall not reveal facts, data or information obtained in a professional capacity without the prior consent of the client or employer except as authorized or required by law or this Code.

    d.   Engineers shall not permit the use of their name or firm name nor associate in business ventures with any person or firm which they have reason to believe is engaging in fraudulent or dishonest business or professional practices.

    e.   Engineers having knowledge of any alleged violation f this Code shall cooperate with the proper authorities in furnishing such information or assistance as may be required.

2.   Engineers shall perform services only in the areas of their competence:

    a.   Engineers shall undertake assignments only when qualified by education or experience in the specific technical fields involved.

    b.   Engineers shall not affix their signatures to any plans or documents dealing with subject matter in which they lack competence, nor to any plan or document not prepared under their direction and control.

    c.   Engineers may accept assignments and assume responsibility for coordination of an entire project and sign and seal the engineering documents for the entire project, provided that each technical segment is signed and sealed only by the qualified engineers who prepared the segment.

3.   Engineers shall issue public statements only in an objective and truthful manner.

    a.   Engineers shall be objective and truthful in professional reports, statements or testimony. they shall include all relevant and pertinent information in such reports, statements or testimony.

    b.   Engineers may express publicly a professional opinion on technical subjects only when that opinion is founded upon adequate knowledge of the facts and competence in the subject matter.

    c.   Engineers shall issue no statements, criticisms or arguments on technical matters which are inspired or paid for by interested parties, unless they have prefaced their comments by explicitly identifying the interested parties on whose behalf they are speaking, and by revealing the existence of any interest the engineers may have in the matters.

4.   Engineers shall act in professional matters for each employer or client as faithful agents or trustees.

    a.   Engineers shall disclose all known or potential conflicts of interest to their employers or clients by promptly informing them of any business association, interest, or other circumstances which could influence or appear to influence their judgment or the quality of their services.

    b.   Engineers shall not accept compensation, financial or otherwise, from more than one party for services on the same project, or for services pertaining to the same project, unless he circumstances are fully disclosed to, and agreed to by, all interested parties.

    c.   Engineers shall not solicit or accept financial or other valuable consideration, directly or indirectly, from contractors, their agents, or other parties in connection with work for employers or clients for which they are responsible.

    d.   Engineers in public service as members, advisors or employees of a governmental body or department shall not participate in decisions with respect to professional services solicited or provided by them or their organizations in private or public engineering practice.

    e.   Engineers shall not solicit or accept a professional contract from a governmental body on which a principal or officer of their organization serves as a member.

5.   Engineers shall avoid deceptive acts in the solicitation of professional employment.

    a.   Engineers shall not falsify or permit misrepresentation of their, or their associates', academic or professional qualifications. They shall not misrepresent or exaggerate their degree of responsibility in or for the subject matter of prior assignments. Brochures or other presentations incident to the solicitation of employment shall not misrepresent pertinent facts concerning employers, employees, associates, joint ventures or past accomplishments with the intent and purpose of enhancing their qualifications and their work.

    b.   Engineers shall not offer, give, solicit or receive, either directly or indirectly, any political contribution in an amount intended to influence the award of a contract by public authority, or which may be reasonably construed by the public of having the effect or intent to influence the award of a contract. They shall not offer any gift, or other valuable consideration in order to secure work. They shall not pay a commission, percentage or brokerage fee in order to secure work except to a bona fide employee or bona fide established commercial or marketing agencies retained by them.

III. PROFESSIONAL OBLIGATIONS

1.   Engineers shall be guided in all their professional relations by the highest standards of integrity.

    a.   Engineers shall admit and accept their own errors when proven wrong and refrain from distorting or altering the facts in an attempt to justify their decisions.

    b.   Engineers shall advise their clients or employers when they believe a project will not be successful.

    c.   Engineers shall not accept outside employment tot he detriment of their regular work or interest. Before accepting any outside employment, they will notify their employers.

    d.   Engineers shall not attempt to attract an engineer from another employer by false or misleading pretense.

e. Engineers shall not actively participate in strikes, picket lines, or other collective coercive action.

f. Engineers shall avoid any act tending to promote their own interest at the expense of the dignity and integrity of the profession.

2. Engineers shall at all times strive to serve the public interest.

a. Engineers shall seek opportunities to be of constructive service in civic affairs and work for the advancement of the safety, health and well-being of their community.

b. Engineers shall not complete, sign, or seal plans and/or specifications that are not of a design safe to the public health and welfare and in conformity with accepted engineering standards. If the client or employer insists on such unprofessional conduct, they shall notify the proper authorities and withdraw from further service on the project,

c. Engineers shall endeavor to extend public knowledge and appreciation of engineering and its achievements and to protect the engineering profession from misrepresentation and misunderstanding.

3. Engineers shall avoid all conduct or practice which is likely to discredit the profession or deceive the public.

a. Engineers shall avoid the use of statements containing a material misrepresentation of fact or omitting a material fact necessary to keep statements from being misleading or intended or likely to create an unjustified expectation; statements containing prediction of future success; statements containing an opinion as to the quality of the Engineer's services; or statements intended or likely to attract clients by the use of showmanship, puffery, or self-laudation, including the use of slogans, jingles, or sensational language or format.

b. Consistent with the foregoing, Engineers may advertise for recruitment of personnel.

c. Consistent with the foregoing, Engineers may prepare articles for the lay or technical press, but such articles shall not imply credit to the author for work performed by others.

4. Engineers shall not disclose confidential information concerning the business affairs or technical processes of any present or former client or employer without his consent.

a. Engineers in the employ of others shall not without the consent of all interested parties enter promotional efforts or negotiations for work or make arrangements for other employment as a principal or to practice in connection with a specific project for which the Engineer has gained particular and specialized knowledge.

b. Engineers shall not, without the consent of all interested parties, participate in or represent an adversary interest in connection with a specific project or proceeding in which the Engineer has gained particular specialized knowledge on behalf of a former client or employer.

5. Engineers shall not be influenced in their professional duties by conflicting interests.
    a. Engineers shall not accept financial or other considerations, including free engineering designs, from material or equipment suppliers for specifying their product.
    b. Engineers shall not accept commissions or allowances, directly or indirectly, from contractors or other parties dealing with clients or employers of the Engineer in connection with work for which the Engineer is responsible.

6. Engineers shall uphold the principle of appropriate and adequate compensation for those engaged in engineering work.
    a. Engineers shall not accept remuneration from either an employee or employment agency for giving employment.
    b. Engineers, when employing other engineers, shall offer a salary according to professional qualifications.

7. Engineers shall not attempt to obtain employment or advancement or professional engagements by untruthfully criticizing other engineers, or by other improper or questionable methods.
    a. Engineers shall not request, propose, or accept a professional commission on a contingent basis under circumstances in which their professional judgment may be compromised.
    b. Engineers in salaried positions shall accept part-time engineering work only to the extent consistent with policies of the employer and in accordance with ethical consideration.
    c. Engineers shall not use equipment, supplies, laboratory, or office facilities of an employer to carry on outside private practice without consent.

8. Engineers shall not attempt to injure, maliciously or falsely, directly or indirectly, the professional reputation, prospects, practice or employment of other engineers, nor untruthfully criticize other engineers' work. Engineers who believe others are guilty or unethical or illegal practice shall present such information to the proper authority for action.
    a. Engineers in private practice shall not review the work of another engineer for the same client, except with the knowledge of such engineer, or unless the connection of such engineer with the work has been terminated.
    b. Engineers in governmental, industrial or educational employ are entitled to review and evaluate the work of other engineers when so required by their employment duties.
    c. Engineers in sales or industrial employ are entitled to make engineering comparisons of represented products with products of other suppliers.

9. Engineers shall accept responsibility for their professional activities; provided, however, that Engineers may seek indemnification for professional services arising out of their practice for other than gross

negligence, where the Engineer's interest cannot otherwise be protected.

    a. Engineers shall conform with state registration laws in the practice of engineering.

    b. Engineers shall not use association with a non-engineer, a corporation, or partnership, as a "cloak" for unethical acts, but must accept personal responsibility for all professional acts.

10. Engineers shall give credit for engineering work to those to whom credit is due, and will recognize the proprietary interests of others.

    a. Engineers shall, whenever possible, name the person or persons who may be individually responsible for designs, inventions, writings, or other accomplishments.

    b. Engineers using designs supplied by a client recognize that the designs remain the property of the client and may not be duplicated by the Engineer for others without express permission.

    c. Engineers, before undertaking work for others in connection with which the Engineer may make improvements, plans, designs, inventions, or other records which may justify copyrights or patents, should enter into a positive agreement regarding ownership.

    d. Engineers' designs, data, records, and notes referring exclusively to an employer's work are the employer's property.

11. Engineers shall cooperate in extending the effectiveness of the profession by interchanging information and experience with other engineers and students, and will endeavor to provide opportunity for the professional development and advancement of engineers under their supervision.

    a. Engineers shall encourage engineering employees' efforts to improve their education.

    b. Engineers shall encourage engineering employees to attend and present papers at professional and technical society meetings.

    c. Engineers shall urge engineering employees to become registered at the earliest possible date.

    d. Engineers shall assign a professional engineer duties of a nature to utilize full training and experience, insofar as possible, and delegate lesser functions to subprofessionals or to technicians.

    e. Engineers shall provide a prospective engineering employee with complete information on working conditions and proposed status of employment, and after employment will keep employees informed of any changes.

"By order of the United States District Court for the District of Columbia, former Section 11(c) of the NSPE Code of Ethics prohibiting competitive bidding, and all policy statements, opinions, rulings or other guidelines interpreting its scope, have been rescinded as lawfully interfering with the legal right of engineers, protected under the antitrust laws, to provide price information to prospective clients; accordingly, nothing contained in the NSPE Code of

Ethics, policy statements, opinions, rulings or other guidelines prohibits the submission of price quotations or competitive bids for engineering services at any time or in any amount".

—————— CODE OF ETHICS For The Project Management Profession——————
(Project Management Institute)

PREAMBLE

Project Managers, in the pursuit of the profession, affect the quality of life for all people in our society. Therefore, it is vital that Project Managers conduct their work in an ethical manner to earn and maintain the confidence of team members, colleagues, employees, employers, clients and the public.

ARTICLE 1

Project Managers shall maintain high standards of personal and professional conduct, and:
a. Accept responsibility for their actions.
b. Undertake projects and accept responsibility only if qualified by training or experience, or after full disclosure to their employers or clients of pertinent qualifications.
c. Maintain their professional skills at the state of the art and recognize the importance of continued personal development and education.
d. Advance the integrity and prestige of the profession by practicing in a dignified manner.
e. Support his code and encourage colleagues and co-workers to act in accordance with this code.
f. Support the professional society by actively participating and encouraging colleagues and co-workers to participate.
g. Obey the laws of the country in which work is being performed.

ARTICLE II

Project Managers shall, in their work:
a. Provide the necessary project leadership to promote maximum productivity while striving to minimize costs.
b. Apply state of the art project management tools and techniques to ensure quality, cost and time objectives, as set forth in the project plan, are met.
c. Treat fairly all project team members, colleagues and co-workers, regardless of race, religion, sex, age or national origin.
d. Protect project team members from physical and mental harm.
e. Provide suitable working conditions and opportunities for project team members.

f. Seek, accept and offer honest criticism of work, and properly credit the contribution of theirs.

g. Assist project team members, colleagues and co-workers in their professional development.

ARTICLE III

Project Managers shall, in their relations with employers and clients:

a. Act as faithful agents or trustees for their employers and clients in professional or business matters.

b. Keep information on the business affairs or technical processes of an employer or client in confidence while employed, and later, until such information is properly released.

c. Inform their employers, clients, professional societies or public agencies of which they are members or to which they may make any presentations, of any circumstances that could lead to a conflict of interest.

d. Neither give nor accept, directly or indirectly, any gift, payment or service of more than nominal value to or from those having business relationships with their employers or client.

e. Be honest and realistic in reporting project quality, cost and time.

ARTICLE IV

Project Managers shall, in fulfilling their responsibilities to the community:

a. Protect the safety, health and welfare of the public and speak out against abuses in the areas affecting the public interest.

b. Seek to extend public knowledge and appreciation of the project management profession and its achievements.

———— Questions and Topics For Discussion ————

1. John Q. Feelgood, M.D. (in partnership with a couple of associates) owns a medical testing lab in the professional building which he occupies. All tests ordered on patients are processed through this lab. Research has shown that a very high percentage of patients get their prescriptions filled at the closest drug store. Based on the preceding Dr. Feelgood and associates open up a drug store at the street level of their building. Discuss the various ethical implications and/or considerations attendant to Dr. Feelgood's ownership of the testing lab and drug store.

2. Discuss in general terms the various ethical issues/considerations attendant to making a profit from sickness or human misery. (Example: Should

hospitals strive to "maximize" profit or should hospitals be non-profit institutions).

3. Uncertain over the legal/contractual implications of a "good faith" decision made with his management's tacit concurrence – or at least lack of objection – a project manager of an aerospace company refers the matter to his corporate legal department. He does so "to insure that there is no problem downstream." The PM is summarily "fired" and the corporation turns the case to the government for investigation (ostensibly to protect "its own interests.") Discuss the ethical issues or considerations involved. Did the firm act ethically?

4. Widget Inc. is acquired by Turbo Widget Incorporated. Following the acquisition, Harry P. Executive and John L. Employee of Widget Inc. are terminated. Mr. Executive has three years with the company and a "golden parachute" worth 9 million dollars. The latter was emplaced by the board of directors in anticipation of the "unfriendly takeover" of Widget Inc. Mr. Employee, a CPA with 27 years of company service, is terminated three years short of his early retirement date. He gets severance pay of 6 months of salary (a week per year of service). Discuss the various moral and ethical considerations/issues involved.

5. I.M. Grunt moonlights to supplement his income. He gets "called in on the carpet" based on a broadly worded conflict of interest policy stated in the company's rules and regulations. Mr. Grunt, as part of his defense, points out that the company's CEO is a member of the Board of Directors of a number of companies that appear to be suppliers and/or possible competitors. He is told that "it's not the same thing; there is no parallel here". Discuss the various moral/ethical issues and considerations.

6. Discuss what types of disclosures are (or should be) mandated by ethics and ethical considerations in the course of contractual negotiations. Should there be a difference between dealing with the Government and the Private sectors; if so why?

7. A Registered Professional Engineer (P.E.) employed by an aerospace company recommends a higher safety margin on some structural member. His supervisor, also an experienced engineer but *non-licensed*, overrules the P.E.'s decision based on cost considerations. What, if any, ethical obligation does the state licensed professional have in this situation?

8. Within a matrix organization, a project manager elects to "carry" an individual on the project for an extra six months (even though the individual's services cannot be fully utilized). If the individual were to return to his (parent) functional organization, at this time, he would most likely be laid off due to a temporary lull in activity. The net result of the preceding is

that the profit to the company is reduced by 25,000 dollars on a project worth 30 million at sales level. Was the PM's decision ethical? How, if at all, would your views of the situation be affected assuming (1) Individual was a long term employee with a large family; (2) Individual was a single person and a relatively new employee; (3) How would you go about establishing "right" vs. "wrong" course of action if more than one individual was affected?

9. You are employed as a design engineer by Shoddyco Inc. At least two of the products marketed by Shoddyco have caused fatal injuries. While outwardly Shoddyco promotes design safety, design engineering is continually and subtly pressured to cut costs wherever and whenever possible even at the expense of *what you consider may be design safety.* Shoddyco has been sued. You have information that would be of significant help to plaintiffs whose child was killed by a Shoddyco product. Discuss/Justify your proposed course of action from the standpoint of moral and ethical considerations/issues involved.

10. Take the above described Shoddyco Inc. case. You were the Project Manager on one of the products described above which caused fatal injuries in the field. Shoddyco, you and two other people have been named in a products liability lawsuit. Shoddyco management decides to settle out of court with plaintiffs (presumably "in the best interests of shareholders") leaving you and the others to "fend" for yourselves. Did Shoddyco Inc. act ethically; why; if not why not?

11. Consider the above case. You ultimately leave the company. You become aware of another lawsuit brought against Shoddyco and have information of material usefulness to plaintiffs. You call them and offer your services. Are you acting ethically given the above background information. Discuss/Justify.

12. Given current trends/thrusts in products liability, procurement integrity etc. (a) under what conditions would you characterize disloyalty to the corporation ethical or (b) under what conditions would you characterize loyalty to the corporation unethical (c) discuss legislation you would propose in this general area.

13. An employee approaches a manager regarding rumored lay-offs in the next six months. Not wishing to "start a stampede" and hurt the company, the manager down plays the rumors and effectively side steps the issue. While the manager did not actually lie to the employee, he did not tell him the truth either. The manager knows that lay-offs are imminent and that the employee's department is one of those particularly affected. He knows that this particular employee along with at least a couple of others have fairly large families and really need job security/stability.

What would you have done if you were the manager and why? Reconcile your answer with a discussion of your ethical obligations towards the company versus another human being and a fellow employee.

References

1. Sir Adrian Cadbury, "Ethical Managers Make Their Own Rules," Harvard Business Review,, (September-October 1987), p. 69-73.
2. LaRue Tone Hosmer, "The Ethics of Management," (Irwin, Homewood, Illinois, 1987), p. 12.
3. James Owens, "Business Ethics: Age Old Idea, Now Real".
4. USN&WR, "A National of Liars," (February 23, 1987), pp. 54-60.
5. Patrick E. Murphy, "Creating Ethical Corporate Structure," Sloan Management Review, (Winter 1989), p. 85.
6. USN&WR, "The State of American Values," (December 9, 1985), p. 55.
7. USN&WR (December 9, 1985).
8. John F. Akers, "Ethics and Competitiveness-Putting First Things First," Sloan Management Review, (Winter 1989), p. 69.
9. USN&WR (December 9, 1985).
10. USN&WR (February 23, 1987).
11. USN&WR, "Stealing 200 Billion the Respectable Way," (May 20, 1985), p. 83.
12. USN&WR (December 9, 1985).
13. Jerry W. Anderson, Jr. "Social Responsibility and the Corporation," Business Horizons , (July-August 1986), p. 23.
14. USN&WR, "Corporate Crime – The Untold Story," (September 6, 1982), p. 25.
15. Ibid.
15(a). Paul Bernstein, "Capitalism's Elusive Constituency:" Business Horizons, (November-December 1986), p. 4.
16. USN&WR, "Happiness – How Americans Pursue It," (March 4, 1985), p. 69.
16(a). J. Irwin Miller, "Looking Out for #1," Business Horizons, (January-February, 1986), p. 9.
17. A Counter Intelligence Awareness Primer II, Hughes Aricraft, A Subsidiary of GM Hughes Electronics, (1988), p. 57.
18. David J. Cherrington, "The Work Ethic," AMACOM, (New York, 1980), p. 13.
19. Ibid.
20. Harvey Hornstein, "Managerial Courage," John Wiley, (New York, 1986), p. 134.
21. USN&WR, "Pay for Performance – Good News or Bad," (March 11, 1985), p. 74.
22. Newsweek, An embarrassment of Riches," (May 14, 1984), p. 51.
23. USN&WR, (September 10, 1984), p. 60.
24. USN&WR, (September 13, 1982), p. 53.
25. USN&WR, (May 21, 1984), p. 79
25(a). Business Week, (May 1, 1989).
25(b). Ibid.
25(c). Ibid.
25(d). Paul Bernstein, "Capitalism's Elusive Constituency," Business Horizons, (November-December, 1986), p. 6.
25(e). J. Irwin Miller, "Looking Out for #1," Business Horizons, (January-February 1986,), p. 6.
25(f). W.D. Litzinger and T.E. Schaefer, "Business Ethics Bogeyman: The Perpetual Paradox," Business Horizons, (March-April 1987), pp. 16-21.
25(g). Ibid.
25(h). Business Month, (May, 1989), pp. 8-9.
26. Peter F. Drucker, "The Changing world of the Executive," Times Books, (New York, 1985), p. 22.
27. Saul W. Gellerman, "Managing Ethics from the Top Down," Sloan Management Review, (Winter 1989), p. 75.

28. Harold M. Williams, "It's time for a Takeover Moratorium," *Fortune*, (July 22, 1985), p. 136.
29. Ernest Conine, "Making Greed Look Respectable," *Los Angeles Times*, (April 29, 1985), Part II, p. 5.
30. Robert J. Samuelson, "A Misuse of Management Power," *Newsweek* (June 25, 1984), p. 56.
31. *Newsweek*, "Days of the Jackals," (March 18,1985), p. 53.
32. Saul W. Gellerman, p. 75.
33. Robert F. Bruner and Lynn Sharp Paine, "Management Buyouts and Managerial Ethics," *California Management Review*, (Winter 1988), p. 89-98.
34. Ibid.
35. Ibid.
36. Thomas C. Haynes, *New York Times*, November 24, 1985.
37. Adolf Berle, Jr., and Gardiner Means, *The Modern Corporation and Private Property: 1933;* Prof Berle carried his analysis of the divorce between property and control even further in his book *Power Without Property,* Harcourt, Brace & World, Inc. New York, 1959, p. 59-60 and 69-76.
38. In: Paul O. Gaddis, *Corporate Accountability*, Harper and Row, 1964, p. 35.
39. Robert J. Larner, *Management Control and the Large Corporation*, Dunellen, New York, p. 12.
40. Thomas M. Jones, "Corporate Control and the Limits to Managerial Power," *Business Forum*, (Winter, 1985), p. 16-21.
41. Ibid.
42. Sir Adrian Cadbury, *Ethical Managers Make Their Own Rules*, p. 70.
43. Charles C. Abbott, "Theories of the Corporation," in: Ernest Dale, *Readings in Management*, McGraw Hill, New York, p. 48.
44. Ichak Adizes, *How to Solve the Mismanagement Crisis*, Adizes Institute, San Diego, 1981, p. 227.
45. Patrick E. Murphy, "Creating Ethical Corporate Structures," *Sloan Management Review*, (Winter, 1989), p. 81-87.
46. Saul W. Gellerman, "Managing Ethics from the Top Down," *Sloan Management Review*, (Winter, 1989), p. 73-79.
47. Robert Chatov, "What Corporate Ethics Statements Say," *California Management Review*, (Summer, 1980), p. 20-29.
48. James L. Hayes, *Memos for Management Leadership*, AMACOM, 1983, p. 99.
48(a). Archie B. Carroll, "In Search of the Moral Manager," *Business Horizons*, (March-April, 1987), p. 7.
49. James L. Hayes, p. 115.
50. James O'Toole, *Making America Work*, Continuum Publishing, New York, 1981.
51. David J. Cherrington, *The Work Ethic*, AMACOM, New York, 1980, p. 20.
52. In: Ernest Dale, *Management Theory and Practice*, McGraw Hill, New York, 1965, p. 204.
53. Cherrington, p. 20.
54. Nancy R. Hauserman, "Whistle-Blowing: Individual Morality in a Corporate Society," *Business Horizons*, (March-April, 1986), p. 6.
55. See *Work in America*, Report of Special Task Force to Secretary of HEW, 1973, p. 20-23.
56. James L. Hayes, p. 155.
57. O'Toole, p. 185-186.
58. Ibid., p. 14.
59. Herman Kahn, *The Next 200 Years*, William Morrow and Co., Inc., 1976, p. 201.
60. Christopher Lasch, *The Culture of Narcissism*, W.W. Norton, New York, 1978.
61. Steiner and Steiner, p. 96-97.
62. N.D. Kondratieff, "The Long Wave in Economic Life," *Review of Economic Statistics*, November, 1935.
63. Hosmer, p. 33 and 90.
64. Jerry Anderson.
65. Steiner and Steiner, p. 107.
66. James O'Toole, *Making America Work*, Continuum Publishing Co., New York, 1981, p. 53.
67. Irving S. Shapiro, *America's Third Revolution*, Harper and Rowe Publishers, New York, 1984, p. ix-x, 4.
67(a). As quoted in *Business Horizons*, (March-April, 1987), p. 25.

68.
69.   Butler D. Shaffer, "The Biggest Lie? 'The System Works for Us,'" *The Orange County Register*, (October 24, 1985). (Mr. Shaffer is associated with Southwestern University).
69(a). J. Irwin Miller.
69(b). "Robots in Mexico? Automation where many are jobless? Sure," *Electronic Business*, (February 15, 1988), p. 110-112.
70.   Nancy R. Hauserman, p. 4.
71.   Murray I. Mantel, *Ethics and Professionalism in Engineering*, MacMillan and Company, New York, 1964, p. 18.
72.   La Rue Tone Hosmer, *The Ethics of Management*, Irwin, Illinois, 1987, p. 94.
73.   James Owens, "Business Ethics: Age Old Ideal, Now Real," *Business Horizons*, (February, 1978), p. 29.
74.   Hosmer, p. 97.
75.   Mantel, p. 57.
76.   G.A. Steiner and J.F. Steiner, *Business, Government and Society: A Managerial Perspective*, Random House, New York, 1980, p. 372, 385.
77.   Aristotle, "The Nicomachean Ethics," English translation by J.A.K. Thomson, Allen and Unwin, London, 1953 in: Robert F. Davidson, *The Search for Meaning in Life*, Holt, Rinehart and Winston, New York, 1962, p. 188-196.
78.   Mantel, p. 22.
79.   William S. Sahakian, *History of Philosophy*, Barnes and Noble, New York, Copyright 1968, Printed 1988, p. 74.
80.   Elmer Sprague, *What is Philosophy?*, New York, Oxford University Press, 1961, p. 103-104.
81.   Robert F. Davidson, p. 218.
82.   William S. Sahakian, p. 230-231.
83.   George A. Steiner and John F. Steiner, *Business, Government and Society: A Managerial Perspective*, Random House, New York, 1980, p.387.
84.   Robert F. Davidson, p. 62.
85.   Ibid.
86.   Davidson, p. 68-71.
87.   Sahakian, p. 217-220.
88.   Ibid, p. 221-222.
89.   Mantel, p. 31.
90.   Steiner and Steiner, p. 389.
91.   James B. Wilbur and Harold J. Allen, *The Worlds of Hume and Kant*, American Book Company, New York, 1967, p. 95.
92.   William S. Sahakian, p. 177.
93.   Mantel, p. 7.
94.   Hosmer, p. 92.
95.   Albert Z. Carr, "Is Business Bluffing Ethical?", *Harvard Business Review*, (January-February, 1968), p. 145.
96.   Ibid, p. 146.
97.   USN&WR, "Plant Closings Spark Fresh Resistance," (April 15, 1985), p. 75.
98.   Donald B. Greenbury, "Strategy for Survival," *Machine and Tool Blue Book*, p. 48.
99.   Doug Brandow, "Indentured Industries," *The Orange County Register*, (November 21, 1985), p. A21.
100. USN&WR, Ibid.
101. Steiner and Steiner, p. 386.
102. Nancy R. Hauserman, "Whistle-Blowing: Individual Morality in a Corporate Society,"*Business Horizons*, (March-April, 1986), p. 6.
103. Steiner and Steiner, p. 365.
104. Hosmer, p. 81-82.
105. Mantel, p. 58.
106. Ibid.

Project Management
And The Industrial Process

——————————————— **Chapter 12** ———————————————

Strategic Planning and
Product Development

12.1   Forces Driving the Need for Strategic Planning

Strategic planning may be defined as the systematic Assessment, Coalescence, and Transcription of Information into an Optimized Network of organizational missions, objectives, goals, and targets. It constitutes an ACTION-oriented effort at suppressing managerial reaction in an increasingly volatile environment. It is proactive rather than reactive; it sets the stage and serves as a precursor for either product or system development and increased productivity. Although strategic planning is an ongoing, forward-looking effort, it is also a vehicle for optimizing short-term gains through the systematic assessment, coalescence, and transcription of the organization's overall posture into a comprehensive and cohesive plan of action. Short-term gain optimization stems from a process of rational reevaluation and an ongoing top-down, bottom-up readjustment of plans in the direction of desired and well-defined results.

To place strategic planning into the proper perspective, consider the chronology of some of the major scientific and technological developments over the past 2,000 years on a compressed scale of the past month. On this scale, Franklin discovered the positive and negative aspects of electricity some four days ago. Approximately three days ago, Volta discovered the battery and Faraday demonstrated the first electric motor. In the past two days, Edison demonstrated the light bulb, Roentgen discovered X-rays, and the first automobile was test driven. A little more than 24 hours ago, Braun demonstrated the first cathode ray tube (CRT), Einstein proposed the theory of relativity, and DeForrest swung the doors open on the era of electronics with his discovery of the triode, while the Wright Brothers were experimenting with the airplane. About the same time, Bohr developed atomic theory and Farnsworth demonstrated the first television. Within the time span equivalent to the past 15 to 20 hours, people flew the first jet, set off a nuclear explosion, developed the transistor, sent the first satellite into orbit, and demonstrated the laser. Within the last 12 hours, the world saw Neil Armstrong make "one small step for man" along with a "giant step for mankind."

Characteristic of this rate of technological innovation are four evolving and interactive factors with a seemingly elusive impact on management philosophy and practice which require a system approach to institutional guidance and management. These factors include increasing complexity, escalating cost and significant development risk, a high rate of change, and scarcity of resources both human and material. The following discussion highlights some of the significant issues in these areas that give rise to the need for strategic planning or an integrated, multidisciplinary approach to the management function.

(a) Complexity

Those electing careers in science or technology today are effectively committing themselves to a lifetime of study. According to a study conducted at Texas Christian University, the average engineer surveyed devoted an average of 16 hours a week outside of work to keep technically current in his specialty.[1] Aside from the depth of individual skill required, successful developments in many engineering and manufacturing areas are becoming heavily dependent on improvements in computer-aided design (CAD) and computer-aided manufacturing (CAM) techniques. A case in point is the current development effort in very high speed integrated circuitry (VHSIC), which is not only dependent on advances in CAD/CAM but also on advances in other areas like electron-beam lithography and materials science, which themselves require highly specialized talent.

For the most part, therefore, successful product development today requires the integration of highly specialized, multidisciplinary talent usually in a project context. It thus requires broader-based participation of such talent in the management and decision-making process involving the development, evaluation, and ultimately successful diffusion of the product.

This is an area to which management, at least in this country, has not adapted itself very successfully. Planning, scheduling, and control in general continue to be very closely and jealously guarded management functions, which consequently suffer from want of participation and commitment of the work force.

The staff report of the Committee on Science and Technology of the 97th Congress contains some interesting observations on the continuing erosion of our competitive position in the international market despite our continuing preeminence in basic and applied research.[2] The report states, for instance, that Japanese success in the marketplace can be attributed to teamwork, an area in which the Japanese excel. "Truly original or creative activity," the report goes on to say, "is largely a function of individuals working alone and, hence, tends to take place in societies like that of the United States which place emphasis upon the individual, rather than in societies like that of Japan which place emphasis on the group." Innovation, or the ability to put available knowledge to practical use, however, is the by-product of group dynamics. Group effort is essential in the pursuit of desired goals and objectives in the conversion process of R&D to commercial application. Included in the group dynamics aspect is the ability of the organization to identify and integrate the various areas of expertise needed to make projects successful.

In our current environment, successful planning, scheduling, and control, whether strategic or tactical, must begin with the involvement of workers themselves rather than with the traditional preprogrammed dictates and expectations of their supervision. The complexity of today's undertakings mandates such an involvement. Complexity also suggests that management must play a different role in all phases of bringing a product to the market. As Leonard Sayles points out, the manager must be

> "like a symphony orchestra conductor, endeavoring to maintain a melodious performance in which the contributions of the various instruments are coordinated and sequenced, patterned and paced, while the orchestra members are having various personal difficulties, stage hands are moving music stands, alternating excessive heat and cold are creating audience and instrument problems, and the sponsor of the concert is insisting on irrational changes in the program."[3]

Unfortunately, in far too many organizations the shared responsibility approach to the managerial function is viewed as far too idealistic. More common is the traditional or centralized, power-oriented approach, which, as Pascale and Athos observe, fosters and reinforces "a macho style of management that is a major cause of our problems today."[4] Much of this stems from the fear of being exiled. As Galbraith points out, the exiled executive or manager is unlike the "politician when he is defeated...the university president when he becomes emeritus, and the peacetime general who fails to become corporation president."[5] The difference between being "in" and "out" is not slight; it is total. Some observers feel that the tendency toward the "macho style of management" in government and industry largely accounts for the current high cost and risk of product development.

(b) Cost and Risk

Booz, Allen, and Hamilton report that of the total funds expended on industrial R&D in this country, typically 70% (or some $45 billion) is spent on unsuccessful efforts. According to their statistics, two-thirds of this amount, is wasted in the development phase on products unlikely to see the light of day.[6,7,8] Other studies support these statistics and underscore the staggering cost and continually rising stakes in product development.

Management has tended to attribute and frequently justify the high cost and risk of development to the complexity of today's undertakings. We cannot deny this complexity. However, we can take exception to the often accompanying implication that today's undertakings somehow defy thoroughness of evaluation, depth of planning, and effectiveness of control and thus involve high cost and risk of development. The high cost and risk of development tends to be more a function of the prevailing management attitude and approach to dealing with complexity rather than a function of the complexity of the undertakings per se. In a study aimed at establishing the technical versus nontechnical failure rates of R&D projects, Gerstenfeld found that only 16% of the projects failed owing to technical causes compared with 52% that failed for non-technical reasons.[9] Such statistics raise basic questions about the reasons for the poor quality of many management decisions.

Despite increasing technological complexity, management functions for the most part remain mechanically structured and individually centered from the middle to upper levels of management. Preprogrammed expectations are frequently passed on to the operating levels for reaffirmation through execution rather than confirmation and contribution by a talented pool of professionals, which management generally assembles at great expense and maintains at high cost. The net result is a tendency at the operating levels to select and implement planning, scheduling, and control techniques to satisfy management's requirement in these areas rather than help evolve a plan of action. Such conditions contribute to a high degree of underemployment, misemployment, and dissatisfaction in professional ranks. Most professionals are keenly aware of their exclusion from the decision-making process.

In many segments of the governmental and industrial communities, the ambivalence toward the multidisciplinary and participative approach to institutional management is expressed in an apparent paranoia over illusions of control. Few at the higher levels of management today would be willing to admit to being unable to "participate in an informed way in the decisions most vital to their future."[10] Even fewer would admit to frequently not understanding "what's going on out there," growing "out of touch and out of date" with the evolving technology. As Bales points out, "In an age...multinational, multiproduct, multimarket, multitechnology, multicompany...many may be on the verge of losing control but continue to as is if nothing has changed."[11] The lack of coupling of mutually supportive goals and objectives throughout the enterprise and the consequent inability of many institutions to adapt in a timely manner to a continually and rapidly changing environment result in substantial waste. Strategic planning offers an effective tool in rectifying this deficiency.

(c) High Rate of Change

Recent history is replete with examples of companies that have suffered significant setbacks because of their inability to foresee and adapt in a timely manner to the rapidly changing environment. Classic examples include Timex and NCR, which faltered under the pressure of advances in large scale integrated (LSI) circuitry. In some cases, advances in technology have caused major erosions in the market position of exceptionally well-established products as in the case of Timex's low-cost mechanical watch. In others, they have forced abandonment of product lines as in the case of NCR's electromechanical calculators and cash registers. It is highly unlikely that such conditions were brought about by either a lack of technical foresight or managerial intransigence. More likely they evolved from the polarization of individually held premises that in the absence of clearly articulated objectives, goals, and targets inhibited the organization from responding in a timely manner to rapid changes in technology and the marketplace. For the farsighted, advances in technology have not only provided an entry into an increasingly saturated marketplace but have also opened up many new and highly lucrative opportunities to promote products that have become identified with our contemporary life-style. The personal computer is an example, as indicated by the success of Apple computers in carving out a market share in an area dominated by giants such as IBM, Honeywell, and others.

The impact of the high rate of change in technological innovation has been twofold: First, product life cycles are becoming progressively shorter. (In some segments of the electronics industry today, innovation has compressed the product life cycles to the range of 18 to 24 months.) The overall trend is consequently away from long runs and large lots in most industries. Second, in cases in which products evolve from complex technologies, product designs tend to be in a continual state of flux and seldom reach classical maturity. Profits are consequently much more speculative and difficult to control.[12]

These factors have imposed a set of conflicting requirements upon management. On one hand, they have fueled diversification and fostered a preoccupation with near-term operations requiring a degree of flexibility and a response that is inconsistent with a long-range commitment of limited personnel and resources to the investigation and development of alternative opportunities. On the other hand, these factors have required a degree of foresight and selectivity that can only be afforded through a significant commitment of personnel and resources to the investigation, evaluation, and development of alternative opportunities. Even in the more progressive organizations that do recognize the need for a participative approach to institutional management, time and cost are frequently cited as major obstacles to plans of action consistent with the rates of change in the technology and the marketplace. This stems in part from a resistance to longer range planning based on a preference for short-term payoffs fueled by capital requirements, overregulation, and shortages of past decades. The rate of change promotes a delicate balancing act between long-range objectives and near-term requirements, which must be dove-tailed through integration and interaction of organizational capabilities in line with the scarcity of human, material, and capital resources.

(d) Scarcity of Resources

The mounting scarcity of human, material, and capital resources is a function of many interacting environmental variables. Technological innovation, economic policies, and social and cultural changes are having a pronounced impact, not only on the selection of opportunities, but also on the day-to-day operations of virtually all institutions. It is becoming increasingly important to the success of organizations to evolve a course of action at the operating levels in response to projected changes in the environment. It is becoming equally important to promote an understanding at all levels of the organization of the factors contributing to the increasing scarcity of resources.

The increasing demand for a higher proportion of scientific and engineering talent across the enterprise and in all phases of product development has created a critical shortage of technical personnel. Currently, the demand for engineers and scientists far outstrips supply. According to some, this shortage poses a potential threat to national security as a strong defense industry cannot be maintained without comparable strength in the U.S. industry as a whole. The Bureau of Labor Statistics projects that as of 1990, 180,000 new engineering positions will go unfilled.[13] To illustrate the magnitude of the problem, the Soviet Union currently outproduces the United States in engineering and science graduates by a factor of six. Considering that it takes some 25 to 30 years to develop a productive engineer or scientist, such a shortage may have a serious impact on efforts to boost national productivity and maintain technological superiority. This trend may not be easily reversed. With demand for engineers and scientists at an all time high, fewer graduates are opting for graduate work and an increasing percentage of faculty is leaving academia for more lucrative industrial jobs. The long-range effect will be a severe shortage of qualified faculty, which will further restrict the output of needed technical talent. The importance of engineering talent to the national well being is underscored by Peter Drucker, who quotes a Japanese economist:

"You in the United States have in the last ten years doubled the number of people in law schools, while you barely even maintained the number of people in engineering schools. We in Japan have not increased the number of lawyers but have doubled the number of engineering students. Lawyers are concerned with dividing the pie, engineers with making it larger."[14] In an increasing number of

countries, technical and professional talent are becoming valued extensions of the nation's natural resources.

Shortages in technical as well as other fields will increase as the effects of the declining birthrate in this country become more pronounced. It has been projected that by the end of the decade, two-thirds or about 60 million households will be without children.[15] Among the first-order impacts of such a decline in the birthrate will be a shortage of entry-level workers. Whereas this problem may in part by mitigated through increased automation, such a development is likely to encounter political resistance as automation would tend to displace minorities and those of limited skills whose unemployment is generally the highest. Political resistance may be greatest in the governmental sector as it will probably be the first to face up to the issue of technological unemployment given the high proportion of clerical, secretarial, and information management positions that lend themselves to elimination through automation. Similar problems will be faced by blue-collar workers as factories of the future become increasingly automated through the proliferation of robotics (see Section 9.5c).

Although it is true that massive unemployment should not result from automation as presumably it leads to growth through increased productivity, it is also true that significant growth may be much more difficult to achieve in an increasingly saturated international market in which no industrialized nation will allow its productivity to fall in relation to that of its competitors. By way of an analogy, consider the case of General Motors and Ford Motor Company in pioneering automated welding and assembly in 1969 and 1978, respectively. Whether based on labor pressures, investment, or other considerations, introduction of industrial robots in the U.S. automobile industry was suspended for a number of years after 1975, whereas Japan and Western Europe moved quickly to implement this technology.* By 1980 the net result was a loss of 400,000 jobs in the automobile and related industries to competitors adapting U.S. technology.[16] Coincidentally, the United States relinquished its lead as the world's largest producer of automobiles (see Section 9.5).

The economic, social, and political impact of these trends and conditions may be far-reaching. They can transcend the problems of a particular industry and can catapult themselves into the national and international arenas involving a broad base of delicate international trade balances. Trade deficits and economic policies can create economic shortages that can be just as crippling as material and personnel shortages. Economic policies evolve in response to a host of political considerations making segregation of technological policy difficult.

In the United States economic shortages are primarily the result of a miscellany of laws and regulations that restrict the economic extraction of resources. As an example, the nonfuel mineral industry in this country is re-

---

* In the United States, the first major labor dispute about automation at GM reportedly occurred in 1972.

portedly regulated through some 80 different laws that are being administered by some 20 different agencies. Many of the problems associated with
the scarcity of resources fall clearly within the purview of the government,
which is often in the difficult position of having to trade off long-term benefits
to society against the short-term needs of special groups. As a consequence,
many policies are neither self-sufficient nor mutually supportive and thus
contribute to added complexity, cost, risk, and scarcity.

12.2 The Role of Government

As a response to increasing complexity, rising cost and risk in development, rapid rates of change, and mounting scarcity of resources most nations
have developed a national science and technology policy. The United States is
the only industrialized nation without such a policy, which is thought to
account for the lagging growth rates in productivity compared with Western
Europe and Japan.[17] There are signs however that serious attempts are being
made to follow the lead of other countries in this area.

In Japan a very close working relationship exists between the industrial
and governmental sectors. The Japanese Ministry of International Trade and
Industry (MITI) was established for the specific purpose of making Japan's
high-technology firms more competitive internationally. This has been accomplished in part through underwriting a substantial part of Japans R&D
efforts. Robert Reich, former director of policy and planning at the FTC, and
others have projected that in the next 10 years Japan would surpass the United
States in industrial robots, laser aircraft, computers, semiconductors, and fiber
optics.[18,19,20]

Faced with stiff international competition and an eroding competitive edge,
the U.S. Congress has been struggling with the issue of the proper role of
government in stimulating technological growth and development, particularly in the transition from R&D to full commercialization. In this undertaking Congress has recognized that the traditional governmental role of correcting "marketing imperfections" is no longer viable.[21] The most significant outgrowth of congressional deliberations has been the passage of the Stevenson-
Wydler Technology Innovation Act, which encourages innovation and transfer of federally funded R&D through (a) creation of organizations within the
executive branch, including the Office of Industrial Technology in the Department of Commerce to address the issue of innovation and develop ways to
stimulate it; (b) institution of a scientific and technical exchange program among
the federal laboratories, industry, and universities; (c) establishment of industrial technology centers partially funded by the federal government; and (d)
improved use of federally funded R&D.[22,23]

The Stevenson-Wydler Act is a first step in dealing with a maze of issues
involving tax policies, economic regulations, technology transfers, R&D funding, and foreign trade, which are very difficult to evaluate because of lack of
knowledge of their individual and interactive effects on innovation. As pointed
out by the staff report of the Congressional Committee on Science and Tech-

nology, in the absence of policy there are no explicit national goals to which industry can contribute. Development by government of an industrial policy on these matters might ease much of the uncertainty of the private sector about the effect of future government activities. Some of these very reasons drive the need and underscore the importance of strategic planning in industry today.

12.3   The Systems Approach to Institutional Management

(a)   The Need for the Systems Approach

The tremendous acceleration in the rate of technological accomplishments can be attributed to the application of the systems approach to the cross-correlation, development, and implementation of accumulating technology. The systems approach to the solution of scientific and engineering problems involving several disciplines is a natural extension of the scientific method. It was successfully spurred by the rapid growth in basic knowledge in the physical sciences.

In contrast with the physical sciences, there is little predictability and less continuity in the social sciences. In some cases, major areas in the social sciences are still in stages of relative infancy as in the case of organizational behavior and management practice. With the possible exception of Maslow's theory of human motivation, the balance of significant work in this area is about 30 years old. Included here are the classic works of Argyris, Homans, Lickert, McGregor, McClelland, Herzberg, and Whyte. The full impact of such advances in the social sciences has been hampered by their slow diffusion and acceptance throughout government and industry by a generation of management whose views and values were forged and tempered by the great depression and whose influence still permeates the corporate structure. Despite corporate pronouncements, some management, notably at the middle and upper levels, continues to be practically out of touch with or chooses to ignore the evolving values and expectations of its work force.

In a survey of the 500 largest industrial corporations and 50 of the largest banking institutions as ranked by Fortune,, nearly two-thirds of the CEOs polled viewed strategic planning as *their* primary responsibility, and placed greater importance upon it than on either management selection, development, capital allocation, profits, policy decisions, or morale.[24] This illustrates the prevailing mechanical and centralized view of the management function and a lack of understanding of the process of strategic planning effort. Each of the functions is an integral part of the strategic planning process; all need integrated consideration rather than dissociated analysis. Consider, for example, that increased profit may be more easily realized by bolstering productivity through improved morale rather than by expectations of an increasing share of an already saturated market. Morale improvement in turn is intimately related to management selection, employee development programs, and policy decisions.

The problem of instituting a systems approach in the organizational realm has been compounded by a number of factors including sociocultural attitudes, economics, politics, and technology. Kahn suggests that the price of success in technological improvements contributes to the encouragement of unrealistic expectations and the imposition of impossible demands.[25] Whether unrealistic or not, societal expectations and demands have had a significant impact upon our environment and have contributed to a degree of uncertainty in the political, social, economic, and technological spheres with which the corporate sector is ill equipped and reluctant to cope but must consider as part of its survival.

The continual evolution of sociocultural factors and the like requires longer-range visibility as part of the successful process of anticipation and accommodation of the institution within such an environment. Paradoxically, such visibility is inconsistent with the rapid rate of change of these factors. A significant number of longer-range decisions vital to the well-being of the organization thus defy risk analysis and must rely primarily on procedural, qualitative approach to dealing with the prevailing level of uncertainty. The number, complexity and rate of evolution of factors having potential impact on the organization, both internal and external, preclude their synthesis, assimilation and integration by a single individual and requires the best efforts of the available pool of specialized talent. This is not to suggest that management should abdicate its decision-making prerogatives or organizational control but merely, to advocate within established guidelines the need for a formalized process of broader-based participation in generating inputs for decision making.

Because of the volatility of the environment, it is highly unlikely that a course of action could be set without accompanying vernier adjustments in the direction of desired results in response to the evolving conditions. The strategic planning process provides the framework for such an effort in response to the trend toward greater complexity, higher cost and risk, rate of change, and scarcity of resources.

(b) Prerequisites for Strategic Planning

Strategic planning is unlikely to succeed without higher management's earnest recognition and acceptance of its need. Sustained higher management commitment, direction and orchestration of the effort, as evolving from such recognition and acceptance of need, are essential to overcoming the antiplanning bias inherent in almost all organizations. Among the more frequently cited reasons for this bias is a reluctance to allocate the requisite time and incur the associated expense, exemplifying the adage, that "There is never enough time or money to do it right, but always enough time and money to do it over."

It is somewhat paradoxical that the search for order and predictability is invariably accompanied by efforts at subverting or circumventing the system instituted to bring about the sought-after order and predictability. In general, the more detailed the requirements for planning, the more planning tends to be perceived as restricting alternative options and pursuits and the more demanding of personal commitment it becomes. In the absence of management direction and insistence upon the progressive differentiation, linkage and dissemination of the corporate creed into meaningful operational guidelines, the general statements of organizational objectives and goals tend to diffuse through the organization according to varying managerial values, preferences and interpretations. The latter are often distorted by political considerations and other constraints, rather than shaped by the broad base of environmental dictates. Under such conditions, key strategic issues tend to suffocate. This is particularly debilitating to the individual with the responsibility for tactical planning who typically has little if any input to the longer-range decision but who may be faced with operationally conflicting requirements, especially in the establishing of priorities, trade-offs, and allocation of resources.

To the extent that planning focuses efforts and narrows choices, it is important that choices reflect not only the best individual judgments of the various elements of the organization but that the integration of such choices also reflect the best possible fit for the entity as a whole. Clearly, this suggests a need for bottom-up integration through successive levels of management, which can only be effected in response to a bottom-down, progressively more detailed differentiation of company objectives into specific goals and targets at each level of the organization. This requires a process of iterative reconciliation through a formalized strategic planning framework. The process cannot be initiated or sustained without top management commitment and direction.

12.4   Implementation of Strategic Planning

The ultimate objective of strategic planning is to evolve a sound, comprehensive, and cohesive course of action within a disorderly and uncertain marketplace. This objective mandates (1) a clear-cut translation of objectives, expectations, needs, and requirements into progressively more explicit direction based on an ongoing evaluation of the organization's overall posture, (2) a projection of the nature, extent, and impact of environmental factors, including anticipated changes, on the determinants of this posture, and (3) a determination of the requisite incremental adjustments to reconcile and minimize the disparity between the organization's prevailing and desired posture in line with the evolving environment changes.

Implementation of strategic planning requires a framework for the systematic assessment, coalescence, and transcription of a broad range of considerations, generally involving key business areas, into a specific and well-coordinated course of action by the different parts of the organization. Such a course of action, however, cannot be evolved without a concentrated effort at structuring a closed loop, iterative process of balancing the global views of top management, which are invariably based on political, financial, marketing, and administrative considerations, against the views of the technical or business professional, which focus on the more elegant and usually farsighted technical aspects and merits of a given case. The success of implementation of strategic planning is contingent upon the institution of a framework that fosters a climate of cooperation at various organizational levels by way of an integrative approach to management, especially in complex undertakings, rather than the more traditional approach based upon dominance, obedience and submission. This latter approach often stems from managerial insecurities or misguided sense of self adequacy characteristic of the management cultist which academia continues to breed and industry tolerates and nurtures.

In almost all organizations there is a tendency of its constituent memberships to espouse and advocate those aspects of an issue they understand best and over which they would individually exercise the greatest amount of control. In view of this, a routine procedural framework must be designed to control such tendencies at all levels of management as they ultimately lead to counterproductive views that devaluate the merits of both technical contributions and management functions. Symptomatic of such conditions are perceptions that engineers do not fully understand that engineering is an economic as well as a technical discipline and that it is not in the company's best interest for them to select their own projects based on their professional interests, career goals, and values, regardless of the relationship of such projects to product usefulness and company goals.[26,27,28] Frequently, however, company goals lack clarity and specificity and reflect varying managerial values. This gives rise to the corollary view that higher management is populated by generalists and "professional bureaucrats who are preoccupied with measuring economic results, oversimplifying problems, getting immediate results and manipulating people to achieve company economic goals,"[29] all of which are inexorably tied to self-enrichment and self-glorification.

Such a disparity in perceptions is symptomatic of both the engineer's need to reorient his thinking and management's need to integrate the engineer into the mainstream of the decision-making function affecting the long-range prospects of the organization as well as his career. Enlightened management recognizes this as no longer an option but a requirement as technology becomes more critical to its survival and technical professionals become more sensitized to the economic value of their contribution.

A general academic reeducation or industrial conditioning of the technical professional, as advocated by some, to develop a greater appreciation for the dynamics of the free enterprise system and corporate objectives and goals appears misguided. His source of frustration does not stem so much from a lack of understanding of the system as from the frequent lack of clear-cut articulation of corporate objectives and goals in meaningful, operationally consistent and measurable terms that reflect consideration of technical decisions, while misdiagnosed competitive developments and the need for "situation management" dictate unrealistic plans and schedules. The net result is a reaction that contributes to the further dissipation of organizational capabilities and erosion of national industrial strength.

Few in management today would deny the need for change. The problem, however, is that needed change is perceived by the individual as falling in areas outside of his immediate sphere of influence. At the lower echelons of management, this need tends to be viewed primarily in terms of streamlining other organizations or a more favorable posture of upper management toward one's own efforts or operations. At the upper echelons of management, change tends to be viewed in terms of legal economic, and political imperatives affecting the industry or company, such as governmental regulation or deregulation, lower interest rates, incentives, and the like. While the debate over the requisite changes persist, Japanese management is deftly applying a 35-year-old American management concept (strategic planning) with devastating effectiveness in the electronics, steel, automotive, and computer markets, to name a few.

Japanese effectiveness in this area is evident from the very high degree of self-sufficiency in key high technology areas. As shown below, the primary technology in most key electronics products is now Japanese:

——————— Table 12.1(a): Extent of Japanese Self-Reliance ———————

Technology Area	Approximate Extent of Self-Reliance (%)	Approximate Extent of External Reliance (%)		
		U.S.	Europe	Others
Assembly Robots	78	14	8	0
CAD/CAM	96	4	0	0
CCDs	80	16	2	2
Communications Satellites	80	16	4	0
Computers	66	30	1	3
Copiers	80	15	4	1
Data Bases	100	0	0	0
Digital PBX	90	7	3	0
Laser Printers	82	12	6	0
Microprocessors	55	35	6	4
Optical Fibers	70	25	5	0
Optomagnetic Disks	61	24	15	0
Semiconductor Memories	51	40	6	3
Superconductive Materials	100	0	0	0
Servomotors	62	38	0	0
VCRs	78	12	6	4

Source: Electronic Business, 12 June 1989

——————— Figure 12.1: Elements in the Implementation of Strategic Planning ———————

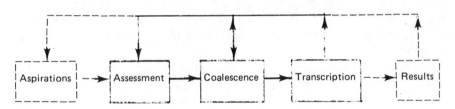

The implementation of strategic planning involves three principal stages (Figure 12.1). These stages include assessment, coalescence, and transcription of dominant business areas and their related aspects into a course of action consistent with unfolding market conditions or the creation of new markets.

In the following discussion we will view strategic planning conceptually delineating some of the key elements of each stage, rather than as a universally applicable step-by-step procedure.

(a) Assessment

In general, the key elements of the assessment stage should include an audit of aspirations along with an iteration of objectives, environmental factors, and product life cycles.

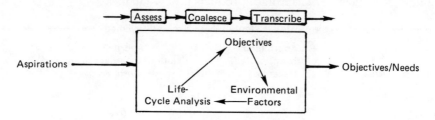

Objectives

Thompson and Strickland[30] suggest that the purpose of an organization must be externally rather than internally oriented, in line with Peter Drucker's view that "there is only one valid definition of business purposes: to create a customer" or effectively develop and satisfy a need.[31] This somewhat obvious proposition is not always that clear cut in practice.

As Hanan notes, companies for the most part are not strictly market oriented; their basic orientation tends to be inward, dominated by a preoccupation with existing "products, properties and processes" rather than with market needs and trends.[32,33] Companies tend to ask, "Given our technology, what product can we make?" rather than the more pragmatic question, "Given our market's needs, what products can we make to satisfy them – using our present technology or utilizing allied or even new technologies?"[34]

This preoccupation with technology rather than overall market needs has brought about the near demise of major industries in this country. Classic examples are the railroads and the movie studios, which failed to recognize soon enough that they were part of the broader transportation and entertainment industry.

There are other parallels today, although the examples are perhaps not as pointed. With the usual infallibility of hindsight, one might ponder, for instance, the belated entry of giant IBM, the computer pioneer, into the personal computer market behind a horde of other companies, some of which owe their

──── **Figure 12.2: Coupling Objectives Within The Organization** ────

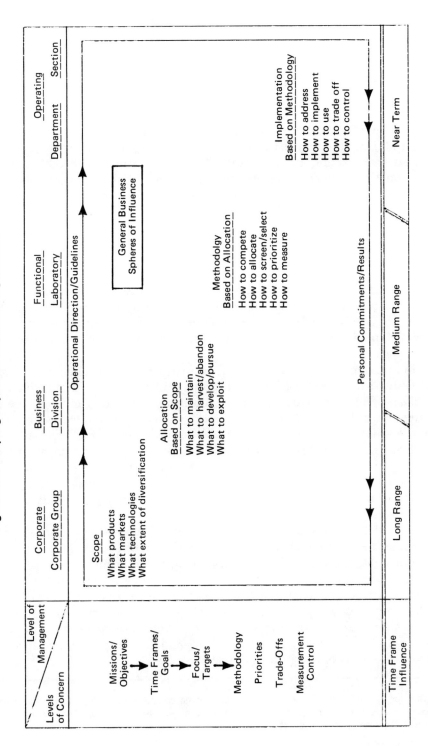

existence to their foresightedness.* Consider also the Xerox corporation, which allowed its virtual monopoly in office copiers to erode to the point of a permanent retrenchment in this area. In 1970 Xerox's share of the market was an enviable 97%. As of 1980 it slipped to 53%, whereas others, including the Japanese, steadily increased their share from 3 to 47%.[35]

The basic questions that must be addressed in the assessment stage both at the macro and the micro level, are definitions of the nature, scope, desirability, and direction of the organization's business interests and the extent of organizational commitment to these interests. Such questions involve an analysis of marketing, technical, manufacturing, financial, and other factors that cannot possibly be performed, assimilated or integrated only at the upper levels of management. As Galbraith suggests, at the present time no single man or group of men within a corporation's hierarchy can ascribe to the philosophy of "l'etat c'est moi."[36]† Sooner or later entrepreneurs and managers must abdicate to groups sharing specialized information essential to the operation of the enterprise. The conclusion reached by Galbraith is that the organization man no longer sustains the organization but is in fact sustained by the organization. This for many is a very bitter pill to swallow. The success of corporate undertakings will thus be largely influenced by the caliber and consistency of the integration of inputs from the base of the corporate pyramid in response to quality and continuity of guidelines transmitted downward.

Delineating such guidelines may be thought of as paralleling the four successive stages of organizational strategy identified by Thompson and Strickland.[37] These include corporate, business, functional, and operational strategies which, although primarily associated with the multitechnology and multiproduct organizations, are adaptable to single business enterprises seeking diversification, redirection, or both. The definition of objectives should be similarly patterned along those stages. The assessment stage should thus involve in part an audit of the extent of coupling of the objectives at each successive level of the organization in line with the sphere of managerial influence at the level (Figure 12.2).

Formulating corporate objectives in terms of successively more specific guidelines helps to maintain the necessary degree of operational continuity without stifling critical issues or organizational commitment.

This framework provides a vehicle for satisfying some of the essential criteria in the development of suitable objectives. It fosters commitment, which in turn promotes a motivating environment. This can be further reinforced through establishing measurable goals and targets through a process of association of progressively shorter time frames and greater quantitative specificity with the string of interlocking operational objectives.

---

* This can be explained by the frequent policy of large companies to wait and see how a new product fares in the marketplace before committing major funds to a competitive product. This may have been the case with IBM.

† "The state is me."

Environmental Factors

The interlocking of organizational objectives is part of a process of crystallization of expected results which must be developed in concert with an evaluation of the impact of both external and internal factors upon the institution and its selected scope of activities. External factors such as political and economic conditions, governmental regulations, technological innovation, competitive conditions, and demographic changes[38] each encompass a broad range of issues that aside from imposing constraints on the organization may promote downstream weaknesses and threats to its well-being.

These external factors generally do not lend themselves to easy quantification or reliable prediction, and the impact of the multitude of constituent issues they encompass cannot be rigorously defined in terms of cost, benefits, and risks. This general problem tends to be amplified by the interaction of issues including tax policies, economic regulation, cost of capital, inflation, material shortages, foreign trade, and so on.

Several forecasting techniques are available to aid in the evaluation and projection of external factors, which are summarized in Table 12.2. These techniques generally fall into one of three basic categories: qualitative, time series, and parametric.[39] Although these techniques have their usefulness, they tend to be narrow in scope. Their application is consequently restricted by a wide range of factors including the specific purpose of the forecast, relevance and availability of data, accuracy desired, time frame being forecast, and cost to the company, to name a few. Newer and potentially more powerful computer-based techniques such as PIMS (profit impact of market strategies) can be found in progressively wider use today.

Many view computer-aided simulation and decision-making techniques as being of limited practical usefulness as they merely suggest possibilities within a narrow band of issues. Management typically approaches such tools with considerable skepticism as it seldom participates in their development or is fully versed in their technical aspects. However, computerization does not automatically lead to improved management as its effectiveness is ultimately dependent on the judgment used in the development of the algorithms and the discrimination and application of generated outputs.

Overall, the problem in evaluating the external environment is to correlate, integrate and interpret qualitative and quantitative data, which typically requires a certain degree of intuitiveness and foresight. Such capability normally develops as a by-product of the synthesis of years of composite experience and may be extracted from within most organizations, often times from across several layers of management.

Objectives must also be compatible with the internal factors which characterize an organization's basic capabilities, resources, and accomplishments. This compatibility evolves from the consideration of such areas as existing product life cycles and their mix, organizational capabilities, past performance and financial conditions, organizational structure, priorities, interests and expectations of the work force. Internal factors are much more easily quantifi-

Table 12.2: Forecasting Techniques

Qualitative/Subjective		Quantitative/Objective	
Individual (visonary)	Consensus	Time Series	Parametric
• **Individual/ Scenario Writing** Generally nonscientific relying on individual immagination, intuition, guesswork, logic, and judgment. Normally performed by an individual expert in underlying discipline/ field.	• **Polls/Market Research** Systematic surveys leading to the evolution and testing of hypotheses relative to real markets. May typically involve individuals active in the field.	• **Mathematical Averaging** Weighted or nonweighted averaging of time-dependent/ phased data.	• **Correlation/ Regression Techniques** Deals primarily with statistical analysis and an attempt at the evolution of a functional relationship between two or more variables of interest.
• **Historical Analogy** Comparative analysis based upon similarity patterns with new products.	• **Panels/Delphi Methods** Expert projections developed either through unstructured interaction or through structured and systematic interrogation.	• **Trend Extrapolation/ Curve Fitting/Smoothing (Linear, Exponential, Polynomial, or Logarithmic)** Involves either weighted or nonweighted mathematical and/or graphic manipulation of time-dependent data. May or may not be subject to judgment modifications.	• **Modeling** Development of algorithms or a system of interdependent regression equations for the purpose of defining/describing input/output relationships, for instance, in economic and economic models.

Table 12.3: Sample Matrix For Evaluating Organizing Activities/Profile

Product Line or Activity / Sample Criteria	A Value	A Score	B Value	B Score	C Value	C Score	D Value	D Score	E Value	E Score
Sales/Total Sales	3%	1	12%	3	20%	4	15%	3	25%	5
Sales/Employee	-	-	-	-	-	-	-	-	-	-
Sales/Sq. Ft.	200	5	150	4	175	4	120	3	95	1
Sales/Investment										
Earnings/Total										
Earnings/Employee										
Earnings/Sq. Ft.										
Investment/Total										
Investment/Employee										
Investment/Sq. Ft.										
Sales/Total Market										
Forecast Sales/Total Market										
Actual Sales/Forecast										
Bid Won/Total Bids										
Bidding Expense/Total Budget										
Bidding Expense/Sales										
Bidding Expense/Forecast										
% Sales Market/Cust. A										
% Sales Market/Cust. B										
% Sales Market/Cust. C										
% Sales Market/Cust. D										
% Sales Market/Cust. E										
% Sales Market/Cust. F										
Engring/Total Labor										
Activity/Org. Personnel										
Staff/Line Personnel										
Employee Turnover, etc.										
Totals										

Notes:
- Scoring, Excellent: 5, Good: 4, Average: 3, Fair: 2, Poor: 1, Problem/ Crisis: 0.
- Maximum score = number of evaluation criteria × 5.
- Evaluate ratios first. Assign relative scores next to each of the activity criterions.
- Total scores for each activity. Address areas with lowest scores first.

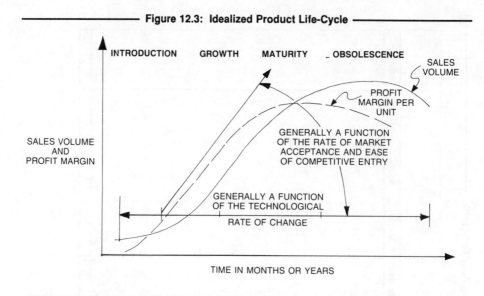

Figure 12.3: Idealized Product Life-Cycle

able than external ones and provide the basis for identifying and classifying activities requiring management attention in line with external conditions.

Quantification of organizational activities may be largely accomplished through an analysis of a wide range of calculable ratios of the type presented in Table 12.2, the primary purpose of which is to establish patterns of organizational development, customer dependence, market penetration, and a broad range of other issues such as product life cycle, resource use, capability, staffing efficiency, productivity, and morale.

Analysis of internal factors lends itself much more readily to the use of computers. Even in cases involving an indirect consideration such as morale, assessments can be made through a number of ratios and percentages relating to the extent of employee turnover, absenteeism, sick leave, tardiness, and quality of output. But although a large number of internal factors do lend themselves to quantification and computerized analysis, current management systems remain predominantly oriented toward the accumulation and stewardship of modularized data in the general areas of financial and management accounting. Thoroughness of analysis is thus typically inhibited not so much by a lack of available data as by its inaccessibility and retrieval in a timely and operationally useful format for a variety of inferential analyses. Strategic planning should address some of the strengths and weaknesses of its management information systems in providing random access to the substantial amount of available data that should be cross-correlated and evaluated as part of this stage of the strategic planning process.

Environmental assessment primarily deals with the interrelationship of external environmental factors and the firm's expectations, activities, achievements, and posture, which collectively comprise its strategic profile. Such assessment consequently shapes the development of organizational objectives and drives the need for their periodic reevaluation.

Product Life-Cycle Analysis

Product life-cycle analysis is perhaps the most important yet neglected aspect of the assessment stage. Clifford points out that most leading companies fail to recognize that their products have a life cycle, much less make an attempt to apply the concept.[40] This is consistent with the previously discussed inward orientation of companies.

Product life-cycle analysis can be an extremely powerful tool in evaluating and fine tuning performance. Properly applied, it can provide significant insight into (a) the position of the product in the marketplace and its contribution to the strength or viability of the overall organization and (b) the nature, priority, and allocation of resources in concert with the assessment of the position of the product, objectives of the organization, and environmental conditions.

As a result of the insights gained, product life-cycle analysis can be used to identify business options, streamline organizational responses, and add an element of control in the pursuit of various opportunities.

The life cycle of products is characterized by four stages: introduction, growth, maturity, and obsolescence. These are further characterized by the relative magnitude and the general trend in the combination of sales volume and profit (Figure 12.3). The duration of the individual phases and the length of the overall cycle will vary from product to product, as will the shape of the sales and profit margin curves.

In the introduction stage, sales volume tends to be very low and correspondingly little if any profit is generated. As the product diffuses into the marketplace and gains acceptance, the rate of sales volume and profit will typically continue to increase up to the point where competition become significant. This stage of the life cycle is known as the development stage. The onset of competition will typically manifest itself by a progressive slowdown in the rate of growth of both sales volume and profit, although in total terms sales volume and profit may continue to increase. This generally signals the beginning of early maturity. With the entrenchment of competition, the sales volume will typically begin to stabilize as will profits. The latter will usually begin to fall off before complete stabilization of the sales volume owing to stiffened competition in pricing and other areas. This stage of the life cycle is known as maturity and is followed by the obsolescence stage in which both the sales volume and profits fall off. Obsolescence may be brought about by any number of reasons such as disappearance of need, technological advances, or the other product's attributes and marketing strategy. Obsolescence in most cases can be held back through product improvement or repackaging efforts. In the case of military systems, for instance, such efforts tend to be preplanned to allow for technological insertion or upgrading consistent with the technological improvements that have taken place since the system's introduction.

Life-cycle analysis can disclose conditions that can lead to the evaluation of a number of business options depending on product line mix, organiza-

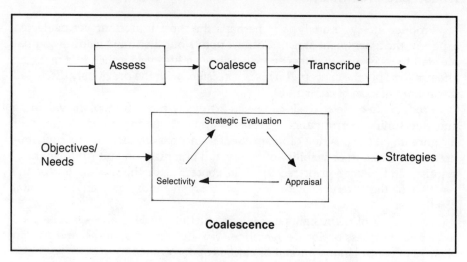

Figure 12.4: Key Elements Of The Coaslescence Stage

tional objectives, and environmental analysis. As an example, an analysis of the percentage of the company's sales falling into each stage of the life cycle may prompt a growth-oriented company to allocate a greater percentage of its resources to the introduction of new products rather than expend them on the improvement or repackaging of products in the latter stages of maturity as a means of extending their life-cycles. Development of target life-cycles, for instance, can be very useful in the pacing of new product development plans and efforts as well as in the timing of the phase-out of matured or obsolete product lines. The specific options that can evolve from such an analysis of the life-cycle profiles will be strongly influenced by the type of industry, the nature of the individual products, their life-cycle stage and overall mix, type of company, its objectives, and environmental factors.

Overall, life-cycle analysis affords a powerful diagnostic check into the range of general options open to the firm, which require further scrutiny, coalescence, and transcription in line with the longer-range needs and expectations of the organization.

(b) Coalescence

The assessment stage typically yields a great deal of relevant data, usually general in nature, requiring further evaluation and processing (Figure 12.4).

Evaluation

A key element in the evaluation, appraisal and screening of indicated pursuits is the recognition that all endeavors must ultimately embody the prospects of economic production and profitable dissemination. This suggests

──────────────── **Figure 12.5: Technology Market Mix Positions** ────────────────

PRODUCT EFFECT	NO TECHNOLOGICAL CHANGE Does not require additional laboratory effort.	IMPROVED TECHNOLOGY Requires laboratory effort utilizing technology presently employed, known, or related to that used in existing company products.	NEW TECHNOLOGY Requires laboratory effort utilizing technology not presently employed in company products.
NO MARKET CHANGE Does not affect marketing programs.		Reformulation	Replacement
STRENGTHENED MARKET Affects marketing programs for classes of consumers not now served.	Remerchandising	Improved Product	Product Line Extension
NEW MARKET Requires marketing programs for classes of consumers not now served.	New Use	Market Extension	Diversification

KEY:

Research and Development Department	Marketing Department
Joint Responsibility of R & D and Marketing Departments	XXXX Boundary Line of Existing Business

Source: Samuel C. Johnson and Conrad Jones, "How to Organize for New Product," *Harvard Business Review* (May-June 1957), pp. 49-62. Reprinted by permission. Copyright © 1957 by the President and Fellows of Harvard College; all rights reserved.

that evaluation of option and pursuits can be considered in terms of existing and projected marketing and technical conditions. The options can be represented by a matrix consisting of the continuum of marketing and technological conditions as shown in Figure 12.5. Each of the points in the matrix indicates the most likely and realistic options for management consideration depending on the posturing of the firm as determined from an audit of its objectives and environmental and life-cycle analyses. These options offer alternatives to the frequently encountered conditions of drift, concession to uncontrollable events, preoccupation with past laurels, or lack of competitive critical mass arising out of failure to rigorously and systematically reevaluate operations.

Figure 12.6: Strategic Alternatives

Product Objectives	No Technological Change	Improved Technology To utilize more fully the company's present scientific knowledge and production skills.	New Technology To acquire scientific knowledge and production skills new to the company.
No Market Change		**Reformulation** To maintain an optimum balance of cost, quality, and availability in the formulas of present company products.	**Replacement** To seek new and better ingredients or formulation for present company products in technology not now employed by the company.
Strengthened Market To exploit more fully the existing markets for the present company products.	**Remerchandising** To increase sales to consumers of types now served by the company.	**Improved Product** To improve present products for greater utility and merchandisability to consumers.	**Product Line Extension** To broaden the line of products offered to present consumers through new technology.
New Market To increase the number of types of consumers served by the company.	**New Use** To find new classes of consumers that can utilize present company products.	**Market Extension** To reach new classes of consumers by modifying present products.	**Diversification** To add to the classes of consumers served by developing new technical knowledge.

Note: Product life cycle will typically dictate where the right kind of competitive advantage is likely to be located.

(Top axis label: Increasing Technological Newness; Left axis label: Increasing Market Newness)

Drift often stems from the inadequate linkage of objectives and goals within an organization, which leads to a course of action influenced not so much by market and technological considerations as by the day-to-day decisions and compromises at or between the operating and administrative levels of management. Emulation of the leading competitor's strategies is similarly symptomatic of drift.

Drift is often accompanied by a tendency in industry to rationalize lackluster performance by appealing to so-called uncontrollable events such as those attributed to technological complexity.

Whether due to technological improvements as proposed by Kahn[41] or not, there has clearly been an attitudinal change in our society affecting expectations, particularly those of the work force. Among the changes cited by Kahn is a "certain loss of uplifting ideals and various distinctions between superior and inferior performance and individuals." In the corporate world the problems attendant to such attitudinal changes are typically consolidated under the umbrella of circumstances beyond managerial control. This phenomenon tends to be more prevalent in larger organizations or bureaucracies and has contributed to the acceptability of normative inadequacy.

Tradition and managerial inertia generally make it exceedingly difficult to reassess and reformulate organizational options, particularly in cases where the organization has enjoyed moderate success. Fear of change is characterized by a reliance upon old rules, methods, and procedures that once may have contributed a measure of success to the organization. Even in cases where changes are made, they tend to be primarily cosmetic, closely patterned on guidelines fashioned in response to different conditions and under different circumstances. Frequently, this leads to situations where much horsepower is generated in the pursuit of opportunities, yet the organizational vehicle fails to develop any significant torque.

There are two basic requirements for the successful pursuit of business options. The first is the so-called differential or distinctive advantage, that is, an advantage unique to the organization that either exists and can be specifically identified or must be developed in a particular sphere of interest. The second is a "critical mass" in terms of a combination of organizational resources and commitment to support such an advantage. The first of these requirements is widely recognized and accepted. The second, however, is often lost in controversies that frequently surround the allocation of organizational resources to various activities in the absence of a systematic reassessment and continuing restatement of organizational objectives.

The matrix of Figure 12.6 offers a number of generalized options to channel organizational pursuits along realistic avenues in accordance with the firm's prevailing fortunes and the constraints imposed by varying market and technological conditions. Recognizing that competitive strategies vary from product to product, time to time, and situation to situation, this matrix can be applied to the organization as a whole in cases of single-product organizations or individually to each of the product lines in cases of multitechnology, multiproduct, or multimarket operations to focus organizational pursuits.

Appraisal

The issues typically faced by an organization are seldom so clear cut as to lend themselves to straightforward packaging in the form of discrete alternative choices. After the assessment stage, strategic alternatives should be further reappraised in conjunction with a wide range of competitive considerations that may tend to modify the suggested course of action. The process of appraisal involves creative reconciliation of the responses to the conditions facing the firm which, parenthetically, need not necessarily be restricted to strategic and competitive issues. This in turn requires iteration, judgment, and creativity at all levels of management supported by a formalized framework designed to elicit and maintain a high level of payoff.

The appraisal stage thus typically addresses issues of recurring, broad-based management interest that usually do not lend themselves to articulation during the more generalized phases of the front end of the strategic planning effort. Consider, for example, an issue such the basis of the coexistence of

——————————— **Figure 12.7: Product/Market Evaluation Matrix** ———————————

Life Cycle Stage \ Competitive Position	Strong	Average	Weak
Development		A	
Growth			B
Shakeout		C	
Maturity/ Saturation		D	
Obsolescence			

Source: Bernard M. Baruch, "Strategic Evaluation and Strategic Choice," in A. A. Thompson and A. J. Strickland, eds., *Strategy Formulation and Implementation* (Dallas: Business Publications), p. 169.

competing approaches and techniques. It can be as significant in the overall evolution of a master strategy at the upper levels of management as in the operating level's decision to pursue a specific opportunity. An appraisal of the impact of the considerations presented in Table 12.3 is an essential element of the coalescence of the organizational response around an effective course of action consistent with the organization's objectives, capabilities, and resources. Aside from the use of checklists, such an appraisal can be supported by general methods discussed in the next section. Other equally important considerations are organizational design and change, integration of resources planning and allocation systems into the process, development of performance measurement methodology and criteria for evaluation.

————————————————— Table 12.4: Improving Selectivity —————————

Spheres of Operation	Relative Weight	Degree of Compatibility of Option Considered											Composite Weight
		0	.1	.2	.3	.4	.5	.6	.7	.8	.9	1.0	
Financial	(.15)						x						.075
Marketing	(.20)								x				.16
R&D program	(.30)				x								.15
Personnel	(.30)				x								.15
Facilities (i.e., capability)	(.05)										x		.05
etc.													
Total	1.00												.585*

*Cutoff may be 0.70 for acceptance.

Source: Adopted with permission from Barry M. Richman, "A Rating Scale for Product Innovation," *Business Horizons* (Summer 1962).

Selectivity

The concept of selectivity is not always clearly understood. This largely stems from the varying perceptions of the importance of products and product lines to the organization as a function of time. Because of such temporal changes in the significance of products and product lines, it becomes desirable to focus organizational pursuits in a direction that will promote the longer-range interests of the organization and will be consistent with its prevailing fortunes and competitive strengths.

A possible tool in developing a greater degree of organizational selectivity is an adaptation of the so-called Hofer and Schendell matrix.[42] The strength of this tool lies in its depiction of the distribution of the firm's business interests across the stages of product-market evolution (Figure 12.7). The size of the market and the organization's share as established in the course of the assessment stage is generally represented by means of circles and pie wedges, respectively. It is subsequently plotted at the coordinates of the matrix representative of the stage of evolution. Such representation can be useful to identify the merits of various products and management options. By way of illustration, consider products A, B, C, and D, which may be interpreted as a developing winner, a potential loser, a source of cash, and definite loser, respectively. It will be noted that whereas Figure 12.7 reflects product evaluation on the basis of competitive positions and market shares, there is no reason why such evaluations cannot be performed using growth rates, profits, or other meaningful parameters.

As the marketplace generally provides a host of alternative opportunities, it becomes exceedingly important to be able to compare and evaluate the merits of the available opportunities with reasonable consistency and in concert with the competitive profile of the organization. This is seldom an easy

Figure 12.8: Key Elements of the Transcription Stage

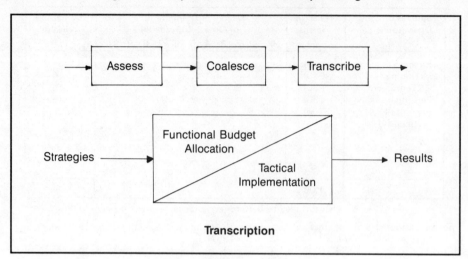

task considering the varying attributes of prospective undertakings relative to the given operational strengths and weaknesses of the organization at a given point in time. Whereas a number of methods have been suggested, among the most effective is the product fit evaluation matrix proposed by Richman.[43] It allows for the evaluation of prospective pursuits based on their compatibility with each of the spheres of company performance rated in relation to their contribution to overall future success. Richman points out that since the overall competitiveness of the company will stem from the performance and relative contribution of the various spheres of operation, it generally follows that optimum competitive advantage is to be found in pursuits that are compatible with and complement the areas of major organizational strength. Each of the company's operational or functional spheres is thus assigned a relative weight in relation to is significance to the company's overall success based on historical considerations or comprehensive appraisal. The sum total of such relative weights should always equal to one (Table 12.4). Similarly, each pursuit is rated in terms of its compatibility with each sphere on a scale of 0 to 1 depending on the degree of its fit with the various elements of the sphere under consideration. The final computation of the relative merit of a given opportunity is calculated as in Table 12.4. This method allows for the establishment of a threshold of acceptability of prospective undertakings in line with past experience or other considerations.

(c) Transcription

Transcription (Figure 12.8) deals with the implementation and control of medium-range and near-term activities, typically within the time frame of one to five years, as suggested by (1) the characterization of the long-range trends

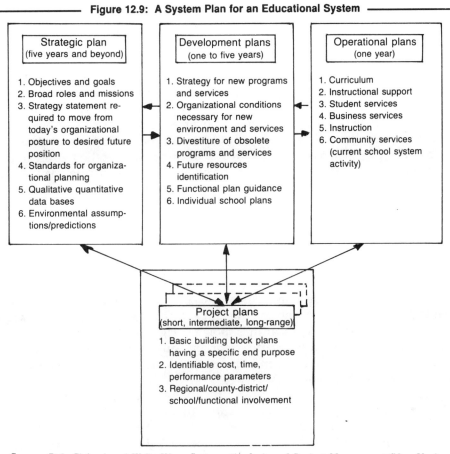

Figure 12.9: A System Plan for an Educational System

Strategic plan (five years and beyond)	Development plans (one to five years)	Operational plans (one year)
1. Objectives and goals 2. Broad roles and missions 3. Strategy statement required to move from today's organizational posture to desired future position 4. Standards for organizational planning 5. Qualitative quantitative data bases 6. Environmental assumptions/predictions	1. Strategy for new programs and services 2. Organizational conditions necessary for new environment and services 3. Divestiture of obsolete programs and services 4. Future resources identification 5. Functional plan guidance 6. Individual school plans	1. Curriculum 2. Instructional support 3. Student services 4. Business services 5. Instruction 6. Community services (current school system activity)

Project plans (short, intermediate, long-range)

1. Basic building block plans having a specific end purpose
2. Identifiable cost, time, performance parameters
3. Regional/county-district/school/functional involvement

Source: D.I. Cleland and W.R. King, *Systems Analysis and Project Management* (New York: McGraw-Hill, 1983), p. 49. Copyright 1983.

and projected developments in the environment and the marketplace extending from five to 15 years into the future; (2) the synthesis of corporate identity or profile in terms of its current competitive position, expectations, pursuits, capabilities, overall resources, and general strengths and weaknesses; and (3) the resultant formulation of indicated adjustments as part of a systematic process of reconciliation of the differences between the aforementioned factors with the desired purpose of developing as unique a capability as possible to inhibit the likelihood of its duplication or erosion.

Functional Budget Allocations

Steiner views the process of transcription as taking place in two steps.[44] The first step is translation of the outputs of the assessment and coalescence stages into functional plans including those elements of the organization essential to the success of contemplated undertakings. This typically involves the allocation of resources to the various functions of the organization in line with the strategic profile and strategic choice. The second step includes funding by the functional organizations of the various near-term activities compatible with the strategic profile and strategic choices.

The first step of the transcription process is primarily to balance available resources against those required by the pursuit of corporate aspirations. If an unreconcilable shortage is projected, it should prompt a further reevaluation and streamlining of strategic options. Conversely, a surplus should prompt a reassessment in line with a broadening of pursuits for the more efficient use of resources. In either case, the resource balancing and allocation effort must incorporate a considerable degree of flexibility to accommodate changes in environmental conditions. The balancing effort typically involves pro forma projections and iteration of functions shown in Figure 12.9.[45]

Tactical Implementation

The second part of the transcription effort is to translate such functional plans into short-range tactical plans by means of budgets, schedules, and organizational adjustments to implement and control day-to-day activities. The general system of plans connecting the three stages of strategic planning with the day-to-day activities of the firm is shown in Figure 12.9.

The transcription process varies from company to company as it is generally driven by both experience and circumstances. There is consequently little uniformity in approach or methodology.

12.5   VHSIC: Sample Catalyst for Radical Innovation

In the introduction to this chapter, we mentioned the growing need for an interdisciplinary approach to management and the strategic planning process and cited very high speed integrated circuit (VHSIC) technology as an example of a development requiring this kind of approach. It might be useful to expand upon the projected impact of this particular development to illustrate the far-reaching effect that R&D efforts, of which there are thousands, can have on the marketplace. Such isolated developments, not all well publicized as VHSIC, may have an equally unsettling impact (from the corporate perspective) on future trends and conditions.

The VHSIC program is a multiyear, multiphased development program heavily subsidized by the Department of Defense that promises to revolutionize the world of electronics and extend its control to areas where size, cost, complexity, reliability, and power requirements have up to now precluded its use.[46,47] It has been projected that in the next decade, the state of the art in signal processing capability will have undergone a staged net improvement by a factor of 1,000 concurrently with a drastic reduction in the spatial dimensions of integrated circuits. Whereas the primary applications at first will be military, the principal long-term market for VHSIC judging by history will be in nonmilitary applications, which today account for 95% of the semiconductor business initially promoted by the defense industry.[48] The prospects are that VHSIC technology will offer the capability of performing hundreds of billions of operations per second. In more tangible terms, this means that certain systems or applications that currently rely on more sophisticated, special purpose, mainframe computers could be made operable at near video rates within a space of a cubic foot or less. The impact of this technology will be profound and far reaching, not only in the area of military systems development but ultimately in the possible development of systems affecting virtually every aspect and facet of our lives. VHSIC goes beyond anticipated improvements in business computers and increased automation in the office, factory and home. It will offer the capability, for instance, to design artificial intelligence systems which, coupled with collateral developments of this technology in other fields, could radically transform the political, economic, social, and cultural profile of our environment. There will be a major impact of such advances on industry and more specifically on a host of predominantly routine office and manufacturing functions. The progressive changes, as the milestones of the VHSIC program are achieved, will further fuel the spirit of innovation and entrepreneurship in this area of technology.

12.6   Strategic Planning and Productivity

Strategic planning is one of the essential building blocks in the improvement of productivity. Commitment of company resources to ill-chosen pursuits cannot possibly improve organizational productivity. However, even well-chosen pursuits provide no assurance of the ultimate productivity of an undertaking because of the criticality of the human factor in the execution phases. As Steiner observes, there are a number of advantages in the process of strategic planning that significantly enhance the prospects of productive selection of pursuits and their ultimate execution.[49] The advantages of strategic planning are as follows:

- Promotes the consideration and treatment of the organization as a system comprised of functional subsystems
- Forces the establishment of objectives and fosters their acceptance through broader-based participation and involvement
- Provides management with an opportunity to consider, evaluate, and select a course of action from among a considerably larger number of alternatives than might be otherwise obvious, identifiable, or considered
- Leads to the establishment of a coordinated resource allocation and performance measurement system
- Identifies strengths and weaknesses along with vulnerabilities that may inhibit attainment of delineated objectives

Strategic planning, if conscientiously and systematically applied, holds out the promise of significant payoff.

———— Questions and Topics for Discussion ————

1. Discuss or rebut a common assertion that a majority of R&D activities and efforts do not lend themselves to effective planning, scheduling and/or budgeting.

2. Discuss the origins and/or the base of support for the "macho style of management" in industry – what, if anything, do you feel can and should be done about it?

3. Discuss the relative effect of company size, product complexity, extent of diversification and availability of resources on the need for and approach to strategic planning.

4. Discuss and describe how you would go about evaluating and measuring the effectiveness of the output of the strategic planning effort instituted by a company.

5. Provide a specific example of the progressive translation and linkage of corporate objectives into operational guidance to your organizational level.

6. How would you go about establishing a business strategy for an existing product line?

7. Prepare an assessment of the likely impact of VHSIC technology upon an industry or company of your choice.

8. Develop a quasi-quantitative basis for the allocation of company resources to prospective pursuits.

————————— References —————————

1. "Nonstop Learning is Engineer's Lot," *Machine Design* (March 11, 1982), p. 436 (attributed to study by Robert G. Rynell).
2. "Survey of Science and Technology Issues Present and Future," *Staff Report of the Committee on Science and Technology*, U. S. House of Representatives, 97th Congress, 1st Session (June 1981), pp. 322-323.
3. Quoted in Henry Mintzberg, "The Manager's Job: Folklore and Fact," *Harvard Business Review* (July-August 1975). Copyright 1975 by the President and Fellows of Harvard College; all rights reserved.
4. Richard Pascale and Anthony Athos, *The Art of Japanese Management*, (New York: Warner Books, 1982), p. 248.
5. J.K. Galbraith, *The New Industrial State* (Boston: Houghton Mifflin, 1967), p. 90.
6. William H. Gruber, *The Strategic Integration of Corporate Research and Development*, (New York: American Management Association, 1981), p. 9.
7. "Uncle Sam Ups Ante for R&D," *Machine Design* (February 25, 1982), p. 182.
8. "U.S. R&D Spending to Rise in 1982," *Los Angeles Times* (May 28, 1982).

9. A. Gerstenfeld, *Effective Management* (Reading, Mass.: Addison-Wesley, 1970), pp. 19, 26.
10. Carter Bales, "Strategic Control: The President's Paradox," *Business Horizons* (August 1977).
11. *Ibid.*
12. A.K. Wikesberg and T.C. Cronin, "Management by Task Force," Harvard Business Review (November-December 1962).
13. "Engineers Never Had It So Good," *Machine Design* (April 8, 1982), p. 150.
14. Quoted in Lawerence A. Skantze, "Productivity: Making It Good Enough, Fast Enough, Soon Enough," *Program Manager* Vol. 10, No. 6(November-December 1981), p. 11-12.
15. Staff Report of the Committee on Science and Technology, U.S. House of Representatives, 97th Congress 1st Session. "Survey of Science and Technology Issues Present and Future." (June 1981), pp. 322-323. "Population Factors and Demographics," p. 217.
16. Walter K. Weisel, "The Robot's Role in Productivity," *Production Engineering* (December 1981), p. 18.
17. "Survey of Science and Technology Issues Present and Future," pp. 322-323.
18. F. Lavoie, "A Battle Won, A War Lost," *Machine Design* (April 8, 1982).
19. "Survey of Science and Technology Issues Present and Future," pp. 322.323.
20. *Aviation Week and Space Technology* (March 8, 1982).
21. "Survey of Science and Technology Issues Present and Future," pp. 146, 150.
22. *Ibid.*, pp. 152, 153.
23. "NTIs: The Door to the Federal Gold Mine," *Government Executive*, Vol. 13, No. 8 (August 1981), pp. 14-20.
24. George A. Steiner, *Strategic Planning* (New York: Free Press, 1979), p. 36.
25. Herman Kahn, *The Next 200 Years* (New York: Hudson Institute William Morrow, 1976), p. 201.
26. M.K. Badawy, *Developing Managerial Skills in Engineers & Scientists* (New York: Van Nostrand, 1982).
27. M.K. Badawy, "What's Wrong with Engineering Management" *Machine Design* (July 22, 1982), pp. 62-66.
28. S.E. Stephenou, *Management: Technology, Innovation & Engineering* (Malibu, Calif.: Daniel Spencer, 1981), pp. 162-164.
29. Badawy, "What's Wrong with Engineering Management," p. 63.
30. A.A. Thompson and A.J. Strickland, "Strategy and Policy: A General Management Overview," in *Strategy and Implementation* (Dallas: Business Publications, 1980), p. 6.
31. Peter F. Drucker, *"Management: Tasks, Responsibilities, Practices"* (New York: Harper and Row, 1974), p. 61.
32. Mack Hanan, *Handbook of Modern Marketing*, ed. Victor Buel (New York: McGraw-Hill, 1970), pp. 17-28.
33. Robert Rothberg, *Corporate Strategy and Product Innovation* (New York: Free Press, 1976), pp. 206-207.
34. Hanan, *Handbook of Modern Marketing*, p. 3:20.
35. Robert Dallos, "Xerox Plans to Eliminate Jobs in US, Abroad," *Los Angeles Times* (September 24, 1981).
36. J.K. Galbraith, *The New Industrial State*, pp. 86-97.
37. Thompson and Strickland, *Strategy and Implementation*, p. 6.
38. Daniel E. Roman, *Science, Technology, and Innovation: A Systems Approach* (Columbus, Ohio: Grid Publishing, 1980).
39. James R. Bright, ed., *Technological Forecasting for Industry and Government: Methods and Applications* (Englewood Cliffs, N.J.: Prentice-Hall, 1968).
40. Donald K. Clifford, "Managing the Product Life Cycle," in Ronald Mann, ed., *The Arts of Top Management: A McKinsey Anthology* (New York: McGraw-Hill, 1971).
41. Herman Kahn, *The Next 200 Years.*
42. Bernard M. Baruch, "Strategic Evaluation and Strategic Choice," in A.A. Thompson and A.J. Strickland, eds., *Strategy Formulation and Implementation* (Dallas: Business Publications, 1980), p. 169.
43. Barry M. Richman, "A Rating Scale for Product Innovation," *Business Horizons* (Summer 1962).
44. Steiner, *Strategic Planning*, pp. 198-204.
45. *Ibid.*

46. D.F. Barbe, "VHSIC Systems and Technology," *Computer* (February 1981), pp. 13-22.
47. John G. Posa, "VHSIC Proposals Take Six Fast Tracks," *Electronics* (September 22, 1981), pp. 89-96.
48. "Very High Speed Integrated Circuits," *Aviation Week and Space Technology* (February 16, 1981), p. 48.
49. Steiner, *Strategic Planning*, pp. 36-43.

——————————————— Chapter 13 ———————————————

Transition to Production

13.1 Introduction
13.2 The Case For A Disciplined Process
13.3 The High Price of Reactive Management
13.4 The Source and Impact of Design Engineering Gaps
13.5 High Payoff Basics
    (a) Simplicity
    (b) Standardization
    (c) Design Tolerances and Safety Margins
    (d) Built in Test Capability
    (e) Manufacturing Involvement
13.6 Evolving a Product Oriented Culture
13.7 CAD/CAM
13.8 Other Important Considerations
    (a) Design-To-Cost
    (b) Configuration Management/Control
    (c) Software Design, Verification and Validation
    (d) Transition Planning
13.8 Strategy That Actually Pays Off

13.1 Introduction

The attainment of cost, schedule and performance criteria is seldom, if ever, an indication of the successful completion of a design and development effort. Many seemingly remarkable design and development triumphs have proven themselves nightmares in production and invariably major disappointments in the field. The combination of these problems have focused attention on the need to address the issue of "transition to production". Generally speaking, the more complex the product or system, the more critical the need to address the issue. In this area, a great many lessons can be learned from the aerospace industry since it deals with the most complex of all "transition" processes. Some of the bitter lessons of the aerospace industry are generally applicable to other industries that deal with transformation of ideas into relatively complex products or systems.

Whether dealing with a military system or a consumer product, rapid transformation of an idea into an end-product typically results in high efficiencies and a significant strategic advantage(s). In the case of military systems, the primary and obvious objective is to obtain a new or upgraded version of a product of value, in the shortest possible time, given a specific mission need. The same is generally true with consumer products. Typically, the

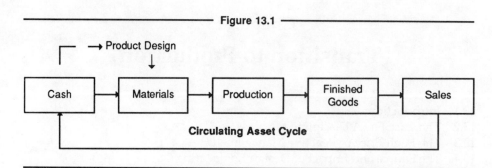

Figure 13.1

objective is to introduce a new or improved product, increase margins or develop other forms of competitive advantage, in the shortest possible time, in line with certain market needs. In either case, reducing the transition time from idea-to-end-product is no longer merely desirable in our highly competitive environment. The ability to do so effectively is critical to the profitability of the organization and hence its survivability.

The above can be conceptually illustrated by using Figure 13.1. The overall investment and amount of capital required over any given period of time is governed by the speed at which the cash cycle of Figure 13.1 is sustained. The faster the cycle, the less investment in circulating capital. The faster the rate of turnover in the elements of the circulating assets, the less the total investment. Scrap and rework, as an example, raise the amount of capital and total investment required; furthermore, they slow down the overall material-product-sales conversion process and thus compound one's losses. It becomes evident that if profits are to be realized, if not maximized, one must focus on factors which *affect cycle time, limit and reduce the amount of capital tied up.*

If cycle times are to be improved, transition to production cannot be treated as a discrete effort to be implemented as of a point in time. *It is a disciplined process that is an integral part of the basic engineering function.* Specifically, that of *effecting and managing* the conversion of viable ideas into *products of value.*

13.2   The Case For A Disciplined Process

In section 11.1(b), we took exception to a frequently heard excuse that today's undertakings somehow defy thoroughness of evaluation, depth of planning, and effectiveness of control and thus inherently involve high risk and cost of development. We proceeded to support our view that: High risk and cost of development are more a function of prevailing *management* attitude and approach to dealing with complexity rather than a function of the complexity of the undertakings per se. As Willis Willoughby, Jr., Chairman of the Defense Science Board Task Force on Transition from Development to Production, notes:

"To my way of thinking, there has been, is now, and may always be one principal area in which we must strive for further improvement.

That principle is *disciplined engineering*...In short, everything...should be subservient to it; yet most of our management systems are designed to circumvent it or excuse its omission."[1]

Most of our major problems stem from what some have described as the "I Can Manage Anything" mentality. In many firms, management seems to operate on the basis of *three implicit assumption* which, in their simplest form, suggest that:

(1) Technical problems can be attacked, solved or eliminated through movement of boxes and lines around the organizational chart. Furthermore, that organization (or reorganization) is the only necessary and sufficient condition to assure success of a project or program.
(2) Movement or re-combination of boxes and lines around the organizational chart will affect the behavior, motivations and/or perceptions of the people involved. Furthermore, that organizational changes reflect an improvement and lead to a greater degree of individual commitment to the success of stated objectives.
(3) Adherence to cost, schedule and performance specifications equates to "quality" of technical effort. Furthermore, that the "quality" of technical effort is primarily, if not exclusively, a function of the "cultural" (re)conditioning of the employee.

The above views are largely responsible for a number of the major problems we appear to be experiencing in developing and maintaining a competitive edge. Tom Woodward* of McKinsey & Co. alludes to the reason:

"In many firms, engineering is still viewed as a narrow technical facility, with its practitioners as in-house vendors to be deployed at the initiative of top management. What is needed is a view of engineering as a discipline that can yield insights about a wide range of functions in a firm, as a vital mediator between vision and reality."[2]

A great deal of this is admittedly perpetuated by scientists and engineers themselves. Many default decision making to the operations and management factions of their company:

"In many enterprises technical management either consciously or unconsciously positions itself apart from the rest of the management team. A technical manager may perceive his role in business as "a capital T, and small m" viewing as his responsibility only the technical aspects of a problem."[3]

---

* Mr. Woodward is a Director in the New York office of McKinsey & Co. specializing in the electronics and telecommunications industries.

A greater number of technical professionals need to recognize that the price of admission into management can often be had for as little as the price of a nice suit and an attractive tie.

"Let's face it. If you enter the meeting with an unknown management group, what do you guess the job is of the guy with the plaid shirt and knit tie? Although stereotypes can be misleading, they also can be symptoms of a problem."[4]

Engineering is a technical *as well as an economic discipline.* Having an engineer run an accounting organization may be just as absurd as having an accountant run an engineering organization. It takes TEAM work. In effect, poor communication along with a lack of effective and pro active technical advocacy at policy and operating levels, tends to be one of the primary causes of our frequent inability to be competitive at home and abroad.

Willoughby concludes:

"It is impossible to describe a management system first that will take care of the fundamentals of the industrial process – engineering and manufacturing...It (the industrial process) will either fail or falter if these processes are not performed in a disciplined manner, because the design, test and production processes are a continuum of interrelated and interdependent disciplines...*Manage the fundamentals of design, test, and production and the management system will describe itself.*"[5]

In the following sections, we present a discussion of concepts aimed at improving the idea-to-end-product cycle time.

13.3 The High Price of Reactive Management

As product life cycles grow progressively shorter (section 11.1(c)), many firms find themselves under increased pressure to accelerate new product development. The need to embark upon and accelerate development, becomes especially intense in the absence of *strategic planning* that sets the stage for a *timely and systematic approach* to the introduction of new products and systems.

"Managers often try to enforce, from the top down, unrealistic scheduling objectives. In other instances, fast development programs are not really planned – they are hastily put together, on an ad hoc basis, when delays become critical. Throwing resources at projects at the last minute...can damage the next product generation, and may leave...organizational problems unresolved for the longer term."[6]

The above conditions are sources of at least two serious and debilitating problems.

First, acceleration of the development effort may not be consistent with the firm's past plans, expectations and strategic choices. In other words, the firm's current strategic profile may be incompatible with what may be required (or was anticipated) in terms of technical accomplishments and capabilities, available facilities and equipment, required staffing and organizational structure, financial condition, preexisting priorities, etc.

Within the constraints of the cost and schedule allocated for development, these situations invariably force very costly compromises that haunt the effort throughout its development and production phases.

Second, development efforts pulled together on an "ad hoc" basis generally suffer from their own unique problems that are aggravated under the above described conditions. Needs and desires are typically expressed and conveyed in terms of *operational* requirements. Operational requirements tend to be performance oriented. Based on the preceding, performance is emphasized at the expense of all other factors and disciplines under the imposed cost and schedule constraints. Since the focus tends to be on performance, state of the art technology is generally used as a basis for the design effort.* Detailed design "requirements" thus typically evolve as the effort progresses. Since the latter tend to be technology driven, they may not necessarily be consistent with operational requirements. This fuels further compromises. The true operational needs and desires which precipitated the cycle are seldom, if ever, rigorously revisited and verified during design. The net result is generally a combination of the following:

- Product or system overdesign.
- Inordinately high engineering change rate (during development and in production) impacting costs and schedules.
- Failure to meet one or more of the operational expectations/requirements.

Regardless of whether the effort is company or customer funded, the preceding suggest two key *preconditions to successful transformation* of an idea into an end product.

(1) Product design, development and implementation must be anticipated by the strategic planning process. More specifically, this process must lead to the emplacement of various "building blocks" within each sphere of the firm's operations to accommodate the specific needs and requirements of planned pursuits in an effective and efficient manner. Unless such building blocks are emplaced within the various organizations, needed contributions cannot be successfully coordinated and sequenced, patterned and paced across the organization.

---

* Versus proven technology or a combination of the two.

(2) Mission profiles and operational requirements including descriptions of environmental use, maintenance, transportation and storage are of little direct value to the product or system **designer**. They must be distilled into specific (i.e. quantitative) performance requirements inclusive of physical attributes such as size, weight, load bearing capability, dynamic properties, thermal performance characteristics, safety, reliability, etc. to guide the overall design process.[7] While operational requirements provide some information relative to the above, this information is generally incomplete and ostensibly qualitative. Sheer complexity frequently imposes subtle and conflicting requirements in some areas, while distorting and obscuring those in others. Studies are often required to *identify, quantify and address the full range of issues and considerations involved.* A disciplined technical effort is a precondition to a successful design, development and production effort. The tendency to misconstrue and transcribe operational requirements *(or market needs)* into a product or system specification format will doom these efforts from the outset.

13.4   The Source and Impact of Design and Engineering Gaps

Any project, be it a feasibility study or a production effort, proceeds through four general phases including: start up and growth, maturity, decline and termination. It is widely and generally accepted that good planning and orderly execution of the effort will result in the commitment of manpower and expenditure of funds, as a function of time, in a manner that approximates the "bell shaped curve" shown in Figure 13.2(a). Clearly, this is somewhat of an idealized view of project/program management.

Whether dealing with in-house or government projects, the actual funding levels and profiles seldom follow the ideal. The reasons for this are many and

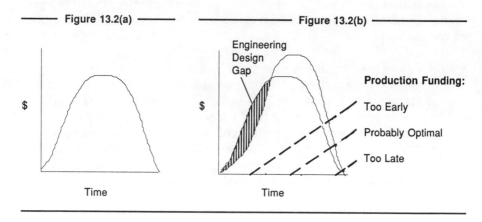

Source: "Solving the Risk Equation in Transitioning from Development to Production," Defense Science Board Task Force on Transitioning from Development to Production. 25 May 1983.

varied and have been addressed throughout this book.* Actual funding pro-files, more often than not, approximate that shown in Figure 13.2(b). The schedule, however, is seldom, if ever, *fully* adjusted to compensate for the phasing of requisite funding. As a result, certain tasks tend to be eliminated or, alternatively, *descoped, deferred or both in line with the available funding and the remaining design/development schedule*. The Defense Science Board has referred to this as the "Design and Engineering Gap"[8]. It results in high risk and cost of development and production depending on the extent of *overlap between the two*. If one commits to production too early, major costs may be incurred in terms of retooling, scrap and rework given the immaturity of design. If one commits too late, the cost of production delays, gaps and restart may be equally significant. Excessive concurrency generally results in high rates of change based on instability in design and also tends to be very costly. The latter, however, may be the optimal middle ground once "the die has been cast".

The following generalized scenario is typical, if not symptomatic, of prob-lems perpetuated by the "Engineering and Design Gap". It is intended as an illustration of the practical progression and interaction of certain aspects of the overall problem and its effects over time.

Phase 1

The need for change is neither apparent nor identifiable. This is largely due to complexity and the fact that transition to production is a continuous process rather than a discrete activity.

Phase 2

As design progresses and engineering change rates increase, the manufac-turing organization's resistance to changes stiffens very rapidly. The growing resistance to engineering changes is understandable as they disrupt produc-tion operations and impact manufacturing/delivery schedules. Design changes are thus frequently suppressed or suspended (except for the most critical) under growing pressure to stabilize the design.

Phase 3

As manufacturing problems begin to overwhelm production costs and schedules, requests for engineering changes spike. Engineering frequently "digs in" for a number of reasons, among them: poor definition and/or articulation of the problem(s), a lack (or inadequacy) of supporting data, etc. A significant number of changes during this phase are "convenience" driven based on inputs from various departments or outside suppliers. Some of the resistance often stems from a tacit concern that high rates of acceptance of requested changes may reflect a shoddy design effort.

---

* As an example, see Section 4.1(a).

Phase 4

Eventually, both engineering and manufacturing concur on the need for certain design changes. At certain stages of the program, however, program management actively begins to resist and suppress changes based on cost, schedule, contractual or other considerations. As an example, management may find certain types of changes very difficult to justify and accept two or three years into production. Invariably, classic questions and issues include: "How did you manage until now?", "Why can't you (or don't you) keep on living with it?", "It will cost more to fix it than live with it".

Phase 5

This phase is typical on government contracts. A point in time is often reached when manufacturing, engineering and project/program management concur on the need for a change. Since the government typically controls the technical data package, changes to the technical data package must be approved by the procuring agency. It is not unusual for the government to disapprove requested changes based on, but not necessarily limited to, logistics considerations. Whereas the change may be clearly desirable, from a reliability or other standpoint, the overall logistics cost impact precludes its implementation. Under such conditions the contractor and the government generally continue to suffer from the legacy of the "Design and Engineering Gap".

As may be seen from the above discussion, the effects of inadequate funding and/or its improper phasing can have far reaching and long lasting effects. Furthermore, it should be noted that the problems discussed in this and preceding sections are not mutually exclusive.

13.5 High Payoff Basics

This section presents a set of general design principles along with suggestions for their implementation as a means of:

(1) Reducing design and technical risks
(2) Improving manufacturability and producibility

These principles and suggestions are generally applicable to the design of virtually any product and its efficient transition to production.

13.5(a) Simplicity

The most important attribute of any design is undoubtedly the degree of its simplicity. Consider what may well be the simplest and functionally most elegant design produced to date: The paper clip. It has no moving parts, it has a very simple shape, does not require tight tolerances, has a very short and simple manufacturing sequence, it does not require assembly or precision adjustment, it is extremely easy to inspect and does not need testing. In addition to the preceding, it is reusable and fulfills its function safely and reliably. In effect and in our judgment a perfect design that ought to be emulated to the maximum extent possible.

Clearly, the functions to be achieved influence the attainable degree of simplicity in design. Given a specific function, two or more *conceptual* approaches can always be evolved to satisfy that function. *All things being equal,* the product with the largest number of design attributes approaching our paper clip ideal will be the least costly to produce, the easiest to maintain and the most reliable in use. *All things, however, are never equal.* On that basis, *Trade off Studies* should be made an integral part of any (conceptual) design effort and thus the implement for the introduction of greater *simplicity* into a product.

Trade off Studies can be an extremely important tool in fine tuning design concepts, simplifying the design, providing for ease of manufacturability, improving product testability and eventually field maintenance. Trade studies that affect *design requirements* should be completed and validated as early as possible and *prior* to the start of full-scale development. Those that relate to *risk reduction* may be conducted up to (and should be completed as of) the point of the critical design review.

13.5(b) Standardization

The benefits of standardizing components and materials tend to be obvious. They stem from either direct or indirect economies of scale associated with the use of "off the shelf" items, frequent elimination of special tooling and test equipment, simplified inventory management and generally faster manufacturing cycles. Standardization of design among similar product lines can yield added benefits and economies of scale in terms of material and component usage, process control, operator training, etc.[9]

These benefits cannot be reaped in the absence of formal *Design Policies and Practices.* Existence and adherence to documented design policies and practices as contained in *controlled engineering manuals and supporting documentation* is essential to:

(1) Implementation of an orderly and disciplined design process *(including formal design reviews)* through a delineation of responsibilities and requirements.
(2) Establishment of a "road map" to the benefits and cost savings attendant to standardization.

These documents must promote and lead to the implementation of design fundamentals, in the form of criteria, standards and practices that are known to yield low-risk, manufacturable, testable and field supportable designs. To do so, engineering manuals must provide a *current and integrated data base,* inclusive of approved parts lists and materials, to help the implementation of the preceding and promote a high degree of standardization. Tailoring policies and manuals to one's product lines leads to the more timely incorporation of current design data and lessons learned from past programs.

13.5(c) Design Tolerance and Safety Margins

The determination of proper tolerances and safety margins is critical to the implementation of low-risk, producible designs. Unfortunately, even seasoned designers frequently do not appear to *fully* appreciate the importance and impact of mechanical and electrical tolerances and safety margins.

There is a tendency to operate on the basis of a premise that: "If some is good, more is better". As an example, unnecessarily tight dimensional tolerances, whether specified out of habit or to "insure" fit, can have a significant impact on costs. In structural design, use of safety margins in excess of those called for by established safety margin criteria, as an "extra safety measure", can add unnecessary weight, volume and/or cost. This may have an adverse impact on other parts of the system. To minimize weight and volume, other components and materials may be subjected to higher operating stress levels to meet performance objectives and requirements.

Tighter tolerances typically result in some combination of the following:[10]

- Extra operations and higher tooling costs.
- Longer operating cycles, more difficult and/or complex inspection and test equipment requirements and procedures.
- Higher scrap and rework rates
- Need for a more skilled and better trained work force.

As a general rule, tolerances should be as "loose" as possible within the constraints imposed by performance specifications. Although the preceding is desirable, it is certainly not a side-effect free antidote for design risk and non-producibility.

Many of the analyses performed by design engineers, albeit thorough, are geared towards *confirming* the product's *compliance with performance specifications*. Little, if any, analysis is performed to *"proof"* a design. Proofing a design involves more *specialized analyses* and hence takes additional time and money. This has encouraged some to view such analyses as generally non-cost effective "options". The real choice faced by management in this regard is to: "Pay for it now or pay for it (a great deal more) later". The latter is being reasserted daily throughout industry. *Specialized Analyses,* including as an example thermal and structural analyses, *are crucial to the validation of the maturity of the design and its proper tolerancing.* Examples of these include:

- *Worse Case Tolerance Analyses:* Effect on product or system performance is evaluated assuming combinations of allowable worse case component (or part) values for the parameter under investigation.

- *Failure Mode Analysis:* Attempts to predict most likely component (or part) failures, collateral damage caused by such failures and effects on system performance. This analysis helps to identify needed design/tolerancing changes.
- *Circuit ("Sneak") Analysis:* Performed to detect unexpected failures modes along with the more obscure cause and effect relationships. It focuses on issues such as latent circuit paths, timing errors, "within spec tolerance build-up" effects, etc.

The lack of such active risk reduction oriented efforts unquestionably causes more schedule, cost and performance problems than any other factor in product development and production. It may well have given birth to the well known adage: "There is never enough time or money to do it right, but always enough to do it over".

13.5(d) Built in Test Capability

Good analysts and design engineers tend to be bright, creative and analytical people. In many respects they are a unique "breed". Their own ability to conceptualize, to visualize and to cope with a considerable amount of ambiguity, often tend to be the very attributes that seemingly keep them from taking into account some of the limitations in manufacturing personnel and processes. It is partly for this reason that products made to work under the watchful eye of engineers – in the "lab" – frequently do not "survive" the high rate production environment of the factory. The opportunities to miscommunicate based on differences in ability, education, training, experience, perceptions and motivations abound, *especially* in such areas as troubleshooting and fault isolation. The frequent inability to articulate *or duplicate intermittent problems* by manufacturing or field personnel, tends to aggravate the preceding and delay implementation of required solutions. This leads to excessive downtime, unnecessary rework and replacement, higher attrition and scrap rates, part shortages, production backlogs and longer cycle times. Parenthetically, all of these are symptoms of an immature design resulting form the violation of one or more of the previously discussed design precepts.

Built-in-testing capability should be a priority from the standpoint of both factory test and production needs and ease of field maintenance. It should be initiated as part of design trade off studies as it affects and influences product cost, risk and produceability through:

(1) Product weight, volume, power consumption and other requirements.
(2) Specification of extent of functional coverage, degree of modularization, visual and physical accessibility.
(3) Definition of inspection and testing requirements; manual and automatic test equipment needs and other related considerations.

(4) Optimization of built-in test allocations between hardware, software and firmware.

13.5(e) Manufacturing Involvement

Early manufacturing involvement in design and development can have a very positive effect on the transition to and subsequent production of a product or system. The concept has undeniable merit and should certainly be encouraged and pursued. As in everything else, there are certain pre-conditions that should temper enthusiasm and expectations.

First, manufacturing must be in a position to provide, *on an extended basis, personnel with extensive practical experience* in manufacturing techniques and technology. Frequently such people are at a premium and cannot be *dedicated* as needed to any one specific program. The inability to commit such people to an effort on a full time basis, as may be required, tends to impact this general activity from the very outset. The suggested answer to this problem invariably tends to be "better management of available resources within the matrix framework". Realistically such vague ideals are seldom successfully achieved. The availability of the above described personnel should be the subject of management's active strategic evaluation and availability planning.

Second, early manufacturing involvement is fruitless unless preceded and accompanied by a disciplined analytical and design engineering effort. Unless designs are "proofed" as discussed in section 13.5(c), the end product will generally reflect a marginally functional but more manufacturable – rather than produceable – design. A "lack of discipline" in a given functional area cannot be offset by efforts of any other. This is part and parcel of the concept of Total Quality Management.

Third, the effort cannot be wished into being, it must be funded. Budgetary constraints and competitive pressures very often lead to either a lack of funding or inadequate funding of this effort. The costs involved can be substantial and the amount of time that needs to be allocated can be significant. This stems from the *iterative* nature of the effort involved. Mere manipulation of budgets and schedules to accommodate this activity, within existing constraints, so as to comply with company policies and/or practices dilutes other functional areas and, at best, leads to marginal results.

Fourth, in organizations in which design, test and production functions tend to be highly fragmented, compartmentalized and matricized, the lack of clear cut responsibility and effective leadership frequently results in lengthy and sub-optimal problem solving and exacerbates any pre-existing problems of the type discussed. This is further aggravated in the absence of clearly quantifiable design-to-cost objectives. Experience in the computer and virtually all other segments of the electronics industry suggests that shortest design-to-market cycle times are achieved when dedicated project teams are formed, to "shepherd" the product or system into being, rather than through assignment or allocations of tasks by functional responsibility.[11]

In general, engineering and manufacturing interactions should address and resolve a number of important issues relating, but not necessarily limited, to the following examples.[12]

Design for Expected Level of Production:

Production methods selected should reflect the most economical choice for the anticipated level of production. As an example, a die casting should be selected over a sand-mold aluminum casting for a mass produced part. Significant cost savings in terms of labor and materials may hinge on a decision that involves such alternatives.

Eliminate Secondary Processing:

Secondary operations such as deburring, inspection, plating, heat treating and associated material handling can be every bit as expensive, if not more so, than the primary manufacturing operation. In reviewing designs, the cost of both primary and secondary operations must be considered. The objective, as noted in Section 13.5(a), should be to simplify the design as much as possible in order to shorten the manufacturing sequence and thus minimize costs.

Use Most Processible Materials/Specials Process Characteristics:

The part's functional characteristics may allow the use of alternative materials. In such cases the one with the most processible characteristics (e.g. feed, cutting speeds, etc.) should clearly be selected for production. Some manufacturing processes have special characteristics that can lead to the elimination of several operations. Injection molding, for instance, allows one to incorporate color and surface texture to plastic parts as extracted from the mold. Other processes may lead to the elimination of the need for separate and frequently expensive components.

Undue Influences

Engineering and manufacturing decisions and choices should not be unduly influenced by the current approach or available technical means of production. Under competitive pressures, older and more labor intensive design approaches are often implemented based on commonality or similarity – and thus perceived economies of scale – with products already in production. Designs may thus fail to reflect maximum available or possible use of "in-house" automation in manufacturing and testing. Established habits, patterns and practices are difficult to break especially under constraints of cost and schedule and in the absence of dissuading feedback. Conversely, when more efficient means of production are either inaccessible or unavailable "in-house", there may be a tendency to "steer" the design in a direction consistent with that which is available and/or under-utilized. Many "make or buy" decisions are often very strongly influenced by such considerations. It is generally

argued that under-utilization of facilities and equipment, along with the attendant loss in the direct labor base, results in higher overhead rates and tends to
off-set savings realizable on the outside. Furthermore, that higher overhead
rates will not only impact the product under development but any concurrent
production as well. The argument is valid but *misguided*. The availability and
accessibility to effective and efficient means of production must be an integral
part of the strategic planning process tied to product research and development (See chapter 11).

The manufacturing organization's key contribution in this general area is
the refinement of the design in line with the *most efficient and cost effective technical means of its implementation.*

13.6   Evolving a Product Oriented Culture

We have alluded to a need for a greater degree of communication and
interaction between the engineering and manufacturing organizations. Generally speaking, there tends to be a sufficient amount of mismatch between
engineering and manufacturing personnel in terms of education, training, experience, interests and motivations to assure the perpetuation of a disparity
between expected, planned and achieved results. Much of this is being driven
by complexity and, consequently, a growing emphasis by most major engineering schools on a more analytical approach to engineering. Some universities have attempted to meet engineering shortages and the "applied" needs of
industry by offering, what some consider to be, "para professional" programs
leading to degrees in *engineering technology* (e.g. manufacturing or industrial
technology degrees with options in electronics, materials, quality, etc.). It has
been suggested that graduates of such programs compare to engineers on the
same basis as para-legals compare to attorneys or paramedics to doctors. On
that basis the gap between engineering and manufacturing is unlikely to ever
close as by-products of advancing technology become more and more complex.

Most managers will tend to agree that there needs to be a greater degree
of mutual awareness and concern among personnel within these organizations as to the nature, impacts and consequences of their independently held
views, approaches to problems and their solution. New products will continue to be conceived, designed and developed by those that by education,
skill, inclination and experience gravitate towards the more analytical applications of science and technology. Their exposure to manufacturing, if any, will
generally continue to be limited and their view of it is likely to remain somewhat distorted.

Manufacturing in general, and the high volume production environment
in particular, must be observed and experienced first hand. If an engineer is to
become an effective designer, he must experience and be immersed in some of
the grief and misery that tends to be brought on by poor design practices,
functional incompatibilities and fault isolation problems under the constant
pressure of manufacturing and contractual delivery schedules. Once exposed

to the preceding, the "lessons" will have been learned and long remembered.

In the military, those that aspire to and attain high ranks typically seek to have their "tickets punched" by assuming various field as well as staff assignments and functions over the course of their career. Similarly, those that aspire to – or are pre-selected for – management positions in the *design engineering or program management* communities should be subjected to a "factory internship" fairly early in their careers as a *precondition to advancement up the management ladder*. Ideally, this internship should be served under the direct supervision of a senior manager in manufacturing, in a meaningful and challenging position.

Experience suggests that benefits of such programs are maximized when:

(1) The internship program is *formulated and presented* as an essential stepping stone to future growth and advancement within the company. Frequently, a factory "liaison" or "support" assignment carries with it a stigma within the engineering community which is unfortunate and needs to be overcome as it is certainly in the best interests of the company.

(2) Selected personnel have nominal experience in design and/or are familiar with the design that is to be or is being produced. This effectively rules out recent graduates or certain others with little experience or actual involvement in analysis and design functions. Ideally, the individual should be in a position to observe, formulate and communicate design problems in a meaningful, forceful and credible manner *to peers* in design engineering organizations.

(3) The factory internship program is followed by an assignment to a function or a program where observations and lessons learned can be transmitted and incorporated in new or follow-on business. Such programs typically promote:

   (1) Faster convergence on sources of persisting functional difficulties and a more rapid resolution of residual, often very subtle, production "throughput" limiters.
   (2) Cross pollination of engineering and manufacturing talent on a daily basis. This leads to a greater degree of technical interchange along with a higher degree of consciousness and *applied understanding* in engineering with respect to producibility. This can be a very effective team building program.
   (3) Development of individuals with major impact on design and development of new business. It broadens technical talent and nurtures the next generation of design engineering and program management with first hand experience in production.

The above tend to be an integral part of our need to manage the "industrial process".

13.7 CAD/CAM

In our chapter on productivity and in the section dealing with the potential of automation, we noted the CAD/CAM had to be addressed as part of the corporated strategic plan. We supported the view that the same kind of rules that apply to the purchase of equipment and facilities *do not apply* to CAD/CAM.

CAD/CAM must be an integral part of the corporate strategy to modernize its operations and introduce *technical discipline* throughout the plant. Haphazard and piecemeal acquisition, development and use of CAD, CAE and CAM, promotes hardware and software incompatibilities along with difficult and costly transitions to production. Under such conditions CAD reduces to a powerful but time consuming drafting tool. On that basis use of CAD becomes too costly in general use and thus, at best, either an optional or a program unique requirement. Full benefits of CAD/CAM are thus never realized.

Based on discussions of section 13.5(b) and 13.5(c), a good CAD system will generally have the following important – basic – characteristics:

(1) It should support a number of *special analyses* previously described and provide simulation capability using finite or solid modelling techniques.
(2) It should contain a controlled design data base consisting of preferred mechanical and electronic parts along with materials information delineating performance, physical characteristics and tolerances.
(3) It should provide design criteria, processes, standards and rules that are consistent with documented company policies and practices.
(4) It should be compatible with other CAD/CAM hardware and software and must allow for the exchange of information with the CAM function.
(5) It should allow for multiple access and use.

Benefits compound when the CAD system can be properly interfaced with the CAM function. Use of computers in fabrication, assembly, test and supporting activities markedly improves material acquisition, production control, inventory management and quality. Their use reduces scrap and rework, work-in-process, floor space utilization and generally leads to increased productivity along with faster material-to-market conversion times (see Figure 13.1). Added benefits include real time monitoring and statusing in such areas as shop floor and test data collection, configuration management, cost accounting, etc. Typical estimates suggest that automated manufacturing and control functions can reduce transition times up to 50 percent. The above noted advantages, however, tend to be purely theoretical to the extent that CAD/CAM capabilities are:

(1) Developed on a modular and accumulating basis *without* the benefit of a well defined, integrated and executed modernization plan.
(2) Lack of an intensive and comprehensive *training and rehabilitation program* for those employees whose jobs are both affected and impacted by this level of automation.

13.8   Other Important Considerations

Four areas are of special importance in assuring a smooth and rapid transition from design and development to successful production. Their importance stems from a combination of general influence and potential cost impacts. They include:

- Design-To-Cost
- Configuration Management/Control
- Software Development, Verification and Validation
- Transition Planning

13.8(a)   Design-To-Cost

Successful implementation and execution of any effort requires the *identification and quantification* of objectives, goals and targets. As noted elsewhere in this text, a successful product must embody the prospects of *economic production and profitable distribution*. Clearly, unless such prospects are present or *attainable* there is no justification, from the firm's viewpoint, for proceeding with design and development.

Given the above, *marketing* involvement in the conceptual definition and early design stages is crucial to the success of the undertaking. The marketing organization must be in a position to provide a host of "tactical" inputs relative to customer needs, preferences and biases, performance requirements, budgets or sensitivity to costs, time lines, market potential, competitive approaches and their advantages along with answers to a number of other issues. If the marketing organization is relegated (or allowed) to function primarily as an aggregation of "order takers", "public relations specialists" or "political and social pundits", the organization *is not doing its job* and the company is suffering.

Marketing inputs of the type noted must be reviewed and evaluated for impact on design requirements and cost considerations. The by-product of such a review should yield, at least in part, a design cost "bogey" (i.e. target). All considered, such "bogeys" are very often inconsistent with preferred or contemplated design approaches. As a result, a creative reconciliation process must be undertaken in the form of a "design-to-cost" effort. A number of approaches can be taken towards that end and *in conjunction with the high pay-off basics* previously discussed. Once a top level "bogey" has been established, a typical approach may consist of the following:

- Allocation (or "flowdown") of target cost to lowest levels of assembly *as a design parameter.*
- Development of top level cost tracking (see discussion on WBS) approach as part of:
    Parametric – top down – modeling (see section 4.3(b))
    Manufacturing cost – bottom up – modeling
  This is essential to the identification, evaluation and iterating of costs based on discrepancies between "should costs" and "estimated costs".
- Risk assessment and management (see section 6.3(c)) including various cost *trade-offs* between technologies and processes available for each activity or function.
- Yield (statistical process control) studies
- Make/Buy decisions including source review, assessment and selection.
- Various cost containment studies and reviews.

As may be seen from the above discussion, the design-to-cost effort is an integral, concurrent and iterative part of the design activity. To be effective, it must be implemented as part of the conceptual design effort – with *support from manufacturing and key suppliers* – and, ideally, completed as of the time that a design is ready for a formal preliminary design review.

13.8(b) Configuration Management/Control

At some point in time, all creative design must stop and a design baseline or "configuration" must be established and documented. This should typically happen by the critical design review. Baseline design provides the basis for a host of production related functions, maintenance and logistics support activities. Once the baseline has been established, it is imperative that requisite changes to the baseline be carefully documented, implemented and controlled (over the life cycle of the product) to preclude adverse impacts on production, product operation, field modifications/retrofit, spares and maintenance. Clearly the importance of this activity cannot be over emphasized. The potential for major cost and schedule impacts, based on inadequate control, is real and over present. Due to its criticality, this function should always be under the *effective* control of project/program management – rather than either engineering and manufacturing.

During transitional stages to production, there is often a tendency to succumb to temptations of expediency by using "redlined" drawings*, issuing pre-

---

* So called because corrections are frequently marked in red and initialed or signed of by the cognizant engineer.

released information or providing advanced release information for a variety of reasons involving "catch-up", "work-around" or "schedule preservation". These generally affect material procurement, fabrication, assembly, test, etc. One should be especially leery of uncoordinated, seemingly benign, "improvement" or "convenience" changes regardless of whether instigated by quality, manufacturing, engineering or suppliers. As a general rule, the above practices should *never* be *allowed* as they invariably break down discipline and lead to a combination of the following:

- As built configuration does not match design configuration.
- Changes generally breed the need for other, frequently very subtle, changes that may go undetected and undocumented for a long time.
- Excessive test, rework and retrofit.
- Eventual spares identification and field maintenance problems.

There is no better antidote for such problems than discipline, an effective change review/control board and status accounting system. The following is a summary list of recommendations that will generally help suppress previously described problems in this area.

- Develop an *operating* configuration management *plan* and tailor the activity to the specific needs and requirements of the program.
- Insure that an effective configuration management system is in place and that the function is staffed by technically competent – rather than strictly administrative – personnel as of the time the design is baselined.
- Promote early coordination of schedule design releases between engineering, manufacturing and procurement and synchronize critical release activity to manufacturing cycle requirements.
- Require concurrent and thorough review of all changes by all functional areas (or disciplines) by the change control board in line with manufacturing cycle priorities.*
- Maintain activity going over the life cycle of the project/program.

13.8(c) Software Design, Verification and Validation

The growing importance of software is underscored by some rather interesting and staggering statistics. It has been estimated, that over the past 25-30 years some 150 *billion* lines of code have been written world wide at a cost – exclusive of documentation, manuals and training – of about 8 *trillion* dollars**.

---

* Change Control Boards should typically be made up of qualified personnel from Engineering, Manufacturing, Quality, Production Control, Procurement, Logistics Support, Quality and Configuration Management. It should be Chaired by the Project/Program Manager.

** Source: Quality Directorate, Electro-Optical Data Systems Group, Hughes Aircraft Company

Reportedly, the major portion of software budgets are currently being spent on maintaining, correcting and modifying developed codes. Approximately 80 percent of the military systems currently under development are very heavily dependent on software. In some cases software development can amount to a gargantuan effort. As an example, the IEEE Computer* has estimated that the Space Defense Initiative (SDI) would eventually require between 30 to 40 *million* lines of code.

Some industry literature suggests that current software error rates run at approximately 5 to 6 percent and that the rate could be reduced to less than about 0.5 percent. U.S. Air Force studies indicate that 85 percent of the total number of software errors present are introduced during analysis and design phases. The balance of the errors is introduced either during coding and test or operations and maintenance. Typically, only 28 percent of the total errors are discovered during analysis and design phases. The remaining 72 percent linger on through coding and test and the operations and maintenance phases. Approximately one in four of the total number of errors is detected in the latter stages.[13]

Various industry estimates suggest that the cost to fix errors run in the range of 10-100 times the cost of fixing them at the time of introduction. Software can thus have major cost and schedule impact on transition to and production of a product.

Based on the above and in line with growing concerns in this area, a Software Engineering Institute (SEI) has been established at Carnegie Mellon University to develop guidelines and procedures for the objective and consistent assessment of the ability of DoD contracts to develop software in accordance with modern software engineering methods.[14] The latter involve three main areas:

- Resources and Organizational Management
- Software Engineering and Management
- Tools and Technology

Guidelines developed by Carnegie Mellon University with assistance from the MITRE Corporation along with the latest revisions of DoD-STD-2167, DoD-STD-2168 and DoD-STD-1679 – covering software development, quality and testing – are valuable references for those involved in this field. A more thorough review of this important subject is clearly beyond the scope of this text. However, a few general observations and guidelines may be appropriate considering the importance of this subject.

Nowhere does *discipline* tend to be more critical than in the design, testing and validation of software. In general, once a product specification has been developed, the overall design is subdivided into modules for detail design by specific individuals. Therein lies the difficulty and the challenge since there is:

---

* IEEE Computer January 1989

(1) No cost effective procedure of *eliminating* errors.
(2) No technique to *fully* test software as it transitions from an aggregation of modules to an integrated hardware/software system.
(3) No accurate means of *measuring failure rates* of software once it has been integrated with hardware.

Clearly under these conditions a disciplined approach to design, development and validation becomes critical. In line with the preceding, the following general rules tend to be of considerable help.

- Company standards, practices, procedures and conventions regulating detail design and coding practices must be developed, emplaced and followed.
- Once a design baseline is established, a clear cut functional description must be generated including a description of the manner in which the system is *structured to perform* its function.
- Given the preceding, design work and coding should be allocated into modules and initiated based on:
  (a) A *painstaking definition of interface requirements.*
  (b) Definition and/or development of an *outline* for a users manual and *test plans* that, in part, will take into consideration and assure "user (tester ?) friendliness".
- A "data" collection and documentation system must be emplaced along with frequently scheduled reviews to verify the compliance of design and coding efforts with specifications.
- Integration of modules should never be attempted prior to the testing and validation of each module.

Following these procedures will not eliminate problems but should reduce their number and speed up the isolation and resolution of those remaining.

13.8(d) Transition Planning

As stated at the outset of this chapter, the process of conversion of an idea into a product involves a great number of interdependent and interactive considerations and activities. It is a *process* rather than a series of discrete functions.

In attempting to understand this complex process, we tend to break it down into constituent elements. We then proceed to erect conceptual fences to help us simplify and assimilate those elements of the process that are consistent with our backgrounds, general interests and experience. We thus condition ourselves into thinking of the process in terms of distinct and separate building blocks such as R&D, Engineering and Test, Manufacturing and Logistics Support. We tend to approach activities within each of these functions much in the same way, on a modular and accumulating basis as shown in

Figure 13.3a. In so doing we lose perspective of the process and interactions stemming from a combination of overlaps and overlays shown in Figure 13.3b. As an example, most people think of a transition plan in terms of a *manufacturing plan* that may typically include:

- Estimates of manufacturing resource requirements
- Timelines and schedules
- Make/Buy decisions
- Facilities planning/implementation requirements

In effect, the approach to along with all of the requirements typically associated with the *initiation and replication* of a released design. That is *not* what is meant by a transition plan. It is, however, one of several inputs or elements of such a plan. A transition plan to full production should be thought of in much broader terms than those described above. It should be an *overall* planning document that addresses and integrates interdependent and interactive issues that are an integral part of functional overlaps shown in Figure 13.3b. Consider the following by way of amplification.

In our discussion of Design-To-Cost, we indicated that marketing inputs can and should have a significant impact on the general attributes and performances characteristic of a design. Typically such inputs lead to trade off studies and design iterations that impact many areas of manufacturing. It is, therefore, necessary to involve manufacturing early on in such efforts to properly influence the design process. The same is true of certain other functions; the prime example being Logistics Support. This suggests a need for a *comprehensive management plan that will describe, integrate and coordinate all of the activities, functions and separate plans* culminating in the final hand-off of the design for full production. Such a plan should be generated and available *prior to* the start of design and should be regularly updated until final hand-off to full production. It is this type of planning and its implementation that typically results in short development times and very profitable production runs.

13.9   Strategy That Actually Pays-Off

Much has been written about successful transitions to production. The following observations reflect current literature on the subject, views of consultants in the field along with some of our own observations and experiences. No single recommendation can assure success; however taken as a package (and a way of life) they promote rapid and successful conversion of ideas into profit. Proven initiatives include:

- Taking a "long look" at market and technology. Specifically, anticipation of *market, technology and company needs*. This is essential to developing an ability to adapt to an environment characterized by growing complexity, high rates of change, risk and cost as well

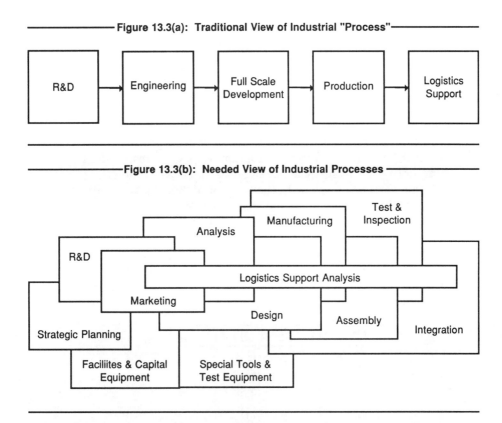

Figure 13.3(a): Traditional View of Industrial "Process"

R&D → Engineering → Full Scale Development → Production → Logistics Support

Figure 13.3(b): Needed View of Industrial Processes

Test & Inspection
Manufacturing
Analysis
R&D
Logistics Support Analysis
Marketing
Design
Assembly
Integration
Strategic Planning
Faciliites & Capital Equipment
Special Tools & Test Equipment

as a scarcity of resources. The importance of this has been addressed in this and other chapters of the book. (See sections 13.3 and 11.4).

- Look for and *insist on excellence* from the very outset and along the way. Start with thorough and comprehensive *planning* and do not succumb to temptations of expediency (See section 5.10). A "total quality" effort starts with quality planning. As part of this process:

  - Use a *balanced team* approach from the outset.
  - Focus team on *cycle times at each step and at every level of the organization*. In many cases such efforts have produced improvements in the range of 25 to 50 percent with comparatively little effort.
  - Identify and *reduce or eliminate barriers and obstacles* including frequently well intentioned but shortsighted or misguided management "policies" and "practices". *Do not constrain but rather empower people as much as possible.*

- Address, readdress and *manage interfaces* on a continuing basis. This is typically an *area of very high payoffs.*

- *Invest* heavily in appropriate areas and key functions. *Do not allow short term budgetary or cost considerations to interfere with longer range profit prospects.* Consider, as an example, parallel pursuit of alternative technologies in line with the established plan and pre-established "start" and "abandon" trigger points. Never "short change" test and integration.

- Recognize the *inclusion* in the decision making process must *never* result in *dilution* of Project/Program Manager's responsibility or authority. Growing evidence suggests that organizations that have become carried away with the concept of "participative management" have done so to the detriment of the Project/Program Manager's authority and responsibility and, in the process, have suffered greatly. **Do not confuse participative management with a democratic process.** It is for this reason that selection of Project/Program Management is very important. The individual, as frequently described, must be a "T" person. That is, the individual must have:

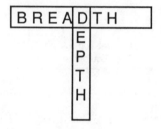

- *Innovate* as in dealing with suppliers. Some companies (such as GM, Ford, Boeing) have reduced the number of suppliers and have strengthened their ties with those remaining through Electronic Data Interchanges. This reduces administrative costs and lead times.

- Insure that people have *access to and use of the right tools at the right time for as long as required* to do a quality job. We are reminded of an example illustrative of the general problem. A few years ago as PCs were being introduced into the work place, managers at Dinko, Inc. were the first to receive their own personal units. For the most part, PCs sat in the managers' offices as underutilized status symbols. A relatively small percentage had gone through any training even fewer had a sustained need for use of the PC. The "worker bees" at the time were being forced to share a limited number of units (within a bull pen) that could never quite accommodate the overall demand for access. Bottom line: Schedule delays, poor quality.

- Consider the implementation of a *low rate initial (or pilot) production* (LRIP) activity to keep the main production facilities from getting tied up and disrupted by initial (i.e. residual design) problems. Some companies have used this approach very successfully on the first 25-150 units produced.

- Look at, consider and *WORK THE OVERALL PROCESS* rather than those areas that appear or are likely to be troublesome based on current assessment.

Success stories typically reflect all of the above as common denominators and have generally resulted in idea-to-end-product conversion time reductions from 20 to as much as 50 percent. In line with the preceding, recall the old adage: **"Time is Money."**

————Questions & Topics For Discussion ————

1. Discuss how the transition plan differs from the engineering, manufacturing or other plans?

2. Project Management is an integral part of the "industrial process". Define and discuss the concept of "industrial process" and the role of the Project Manager in this process.

3. Discuss when and how a transition plan should be pulled together. Who should be the focal point for this effort and how early should it be started?

4. Why is it that transition to production cannot be treated as a discrete point in time?

5. You have been assigned the task of developing a transition to production plan for your company for its Turbo Widget. Develop an outline for such a plan and review it for completeness/content with associates.

6. What elements of the transition plan are part of the overall strategic planning process. Discuss what elements of this plan fall in the "long range", "medium range" and "short term" spheres? Where does the majority of key considerations fall?

7. Pick one or a combination of marketing, engineering, manufacturing or management functions. Develop and discuss a list of "rationalizations" or practices that may tend to undermine rapid transition to production within each of these areas.

8. In the "overall scheme of things" where does the design-to-cost effort fit

in? Could it be performed earlier? Discuss the pros and the cons.

9. Prepare a project plan/schedule reflecting the full scale engineering development of a turbo widget (some hypothetical electro-mechanical device). Show how/where you would incorporate all of the various "design proofing" analyses/tests to (i) minimize engineering changes and (ii) assure a high quality build-to-print effort.

—————————————— References ——————————————

1. "Solving The Risk Equation in Transitioning from Development to Production", *Defense Science Board Task Force on Transitioning from Development to Production*, (May 25, 1983), pp. 4-4 (emphasis ours).
2. Tom Woodward, "How to win in the marketplace with competitive engineering", *Electronic Business* (January 9, 1989), p. 40 (emphasis ours).
3. Skip Jones, "Technical Managers Blamed for Communication Gap, Technological Decline", *Automation* (June 1989), p. 78: Note: Skip Jones is CEO, Data Acquisition Systems, Inc., Boston, Mass.
4. Ibid.
5. See Ref (1).
6. E.G. Krubasic and L. Stein, "Reducing time-to-market boosts the bottom line", *Electronic Business* (May 1, 1989), p. 57.
7. Department of the Navy, "Best Practices: How to Avoid Surprises in the World's Most Complicated Technical Process", *NAVSO P-6071* (March 1986).
8. "Solving The Risk Equation in Transitioning from Development to Production", *Defense Science Board Task Force on Transitioning from Development to Production* (May 25, 1983), pp. 16-17.
9. J. G. Bralla, "Handbook of Product Design for Manufacturing", (McGraw-Hill, New York, 1986), p. 15.
10. Ibid.
11. Dwight B. Davis, "Beating the Clock", *Electronic Business* (May 29, 1989), p. 29.
12. J.G. Brailia, p. 1-18.
13. AFSCP 800-14.
14. See: "A Method for Assessing the Software Capability of Contractors", *Technical Report CMU/SEI-87-TR-23; ESD/TR-87-186,* Carnegie Mellon University (September 1987); Prepared for: SEI Joint Program Office, ESD/XRS, Hanscom AFB, MA 01731.

——————————————— Chapter 14 ———————————————

Future Trends in Project Management

14.1 The Changing Environment
14.2 Project Teams and New Ventures
14.3 Impact of Computer and Automation
      (a) Near-Term Effects
      (b) Long-Range Effects
      (c) Research and Development Projects
14.4 The Project Manager: A Target for Product Liability

14.1 The Changing Environment

Projects will proliferate because of the continuing need for organizations to respond rapidly to a constantly changing technological, socio-economic environment and marketing conditions. Increasing costs, scarcity of resources, advancing technology, and the multidisciplinary nature of most new problems will continue to underscore this need. The pressures of competition (national and international) fueled by widespread computerization, robotics, computer-aided design (CAD) and manufacturing (CAM) have created a climate of "innovation or evaporation." Product liability and environmental changes will further exacerbate the problems of new product and process development and make the requirements for a multidisciplinary project approach even more critical. The continued and time-proven use of project management as a principal way of doing business in engineering, construction, and aerospace will continue unabated.

14.2 Project Teams and New Ventures

The use of task forces or project teams and project centers in major companies can be expected to proliferate. Peters and Waterman report, for example, that General Motors took 1,200 key people from the historically autonomous GM division and put them in a project center.[1] The principal task of the center was to start the downsizing of GM automobiles. The job was accomplished in four years, the implementation was passed back to the division, and the center was dissolved. Other organizations not usually thought of as project oriented, such as Security Pacific National Bank and McDonald's, are using task forces or projects with members taken from various segments of the company to solve special problems or set up new operational procedures. These ad hoc groups possess all the characteristics of a project; that is, they have limited life span, a predetermined budget, fixed goals and objectives, and report to a level consistent with the importance of the problem being attacked. Personnel return to their previous positions when the project is completed or become part of a new operation or segment of the company.

The use of special project teams that can be set up to react rapidly to the changing market, technical, social, and political environment will be a must for progressive and viable companies. Their use will be an important activity in all types of companies, including service as well as manufacturing and process industries. Financial institutions and insurance and advertising companies are already using projects to evaluate and incorporate new technology into their operations. Project teams of the future will have a high degree of interdisciplinary character, including the soft as well as the hard sciences, so that they can relate to all the facets of problems that must be solved when developing a new product or process. The team approach can allow for the rapid transition from design to experimental models, testing, and final production, minimizing the time and cost of introducing new products.[2]

Many companies will set up a project center or a project office that will be in charge of the administrative details involved in the execution of projects. The director of the project office will report at a relatively high level and will have at his disposal a cadre of project managers that can lead new product developments.

In some cases, companies will deliberately separate out small segments of the company to investigate and develop a new promising product area. These ventures will be in the nature of projects and will be set up as independent entities either singly by the company or jointly with one or more other companies. This type of joint venture has already been carried out in the United States in the form of research consortiums in which a number of companies decide to collaborate on a long-term risky research venture that would be too expensive for any one company. Consortiums have been reported with as many as 24 members.[3] Because of the high failure rate of many high-technology projects, this method of distributing cost minimizes the risk taken by individual member firms. To encourage this type of entrepreneurship, the federal government has offered a number of incentives including tax credits, faster depreciation of laboratory equipment, and patent law changes.* Companies can set up research and development limited partnerships (RDLPs), which can offer the limited partners potential licensing royalties and impressive tax savings. On the negative side, the limited partners can lose their entire investment if the project fails.[4] Individual entrepreneurs with venture capital can also band together to form RDLPs to realize potential profits and more certain tax savings. These small development groups operate as projects to test and market new, promising concepts. This also have been occurring to a limited extent and is expected to be even more prevalent in the future. The overall objective of this type of organization, as in the case of the company consortiums, is to respond to the Japanese and European challenge to American leadership in technology – a challenge that can be expected to continue unabated.

---

* See Section 9.4, especially the discussion of the project impact of 1981 ERTA on R&D.

Figure 14.1: Historical Change in the Use of Computers

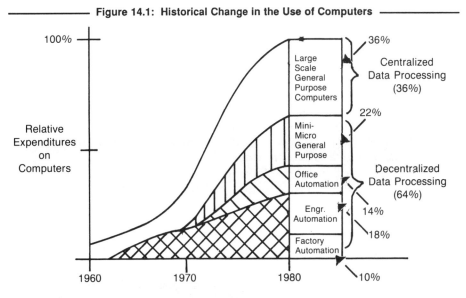

Source: Nolan, Norton & Co., *Stage by Stage*, Vol. 2, No. 1 (1982), p. 3. Used with permission.

14.3   Impact of the Computer and Automation

Since 1960 there has been a progressive and dramatic structural shift in the use of computers (Figure 14.1). This shift has been prompted by both the increasing complexity of the business environment and the rapid advances and innovations in computer technology. Further advances in minicomputers and microcomputer systems will most likely bring profound changes in management philosophy, organizational structures, and approaches to the solution of problems as well as their modes of execution. As Allen Puckett, former chairman of the board and CEO of Hughes Aircraft company has observed:

> Rather than a role as a tool, the digital data-processing system is becoming the backbone or framework around which we will plan, organize, and operate in most of our business and industrial functions. The organization of the data-processing system and in particular of its software – the hierarchy in the system of information handling – will determine the organization of our people and the way they work together.[5]

With the overall trend toward distributed and dedicated processing with an increasing degree of localized computing ability, a number of factors will significantly affect the future role of the project manager. For the most part, the trend is positive, leading to the development and use of fully integrated project management systems through linking of computer-integrated design and manufacturing with cost/schedule/WBS data management systems and incorporating such features as prompting and interactive graphics. Other key features of such systems will be as follows:[6,7]

- Widespread use of simulation and modeling techniques including complex man-in-the-loop dynamic systems.
- Greater time and cost effectiveness, stemming not only from automation per se but also from a combination of error-inhibiting design, drafting, and manufacturing software and prompting software designed to flag more effective alternatives
- Greater flexibility to implementation time and cost and in scheduling facilities and equipment for changeover to other products
- More rapid and effective transmission of lessons learned from one project to another through the updating/reprogramming of affected data bases
- Real or near-real time statusing of the project

Although these developments will clearly provide the project manager with powerful tools, they may not necessarily make his job easier since they have certain liabilities. In the following discussion, some key issues are addressed that may have a significant impact upon the role, function and effectiveness of the project manager both in the near-term and the long-range.

(a) Near-Term Effects

In the near future a trend toward greater physical separation and isolation of project team members can be expected as more and more employers are pressured into allowing the home use of either company or employee-furnished computers. This trend is a result of a number of factors including extended use of flex-time, space and parking limitations, traffic congestion, energy conservation measures, and a host of overhead, employee recruitment, compensation, and retention considerations.* It has been estimated, for instance, that if just 12 to 14% of the work force were to "telecommute," the United States would save 75 million barrels of gasoline a year, ending the need for all gasoline imports.[8] The more immediate impetus for this trend, however, may be the growing need of the employee for a greater sense of independence, freedom, and desire for detachment from the day-to-day corporate life-style (see Section 9.6).

Such a trend, however, raises a wide range of sensitive legal, ethical, security, and productivity issues that require in-depth consideration. Despite po-

---

* Flex-time or flexible working schedule allows the employee to arrange his work hours so that he has some free daytime hours to carry out his personal obligations (family, social, and other) and yet perform the work expected of him by the organization. It may become commonplace for the professional to work at home using a home computer or terminal linked to a central computer at the main company facility. Direct communication with his peers and superiors would be by phone or possibly by videophone.

tential problems, it is anticipated that this trend will accelerate. Several major corporations including Control Data, Chase Manhattan Bank, Aetna Life and Casualty, New York Telephone, and Ford Motor Company already have employees who telecommute.[9] This development could have at least two important effects: First, innovation may suffer. As Thomas J. Allen of MIT suggests, staff productivity is directly proportional to the ease of direct communication.[10] His research findings indicate that engineers get more than 80% of their ideas through direct interaction with peers, that they are not inclined to walk more than 100 feet to share ideas with colleagues, and that they greatly dislike using the telephone. Engineers are not unique in this regard; other professionals tend to be similarly disposed. As a result, increased physical isolation of team members may have an adverse effect on project management's ability to stimulate, coordinate, and control the execution as well as the integration process. Second, it is anticipated that with telecommunication, overall technical integration may become much more demanding of the project manager as he undertakes to screen, interpret, cross-correlate, direct, and coordinate the reiteration and integration of the accumulating inflow of inputs and work products.

This trend must be considered against the backdrop of the current information explosion. Clearly, a great deal of it has been the result of the increasing complexity of our technological and business environments and hence the need to evaluate a growing number of issues. An increasing supply of computer-based information and data promotes a spiraling demand for such information and data even when the supply originates in a centralized information processing and management system. This can be attributed, at least in part, to a perceptual or cognitive overload stemming from the large number of variables that typically influence today's technical problems and business decisions and that often do not lend themselves to easy modeling. This overload makes it difficult if not impossible to assimilate all of the possible outcomes given the large number of variables often involved. The growing need for information is thus driven not only by the number of variables but also by the number of distinct outcomes based upon a permutation of frequently complex dependent and independent variables.

The current proliferation of self-prompting systems requiring little if any operator sophistication and further enhanced by expanding applications portfolios and user awareness has promoted the ability of an unprecedented number of individuals across and up and down the organization to manipulate data and disseminate information. Outputs invariably become inputs subject to further interpretation, manipulation, distortion, dissemination, and storage. This raises the issue of controlling such information handling in the absence of direct coordination and supervision. The role of the project manager may in time include that of a system technical specialist with a greater degree of personal influence and responsibility over the end product. His functions may become much more specialized and challenging and his role more crucial to the success of the enterprise.

(b) Long-Range Effects

In the long run, the anticipated growth of integrated, self-monitoring, automated systems, and the growing portfolio of user-friendly software, along with telecommuting will not only have structural and operational impact upon the organization but an impact on management philosophy as well. There is no question that increased computer use and automation will take over a large number of traditional functions. Nevertheless, project management will survive and evolve as it will continue in many cases to be the crucial link between upper management and the technologist.

To place the long-range in perspective, the following scenario appears likely: The rate and extent of organizational streamlining will depend more on social, cultural, and political considerations than on either technological or economic capabilities. The structural evolution of the organization will proceed in two stages. The first stage will be characterized by the marked resurgence of featherbedding as automation begins to displace the work force at a rate higher than that at which it can be reabsorbed into the economy. During this stage top management will continue to trade some of its prerogatives for employee benefits (for example, stability of employment for reduced wages) to finance corporate reindustrialization. This stage will tend to perpetuate a considerable amount of duplication, waste, miscommunication, overcoordination, and employee accommodation, which the project manager will be expected to offset through greater technological innovation and creativity. A growing number of companies, such as AT&T during its 1983 strike, will possess the capability to operate unimpaired despite labor walkouts and will indeed show improved profitability, as AT&T did over the period of such walkouts. For the most part, automation will be used judiciously and conservatively, for instance, to fill voids created by normal attrition and retirement. The use of overtime as a means of meeting peak demand will likely disappear. Selective retraining and lateral transfers will be used to allow for the activation of automation in areas of gross inefficiency, hazardous areas, or in areas where employee attrition and retirement rates do not keep pace with corporate expectations. In the latter phases of this stage, a significant percentage of the corporate work force may be carried as a cost of doing business. The automation squeeze will be reflected in the widespread conversion in leading industries to a (shorter) four-day work week, which will affect a growing number of employees.

The second stage of the structural evolution of the organization will include the activation of the automated infrastructure and will be accompanied by the institution of lifetime severance benefits to employees displaced by automation. Such settlements would in turn become an integral part of the fixed cost of automation and hence possibly a part of the future asset depreciation base. The public perception will gradually have been conditioned to accept rates of unemployment at least equal to those we currently associate with recessionary periods. Unemployment will probably be exacerbated by the near saturation of the service sector industries like banking that themselves may rely on a considerable amount of automation. Technological advances will likely not provide employment for those already displaced by automation.

Through the "magic" of computer-aided design (CAD), computer-aided manufacturing (CAM), computerized information management (CIM), general office automation, and telecommunication, organizations of the future will tend to be run by small enclaves of specialists inextricably linked to one another. As Thompson points out, the high level of automation, along with its attendant flexibility, will remove many limitations and make many concepts and premises obsolete, and in the process will radically transform management philosophy and practice.[11] He further states that the attainable degree of automation will (a) integrate or merge many functions such as manufacturing and engineering to the point of making them indistinguishable;* (b) make production changeover costs nearly negligible and short runs as economical as long runs; (c) drive individual economic ordering quantities (EOQs) close to one, partly because of the obsolescence of the learning curve concept; and (d) make obsolete return on investment or assets as criteria in the evaluation of a product, given the accrued cost of automation.

Given such an environment, corporate management in deciding which projects to pursue will have to (a) become more sensitized to strategic choices and marketing opportunities through much closer interaction of marketing and financial units with the technical unit; (b) develop a greater diversity of products because of high fixed cost of equipment and facilities; and (c) be more flexible and responsive to consumer needs, reactions, and preferences given future ease of replication of products by competitors through software reprogramming.[12]

(c) Research and Development Projects

The increased number of computers will encompass both minicomputers that can be used by R&D engineers, scientists, and project managers and mainframe computers that are accessible through terminals appropriately located in the various laboratories and offices. The number and scope of computerized data bases that can be used for extracting valuable background information (both current and archive) needed for planning and carrying out advanced research and development will increase markedly. Improved programming techniques for indexing and selecting information will facilitate the search and use process. R&D project managers will be able to access extensive research and marketing data stored by the company data management and communications system (see Figure 9.3). The decision-making process will be aided by data banks that will list prospective and past sales, profit, capital investment, labor, and facility costs for various product areas. Teleconfer-

---

* As an example, functions currently performed by manufacturing engineers will be performed by the design engineer at the computer terminal (See Section 8.5b).

encing will allow for rapid, direct questioning and discussions with key individuals of the company to reinforce or modify technical efforts. In a similar manner, the use of system dynamics and special computer programs will allow the manager to prepare alternative research programs based on changes in governmental or company policy and market demand.

14.4   Project Manager: A Target for Products Liability

In 1842 in the case of *Winterbottom vs. Wright,* an English court ruled that a coach driver could not recover damages from the coach builder for injuries sustained because of a defect. In the court's opinion, recovery of damages by the coach driver would have constituted a basis for the "most absurd and outrageous consequences" without any apparent future limits.[13] By 1916 the change in societal values was reflected in *McPherson vs. Buick Motor Company* in which the plaintiff prevailed in a nearly identical case (see Section 10.6 on products liability). For years following, products liability cases were adjudicated on the grounds of breach of warranties and negligence. By the early-sixties, the theory of strict liability in tort emerged in the courts and was soon adopted by the American Law Institute.* This theory vastly expanded the vulnerability of manufacturers to product liability claims.

A number of recent decisions, including that of the Illinois Supreme Court with respect to the total irrelevance of the state of the art in products liability cases, have led some to comment that as a practical matter we are gravitating toward the concept of absolute liability.[14]

As of the time of the espousal of the theory of strict liability by the nation's courts, considerable debate has taken place on the possible extension of this theory to include corporate employees who have traditionally been safeguarded from legal responsibility in products liability cases by corporate shield laws. With the possible exception of areas involving public health and safety, there does not appear to have been a perceptible trend in this area. Nonetheless, in a recent case, a top corporate official was charged with the violation of the Federal Food, Drug and Cosmetic Act for allowing exposure of food to contamination.[15] The Supreme Court adjudicated the case and in the process imposed a duty upon corporate officials not only to search out and remedy hazardous situations but also to implement systems and procedures to preclude their recurrence. Admittedly, the case involved food, an area in which public health is at stake and the public is justified in expecting the courts to impose the highest standards of care. However, are there not other areas within our complex, changing society in which public interest runs equally high? Based upon such broader public interests, it is unreasonable to expect that the law and public policy will involve lower levels of management? The extension of personal liability to the project manager's level may only be speculative at this time. However, the idea may not be as farfetched nor as

---

* The first notable case was *Greenman vs. Yuba Power Products, Inc.*, California, 1963. The Greenman decision was made two years before the final draft of the Restatement, Torts § 402 A.

long in coming as one may be inclined to believe.

As Freeman points out, based on Prosser's treatment of torts, any specialized corporate manager such as the head of quality control, manufacturing, or engineering, "assuming the proper factual background...merely becomes another link in the chain which runs from design to supply of raw materials and purchased parts, to manufacture, distribution and ultimate retail sale. It is current legal practice to bring suit against as many of the links in the chain as possible."[16,17] Freeman goes on to cite several compelling reasons for the inclusion of individual corporate employees in product liability cases:[18]

- The individual may be the only person accessible to the plaintiff as the corporate entity may have either dissolved, merged, or gone bankrupt.
- The plaintiff may be inclined to seek a more advantageous legal posture based on the prevailing laws within the individual's home state.
- The plaintiff may seek to disrupt the corporate defense by assuring the presence of an individual as a target for accusations (thereby precluding the shifting of blame to an individual unavailable for comment).
- The plaintiff may seek to gain a tactical advantage by stampeding defendants into a fight among themselves.
- The situation and justice demand that the individual be held accountable.
- It might be either impossible or unreasonable to claim the personal involvement and knowledge of top corporate executives increasingly decoupled from the day-to-day product line decision-making process, especially in our "Multinational, multimarket, multicompany, multiproduct and multitechnology organizations."[19,20]

The main function of the project manager, namely, that of an *integrator* of diverse expertise, is the function most likely to make him vulnerable and a target of a products liability case. In the past, corporate employees have been shielded by claims of being a member of a team effort with limited involvement in the overall product. A project manager can make no such claims as he is typically held accountable for all aspects of product development and is often involved in its subsequent introduction in the marketplace. He often acts with the delegated authority of a corporate executive, and it is this that may make him vulnerable to attack. (See Section 10.7c).

Whereas the general public expects economic growth as a by-product of technological innovation, it is increasingly uninclined to accept the risks often accompanying such innovation given the level of training, specialized knowledge and experience which brings it about. This and other factors may focus personal responsibility on the project manager, who is the key element in the transformation of an idea into a product. If this in fact occurs, then products liability should receive even greater emphasis in the training and operations of future project managers.(see Section 10.6).

———————— **Questions and Topics for Discussion** ————————

1. How can companies such as McDonald's, Hertz Rental, and Century 21 real estate use the project concept in developing new business opportunities or improvements? Choose one of the three companies and outline a project that could be useful for this purpose.

2. What are the pros and cons for an investor to consider in risking venture capital in a high-technology research consortium?

3. Why would a project office in a high-technology company of the future be advantageous? In your answer indicate what functions such an office could carry out.

4. How can increasing use of CAD/CAM affect project management?

5. How can carrying out work on a project (using a minicomputer) at home by some personnel affect the managerial functions and operations of the project manager?

6. What type of project would be the most likely to involve the project manager in a potential lawsuit? What are the present factors that mitigate the possibility that a lawsuit would be initiated against a project manager?

7. What are some problems that project managers will face in the nineties?

8. It has been frequently stated that our society and industry are going to become information and service based. How will project management fit into such an environment?

——————————————— **References** ———————————————

1. T.J. Peters and R.H. Waterman, Jr., *In Search of Excellence* (New York: Harper and Row, 1982), p. 132.
2. *Ibid.*, pp. 134-135.
3. "RDLPs and Research Consortiums: The New Wave in R&D," *Compressed Air* (March 1984), p. 23.
4. *Ibid.*, p. 20.
5. Allen E. Puckett, "The Changing Role of Electronics," *Vectors*, Hughes Aircraft Co. (June 1980).
6. Harry B. Thompson, "CAD/CAM and the Factory of the Future," *Management Review* (May 1983), p. 27.
7. "The Automated Factory: Technology Paves the Way to Improved Productivity," *Compressed Air* (September 1982), p. 7.

8. Marianne McGlynn, "Telecommuters Let Their Fingers Do the Working," *Los Angeles Times* (September 16, 1983), pt. V, p.1.

9. *Ibid.*

10. Reported in *Machine Design* (November 26, 1981), p. 2; see also, David Liebson, "How Corning Designed a Talking Building to Spur Productivity," *Management Review* (September 1981), p. 8.

11. Thompson, "CAD/CAM and the Factory of the Future," p. 27.

12. McGlynn, "Telecommuters Let Their Fingers Do the Working."

13. John J. Kirchner, "Product Liability – Current State of the Law," *Proceedings of the Product Liability Prevention Conference,* American Society for Quality Control Inc. (1978), p. 1.

14. Mel Furman, "Defending Product Liability Litigation." *Proceedings of the Product Liability Prevention Conference,* American Society for Quality Control (1978), p. 1.

15. James A. Freeman, "Personal Responsibility and Personal Liability," *Proceedings of the Product Liability Prevention Conference,* American Society for Quality Control (1978), p. 89.

16. *Ibid.*

17. William Prosser, "The Assault upon the Citadel," *Yale Law Journal* 1099 (1966).

18. Freeman, "Personal Responsibility and Personal Liability."

19. Henry Mintzberg, "The Manager's Job: Folklore and Fact," *Harvard Business Review* (July-August 1975).

20. Carter F. Bales, "Strategic Control: The President's Paradox," *Business Horizons* (August 1977).

———————— Appendices ————————

The appendices deal with subject areas of importance to project managers. The object in each case is to identify the subject and describe it briefly. References where detailed information can be found are given at the end of each appendix. In Appendices C and J, more material is provided because of the special importance of these subjects to project success and product performance. The appendices are as follows:

A: **Oral Communication**
B: **Product Assurance**
C: **Produce and System Reliability**
D: **Configuration Management**
E: **Value Engineering**
F: **System Requirements and Specifications**
G: **Logistic Support Requirements**
H: **Risk Assessment**
I: **Quality Circles and Project Management**
J: **Statistics**
K: **Total Quality Management**

Appendices

———————————— **Appendix A:** ————————————
Oral Communication

1.0 General Remarks

- The importance for a project manager to communicate effectively cannot be overemphasized.
- In business and industry it has been found that more than 70% of communication is oral.
- Communication is a two-way process – sending and receiving – during which an idea is transferred from one person to another.
- Unfortunately, most people are more interested in sending than receiving:
    - People tend to be poor listeners; they are often thinking of other subjects or of what they are going to say next.
    - Although much time and energy is spent teaching children to read and write, there is no time spent in teaching students how to listen.
- In addition to the listening problem, there is also a semantic problem arising in part from sociocultural and other differences.

2.0 Estimate of Oral Communication Effectiveness

- Likelihood of sender's expression of thoughts and instructions being accurate in phrasing and terminology (~80%).
- Likelihood of receiver listening attentively and hearing the complete instruction (~80%).
- Likelihood of receiver interpreting what he heard correctly and not misunderstanding owing to semantics, noise level, and other reasons (~80%).
- Probability that the message was sent and headr correctly:

$$P_{total} = (P_1)(P_2)(P_3) = (0.80)^3 = 0.51 \text{ or } 51\%.$$

In other words, there is about a 50% chance that you were not heard completely or correctly or have been misunderstood.

3.0 Results of Poor Communication

- The results of poor communication are invariably negative.
- Distortion and misunderstanding of the idea or instruction can cause
    - Incorrect execution of instruction
    - Bad feelings (loss of friendship or confidence)

- Unnecessary arguments/explanations
- Confusion (not understanding may or may not be recognized or acknowledged by the receiver)

4.0 Common Sense Ways to Improve Oral Communication

- Maintain good eye contact.
- Be careful of voice quality and tone:
  - Keep tone of voice pleasant and relaxed (not irritating).
  - Don't speak in a monotone.
  - Change tone and tempo.
- Speak in a relaxed manner and with relaxed facial expressions:
  - Some goal-oriented, aspiring, executives have practice sessions in front of the mirror, studying and improving their facial expressions and appearance when speaking.
  - Check yourself for nervous mannerisms that may annoy the person you are talking to.
  - Do not hesitate when speaking, this may indicate that you are not sure of yourself.
  - Gestures are sometimes effective but they must be natural and not distracting.
- Choose words carefully:
  - Sometimes choice of the wrong words can trigger people negatively. Do not use inflammatory or "loaded" words.
  - Be diplomatic and polite.
- State all the information necessary:
  - Don't leave out any important points.
  - Seek feedback to preclude misunderstandings.
- Convey clear messages:
  - Be *direct* and *concise.*
  - Be fully informed about what you are saying.
  - Use examples when appropriate.
- Speak to personnel on grounds of common experience. Relate the conversation to the receiver.
- In discussion use empathy – try to see the situation through other persons' eyes. Be responsive to their remarks.
- Be careful of your beginning remarks (don't turn listeners off).
- Listen:
  - Don't think about other things.
  - Concentrate on what the speaker is saying.
  - Sometimes it helps to use responses that indicate you are listening (such as nodding head to encourage speaker, asking clarifying questions).
  - Do not interrupt.

5.0 Summary and References

Interpersonal communication, be it with one, two, or a group of people, is an extremely complex phenomenon. There are barriers complicating effective oral communication that can be categorized as perceptual, psychological, social, cultural, semantic, and physical. For further reading on this most important subject, the following references are suggested:

1. Amos, J.M., and Sarchet, B.R., *Management for Engineers*, (Englewood Cliffs, N.J.: Prentice-Hall, 1981), pp. 262-285.
2. Mitton, D.G., and Mitton, B.L., *Managerial Clout*, (Englewood Cliffs, N.J.: Prentice-Hall, 1980).
3. Murdick, R.G., and Ross, J.E., *Information Systems for Modern Management*, (Englewood Cliffs, N.J.: Prentice-Hall, 1975), pp. 457-462.
4. Steers, R.M., *Introduction to Organizational Behavior*, (Santa Monica, Calif: Goodyear 1981), pp. 208-231.
5. Steil, L.K. et al, *Listening: It Can Change Your Life*, (Somerset, N.J.: John Wiley, 1983).

—————————————— **Appendix B:** ——————————————
Product Assurance

1.0 General Remarks

- A project manager must be concerned about a number of product or system characteristics during system design and development which have to do with quality and that are directed toward customer satisfaction.
- To achieve these characteristics, the company must carry out activities in the following areas:
  - Quality control
  - Reliability
  - Maintainability
  - Human factors
  - System Safety
- Responsibility for these activities can be divided among various engineering and design groups within the company or project; or, they can be organized in one or more groups serving all the projects of the company.
- Large companies or organizations often group these activities together under the general title of Product Assurance or Quality Assurance and Product Effectiveness with a corresponding group or department. The group or department may have status in the corporate structure equal to engineering or manufacturing with a director reporting to a division manager or vice president.
- In small companies the project manager frequently assigns responsibility for these systems properties and development activities to the design and test engineering groups or to one or more individuals, who act as staff to him.
- It is essential that these characteristics be taken into account in system design and development.

2.0 Quality Control (QC)

- QC group personnel are usually responsible for ensuring that
  - Appropriate test procedures are set up
  - All test procedures are followed
  - All specification and requirements are met
- QC can be carried out at various stages of the manufacturing process:
  - Incoming materials and components
  - Fabrication of parts (tolerance checks and measurements)
  - Manufacturing procedures and processes
  - Assembly of components into subsystems

– Packaging and shipping

3.0 Reliability (discussed in more detail in Appendix C)

- The reliability group is generally responsible for
  – Determining failure rates
  – Determining modes of failure
  – Predicting the lifetime of the product or system (reliability of the system under the conditions of use)
  – Analysis of test data
  – Recommendations about whether system redesign or modification is needed

4.0 Maintainability

- The maintainability group is generally responsible for ensuring that maintenance has been appropriately considered during the design and development of the system. This includes
  – Ease of maintenance (modular concept – use of readily replaceable modules where possible; accessibility of components, commonality, or interchangeability)
  – Minimization of cost of maintenance (use of high-reliability components)
  – Built-in capability for scheduled preventive maintenance
  – Minimization of downtime
- Maintainability may be a separate group or it may be included in the quality control, reliability, or logistics groups.

5.0 Human Factors

- The human factors group is responsible for ensuring that the human in-the-loop (for reliability and consistency of operation, service, maintenance, and so on) is appropriately considered during the design phase.
- The group considers human/machine interface problems.
- The activity of designing a system for ease and convenience in use by people is called human engineering.

6.0 Systems Safety

- The systems safety group is responsible for identifying all potential hazards of the system being developed, along with recommending appropriate action to minimize or control these hazards (qualitative and quantitative). The safety factor is also related to product liability evaluation and environmental impacts. Errors in design and fabrication can result in injury to humans and destruction of property when the system is used.

7.0 Summary and References

The subjects of product assurance and quality control are intimately related and go far beyond the preceding brief descriptions and comments. For in-depth coverage, readers can refer to the following:

1. Blanchard, B., and Lowery, E., *Maintainability: Principles and Practice,* (New York: McGraw-Hill, 1969).
2. Cunningham, C., and Cox, W., *Applied Maintainability,* (New York: John Wiley, 1972).
3. Duncan, A.J., *Quality Control and Industrial Statistics,* (Homewood, Ill.: Richard D. Irwin, 1972).
4. Feignbaum, A.V., *Quality Control: Principles, Practices and Administrations,* (New York: McGraw-Hill, 1951).
5. Feignbaum, A.V., *Total Quality Control Engineering and Management,* (New York: McGraw-Hill, 1951).
6. Harris, D.H., and Chaney, F.B., *Human Factors in Quality Assurance,* (New York: John Wiley, 1969).
7. Juran, J.M., *Quality Control Handbook,* (New York: McGraw-Hill, 1962).
8. McCormick, E.J., *Human Factors Engineering,* (New York: McGraw-Hill, 1970).

——————————— Appendix C: ———————————
Product and System Reliability

1.0 Definition

- Reliability is defined as the probability that a system or device will perform without failure under given conditions for a specified period of time. The period of time referred to is usually the operational or use time.
- We can also speak of the reliability of a component or system at time t as the probability that the equipment will be operational at time t.
- The reliability of an item (component or system) can be determined by testing a number of identical items. By noting the number that fail as a function of time, the reliability can be determined (see Section 3.0).

2.0 Why Reliability Is Important

- For companies reliability is a matter of:
  - Minimizing servicing of products
  - Minimizing customer complaints
  - Protecting the company's reputation
  - Product liability considerations
- Reliability must be designed into the system design from the start of the development process.
- Taking reliability into account in system design and development process can
  - Decrease operating cost
  - Decrease downtime of the system when it is finally developed
  - Decrease the risk of loss of life or property
  - Decrease logistic support requirements

3.0 Arithmetic Formula For Reliability

$$R(A) = \frac{N_s(t)}{N_o}$$
$$N_o = N_s(t) + N_f(t)$$

Where $R(A)$ is the reliability of the component

$N_s(t)$ is the number of surviving units at time t

t is usually the operational time

N_o is the total number of units being tested

$N_f(t)$ is the number of units that have failed at time t

- The more units tested, the more accurate the reliability R(A) value. Ideally, a statistical number of units should be tested, but this may not be practical, particularly if there are only a few systems, the items are expended when tested, or they are very expensive.

4.0 Failure Rates

- Instantaneous failure rate: l is the number of units failing/unit time at time t.

$$ l = \frac{\Delta N_f}{\Delta t} \quad \text{or} \quad \left(\frac{dN}{dt}\right)_f t $$

- Failure rate as a function of time: If a number of identical components or systems tested as a function of time and the failure rate calculated from the test data the following curve is obtained:

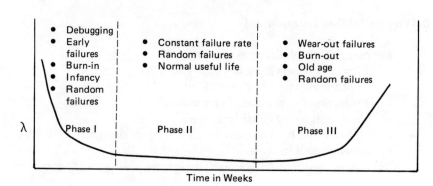

Time in Weeks

5.0 Early System Failures (Phase 1)

- Failures may be due to faulty components, poor assembly, random failures, or the like.
- Weaknesses may be exhibited early in the life of the product (rejects).
- Early failures are referred to as "infant mortality."
- Faulty *components* can be weeded out by preliminary testing, break-in, or burn-in.
- Early *system* failure may often be taken care of by
  (a) Preliminary testing or break-in, done by companies in an initial brief run of the system (also to make sure it works).
  (b) Warranty or guarantee to fix defective components within a certain time period.
    – These depend on the manufacturer's need and desire to back up his product.

  - It may not be economical to give too long a guarantee period.
  - Ideally, the guarantee period should take the product into the low failure region.
  - Such warranties are common with electric appliances, automobiles, and so on.

6.0 Random Failures (Phase II)

- During this phase the failure rate (1) is constant.
- Failure occurrence is due more to chance or overstress than deficiency in fabrication and manufacture.
- This is the failure rate of the system during its normal use.
- Mean-time before failure (MTBF):*
  - Defined as:

$$\text{MTBF} = \frac{1}{\lambda} \text{ (time units) where } \lambda = \left(\frac{dN_f}{dt}\right)_t = \frac{\text{no. of units failing}}{\text{time}}$$

  - This can be determined by testing many like items.

7.0 Wearout Failure (Phase III)

- Components or product finally wear out.
- The equation shows that reliability is decreasing rapidly in wearout phase as both 1 and t are increasing; more and more components fail.

8.0 The Reliability Equation

- Experimental data for a large population of components or systems tested show the following equation to hold:

$$R_A(t) = e^{-\int_o^t \lambda dt} = 1/e^{\int_o^t \lambda dt}$$

Where $R_A(t)$ is the reliability of component A at time t

  e is the exponential constant
  1   is the failure rate of component A
  t is the time of use

- To use this equation, 1 must be a known constant or a known function of t, for example,

---

* Can also mean the mean-time between failure – not treated here.

$$\lambda = A$$
$$\lambda = Kt$$
$$\lambda = A + Kt$$
$$\lambda = f(t)$$

actually, l has different values for the various phases of use discussed above, for example, possible values could be

Phase I $\lambda = -Kt$
Phase II $\lambda = $ constant
Phase III $\lambda = +Kt$

9.0 Determination and Calculation of Systems Reliability

- This can be accomplished by testing the whole system as an entity.
- In the design and development phase system, reliability can be estimated from the reliability of its parts.

9.1 When Components Are in Series

(a) System has n different components:

- If one component fails, the system fails.
- *Example*

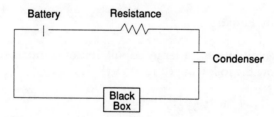

(b) System has n identical components:

$$R_1 = R_2 = R_3 = ...R_n = R$$
$$R_{syst}(t) = (R_1)(R_2)(R_3)...R_n = R^n$$

(c) Effect of component reliability on subsystem reliability:
Example: A system consisting of 10 components in series:
Case 1. Each component has reliability of 0.90 at time t

$$R_{syst}(t) = (0.90)^{10} = 0.35$$

Case 2. Each component has reliability of 0.99 at time t

$$R_{syst}(t) = (0.99)^{10} = 0.90$$

Case 3. Each component has reliability of 0.999 at time t

$$R_{syst}(t) = (0.999)^{10} = 0.99$$

9.2 Components Are in Parallel (Redundancy)

(a) System consists of n different components:
- If one component fails, the system continues to operate.
- General equation:

$$R_{syst} = 1 - (1-R_1)(1-R_2)(1-R_{3)}\ldots(1-R_n)$$

(b) System consists of n identical components

$$(R_1 = R_2 = \ldots R_n):$$

- General equation: $R_{syst} = 1 - (1-R)^n$
- *Example:* Assume a system of two components in parallel

$$R_1 = R_2 = 90$$

$$R_{syst} = 1-(1-0.90)2 = 0.99$$

Note: There is higher reliability of two components in parallel (0.99) compared with one component (0.90); this shows the advantage of redundancy.

10.0 Functional Factors Affecting Component and Systems Reliability (Hardware System)

(a) Development factors

- Design
- Materials used
- Fabrication technique
- Assembly
- Process

These factors determine the initial strength capability.

(b) Preoperational environment:

- Installation
- Shipment
- Quality control

(c) Operational environment

- How system is operated
  - Maintenance
  - Service

11.0 Methods of Improving Systems Reliability

(a) Simplify the design as much as possible without sacrificing perform-
    ance. Reduce number of components to a minimum.
(b) Use the most reliable components available, commensurate with cost.
  - Preferably use standard proven components rather than advanced
    SOA.
  - Make a trade-off study evaluating the use of the most advanced,
    sophisticated equipment available according to reliability, main-
    tainability, and *cost*.
  - The question that must be answered is whether the increased so-
    phistication is worth the increased cost and possible decreased
    reliability and maintainability.
(c) Improved quality control:
  - Better test procedures for identifying faulty units
  - Better manufacturing techniques (such as use of a clean room and
    the like)
(d) Use of redundancy of standby systems where possible. Cost, weight,
    volume restrictions, and other constraints must be taken into account
    and trade-offs made.
  - Redundant systems:
    - Components are in parallel.
    - Components are identical.
    - Two or more systems are operational all the time.
    - If one system fails (for example, see Figure C.1) the other can
      still meet the demand.
  - Standby systems:
    - These are back-up systems (secondary systems).
    - They are not used unless the primary system fails.
    - A sensing and control system is needed to recognize when a
      failure has occurred and to initiate transfer to the standby
      system.
(e) Use of safety factors:
  - Many systems are designed to withstand loading or use beyond
    that to which they would normally be exposed.

—— Figure C.1: Example of a Redundant System: Pressurized Fuel Supply System ——

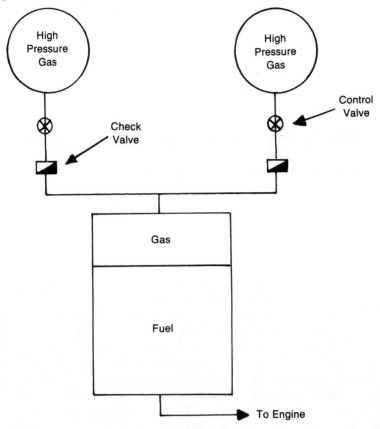

Notes: (a) Redundancy occurs here in the portion of the system starting from the gas tanks and ending at the line to the fuel tank.

(b) If a control valve or check valve fails closed, there will still be gas pressure supplied to the fuel tank.

- Examples
  - Commercial aircraft are designed to be able to withstand 1.5 times the loadings they are normally exposed to.
  - Pressurized tanks are designed and must pass tests for pressures 1.2 to 1.5 times what they will be normally exposed to.
- Operate the system at less than its rated full capacity. There will be less chance of overstress or fatigue.
  Examples:
  - A vehicle such as an aircraft may be off-loaded to provide increased safety and reliability. An aircraft built to carry a maximum load of 120,000 lbs is only loaded to 100,000 lbs (S.F. = 1.2).
  - A 10 kw motor is never operated above 8 kw.

The term *safety factor* indicates the degree of safety – therefore, reliability.

(f) Design reviews by experienced personnel.
(g) Provide all the necessary maintenance and service to the system during its lifetime to maintain highest possible reliability.

12.0 Confidence Level

The degree of confidence in the reliability is the confidence level.

- To establish confidence level it is necessary to know
  - How many components or systems should be tested
  - How the number of components tested relate to the conclusions about the reliability of the total population
  - How close the test conditions simulate the actual use conditions
- Confidence level gives the probability that a certain percentage of the product items will have certain performance characteristics or, in this case, reliability. Confidence level increases with the number of items tested or the length of time the system is tested.
- A 100% confidence level would be achieved if you tested every item in the population for a period equal to its operating time.
  - This could be unrealistic if the items were used up when tested. There would be none left to use in the system application.
  - Cost becomes prohibitive if too many items are tested, for example, Minuteman ICBMs. Also, you may not have a sufficiently large (statistical) number of items in the inventory.
- Tables relating sample size, reliability, and confidence level have been worked out by statisticians. This allows the systems manager to make decision about how many items or systems should be tested for various levels of confidence.
- Problems in determining confidence level:
  - How random is the sample?
  - Are the tests of the item or system under truly operational conditions?
  - What confidence level is reasonable?

13.0 References

1. Bazovsky, I., *Reliability Theory and Practices.* (Englewood Cliffs, N.J.: Prentice-Hall, 1961).
2. Calabro, S.R., *Reliability Principles and Practices.* (New York: McGraw-Hill, 1962).
3. Ireson, W., ed., *Reliability Handbook.* (New York: McGraw-Hill, 1966).
4. *Proceedings of the Annual Reliability and Maintainability Symposium,* Philadelphia, Pa., January 27-29, 1981.
5. Smith, D.J., *Reliability Engineering,* (New York: Pitman, 1972).

— Appendix D: —
Configuration Management

1.0 General Remarks

- Configuration management is a management planning andcontrol technique used by companies that develop complex systems having many subsystems and components.

- It has as its objectives

  (a) Accurate and complete identification of each material, part, subassembly, and assembly that goes into the product
  (b) Accurate and complete accounting of all changes to product descriptions and to the product itself

- Configuration management can be defined as management procedures and operations for providing uniform product descriptions, status records, and the control and documentation of all changes; or, "the discipline of ensuring that equipment or hardware meets carefully defined functional, mechanical, and electrical requirements and that any chnages in these requirements are rigidly controlled, carefully identified, and accurately recorded" (Samares and Czerwinski, see references).
- The term *configuration* refers to a complete description of the physical and functional characteristics of a product and its components. This includes:

Size	Material
Weight	Power requirements
Location	Performance
Interfaces	Changes in components and subsystems
Test Procedures	(including dates of change)
Operational procedures	
Repair procedures	

- Configuration management for a large, complex hardware system having many subsystems and components involves the following phases of activity:

  (a) Setting up and monitoring baseline requirements during the system development
  (b) Identification of parts, subsystems, and systems

(c) Accounting – keeping records of parts, tests, and so on.
(d) Change control – keeping track of changes in the system

- Configuration management must be carried out in the planning phase and also during the complete lifetime of the system development process.

2.0 Organization for Carrying Out Configuration Management

- Some companies have a separate organization that is independent of the engineering, testing, manufacturing, and quality assurance departments.
- Other companies – usually smaller companies – designate a staff specialist for this assignment.
- Still other companies integrate configuration management into the engineering division.
- For small projects the project manager may appoint a staff person or be his own configuration manager.

3.0 Baseline Requirements for a Large Complex System

- Initial baseline requirements are set up for the system:

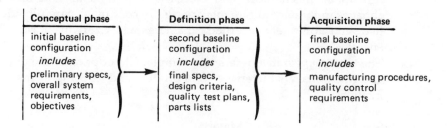

Conceptual phase	Definition phase	Acquisition phase
initial baseline configuration *includes* preliminary specs, overall system requirements, objectives	second baseline configuration *includes* final specs, design criteria, quality test plans, parts lists	final baseline configuration *includes* manufacturing procedures, quality control requirements

- The contract between the buyer and seller spells out the baseline requirements for each phase of the system development process. These have some degree of flexibility.
- During the course of system development, the configuration management group maintains a check on how the actual configuration is working out in comparison with the original baseline requirements (called "baseline management").
    - The initial baseline configuration is established from the system performance requirements and objectives (preliminary specs, design criteria, and so on).
    - The second baseline configuration is based on design requirements and is backed up by such items as model-testing results, engineering drawings, and other supportive information.

   – The last baseline configuration is a production baseline with backup of manufacturing prototype results, full detailed engineering drawings, quality assurance data, test procedures, and the like.
   – The system is finally built according to the last baseline.

4.0 Configuration Identification

4.1 What Is It?

- Configuration identification is the process of identifying specifications, hardware, and data available at the start of a system development.

4.2 Key Requirements for Successful Configuration Identification

- All available initial data and equipment items must be identified.
- There must be a system with documented procedures developed for controlling and monitoring the hardware items that are to be fabricated.
- One individual or group must be designated for issuing and controlling all configuration item identification.

4.3 Software Items That Must Be Initially Identified

- Contractual documents
  - Work statement
  - Special customer requirements
  - Delivery schedule of hardware or software
  - Reporting schedule
- Preliminary study information
  - Drawing and engineering data
  - Preliminary study report
  - Preliminary specifications
  - Test procedures
  - Anticipated parts lists, spares required, and so on

4.4 System for Identifying Hardware Items

- See Table D1 for example.
  - Configured item number
  - C.I. description
  - Specification number
  - C.I. number
  - Responsible engineer

The six standard configuration identifiers used by government agencies and industry for hardware items are as follows (a combination of these will be used):

Table D.1: Hardware Item Identification

Configured Item	Configured Item Description	Specification	C.I. Number	Responsibility
	Stabilization and Control Subsystem (con't)			
	Sensor and Drive Electronics Assembly		AK100 (Ref.)	M. Nelson
236880	Chassis Assy, SSE-1020A1	EQ4-432	AK116	L. M. Lewis
236884	Chassis Assy, SIE-1010	EQ4-431	AK118	L. M. Lewis
236883	Chassis Assy, DAE-1030A1	EQ4-430	AK127	L. M. Lewis
236885	Chassis Assy, DAE-1030A2	EQ4-430	AK128	L. M. Lewis
236886	Chassis Assy, ESE-710A1	EQ4-419	AK129	L. M. Lewis
236830	Chassis Assy, ESE-710A2	EQ4-419	AK130	L. M. Lewis
236834	Chassis Assy, SRE-810A1	EQ4-426	AK131	L. M. Lewis
236744	Chassis Assy, SRE-810A2	EQ4-426	AK132	L. M. Lewis
236743				
	Electrical Power Subsystem	SS14-03	AK200	H. Kelly
237034	Battery	EQ3-168	AK201	R. Weber
237032	Converter No. 1	EQ3-161	AK202	M. Monaco
241198	Solar Paddle	EQ3-167	AK203	C. Lindley
235118	Shunt Element Assembly	EQ3-162	AK204	R. Rubin
235119	Power Control Unit	EQ3-163	AK205	R. Rubin
237033	Converter No. 2A	EQ3-164	AK206	M. Monaco
237031	Converter No. 2B	EQ3-164	AK207	M. Monaco
	Telemetry Subsystem	SS6-17	AK300	A. Anderson
236408	PCM Encoder	EQ4-437	AK301	E. B. Smith
238763	"S" Band Transmitter	EQ4-438	AK302	J. Olsen
237028	Antenna Assy, "S" Band	EQ4-439	AK303	B. Ash
235800	Command Decoder	EQ4-440	AK304	S. Cobb
H244904	Transport Case		AK305	F. White
F240632	Antenna Hat Assy		AK306	F. White
EG238047	Telemetry Demodulator	EQ4-442	AK350	B. March
EG238048	Command Demodulator	EQ4-443	AK360	B. March
	Electrical Integration Subsystem	SS4-07	AK400	C. R. Bennett
237955	Electrical Integration Assy	EQ3-158	AK401	M. Harris
240369	Cabling	EQ3-160	AK402	L. DeSilva
237956	Auxiliary Electrical Integration Assy	EQ3-159	AK403	M. Hoffman

1. Specification number
2. Equipment number
3. Drawing and part number
4. Equipment and item serialization number
5. Change identification number
6. Manufacturer's code identification number – coding by location or by use of a system tree

5.0 Configuration Accounting

5.1 What Is It?

- Configuration accounting refers to the reporting and documenting of activities involved in keeping track of the status of configuration at all times after the system development has started and often during the whole lifetime of the system.

5.2 Why Is It Important?

- It provides the customer with the documentation that describes the status of the configured components and subsystems and the final configuration of each item as well as the final total system.
- It keeps records on all approved changes made to each C.I. and the configuration as a whole (the total system).
- It keeps records on the location of each C.I. during the acquisition phase.

5.3 Documentation

- In addition to the software items that were originally identified, there are additional
  - Engineering drawings and changes to drawings
  - Specifications and changes to specs
  - Test procedures
  - Test results
  - Shipping and handling instructions
  - Technical manuals

5.4 Data Management Group

- A data management group is often used as part of configuration management organization to keep the records and disseminate information.
- An information system must be set up to keep all the concerned groups property informed including management, engineering, manufacturing, and the customer.

- Decisions must be made about
  - Who to inform
  - What to tell
  - How often to report

6.0 Configuration Change Control

6.1 What Is It?

- Configuration control refers to the procedure by which changes to baseline configured items are proposed and formally processed.
- It involves
  1. Analysis of the need for the change
  2. Alternative approaches
  3. Interface effects on other components and subsystems
  4. Effects on resources and schedule
  5. Effect on the baselines

6.2 Why Is It Important?

- Each change in a system during development or manufacture is like a new contract concerned not only with the projection of effort but also with the effect on completed and in-process work.
- As systems designers, engineers, and others work on building new systems, important changes come to mind that have the potential of
  - Improving performance
  - Reducing complexity
  - Decreasing costs
- The customer also has ideas and desires for improvement of the product and decreasing costs.
- Changes in design and configuration can often be brought about as a result of design reviews held within the company or with the customer upon demand.

6.3 Design Reviews

- Design reviews are a series of formal meetings held internally by the company during the design process.
- The customer may or may not be invited to participate, although he can ask for a design review.
- Company experts and key personnel examine the following:
  - Product design
  - Configuration
  - Test program
  - Test data
- A mock-up or model of the system may have been prepared to show how the components and subsystems fit.

- Specific objectives are to
  1. Examine design for flaws or errors
  2. Confirm that the design is in fact the optimum one
  3. Detect interface problems of components or subsystems
- Each attendee fills out critique sheet.
- Results of design review are recommendations by the attendees for changes and improvements in the design.

6.4 Change Control Procedures

(a) Request for change can originate from the customer or from company personnel.
(b) Change request is processed.
(c) Following approval by the change control board (CCB), top management and the customer must approve.

6.5   Change Control Board (CCB)

- The change control board, also called the configuration control board, is set up to approve or disapprove recommended changes.
- The board often includes representatives selected from the following groups: engineering, production, control, purchasing, contracts, and quality assurance.
- CCB is usually headed by the configuration department managers or the project manager or assistant project manager.
- CCB must verify the following:
  1. The change is necessary.
  2. The method of implementation is feasible.
  3. The change can be accomplished within cost and schedule requirements.
- If the change in a design improvement, additional component, schedule change, or any change that will increase cost above the negotiated contract cost, then an engineering change proposal (ECP) is drawn up, priced, and submitted to the customer for his approval.*
- An example of the configuration management change process would be the following:
  - An engineering change is found necessary.
  - The change in design is determined by the groups involved.
  - Approval of the change is sought from the project manager and/or the change control board.
  - PM and CCB evaluate the effect of the change.

---

* Many contracts (particularly government contracts) have more than doubled in final price owing to engineering changes (known as cost growth).

- Approval is then sought from upper management or the customer.
- The proposed changes are documented.
- The changes are implemented.

7.0 References

1. Archibald, R.D., *Managing, High-Technology Programs and Projects.* (New York: Wiley-Interscience, 1976), p. 190.
2. Blanchard, B.S., *Engineering Organizations and Management.* (Englewood Cliffs, N.J.: Prentice-Hall, 1976), pp. 188-191.
3. Samares, T.T., and Czerwinski, F.L., *Fundamentals of Configuration Management.* (New York: Wiley-Interscience, 1971).

Appendix E:
Value Engineering

- Value engineering is defined and used in a variety of ways. One common definition is a concerted effort to produce the end item as inexpensively as possible without any degradation in performance or quality. It is also sometimes referred to as value analysis.
- Following system design and development, new technical developments and improvements in materials, manufacturing procedures, and so on often occur. It is the responsibility of the value engineering group to become aware of these changes and incorporate them into the systems if they will decrease cost and not affect performance or quality.
- For example, it may become evident that an expensive metal part can be replaced by an equally effective but much less expensive plastic part. Another example would be the awareness that a particular molded component can be more economically stamped out from thin metal using a continuously operating machine.
- There may also be improvements in the design that can bring about cost reduction. If the system designer were perfect, then no improvements would be possible, but since designers are human they may have overlooked some detail that would make the system cheaper to produce. Continued study of the product and its details of manufacture can lead to improvements through effective value engineering.
- Strictly speaking, value engineering should be applied before engineering drawings are finalized and during the system design and development phase. That is the period when savings can be greatest. However, considerable savings are commonly experienced after the system design and development phase has been completed.
- Value engineering has been used in industry extensively and also in Department of Defense procurements. It has been a requirement in many DOD system development contracts. Here again the principal objective has been to decrease cost.

References:

1. Clawson, R.H., *Value Engineering for Management.* (Princeton, N.J.: Auerback, 1970).
2. Crum, L.W., *Value Engineering.* (London: Longman, 1971).
3. Heller, E.D., *Value Management: Value Engineering and Cost Reduction.* (Reading, Mass.: Addison-Wesley, 1971).
4. Mudge, A.E., *Value Engineering: A systematic Approach* (New York: McGraw-Hill, 1971).

Appendix F:
System Requirements and Specifications

1.0 What Are System Requirements or Specifications?

- They are the definitions of the functional and physical requirements of the components, subsystems, or systems.
- They state exactly what components, subsystems, and systems are supposed to do and what they look like quantitatively.
- They are determined on the basis of customer needs or requirements and what is feasible.
- They serve as references for describing important design characteristics or components, subsystems, and systems.
- They should be set up so that if each component and subsystem meets its specification, the total system will meet its specifications and objectives.
- They can be and usually are the basis for contractual agreements between buyer and seller.
- They must conform to the standards imposed by
  - Groups having authority to impose restrictions and regulations:
    - (a) Federal, state, and municipal agencies
    - (b) National standard groups
  - Company standards and practices
- They can be used for
  - The performance of the final product or system
  - Incoming materials
  - Manufacturing
  - Packaging
  - Shipping

2.0 Common Specifications Used in Systems Procurements

- There are many kinds of specifications, but in major systems procurement design specs and performance specs are the most common and the most important.
- Examples of other types of specifications are process, manufacturing, packaging, storage, and shipping.

2.1 Customer Specifications
(a) Design Specifications
  - Materials, dimensions, and configurations of item are specified in detail so that item can be produced.
  - Allowable tolerances are usually specified.

- Weight, size, and other physical requirements may also be speci-fied.

(b) Performance Specifications

- These spell out the functions that the product must be able to perform to be acceptable.
- They are usually spelled out as tests that the product must be able to meet.
- Performance specs may be rigid; if the product does not meet tests within allowable limits the product or project is canceled.
- Performance specs may be loose; the designer works toward a desired goal but the customer is aware that full realization of the ultimate goal may be
  - Too costly
  - Too time consuming
  - Not presently within the state of the art (SOA)
  Under these conditions the ultimate goals may be compromised.
- Of the two types of specifications, performance specifications are pre-ferred because they test the ability of the product or system to meet its objective function.
- More often than not performance specs are the basis for contractual agreement.

2.2 Company Specifications

- These requirements set up by an individual company for their prod-uct.
- They can include material specs, tolerances, and so on.

3.0 Development of Specifications

3.1 Preliminary Specifications

- These can include some or all of the following:
  - Identification of design specs
  - Identification of performance specs and system requirements
  - Spelling out development and operational plans
  - Spelling out maintenance and logistic plans
- Preliminary specs have the following characteristics:
  (a) They are necessary to initiate the design effort.
  (b) They should be broad documents indicating objectives but no so rigid so that minor changes cannot be made.
  (c) They are a "living" document.

3.2 Preliminary Design Review (PDR)

This review usually involves evaluation of software such as
- Blueprints, plans, and sketches
- Design approach work descriptions
- All documentation prepared to date

3.3 Changes in Specifications and Design

- Spec changes (usually accomplished by memo)–engineering change request (ECR)
- Alteration notices (usually minor changes)
- Major modification changes (mod change)
  (a) To improve system in major way
  (b) To correct a deficiency
- Major changes should be timed so that
  (a) Several changes can be made at the same time
  (b) Changeover occurs at a shutdown time or major maintenance event

3.4 Final Design Specifications and System Requirements

- These are developed from systems analysis, modeling, simulation, optimization, and prototype testing.
- The design "freeze date" is important because after that date no further engineering changes are allowed except by high-level approval and for very important reasons.

4.0 Format for Specifications

4.1 Industrial

There is no standard format–each company has its own.

4.2 Military (ML specs)

- Military specs are fairly well organized.
- They often include the following items (see Table F.1):
  (a) Scope
  (b) Applicable documents
  (c) Requirements
  (d) Quality assurance
  (e) Packaging (preparation for delivery)
  (f) Use

———————————— **Table F.1: Checklist for Design Specifications*** ————————————

1. Warning notice (if classified)
2. Specification symbols and numbers
3. Heading
4. Preamble
5. Title and date
6. Supersession data

Section 1: Scope

7. Scope
8. Classification (grades, classes, reliability levels, etc.)

Section 2: Applicable Documents

9. Furnished documents
10. Proper sequence of listings
11. Titles and symbols same as on documents
12. Other publications with source identified

Section 3: Requirements

13. Paragraph on detail specifications, specification, or specification sheets
14. Organization of requirements
15. Qualification clause
    a. Qualification for initial level
    b. Qualification for other levels
    c. Periodic qualification reevaluation
16. Standard sample
17. First article
18. Materials (including statement on toxic products and formulations)
19. Reliability
20. Construction
21. Maintainability
22. Transportability
23. Performance characteristics
24. Details on components
25. Chemical and physical properties
26. Radio interference suppression
27. Dimensions
28. Weight
29. Color
30. Finish
31. Nameplate or product markings
32. Furnished property
33. Loaned property
34. Workmanship
35. All requirements covered by tests in Section 4.

Section 4: Quality Assurance

36. Responsibility for inspection clause
37. Organization of examination and tests
38. First article inspection
39. Qualification
    a. Qualification for initial level
    b. Qualification for other reliability levels
    c. Periodic qualification reevaluation
40. Quality conformance inspection
41. Test methods

Section 5: Packaging (Prep for Delivery)

42. Preservation and packaging
43. Packing
44. Marking (packages and shipping containers)
45. Labeling

Section 6: Use (Notes)

46. Intended use
47. Ordering data
48. Standard sample information
49. Qualification
50. Definitions
51. Cross-referencing for changes or clarification of types
52. Miscellaneous notes such as levels or packaging and preservation
53. Purchase description supersession data
54. International interest

Appendix

*DOD 4120.3-M

5.0 Conforming to Group and Association Standards

- There are many organizations that set standards for various products. Of these only governmental agencies and certain organizations are controlling.
- The design must be such that the final product will conform to all city, county, state, and federal regulations.
- State registration laws require that design engineers involved in public works be registered.
- The product must not be dangerous to humans or property.

- Federal statute (Public Law 90-146) has provided for a National Commission of Product Safety.
  - The commission consists of seven members appointed by the president.
  - Its purpose is to protect consumers against hazardous household products.

6.0   Conforming to Group and Association Standards

There are many private organizations in the country that have been set up to develop and maintain standards. Some of these are the following:

- The American Society for Testing Materials (ASTM)
  - The source of the most widely used industrial standardization documents in the United States.
- The American National Standards Institute (ANSI)
  - Serves as a control repository and distribution center for widely accepted standards in all fields
  - Develops standards when an important void exists
- The Society of Automotive Engineers (SAE)
  - Develops, publishes, and sells
    (a) Aerospace Material Specifications (AMS)
    (b) Aerospace Standards (AS)
    (c) Aerospace Recommended Practice (ARP)
- National Electrical Manufacturers Association (NEMA)
  - Develops standards for electrical power equipment

In addition, there are a number of other organizations involved in the development and distribution of standards including the following:

- The American Society of Mechanical Engineers (ASME)
- The Electronic Industries Associations (EIA)
- The National Fire Protection Association (NFPA)
- The National Aerospace Standards Committee (NASC)
- The Underwriters Laboratories (UL)

Note: Companies or government agencies often require, in their system requirements or specifications for project involving system development, that certain standards or associations codes be followed.

7.0 References

1. American Standards Institute, 10 E, 40th St., New York, NY (for information on standards).
2. Blanchard, B.S., *Engineering Organization & Management*, (Englewood cliffs, N.J.: Prentice-Hall, 1976). pp. 70-74.

3. Eshbach, O.W., ed., *Handbook of Engineering Fundamentals*. (New York: John Wiley, 1965), pp. 17-23.
4. "Seals of Approval: What They Do for Your Product.: *Product Engineering* (November 21, 1966), pp. 139-139.
5. "Specification Practice," Mil-STO-490. U.S. Department of Defense, Government Printing Office, Washington, D.C. (October 30, 1968).
6. A number of commercial information selling companies offer microfiche services for almost every type of industrial code and standards.

--------------------------- Appendix G: ---------------------------
Logistics Support Requirements

In both the private and the public sector, many projects involve the development of systems that will require servicing and maintenance when they become operational. Planning for implementation, servicing, maintenance, and other requirements for successful operation must be done during the design and development (project) phase if the operational and maintenance costs are to be minimized. Although the emphasis for such logistic support requirements is different for government agencies (such as DOD) and commercial projects, the general concepts are similar. In DOD-type procurements, for example, provisions for spare parts, servicing, maintenance, personnel training, instruction, parts manuals, and computer and software support are extremely important. In commercial systems similar factors must be considered in the system design and development, but the matter of sales personnel and outlets, distribution, transportation, warehousing, and other profit-oriented factors are of even greater importance.

References

1. Blanchard, B., *Logistics Engineering and Management.* (Englewood Cliffs, N.J.: Prentice-Hall, 1974).
2. Bowerson, Donald J., *Logistical Management.* (New York: MacMillan, 1974).
3. Fair, Marvin L., and Williams, Earnest W., Jr., *Economics of Transportation and Logistics.* (Dallas: Business Publications, 1975).
4. Heskett, James L., et al, *Business Logistics.* (New York: Ronald Press, 1973).
5. Lambert, D.M., and Stock, J.R., *Strategic Physical Distribution Management.* (Homewood, Ill.: Richard D. Irwin, 1982).
6. Mossman, F.H., *Logistic Systems Analysis.* (Washington, D.C.: University Press of America, 1977).

—————————— Appendix H: ——————————
Risk Assessment

1.0 Introduction

Although the subjects of risk management, risk assessment, and risk analysis are closely related, each deals with different considerations of the risk problem. Areas where the element of risk has been studied include safety (hazard), capital investment, and project decision making and appraisals. This last area of application is the subject of this appendix.

2.0 What Is Risk Assessment?*

In the context of program management, the term *risk assessment* refers to the risk of failure to meet cost, schedule, or performance goals. *Risk* as used here denotes the probability that an event will occur and its consequences. An event with a high probability of occurrence but an unimportant consequence is considered as having a low risk, whereas an event with an important undesirable consequence and a moderate probability of occurrence is rated as having a high risk. Although the terms *high, medium,* and *low* can be used to describe the degree of risk that is expected, the quantification of risk is a desirable and rewarding objective. This concept and terminology is particularly applicable to systems acquisition programs where there are not a statistical number of events (acquisitions of the particular item) from which to draw. Instead, the experience of experts is used to synthesize a model and provide a quantitative expression for the degree of uncertainty. Such quantification depends on the use of probability distribution functions (PDFs) and cumulative distribution functions (CDFs). PDFs may be Gaussian, skewed, and so on. CDFs allow for the determination of confidence level.

3.0 Why Is It Important for Project Management?

Quantification of risk assessment can be a valuable tool in the planning process for several reasons:

1. It helps identify problem areas (high-risk elements) in the execution of the project.
2. It tends to bring into focus areas of disagreements about assumptions and methods of project execution.

---

* The following material is taken primarily from a handbook, *Risk Assessment Techniques*, 1st ed. (July 1983), prepared by personnel of the Defense Systems Management College at Fort Belvoir, Virginia. Copies can be obtained by writing to the Superintendent of Documents, U.S. Government Printing Office, Washington, D.C. 20402.

3. It can consider a large number of variables and provide evaluations that otherwise would not be attainable.
4. It allows for the evaluations of the variation of risk at different funding levels.

Cost of risk assessment versus benefits is an important consideration in deciding where to proceed with a quantitative risk assessment. Direct benefits can include the determination of the likelihood of an overrun and the effect of alternative schedules including their probability of success and their funding requirements. Indirect benefits include improvement of program definition for both management and the team members.

4.0 What Techniques Are Available?

The predominant techniques that are currently in use include

- Network analysis (for example, the use of PERT–see Chapter 6)
- The method of moments
- Decision analysis
- WBS simulation
- Graphics
- Estimating relationships
- Risk factors

5.0 How Does One Select the Best Technique?

Selection of the optimum technique for a particular project is dependent on the type of project and the project emphasis, whether cost, schedule, or technical performance. If there is sufficient funding, a combination of methods is advisable. Each technique has its specific features that make it more amenable to particular types of projects.

6.0 Summary

The problems or risk related to program/project decision making can be treated in several different ways. Possible approaches are making decisions under certainty, making decisions under risk, or making decisions under uncertainty. Each of these approaches has its own specific techniques and applicability. Considerations of typical project/program efforts involving high technology indicate that the use of a mixed risk-uncertainty type of approach can be advantageous in decision making.

7.0 References

1. Crouch, E.A.C., and Wilson, R., *Risk Benefit Analysis.* (Cambridge, Mass.: Ballinger, 1982).

2. Griffith, R.F., ed., *Dealing with Risk: The Planning Management, and Acceptability of Technology Risk.* (New York: John Wiley, 1981).
3. Hertz, David B., *Risk Analysis and Its Applications.* (New York: John Wiley, 1983).
4. Pouliquen, Y., *Risk Analysis in Project Appraisal.* (Baltimore: Johns Hopkins University Press, 1979).
5. Raiffa, H., *Decision Analysis: Introductory Lectures on Choices Under Uncertainty.* (Reading, Mass.: Addison-Wesley, 1968).
6. *Risk Assessment Techniques.* Defense Systems Management College, Fort Belvoir, Va. Superintendent of Documents, U.S. Government Printing Office, Washington, D.C. 20402.
7. Rowe, W.D., *An Anatomy of Risk.* (New York: John Wiley, 1977).

Appendix I:
Quality Circles and Project Management

The use of quality circles has achieved much notoriety in the management literature and elsewhere as a means of improving productivity. Quality circles, which are part of the Japanese philosophy and management style, emphasize group as well as individual participation in increasing company effectiveness and hence product quality and profits. It attempts to apply this type of activity to American companies, quality circles have become a passing fad for some organizations and a way of life for others.

A quality circle consists of a small voluntary group of employees and their supervisor from the same work area, who meet on a regular basis to study quality control and productivity improvement techniques. The members apply these techniques to identify and solve work-related problems and offer their solutions to management for approval. It is most effective to keep the groups small, four to fifteen members; about eight members is optimum. Members are taught brainstorming, data analysis, and other methods of analyzing and solving production and work-related problems.* There may be a special facilitator or specialist included in the circle to guide the group. Sometimes one or more consultants are brought in to assist setting up the quality circles and determining their functions.

There have been many claims for the effectiveness of quality circles. This is not unexpected since failures would less likely be publicized. The following examples of successes have been cited (see Tortorich, et al in references):

- Honeywell: Nonunion electronics shop, 10 circles with 120 members reduced costs by 46% over a two-year period.
- Martin Marietta Corp.: In a facility dedicated to mechanical and weld assemblies and to the application of various thermal protection materials, 142 circle members improved their rate of defects per person from .49 for the six months before the circles to .20 for six months after.

Although the use of quality circles has been mainly in production-type operations, it has also found utility in project-oriented companies. It can be an effective tool for the project manager because it draws together personnel with different departmental viewpoints to solve project problems, including not only improving the quality of the work or new product but also cutting costs.

The selection of a competent facilitator/coordinator is probably the most important feature of the implementation process, along with the inclusion of people who are genuinely interested in the ultimate success of the project.

---

* Common techniques include Pareto diagrams, cause-and-effect diagrams, flowcharts, histograms, checklists, and graphical representations.

It is essential that management be completely supportive of the circles as well as responsive to their recommendations. Being responsive does not necessarily mean that all recommendations are accepted and implemented, but simply that they are given full consideration.

Although quality circles have advantages and disadvantages and some fail, nevertheless, their overall impact on American industry, as in Japan, has been positive. The technique reflects the importance of personnel involvement and participation in the achievement of project and organizational goals.

References

1. Dewar, D., *Quality Circle Guide to Participative Management*. (Englewood Cliffs, N.J.: Prentice-Hall, 1980).
2. Patchin, R.I., *Management and Maintenance of Quality Circles*. (Homewood, Ill.: Dow Jones-Irwin, 1983).
3. *Quality Circle Techniques*. Hughes Aircraft Co., Training Department, 1982.
4. Thompson, P.C., *Quality Circles–How to Make Them Work in America*. (New York: American Management Association, 1982).
5. Tortorich, R., et al, "Measuring the Organizational Impact of Quality Circles," *Quality Circle Journal* (Novmeber 1981).

———————— Appendix J: ————————
Elementary Statistics (Brief Review)

1.0 General Remarks

The subject of statistics is of major importance to the project manager for a variety of reasons. Of these the most basic are:

- In evaluating and testing systems, subsystems and components, statistical treatment is often required in order to minimize cost and determine whether prescribed levels of performance can or are being met.

- In planning and executing the project, the risk factors or probabilities of success of various courses of action must be assessed so that appropriate choices can be made.

Although comprehensive identification and understanding of the many possible applications of statistics to project management would involve a high level of mathematical complexity, considerable benefit can be realized using a relatively modest knowledge of mathematics. In fact, a knowledge of basic algebra can provide an adequate background for the major subject areas important to the project manager. These and other related topics of statistics are necessary tools for successful project management.

There are two broad categories of statistical techniques: descriptive and inferential. The methods of inferential statistics are used extensively in "decision theory."

2.0 Descriptive Statistics:

- Presents or summarizes data in various ways without attempting to infer anything that goes beyond the data itself (e.g. the U.S. census; the determination and presentation of means, medians and modes of sets of data.)

- The data can be presented in summary statements, tables, graphs or charts as shown in Figures 8.1 and 8.2 of Chapter 8. Bar charts are an example of descriptive statistics.

- Constituted the main body of statistics years ago. Although still important and frequently used, the shift of emphasis has been to inferential statistics and probability theory.

3.0 Inferential Statistics:

- Conclusions can be drawn about large populations based on a limited amount of sampling (data).

- Generalizations go beyond the data and have a probability factor attached to them as to their validity or likelihood of being correct.

- Constitute the main body of current statistical study and use.

- An example of inferential statistics would be the estimate of what percentage of components would be within specifications given the results of testing a limited number of the components. Along with this estimate, a confidence level would have to be provided.

- Inferential statistics can be used when there is only partial, incomplete or indirect information available. Predictions or recommendations are made accordingly based on probability theory.

4.0 Probability

- If there are "n" equally likely outcomes or events, of which only one can occur and "s" represents the number of possible favorable events, then the probability of success is given by the ratio "s/n".

- In this definition of probability the value of probability can vary from 0 to 1.00. However, probability can also be expressed as percentages varying from 0 to 100.

- Another definition of probability: The probability of an event happening is the proportion of the time that events of the same kind will occur in the long run e.g. 40% chance of rain means that under the existing weather conditions it will rain 40% of the time.

- There are a number of rules for calculating probability:

  (a) The probability of an event A can be determined by summing up the probabilities of the individual events comprising A. $P(A) = P(A1) + P(A2) + P(A3) + \ldots + P(AK)$.

  (b) If two events are possible and they are mutually exclusive, i.e. dependent, the probability that one of the two will occur is equal to the sum of their probabilities. $P(A \text{ or } B) = P(A) + P(B)$

  (c) The probability that two sequential or independent events will both occur is the product of their individual probabilities. $P(AB) = P(A).P(B)$.

In such cases, the occurrence of one event must not preclude the occurrence of the other. For example, the development and success of a new product can depend upon the obtaining of funding for the new product development and effective marketing of the new product. Assuming equal probabilities of 50% for the two endeavors, the overall probability of success for the new product becomes 25%. Similar considerations can be made for more than two sequentially occurring events.

- These are just a few of the simple rules of probability. Some of the many other rules and subjects related to probability that can be of value to the project manager are: conditional probability, Bayes Theorem and probability distributions.

5.0 Expected Values

- Expected value is a measure of what is expected mathematically.

- It can best be explained by an example: If 1,000 tickets are sold for a raffle at a price of $10 per ticket, the expected value or mathematical expectation of each ticket buyer is one cent. The expected value is the product of the probability of the event occurring and the value of the event or item./

- If there are several events or items involved the expected value can be arrived at by summing the products for each event and its respective probability.

$$E.V. = v_1P_1 + v_2P_2 + v_3P_3 + ...v_KP_K.$$

6.0 Decision Theory

- Many important decisions made by the project manager are made under conditions of uncertainty, because seldom is complete information available.

- In the use of decision theory a choice is made between alternatives such that the economic consequence is the most promising.

- Example: An appliance manufacturer is considering expanding his plant and his consultants give him the following projected profit information for the upcoming fiscal year:

	Expand Now	Do Not Expand
economic conditions favorable	$480,000	$220,000
a recession occurs this year	$60,000	$140,000

If the manufacturer believes there is a better than 50:50 (say 60%) chance that there will be a recession, the expected profit will be $228,000 if he expands now.

$$(480,000)(0.40) + (60,000)(0.60) = 228,000$$

If he does not expand, his expected profit for the year will be $172,000.

$$(220,000)(0.40) + (140,000)(0.60) = 172,000$$

Since the former value is greater, proceeding with the plant expansion would yield the greatest profit.

7.0 Other Pertinent Topics

- There are numerous other rules and subject of Statistics that could be discussed but they fall beyond the scope of this text.

- Such subject areas include regression and correlation analysis, chi square tests and the analysis of variance, queueing, game theory, Monte Carlo simulation, etc.

8.0 Some Key Formulas Used in Statistics

Mean value for sample

$$\bar{x} = \frac{\Sigma x}{n}$$

Standard deviation for sample

$$s = \sqrt{\frac{\Sigma (x-\bar{x})^2}{n-1}}$$

Standard units (z-values)

$$z = \frac{x-\bar{x}}{s} \text{ or } \frac{x-\mu}{\sigma}$$

Confidence interval for small sample (n<30)

$$\bar{x} - t_{\alpha/2} \cdot \frac{s}{\sqrt{n}} < \mu < \bar{x} + t_{\alpha/2} \cdot \frac{s}{\sqrt{n}}$$

Confidence interval for large sample (n≥30)

$$\bar{x} - z_{\alpha/2} \cdot \frac{\sigma}{\sqrt{n}} < \mu < \bar{x} + z_{\alpha/2} \cdot \frac{\sigma}{\sqrt{n}}$$

Maximum error of the mean

$$E = z_{\alpha/2} \cdot \frac{\sigma}{\sqrt{n}}$$

Sample size and maximum error

$$n = \left(\frac{z_{\alpha/2} \cdot \sigma}{E}\right)^2$$

Weighted mean
$$\overline{X}_w = \frac{w_1 x_1 + w_2 x_2 + \text{-----} w_n x_n}{w_1 + w_2 + \text{----} w_3}$$

9.0 References

1. Bierman, Jr., H., Bonini, C.P. and Hausman, W.H., "Quantitative Analysis for Business Decisions", 5th Edition (Homewood, Illinois: Richard D. Irwin, 1977).
2. Dinkel, J.K., Kochenberger, G.A. and Plane, D.R., "Management Science: Text and Applications" (Homewood, Illinois: Richard D. Irwin, 1978).
3. Freund, J.K., Kochenberger, G.A. and Plane, D.R., "Management Science: Text and Applications" (Homewood, Illinois: Richard D. Irwin, 1978).
4. Freund, J.E., "Modern Elementary Statistics", 6th edition (Englewood Cliffs, N.J.: Prentice-Hall, 1984).
5. Groebner, D.F. and Shannon, P.W., "Essentials of Business Statistics" (Columbus, Ohio: Merrill, 1987).
6. Hamburg, M., "Basic Statistics", 2nd Edition (New York, N.Y.: Harcourt-Brace-Jovanovich, 1979).
7. Hamburg, M., "Statistical Analysis for Decision Making", 3rd Edition (New York, N.Y.: Harcourt-Brace-Jovanovich, 1983).
8. Jedamus, P. and Frame, R., "Business Decision Theory" (New York, N.Y.: McGraw-Hill, 1969).
9. Lapin, L.L., "Quantitative Methods for Business Decisions with Cases", 3rd Edition (New York, N.Y.: Harcourt-Brace-Jovanovich, 1985).
10. Levin, R.I., "Statistics for Management", 4th Edition (Englewood Cliffs, N.J.: Prentice-Hall, 1987).
11. Thierauf, R.J. and Klekamp, R.C., "Decision Making Through Operations Research", 2nd Edition (New York, N.Y.: John Wiley and Sons, 1975).
12. Trueman, R.E., "An Introduction to Quantitative Methods of Decision Making." 2nd Edition (New York, N.Y.: Holt, Rinehart and Winston, 1977.)

─────────────────── **Appendix K:** ───────────────────
Total Quality Management

In 1979, Konosuke Matsushita of Matsushita Electric observed:

"We are going to win and the industrial West is going to lose out. There's nothing much you can do about it, because the reasons for your failure are within yourselves".

It is no secret that the U.S. is under intense and unparalleled pressure from a variety of threats including not only the Pacific rim countries but now the "United (1992) States of Western Europe" as well. This intense competitive pressure is to be found in both the commercial and defense industries. American industry must remain and become even more commercially competitive. It is simply a matter of survival within a world economy.

In 1988, for reasons discussed in many parts of this book, the Secretary of Defense issued a posture statement giving top priority to the implementation of *Total Quality Management* (TQM) within DoD and its contractor base. He did so pursuant to Executive (Presidential) Order 12552 that focussed on productivity and a need for continuous improvement in product quality. However, the DoD by itself cannot "lead the industrial horse to water". American industry by itself must espouse and press forward with the concept of "Total Quality".

In Japan, TQM is known as *KAIZEN*. It's objective is a *progressive and unending improvement in the environment, quality of life, work process and work products based on the establishment of ever-higher standards*. It applies equally to *managers and workers* alike. Ironically, Japan's success including it's economic miracle demonstrates the validity of primarily western (i.e. American) industrial philosophy and thought. TQM or KAIZEN was evolved by quality experts including Crosby, Deming, Fiegenbaum, Ishikawa and Juran as based largely on the works of Walter Shewhart during the 1920's. It has become painfully apparent that neither quantity, styling nor price are a substitute for quality. In fact, *there is no substitute for quality*. The question is what is the best approach to achieving it?

There are *two basic components in TQM:* The philosophical and the technical.

Philosophical: The philosophical component involves the need and attempt to *tap the full potential of human resources through participation in strategic thinking and achievement of productivity through fairness and ethical behavior*. Please note that each and every one of these aspects is addressed and stressed in a number of chapters of this text. Guiding philosophical principles of TQM include:

- *Top* Management commitment and leadership
- Intensive training and employee involvement *along with supplier participation*
- *Clarity and consistency of purpose along with streamlining and standardization of effort.*

Technical: The technical component involves the use of a wide range of technical tools that can and must be brought to bear in the *continuous improvement of quality.* These may include use of:

- Experimental validation
- Statistical methodology and graphical techniques
- Performance (scrap, rework, etc.) indicators
- Audits, Reviews, *Root Cause Analysis and Corrective Action.*

What many fail to recognize is that the primary aim and function of management and the organization must be to *facilitate and/or incorporate the concept of continuous (measurable) improvement into each employee's daily life by promoting individual thinking and independent action.* Unless this can be accomplished, namely TQM becomes an individual's second nature and a way of life, TQM will revert to another (seemingly) useless "magic wand" – refer to page 188.

The government's TQM program as implemented in 1988 included a number of efforts as strategic components. Among them:

- Acquisition Streamlining (see DoD Directive 5000.43, January 1986). In general, promotes innovation and cost-effective design throughout the entire spectrum of acquisition functions and activities.
- "Could Cost". Imposes the "commercial market challenge" upon weapon system cost and quality. Extension of "value engineering" beyond mere "should cost" is advocated to minimize non value added work contractors.
- Reliability and Maintainability 2000. A major (1988) initiative of Headquarters, USAF. Focuses on reliability and maintainability improvement through design optimization (robust design) and variability reduction based on the use of various statistical and other tools and techniques.

Other "strategic" components of this program include:

- Certified Contractor Programs
- Warranties
- Risk Reduction

Parenthetically, as part of "risk reduction" *two outstanding documents published under the auspices of the Defense Science Board Task Force. Transition from Development to Production, include: DoD Transition Templates and the Navy's Best*

Practices. Familiarity with these is essential to the understanding and appreciation of TQM regardless of whether one is part of the defense or commercial sectors. These reports are MUST READING for *both the student and the seasoned professional.*

A number of other improvement techniques, applicable to both military and commercial programs, are an integral part of TQM and the lexicon with which the reader should be familiar.

Concurrent or Simultaneous Engineering: A combination of methods, techniques and practices that, *from the outset,* take into consideration (1) factors and parameters of importance in latter stages of the product's life cycle (2) consider and design processes for use in future stage of product implementation and deployment, and, (3) focus on reducing transition times from development to production. In effect, the objective is a "concurrent system" approach (rather than the more traditional "sequential" approach) to product design along with its implementation and overall operational considerations.

Quality Function Deployment: A systematic approach that employs a series of matricies to translate user requirements into process and product characteristics. The matricies are used to identify conflicting requirements; requisite tools, applicable techniques, associated risks and indicated priorities.

(Dr. Genchi) Taguchi Methods: Techniques for optimizing and integrating product design and manufacturing processes on the basis of a combination of engineering and statistical methods. *The Quality Loss Function* is a by product of Taguchi's efforts in this area. It is a mathematical theory that relates loss to customer and society based on product variation from target value. Loss is viewed in very broad terms including both tangible (performance) as well as intangible considerations (dissatisfaction). Taguchi's *Parameter Design* is an optimization procedure to determine product design or process levels such as to minimize sensitivity of *output* to *input* variations.

Cycle Time Management: Basically a time management technique designed to *identify and eliminate non value added activities.* The fallout of this technique is generally a combination of better quality and higher productivity at a reduced cost.

Deming Cycle: A structured problem solving technique nearly identical to the "scientific method". The cycle includes (1) examination of the process (2) identification of likely causes of variation (3) collection and reduction of data (4) identification or recommended corrective action (5) testing and monitoring of results of action taken. In effect, the cycle consists of "plan", "do", "check" and "act" (PDCA).

As may be seen from the preceding discussion, TQM involves a "disciplined" network of systems and processes implemented and administered through team work within a supportive environment. Central to TQM is customer satisfaction (i.e. organizational survival). Figures K.1 and K.2 show what TQM implementation involves along with the tools and techniques of TQM.

Overall industry reaction to TQM has been mixed. The process is yet to be fully embraced. While a number of companies have reported very impressive improvements in quality and productivity (e.g. Ford), the implementation of "TQM" in others has been an extremely costly and painful experience (a possible example of the latter being Douglas Aircraft Company).

TQM is impeded and/or falls short of expectations whenever the following general conditions exist:

- Lack of overall perspective as to the essence of TQM or its criticality (i.e. TQM is a disciplined approach to the *management of the overall industrial process that must integrate individual skill and will.*)
- Failure to recognize that even planning requires some planning (i.e. so does TQM and how!)
- Failure to define and articulate an unswerving commitment to quality
- Expectations of immediate results – The "magic wand" syndrome
- Isolation and insulation of top management – relegation of responsibility and accountability to lower echelons of management or to supervisory levels – the "Hawthorne Experiment" syndrome: "first level supervision does it best!"
- Temptations of expediency stemming out of operational considerations such as quantity, cost or schedule that undermine quality.
- Making management decisions based on the face value of figures
- Lack of (or inattention to) customer feedback

Supplemental Bibliography/Suggested Readings:

1. DoD Manual 4245.7 Transition from Development to Production, September 1985.
2. NAVSO P-6071, Best Practices – How to Avoid Surprises in the World's Most Complicated Technical Process, March 1986.
3. George Stalk, Jr., "Time – The Next Source of Competitive Advantage", Harvard Business Review, Jul-Aug 1988.
4. J.M. Juran and F.M. Gryna, Jr. "Quality Planning and Analysis From Product Development Through Usage", McGraw-Hill Book Co.
5. Kaoru Ishikawa, "Guide to Quality Control" UNIPUB 1976 and "What is Quality Control? The Japanese Way", Prentice-Hall, 1985.
6. Masaaki Imai, "Kaizen – The Key to Japan's Competitive Success", Random House, 1986.
7. P. L. Townsend, "Commit to Quality", John Wiley and Sons, 1986.
8. J.M. Juran, "Managerial Breakthrough – A new Concept of the Manager's ", McGraw-Hill Book Company, 1964.
9. A.V. Feigenbaum, "Total Quality Control", McGraw-Hill Co., 1986.
10. W.E. Deming, "Out of the Crisis", MIT Center for Advanced Engineering Study, Cambridge, Mass., 1966.
11. J.H. Harrington, "The Improvement Process", McGraw-Hill Book Co., 1987.
12. Bob King, "Better Designs in Half the Time: Implementing QFD in America", GOAL/QPC, Methew, Mass, 1987.
13. "Quest for Quality", Special Issue, Electronic Business, October 16, 1989.

————————— **Figure K.1: TQM Implementation** —————————

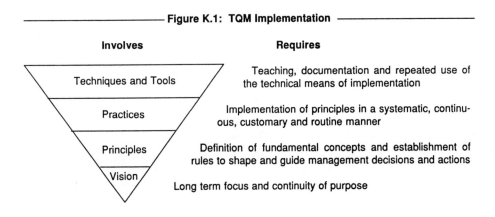

Involves	**Requires**
Techniques and Tools	Teaching, documentation and repeated use of the technical means of implementation
Practices	Implementation of principles in a systematic, continuous, customary and routine manner
Principles	Definition of fundamental concepts and establishment of rules to shape and guide management decisions and actions
Vision	Long term focus and continuity of purpose

Source: Total Quality Management Pamphlet of the Department of Defense, Washington D.C.

————————— **Figure K.2: TQM Techniques and Tools** —————————

Source: Total Quality Management Pamphlet of the Department of Defense, Washington D.C.

Index

DATE DUE
